Tracing the Veins

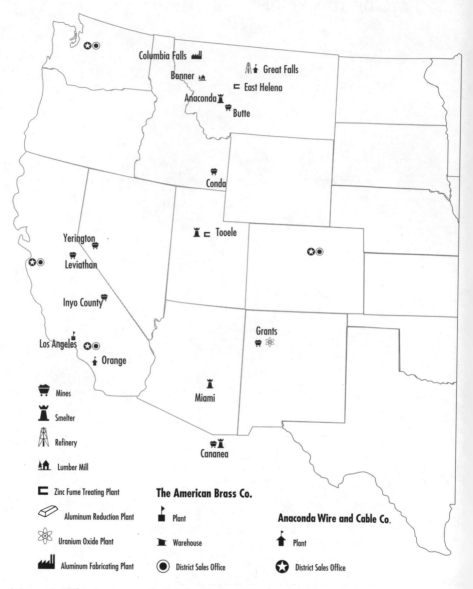

Map 1. "This Is Anaconda." Adapted from Anaconda Company Annual Report, 1959. Map design by Nick Baker/ArtText.

New Toronto

Muskegon

Buffalo

Hastings

Providence

Miilwaukee

Detroit

Torrington

Kenosha

Philadelphia

Waterbury

Chicago

Ansonia

Cleveland

Sycamore

Perth
Amboy

Marion

Anderson

Mattoon

Terre Haute

Dallas

Map 2. "Anaconda Operations in Chile." Adapted from Anaconda
Company Annual Report, 1959. Map design by Nick Baker/ArtText.

Tracing the Veins

Of Copper, Culture, and Community from Butte to Chuquicamata

Janet L. Finn

UNIVERSITY OF CALIFORNIA PRESS
Berkeley · Los Angeles · London

338.2743
F51t

University of California Press
Berkeley and Los Angeles, California

University of California Press, Ltd.
London, England

© 1998 by
The Regents of the University of California

Library of Congress Cataloging-in-Publication Data

Finn, Janet L., 1956–
    Tracing the veins : of copper, culture, and
community from Butte to Chuquicamata/Janet L.
Finn
       p.   cm.
    Includes bibliographic references and index.
    ISBN 0–520-21136-7 (cloth : alk. paper). —
ISBN 0–520-21137-5 (pbk. : alk. paper).
    1. Anaconda Company.   2. Copper industry
and trade—Social aspects—Montana—Butte.
3. Copper industry and trade—Social aspects—
Chile—Chuquicamata.   I. Title.
HD9539.C7U539   1998
338.2'743'0978668 — dc21   97-45120
                                          CIP

Printed in the United States of America
9   8   7   6   5   4   3   2   1

*To the women and men of Butte,
Chuquicamata, and Calama, who offered
me their courage, wit, and wisdom.*

Butte, Montana (1988)

I cannot sleep in this silence.

All my young life I could hear
thrumming of the mines beneath my feet.
Beneath my bed the rumbling pumps,
the feet of my uncles rising
and falling, heavy in the shafts.
Electric roar of mine yard lights
up on the hill where they gave
limbs, lungs and finally, lives
to the machines and copper dust.

I cannot hear tonight
the distant voices of outrage
that were the very walls
of the Miner's Union Hall.
In the end, there was a price
the company found for that.

Awake now, I drift ever downward
through black, collapsing tunnels.
Jobless, I wail and wander beneath
the streets, offering poor comfort
to the children of this city.

John McGinley 1992

Contents

Illustrations

Preface

It is springtime in the Rockies and once again I am on the verge of departure, heading south for my sixth consecutive winter in the Andes. In recent weeks I have been gathering materials for a seminar on gender, community, and social action that I will present at the University of Concepción. Another file is filled with notes and questions regarding my work in Northern Chile. I look forward to conversations with friends and colleagues, who continue to challenge and change my thinking about the story I tell. I wonder what I will encounter on my return to Chuquicamata. Layoffs and early retirements are a fact of life in the Chuquicamata mines these days. Who will be leaving this year, and who has already moved on?

I recently made a trip to Butte in search of images to enliven what I have written. As I pored over photo collections in the Butte-Silver Bow Public Archives, the human consequences of mining history weighed heavily on me. There was both vitality and vulnerability in the faces of those who have lived this story of copper and community. I hope my words do them justice. During the last year, three of the Butte residents whose stories I tell here have passed away. Their words brought life to this book. I am grateful for the time and wisdom they so generously shared with me and sorry that I cannot share this final product with them.

This book is truly a work in progress. From its modest beginnings in Butte, the project has offered me opportunities beyond my imagining and lessons in humility that remind me of how much I have to learn. When I first embarked on this journey in 1991, I did not imagine a single trip out of the country, let alone a life built around transnational ties. Those ties now bind me to the telling and living of a larger story. It is that larger story that informs my perspectives on and commitment to the teaching, research, and practice of social change. In 1996, thanks to support from the Montana Committee for the Humanities and the University of Montana Visiting Scholar Grants Program, I was able to bring two women from Northern Chile to Montana for an extended visit. Community and university audiences learned firsthand of their courageous search for the remains of their loved ones who were "disappeared" under Chile's military dictatorship and of their ongoing demands for truth and justice. As local audiences witnessed these women's testimonies, their understandings of boundaries and difference — north and south, we and they — were challenged. The experience helped me see new directions that my journey will take. It convinced me of the value of learning through careful listening, critical dialogue, and the disruption of our certainties.

I am deeply indebted to the wonderful faculty, mentors, and colleagues in the Department of Anthropology and School of Social Work at the University of Michigan who disrupted my thinking, challenged my certainties, and opened new possibilities for discovering patterns that connect. I owe a special thanks to the members of my dissertation committee, who posed the intellectual challenges that opened new worlds to me and offered the support that enabled me to see and pursue the larger vision of this project: Sherry Ortner, whose ongoing critical engagement with feminist and practice theory has informed and inspired my thinking and whose pithy words of advice always come at the right time; Rosemary Sarri, who taught me what it means to make a lifetime commitment to social work and to continually question what we think we know about social change; Ann Stoler, whose depth and breadth of intellectual energy sparked my passion for anthropology and taught me the importance of history; Barry Checkoway who taught me the importance of community and participation, not merely as theoretical concepts but as essential elements in daily life; and Roger Rouse, who encouraged me to enter the complicated terrain of postmodernity and transnationalism and gave generously of his time and ideas along the way. He made the project seem both possible and important when something of a more limited scale would have been the practical choice. I also thank Ruth Behar for encouraging me to write from the heart as well as the head about people and places I care about.

I was able to devote two years to research and writing thanks to the

generous support of the Mary Malcomson Raphael Fellowship awarded
by the University of Michigan's Center for the Continuing Education of
Women and a predoctoral fellowship awarded by the University of
Michigan's Horace H. Rackham School of Graduate Studies. I thank Jim
Flightner, dean of the College of Arts and Sciences at the University of
Montana, for granting me a research sabbatical when I needed it most.
    Support for this project has come in so many forms. I owe special
thanks to Ellen Crain, Jim Harrington, and Marilyn Maney of the
Butte-Silver Bow Public Archives and Butte Historical Society and John
Hughes of the Butte-Silver Bow Public Library for their ongoing assis-
tance and support; John Stiles, Yvonne Williams, Vivian Dames,
Gerhard Schwab, Dorothy Hodgson, Laura Dresser, Jennifer Stucker,
and M. Z. Morgan for their good humor, patient friendship, and stimu-
lating conversations as the ideas for this project began to take shape;
John McGinley, Margaret Power, Lessie Jo Frazier, and Rita Pickering
for their helpful suggestions on early drafts; Angélica Gimpel Smith and
Teresa Lopez for many conversations about the Chilean side of this story
and for the opportunity to tell parts of this story to university audiences
in Santiago; Paula Allen and members of the *agrupación* who invited me
into their lives and taught me to think of research as a long-term relationship; friends in Chuqui, Calama, and Santiago, who gave me many
reasons and opportunities to improve my Spanish; Laura Ahearn for
inviting me to participate in the Agency panel at the 1995 American
Anthropological Association Meetings, which enabled me to think more
carefully through the questions of agency addressed here; my colleagues
and students at the University of Montana, in social work and beyond,
who continue to inspire and challenge me; and Stan Holwitz, Harry
Asforis, Rose Anne White, Carolyn Hill, and the anonymous reviewers
at the University of California Press for the heartening support and valuable criticism that helped me see the forest through the trees.

In 1994, I began my academic career at the University of Montana,
returning as teacher to my undergraduate alma mater. I have given
numerous readings from this work to classes and community groups,
and I invariably receive thoughtful and critical comments from listeners
who have lived parts of this history. They engage me in lively debate and
help me hone my arguments, seek additional data, and revisit my ethnographic material with fresh perspectives. But as deeply as I care about
the project, I found myself more invested in its final presentation in
book form than in the complicated histories and experiences from which
it emerged. That changed abruptly in December 1996, when I was diag-

nosed with cancer. I was faced with the meaning and power of "lived experience." It was one thing to write of local knowledge of cancer and its place in a toxic way of life, as I had in chapter 6 of this book. It was quite another to live it. Good luck, good friends, good medical care (and insurance), along with my own bravado, got me through a few difficult months. I came through this experience more convinced than ever of the "human" in agency and subjectivity. I do not claim any connection between my illness and mining life. But I understand the power of this diagnosis and the search for explanation in a very different way than my writing in chapter 6 suggests.

I also learned important lessons about the meaning of community through the unconditional support of family and friends who keep me smiling, appreciate my sarcasm, and put up with my quirks. Thanks to all of you. You know who you are. To Don, Mick, and Cathy, thanks for being there when I needed you. And to my parents, thank you for your unflagging support, and especially for valuing education and encouraging my pursuits, even when I was not so sure where they were taking me.

ONE

Tracing the Veins

The Story of the Anaconda Company is a major chapter in the epic
of American industry. Its name is synonymous with copper. From a
hole in the ground — the fabulous Anaconda mine — on Butte Hill . . .
stemmed an empire that today stretches from the Rockies to the Andes
with a constructive impress laid on two continents.

Isaac Marcosson 1957

This is a tale of two cities: Butte, Montana, USA, and Chuquicamata,
Chile, intimate strangers, linked through their histories as the copper
producing hubs of the Anaconda Company. From the 1920s to the
1970s, their rich copper deposits served as the corporate anchors for
Anaconda, a giant of the mining industry.[1] On their scarred surfaces,
these towns appear as mirror images, reflecting the hope and pain of
their copper-plated pasts. Their differences, though, are as deep as the
veins of copper that coursed beneath them. Like the veins themselves,
Butte and Chuquicamata are connected in a labyrinthine history of
political and economic intrigues that defy above-ground detection.

This book tells the story of a powerful corporation that left its impress on community life from the Rockies to the Andes and of the creative agency of men and women who built community and carved their
own histories and futures in two isolated corners of the world. The story
contributes to transnational understanding and the understanding of
transnationals as it traces the relationship of capitalism and community
across cultural, national, and geographic boundaries. It challenges the
limits of comparative study by situating Butte and Chuquicamata not
merely as comparable sites of copper extraction but as mutually enlight-
ening sides of a larger, and largely obscured reality. In the process, it disrupts the limiting assumptions about North and South, we and they, and
development and "underdevelopment" that are often predicated on
views from the North.

This study responds to the call for the engagement of history and
ethnography in understanding the intersection of global processes and

local life. It enables us to take a long-term look at large-scale political and economic shifts, patterns of corporate practice, and the articulation of these forces with peoples' lived experiences.[2] Questions of gender and power, class and community are at the center of a story that moves beyond abstractions to a concrete and culturally informed analysis of the making of a mining way of life.

This is also a story of a personal journey from Butte, my childhood home, to Chuquicamata, our unofficial sister city. It speaks to the meaning and power of engaged research, where the author is deeply implicated in her subject of study. This work resonates with the voices of many, though it is the writer who has chosen how to arrange and represent those voices. I am deeply grateful to the many people whose stories enrich this work. I hope that my contextualizing of those many voices has done justice to the lives represented here.

As a point of entry, let me tell you how a simple three-month project turned into a three-year personal and professional odyssey. This study has its roots in Butte. So do I. I lived in Butte most of my childhood and returned in 1991 to write about women's perspectives and experiences during the devastating copper strike of 1967. I was eleven years old when the strike began. It was the longest in Butte's history and the one that stood out in my childhood memories. My family was not a "mining family," but the ripple effects of the nine-month strike were felt throughout the community. It was the moment when the words *strike*, *scab*, and *picket line* took on meaning for me.

In 1989, fifteen years after my departure from Butte, I set aside my social-work career in child and family services and returned to the university. I needed new ways to think about and act on the social dilemmas that confronted me each day. I immersed myself in the study of gender, culture, and social change. I was drawn back to the community I had left behind and to the questions of power, meaning, and women's practice embedded in its history.

Much of the literature I read on women's social action in the U.S. labor movement focused on the moments when women took to the streets or joined men on picket lines.[3] Other works illustrated women's public actions in the face of resistance from union men and corporate bosses.[4] Yet I did not recall seeing Butte women in the streets or on the lines. I wondered what it was women were doing when they weren't doing what men did during a strike. I decided to record accounts of the 1967 strike given by wives, mothers, and daughters of men who worked in the mines.

I soon discovered that my informants in Butte had a hard time staying on the subject at hand. Despite my early efforts to direct our conversations, by the third cup of coffee we invariably shifted from the 1967 strike to strikes in the thirties, forties, fifties, and seventies and the closure of the mines in the eighties. Once I learned to listen more carefully and deeply to women's stories, I realized they were challenging the way I had framed the study. A strike in Butte could not be understood in the singular, as a discrete action contained by the date of the walkout and that of the contract settlement. Strikes were a plural concept, linked together in a larger story of community struggle.

Butte women described strikes not in terms of an event but as part of an ongoing cycle of community life, modulated by three-year labor contracts.[5] Their stories revealed a patterned shift in gender relations during strikes. Women's social participation increased as they sought wage labor and mobilized informal networks of support, usually behind the scenes. They talked of self-conscious practices of community caregiving to assuage a sense of crisis during hard times, a practice I have come to call "crafting the everyday." Women offered rich insights into the power of relationships among women and the negotiation of relationships between women and men. The stories of miners' wives and "company" wives spoke to complex webs of relationships not clearly delineated along class lines. They illustrated the love, humor, and support that rendered their lives so much more than worlds of privilege or "worlds of pain."[6]

Their stories demanded that I turn to history. I abandoned my plan to study a single strike. I listened to the cadence of the corporate-community relationship, modulated over time by labor contracts, strikes, lockouts, and layoffs. I spent hours in the local archives, reading accounts of Butte's labor history. The cryptic presence of Chile lurking in the shadows of Butte's history captured my attention. I explored the connections, tracing history through the veins of copper mined by the Anaconda Company. I became convinced that I could not understand Butte's tumultuous past without looking critically at the Anaconda Company's operations abroad, and specifically at the relationship to Chuquicamata.[7] As I listened to women's stories in Butte, I wondered about the stories of women in Chuquicamata (or "Chuqui" as the residents say). Where might be the common ground and what might be the important differences? I also listened to men's stories and was struck by the frequent comment, "The company never had a strike it didn't want." What might I find if I took that seemingly simple phrase as another research question?

I located Chuquicamata on a map and read a travel-guide description of this place I could barely pronounce. I learned that Chuqui "is the largest open pit copper mine, and the largest single supplier of copper in the world. This pit is 350–400 meters deep and is responsible for half of Chile's total copper output and at least 25% of Chile's total annual export income" (Samagalski 1990, 85). To the girl who had grown up on the "Richest Hill on Earth" and the woman who was now living alongside "America's Largest Toxic Waste Site," these superlative figures had an impact.[8] I wanted to know more about this strange place that was beginning to sound familiar. I embarked on a crash course in Spanish and twentieth-century Chilean history and politics, with the copper connections as my guide.

In 1992, I made my first trip to Chile to see if my notion of a two-site community project was feasible. I worked on my Spanish and plumbed the archives of Santiago. The folk theory of the Butte miners fueled my curiosity as I immersed myself in a detective story of corporate intrigues. The tone of this work reflects my own growing acceptance of the truth in the assertion that "the company never had a strike it didn't want." I do not claim to have proven this, only to believe it. My beliefs are grounded in my complicated positions of Butte girl and cultural scholar.[9] None of these academic endeavors prepared me for my arrival in Chuquicamata and my tour of the open-pit mine. I stood among tourists who gawked into the gaping hole in the earth. I listened to their comments of awe and disbelief and took note of their expressed apprehension. But this foreign place was comfortingly familiar to me: I felt right at home. Whatever the obstacles, the project seemed possible, and in that moment, I knew I was going to return.

I did return to Chile for several months in 1993 and 1994. Once again, the stories I listened to profoundly challenged the meager, if expanded, parameters of my research and boundaries of my comprehension. The Anaconda Company, which left Chile in 1971, still loomed large in the popular imagination and conversation in Chuquicamata. I could not comprehend its historical force without grappling with its presence in the present. Likewise, I learned that I could not speak of the Anaconda Company era (1923–1971) without addressing the military dictatorship (1973–1990) that followed the company's departure.[10] The more closely I listened, the more I came to hear a curious local discourse in which the Anaconda Company was variably cast as villain and hero in hotly contested versions of mining history. Anaconda may be gone, but the meaning and power of both its presence and absence have carved out an enduring arena of struggle.

Through the words of women in Chuquicamata, I learned about variations on the theme of "crafting the everyday." A different rhythm modulated their accounts, and the raw force of Chile's Atacama Desert formed a powerful backdrop to memories of life in the Anaconda days. I also learned about violence and fear under dictatorship and democracy. These lessons have cautioned me not to draw too firm a line between the two.

I spent two years moving between Butte and Chuquicamata, digging through documents, reading disparate accounts of history, listening to stories, and joining in community life. I began to grasp patterns and rhythms of change and continuity in Butte and Chuquicamata as I pondered their parallel histories and considered their embeddedness in a transnational political economy of copper. Over the course of the study, those presumed boundaries I had imagined did not pose many problems. It was the seemingly clear and bounded concepts, "culture," "nation," and "place," that became and remain problematic. They were variably defined, defended, and transgressed in the making of mining life. So I made my way through a topsy-turvy world, where the map was not the territory and history relentlessly intruded on the present. A commitment to build relationships and earn trust became my grounding force.

I returned to Butte in 1994 to write my dissertation on the making of gender, class, and community. I had a much more complicated story to tell than that which I had imagined when I embarked on the initial project in 1991. It is this complicated story that I offer here: a cultural and political account of a mining community that spans one century and two continents.

The notion of cultural politics addressed in this book refers to two concepts central to anthropology: meaning and power.[11] How do we as social and cultural actors give meaning to powerful events and power to meaningful events that touch our lives? How is our understanding of and action in the world shaped by the complex relations of power in which we are embedded? How are we ourselves constructed through this melding of meaning and power? These questions are key to grasping the richly textured relationship between emotion and economy prevalent in this story.

Through their stories and daily lives, the residents of Butte and Chuquicamata tackled these questions of cultural politics. They articulated their visions of the limits and possibilities of their social worlds. They situated themselves as both subjects and actors in the making of mining history. They spoke of the contradictions they faced as corporate power collided with community life and of the resources they drew on in confronting those contradictions. On a daily basis, they faced the daunting task this project has posed for me: the struggle to engage with and make sense of a culturally and politically striated story of copper and community in the making. I turn now to the social and theoretical terrain on which this story is built.

INTIMATE STRANGERS

Copper mining has shaped the social and spatial landscape of Butte, Montana, and Chuquicamata, Chile. Butte is situated at the foot of the Continental Divide, in a mountain range known locally as the East Ridge, a rugged vertebrae of the Rocky Mountains. Butte has a colorful history linked to its rich copper resources. This town of thirty-five thousand people has shrunk considerably from its heyday in the early 1900s, when its population swelled to nearly one hundred thousand, and it boasted a reputation for culture and nightlife.[12]

Though copper mining has lost its central place in the local economy in recent years, remnants of the industry still dominate the terrain. A dozen "gallows frames" mark the entrances to the labyrinth of underground mines. These frames supported the hoists that carried miners to the rich veins of copper lying nearly a mile underground. The vast expanse of the Berkeley Pit, the open-pit mine, carved out the northeast boundary of Butte. The surrounding hillsides are largely barren as a result of the combined effects of high altitude and heavy-metal deposits in the soil, the by-product of one hundred years of copper production. Only the hardiest shrubs take root. Many residents find this an apt metaphor for the tenacity of Butte people (see figs. 1 and 2).

Butte is physically and socially divided into The Hill and The Flats. The Hill is home to Butte's original neighborhoods, clustered around the entrances to the many underground mines. The neighborhoods are a colorful mix of worn apartments, modest and stately family homes, and aging mansions in various stages of disrepair and gentrification. Though there is considerable effort to keep Uptown Butte alive, the major commercial development in recent years has occurred on The Flats. The Flats, a sprawling plateau south of the Butte Hill, is a patchwork of middle-class neighborhoods, tract homes, commercial strips, and islands of

Figure 1.   Butte street and gallows frames circa 1960. Courtesy of Butte-Silver Bow Public Archives.

Figure 2.   Berkeley Pit, Butte. Photo by Tony Difronzo, Rainbow Photo, Butte.

the nouveau riche. But the Butte Hill is Butte history. It was from the rich veins of copper that the lifeblood of community emerged.

Local merchants and political leaders have capitalized on Butte's gritty charm and staked claims to its turbulent past in the interest of tourism and community revitalization. Many uptown buildings have gotten facelifts and historic landmark status. Visitors can tour Butte's superlative sites: from the "World Museum of Mining," past the remnants of the "Richest Hill on Earth," to the viewing deck of the Berkeley Pit, which is now filled with billions of gallons of sulfuric sludge — the world's largest toxic lake. Longtime residents remain the city's ardent supporters, always quick with a story and lesson in history for the newcomers recoiling from their first encounter with this wounded terrain.

Chuquicamata is a company town situated in the high mountain desert of northern Chile. Chuqui is known as the place where the sun strikes the red metal. The intensity of blue sky is challenged only by the constant wind that leaves the air thick with smelter smoke and mine dust. Chuquicamata first struck me as one of the few places in the world that makes Butte seem pretty by comparison. Monotonous rows of concrete-block houses and apartments blend into the bleak desert terrain. The tree-lined central Plaza de los Heroes offers blessed shade in this spot that receives less than an inch of rain annually. The plaza is also an important cultural marker, figuring prominently in popular memory as a community gathering place and site of struggles.[13]

Chuquicamata was known as the Greatest Mining Camp in the World. For nearly fifty years, it was the source of two-thirds to three-quarters of the Anaconda Company profits.[14] But the mining industry is shrinking. Chuqui once supported a population of twenty-five thousand people, but that has dwindled by half in recent years. Though nearly ten thousand people still work in the mine, shifting corporate practices in the mid 1990s have resulted in nearly two thousand layoffs and early retirements and the replacement of many union workers with nonunion contracted laborers.[15] Many residents have moved to the neighboring commercial center of Calama, a few miles down the road.

Chuquicamata is perched on a hilltop alongside the yawning open-pit mine. The social structure was set in concrete when the town was built in the early 1900s. Well-appointed management houses overlook the rows of worker housing below. Chileans have replaced Yankee managers, and comfortable "ranch style" homes have replaced the Victorian buildings of the gringos, but the social structure remains in place. Since the early 1970s, company tract homes and apartment complexes have been built in Calama, and Chuqui has become more workplace than home for many mining families.

Calama now reflects many of the social and economic disparities that Chuquicamata once maintained. There are neighborhoods of middle-class homes, some built in the last years of Anaconda's operations and some by CODELCO (*Corporación Nacional del Cobre*), the national mining corporation. Workers are now able to buy their own homes. Around the outskirts of Calama are the *poblaciones*, poor neighborhoods, where the unemployed, underemployed, and poorly paid contracted laborers in the mines make their homes.

Although the Chilean government has run the mines since 1971, signs of the Anaconda Company's influence linger. Public buildings, streets, and neighborhoods are named for Anaconda officials, and soccer games are played in the Anaconda Stadium. The towering Chile Theater and the once-grand Hotel Washington stand as Main Street icons of the corporate legacy (see figs. 3 and 4). Nearly every home has a car out front, not a usual sight in most Chilean towns. Many of the cars have protective covers, guarding against the sun and wind. Every few blocks, there is a car wearing a slipcover fashioned from a U.S. flag. I wondered if the ubiquitous presence of the stars and stripes was a remnant of heavy-handed imperialism from the Anaconda days. Locals assured me that, no, most of these flags arrive in the bulk shipments of used clothes and fabric, supposedly destined for charitable ends, but usually diverted into the vast gray market of secondhand stores. Perhaps the flags stand as more apt symbols of the diffuse forms of imperialism that have followed old-style flag waving.

Butte and Chuquicamata have been the sites of labor struggles, punctuated by long and, at times, violent strikes. In recent years, both communities have weathered political and economic upheavals. There was long-standing resentment in Chile of the power held by foreign corporations and a growing interest in reclaiming the country's natural resources. In 1971, under the Popular Unity government of Salvador Allende, Chile nationalized the copper industry.[16] People in Butte were initially optimistic, hoping to regain center stage in Anaconda's operations without the competition of Chuquicamata. Those hopes were short-lived. The loss of its Chilean riches spelled economic trouble for Anaconda. In 1977, the Anaconda Company was purchased by Atlantic Richfield Corporation (ARCO), a major oil company. After a series of labor conflicts and layoffs, the Butte mines were closed in 1983. Thousands of people were out of work. In 1986, mining resumed in Butte, with one profound difference: the mines were nonunion.[17]

Figure 3.   Anaconda Stadium, Chuquicamata (author photo).

Chuquicamata suffered a different fate. Allende's troubled government felt the pressure of political and economic sanctions imposed by
the United States in response to nationalization of the mining industry.
In September 1973, Allende's government was toppled by a military
coup in which Allende died. Chile was controlled by the military dictatorship of Augusto Pinochet for seventeen years. Labor leaders, executives, and workers in the copper mines were among the thousands of
Chileans executed, imprisoned, or "disappeared" under the brutally repressive dictatorship.[18]

In the early 1980s, many of Chuquicamata's copper miners were in
the vanguard of opposition mobilized against the Pinochet government.[19] The dictatorship gave way to free elections in 1989. The country is now actively rebuilding its fractured democracy. Economic crises
in copper have overshadowed Chuquicamata's newfound political freedom.[20] Fear and uncertainty prevail as the community faces thousands
of layoffs, disabling of union power, and talk of reprivatization of the
mines.[21] Like Butte's residents, the people of Chuquicamata are struggling to imagine a way of life beyond copper. Both communities are
bound together as intimate strangers in a political economy that has
shaped their interlocking histories.

MAPPING THE THEORETICAL TERRAIN

Throughout this work, I build on and critique a theory of practice as I
grapple with the questions of cultural politics. A theory of practice seeks

Figure 4.   Hotel Washington, Chuquicamata (author photo).

to grasp the dynamics of structure and human action as they unfold over time.[22] In something of a rapprochement of the contributions of Marx and Weber, this approach addresses the confluence of power and meaning in the construction of social reality.[23] As anthropologist Sherry Ortner describes, "Within a practice framework, there is an insistence, as in earlier structural-determinist models, that human action is constrained by the given social and cultural order (often condensed in the term 'structure'); but there is also insistence that human action *makes* 'structure' — reproduces or transforms it, or both" (1996, 2). A practice perspective is both political and humanistic. It draws attention to ways in which people embody and carry the weight of determining social forces, to creative human actions that expose the gaps and challenge the "wholeness of the system," and to the making of social actors as they reproduce and change the system.[24] The perspective calls for what Anthony Kelly and Sandra Sewell have termed a "trialectic" approach, one that attends to the mutual constitution of this trinity of social reality.[25]

Prac-
Theory

    The practice perspective has been challenged for its all-encompassing generality, questioned in terms of its status as "theory," and critiqued for its "modernist" insistence on the human in agency and subjectivity. Most recently, Ortner has addressed the need to bridge the gaps between practice theory and bodies of feminist and other subaltern theories (1996, 17–20). My work responds to these challenges through an ethnographically and historically grounded account that reads the structuring of social life and human subjectivity against the creative and crit-

ical capacities of social actors. The practice perspective offers an organizing frame for examining the myriad ways in which people confront,
interpret, and negotiate power, follow and break the rules of order, and
craft a sense of meaning in their lives. I attend to power, gender, class,
and community not as abstract concepts but as concrete, mutually constituting practices. My study, situated in the ambiguous space between
practice and feminist theories, provides a basis for both critical reflection and for the elaboration of new theoretical possibilities.

I have tried to keep the "trialectic" image in mind in bringing a theory of practice to bear on understanding the relationship between capitalism and community. I focus on three key aspects. First, I dig beneath
and disrupt surface images of wholeness. For example, the Anaconda
Company claimed to have "laid its impress on two continents." The
analysis offered here disputes this notion of corporate determinism,
revealing instead a complicated history of collaboration and contest. It
also challenges notions of community as a bounded whole.

In chapter 2, I chronicle nearly a century of Anaconda Company
operations, linking the histories of Butte and Chuquicamata and situating them in the larger story of transnational capitalism.[26] I argue that it
is impossible to grasp the cultural, historical, political, and social implications of copper production in one locale without viewing it in relation
to the other and to the cultural politics of copper writ large. A number
of authors have written political and social histories of Butte and
Chuquicamata.[27] However, none address the meaning and power of the
communities' historic intimacy. An uncritical acceptance of boundaries
has constricted the vision of these accounts. Like the Anaconda
Company itself, I have sought to unearth a wealth of knowledge by
crossing over and tunneling under presumed boundaries. In so doing, I
offer an alternative model for the practice of transnational research and
the research of transnational practices.

Let me develop this point further. At one level, Butte and Chuquicamata offer the ideal settings for a comparative study. These communities, linked to the same corporation, shared features common to many
mining towns: isolated terrain, intensive industrialization in an otherwise rural context, dependence on large investments of outside capital,
far-reaching company control of community life, dangerous work,
strong masculine work culture, and a long history of environmental
degradation.[28] At the same time, they are situated in presumably distinct
political and cultural contexts. The stage is set for an informative look
at the similarities and differences in cross-national corporate-commu-

nity relations. However, to focus only on comparison is to miss the fundamental connections between these communities. The validity of certain boundaries is assumed, whereas others, and the contested borderlands they delineate, are obscured. It is necessary, then, to push beyond comparison in order to grasp the complexity of transnational practices.

Second, this study brings structure and practice to life, illustrating their complex interplay. Tensions of structure and agency are articulated through the dilemmas residents faced as a powerful company gave with one hand while it took with the other. It is through movement back and forth between the texture of people's lives and their perceptions of the forces working for and against them that we come to appreciate their concerns and confusions, aspirations and actions. For three generations, residents of Butte and Chuquicamata partially understood and earnestly practiced a mining life orchestrated by the Anaconda Company.[29] The ethnographic data allow for detailed exploration of perceptions, actions, and their consequences as residents differently scripted their variations on the corporate theme.

Systemic forces and human action are intimately engaged. Engagement, however, does not imply determinism. In the slip between the cup of structure and the lip of practice lie uncertainty and possibility. A key theoretical task, then, is not to analytically disengage structure and practice, but to grapple with their engagement and slippage. I reach inside this complexity through ethnographic analysis of the contradictions people faced as "conflicting discourses and patterns of practice" repeatedly posed problems for them.[30] This study sheds light on the ways in which a single company deftly utilized a global perspective and local control in confronting contradictions inherent in the shifting logics of capitalism. I look to the predicaments residents faced as the power of corporate control fused with the possibilities of community life.

The question of contradiction has a central place in social theory. Structural definitions of the capitalist contradiction are often presented in terms of private appropriation and social production, or of the hegemony of the nation-state and the internationalization of capital.[31] Such definitions do not tell us much about the ways in which macro processes translate into the double binds of daily living. Abstract predicaments gain concrete reality in the stories of miners' wives who describe their men as "squeezed in the middle" by the demands of labor and capital. Bodies that bear the toxic consequences of mining life also bear witness to contradictions of exploitation and profit that reach beyond the mines into the most intimate spaces of daily life. And it is in the silences within women's stories of crafting the everyday that we come to appreciate their own deeply compromised relationships to men and mining.

Attention to the ethnographic data reveals another meaning of contradiction. As folks faced the dilemmas of mining life, they developed their own critical practice of contra-diction, talking back to the forces that shape their lives. I borrow this notion of contra-diction as back talk from Kathleen Stewart's work, "Back Talking the Wilderness" (1990, 43–48)."[32] Her discussion of Appalachian women talking back to men, mines, and one another illustrates ways in which gender and power relations are contested and negotiated. She depicts back talk (contra-diction) as a dynamic practice that both creates and pushes against the bounds of the talkable. As these boundaries are stretched, new forms of talk, previously unspeakable, may be spoken. Throughout this work, I illustrate ways in which men and women talk back to one another and the forces shaping their lives. This sense of contra-diction implies more than word play. Attention to back talk offers clues as to how people define what is at stake in their struggles. Where do the axes of struggle lie and how are the double binds of daily living articulated? As people speak against forces that confuse, threaten, or attempt to silence them, they claim the value of their knowledge, histories, dignity, and identity.

Third, this work offers a complicated view of agency that is not reducible to actors strategically deploying symbols and resources in pursuit of their own interests.[33] A better image is that of people as works in progress, shaped by attachments, aspirations, interests, and the rhythmic practices of social life. Practice theorists have focused on cultural actors as they confront problems posed by their belief systems and their social and economic realities in particular historic and political contexts. However, the question of actor and agency remains thinly theorized.[34] The ethnographic data presented here offer a thicker understanding of actors as "dividuals" in the making, curious conglomerates of life experiences.[35]

Agency must be understood in terms of the intimate contradictions and confusions posed by mining life, where residents were both beneficiaries and victims of corporate largesse and exploitation. Lessons of agency are embedded in the stories of bravado that mask fear of that life's real dangers. Likewise, agency is encoded in the stories of crafts(wo)manship, the creative making of self and circumstance out of the cultural material at hand.

The trialectic perspective has provided me an image for grasping the dynamic relationships among community, class, and gender at the heart of this work. I move beyond abstractions and explore the ways in which community, class, and gender are constructed and practiced in lived experience. Throughout this work, I consider the gendered terrain on and through which women and men have worked together and against each other in defining, constituting, and defending community. Critical engagement with a mining way of life shed light on community, class, and gender not as "thinglike structures" but as dynamic, mutually constituting, social processes.[36]

In chapter 3, I examine the competing formations of community that linked and separated the people of Butte and Chuquicamata.[37] Community is at once a negotiated reality in the making and an arena in which other forms of struggle and support play out. I explore the communities that were made and not made as corporate and on-the-ground visions of belonging overlapped and collided. Likewise, I consider the constructions of difference through which certain boundaries were created and maintained, often in the service of corporate visions of community. A focus on the corporate imagination allows us to see ways in which the Anaconda Company worked to create a sense of community in Butte and Chuquicamata. Though Anaconda imagined a benevolent patriarchy in Chuquicamata, it often propagated a sense of democratic "we're all in the same boat" struggle in Butte.

I bring a gender lens to this story, countering a history in which women have been cast in cameo roles as the matrons of boardinghouses and the madams of bordellos. I do not merely "add women" to the story. I offer a careful study of gender and class relations in the making. As Sally Alexander (1994) argues, the experience of social class is not equally shared by men and women. Likewise, their different experiences of class contribute to differential formations of gendered consciousness and practice. The key to understanding this mutual constitution lies in the exploration of ways in which the experiences of class and gender are constructed and articulated, variably reinforcing and repelling one another.[38]

I start from the assumption that class and gender are not neutral descriptors. They are grounded in and constructed through relations of social inequality. Cultural Marxists such as Raymond Williams have drawn attention to the cultural as well as to the economic dimensions of domination and exploitation that shape the experience of social class.[39] Feminist theorists have contributed similar critical analyses of patriarchy and gender. Others have argued the need to link capitalism and patriarchy in theory, as they are intimately linked in practice, in order to understand the mutual construction of class and gender. My thinking has been shaped by their critical insights.[40] But as I sat at kitchen tables and in union offices, talking to folks in Butte and Chuquicamata, words such as *capitalism, patriarchy, class,* and *gender* did not come up often. I needed ways to think about how their stories might encode languages and practices of class and gender that meant something to social actors as well as to cultural scholars.

I looked at critical ethnographic works for help in locating the power behind the words. For example, Ann Stoler, in her study of Javanese workers in Sumatran rubber plantations, cautions against extracting class consciousness from its larger cultural context. She argues the need to examine social realities of class relations as lived, mediated, obscured, and transgressed. She finds that class relations were embedded in and expressed through elite discourses on the colonial order of things, manipulation of gender and ethnic hierarchies, and control of sexuality. She turns to analysis of daily confrontations to examine ways in which class interests are obscured and expressed along race, gender, and ethnic lines (Stoler 1985).

In a similar vein, Verena Stolcke, in her book *Coffee Planters, Workers and Wives* (1988), grasps what it meant to be a man, woman, and worker in a São Paulo coffee plantation. Stolcke argues that workers' class consciousness was mediated by gender consciousness. She illustrates this mediation in an account of young women, proud of their capacity as laborers, who nevertheless wrapped their hands each day so that calluses would not reveal them to be poor and "unfeminine" and limit their marriage prospects. In her work *Landscape for a Good Woman* (1987), Carolyn Steedman delicately crafts a portrait of the politics of longing and envy that filtered through her own mother's complicated relationship to mothering and to working-class identification. From her subtle details of the meaning and power of a hemline, to painful vignettes of the daughters who bore their mother's burdens of longing, Steedman captures the complex fusions of class and gender as lived experience rather than analytic categories. The insights of these writers and others have helped me think about the ways in which gender and class are intimately enmeshed. More important, they capture ways in which gender and class are infused with and articulated through the particular languages and practices of the moment and place.[41]

In chapter 4, I examine the construction of gendered subjectivities and the ways in which men and women reinforced, challenged, and acquiesced to those images. Constructions of man and womanhood and their relations to mining life distinctly shaped the contours of consciousness and action in Butte and Chuquicamata. Drawing from the ethnographic data, I illustrate how men and women talk back to these images as they talk of labor, friendship, intimacy, and one another. I consider not only the mutual construction of gender and class identities and relations, but also the ways in which they are marked by the politics of race and the meanings of "whiteness."

Throughout this work, I try to craft a deeper understanding of the trialectic of social reality in the making as I rework and elaborate themes of community, class, and gender with the ethnographic materials at hand. In so doing, I arrive at an ethnographically informed understanding of the problems and possibilities of mining life. Several themes resonate through the stories told by people in Butte and Chuquicamata: crafting the everyday, consumption, trust and betrayal, and reclamation. They encompass the ways in which people (re)produce themselves within a dynamic system of gender and class relations, talk about their "relations to the means of production," and give meaning to the power of exploitation, acquiescence, and resistance. They provide keys to understanding the contradictions residents faced and their strategies for confronting those contradictions.

In chapter 5, I develop the theme of crafting the everyday by taking a comparative look at "working-class" women's experiences in Butte and Chuquicamata. Women's stories encode a language and practice of class that is absent in men's accounts. Differing temporal and spatial patternings molded women's lives in Butte and Chuquicamata. In Butte, the three-year cycle of labor contracts created temporal rhythms of community life that profoundly shaped women's social reality. In Chuquicamata, lives were spatially structured around the lines at the communal water pumps and company stores, where waiting was women's work. These gendered practices of daily life posed distinct challenges to consciousness and action. Through a close examination of women's social practice, I come to an appreciation of agency as crafts(wo)manship, a process of creatively defining, reworking, and mobilizing the resource potential of their situations, and, at times, shifting the balance of power along the way.

In chapter 6, I draw on the popular name for silicosis — "miner's consumption" — as a powerful metaphor for the many forms of wasting that penetrated mining life. I shift to a symbolic level of analysis to explore the many and varied manifestations of "consumption." Throughout my fieldwork, I listened to countless stories of the consumption of health, lives, values, and the fabric of community. However, the plots, the actors, and the nature and consequences of the consumptive forces varied with the storyteller and setting. Through their stories of consumption, men and women speak to their differing experiences of class relations and to the struggles along gender lines that those experiences entailed. Mining men faced the threat of consumption in a literal sense through their daily encounters with the dangerous conditions of labor. Working-class women's experiences were often articulated through the discourse and practices of consumption as they struggled to fulfill their responsibilities as stewards of family and community. By attending to "relations of consumption," we may grasp a richer understanding of class and gender-based social experience than analyses of relations of production and reproduction have allowed.[42]

A powerful discourse of trust and betrayal reverberates throughout the histories of Butte and Chuquicamata. In chapter 7, I explore the ways in which the theme of trust and betrayal has manifested in labor-company relations, in gender relations, and in political promises made and broken. In materially and symbolically loaded ways, trust and betrayal have been encoded in social consciousness and practice. Workers in Butte and Chuquicamata have variably expressed their sense of betrayal by both union and company practices. They have found themselves the targets of blame for problems beyond their control. They are deeply skeptical of the calls for worker participation in the new forms of labor discipline they face. I argue that, ironically, this tension of trust and betrayal and its concomitant practices of resistance are key to the retooling of workers for their transient positions in the labor discipline of postmodern capitalism.

However, residents are not simply acquiescing to new forms of discipline and disposition. They are talking back, challenging the remaking of their histories and futures, even as they craft their own (re)visions of the past. I turn to the concept of "reclamation" as a key word for articulating this emerging arena of struggle. I draw from the Spanish, *reclamar*, "to make claims or to demand," in addressing the reclamation of histories, identities, and dignity underway on many fronts in Butte and Chuquicamata. I do not use the notion of reclamation merely as a metaphor for nostalgic yearnings for a romanticized past when copper was king. There is something more complicated at work here. In Butte, an emerging political economy of reclamation, from toxic waste cleanup to the marketing of labor history for tourism, suggests the possibilities for a curious revival of king copper at the turn of the century. In

Chuquicamata, residents are staking claims to the Anaconda legacy as evidence of their struggles and successes. They are demanding their fair share from the promise of nationalization, in which "copper belongs to all Chileans," and in the process challenging both the foreign and "domestic" occupiers of their desolate homeland. Perhaps these struggles for reclamation may reconfigure boundaries and fuel new border clashes, or perhaps they may spark new imaginings of common ground.

The many stories told throughout this book speak to the translation of global politics into local pain and possibility. In chapter 8, I return to broader questions of community and transnationalism. I reflect on the theoretical implications of this work and consider the lessons learned here in light of current cultural and political debates. Perhaps this history can inform us about the dangers and possibilities of the present systemic moment marked by global integration, brutal inequality, and a growing infatuation with free-trade agreements. Embedded in the fields of struggle addressed throughout the book — community, consumption, trust and betrayal, and reclamation — are lessons for social transformation. These lessons serve as both cautions and guides for envisioning alternative forms of alliance that challenge presumed boundaries and for discovering new possibilities in forging common ground.

THE PRACTICE OF RESEARCH

The practice of social research is intimately tied to the research of social practice. My research process was a trialectic one of being, doing, and becoming.[43] I became a traveler across many borders. I learned the importance of being in and with the many communities that I came to know, absorbing more than analyzing their complexity. The process of "doing research" meant being with people, hearing their stories, and telling a few of my own. I learned not only to allow but also to appreciate the intrusion of histories in the present and the meddling of the present in past affairs. I started from a place of partial knowledge and became a critical actor in my own history as I immersed myself in these stories of struggles and successes.

Connections of friendship and kinship were central to my Butte-based research. Through these ties, I met women who offered the wisdom and experience of getting by during the strike years. I came to know informal, neighborhood women's groups and gathered with them for coffee and conversation. I also participated in formal women's organizations and interviewed members regarding their recollections of fam-

ily and community life during the Anaconda years. For example, I met
the president of the Butte Business and Professional Women shortly after
arriving in Butte. She invited me to give a presentation on my project at
one of the group's monthly meetings. I agreed, and soon found myself in
the company of a dynamic group of older women with a wealth of
knowledge about Butte's labor history. Our friendships opened doors to
insightful conversations about coming of age as women in this masculine world of mining.

I followed their leads to other residents whose lives were tied to mining. I spoke with retired miners, labor leaders, and others who had lost
their livelihood when the mines closed. I asked about recollections of
family and community life during the Anaconda era and about their perspectives on community continuity and change in the ensuing years.
Their stories intermingled pain and pride as they excavated memories of
labor, copper, and community. Through these overlapping networks, I
grasped a broader sense of the history and practice of community and
came to appreciate the "complex webs of significance" in which peoples' lives were embedded.

I drew upon my past social work while living in Butte: for six
months, I facilitated the support group at Butte's battered women's shelter. Through this powerful personal and professional experience, I
gained a deeper appreciation of the complexities of women's suffering
and survival. As I listened to women's stories and witnessed the nurtur-
ing of support in the face of fear, I wondered about the connections to
women in Chile who have survived both personal and political violence.
My acquaintance with the diverse group of volunteers at the shelter
offered further opportunities to hear stories of women's social action in
the process of community change.

While in Butte, I attended regular meetings of the Citizen's Technical
Environmental Committee (CTEC), a watchdog group on environmental cleanup. Their purpose is to translate technical discourse into meaningful talk and action. The meetings revealed the tensions between high-
tech talk and local back talk. Themes of trust and betrayal, which
resonate throughout Butte's mining history, marked exchanges among
"outside experts" and local skeptics. These meetings highlighted and
articulated many levels of concern about the convulsive changes Butte
has experienced and the unsteady ground on which the community
stands.

I spent hours engaged in historical research in the Butte Pubic
Library, the Butte-Silver Bow Public Archives, and the Montana State

Historical Society Library, which houses the Anaconda Company papers. Daily conversations with local historians, archivists, and interested patrons were as valuable as the documents. These conversations helped me think about the data in different ways, discover new source material, and learn what other people believed to be important, interesting, and "true" when speaking of company-community relations.

Before I describe my Chilean-based research, I must speak of my own history. All researchers bring the baggage of their own "power-knowledge" and histories with them to the field.[44] Some, however, are more personally implicated in their subject of study than others. I am one such case. When I began fieldwork in 1991, I returned to Butte to live for the first time in seventeen years. My father closed his laundry business during Butte's hard times in the late 1970s, and he, like the unemployed miners, was one of many men who went elsewhere in search of work. But his name was well known among business and bar-room circles. Frequently, I made my introduction not as cultural researcher but as Tom's daughter. I built credibility through kinship rather than scholarship.

My father was born in Butte, with family ties to one of the close-knit neighborhoods perched atop the Butte Hill. Life took him in many directions, including a return to Butte in 1961 to pursue his dream of "getting ahead" by running his own business. My mother, born and raised in the "Garden City" of Missoula, 120 miles from Butte, experienced the dislocations of a foreigner upon arrival in the mining city. I grew up amid the complicated "structures of feeling" emanating from my father's working-class and my mother's middle-class roots.[45] We lived in a middle-class neighborhood on The Flats, comfortably distant from the hungry pit. I was the youngest of four children, all with reputations as good students — not necessarily an honor in a town where jocks were the heroes. Rhythms outside of mining created the tempo of our family life.

Butte was my father's town. My mother crafted a way of life through participation in service and social organizations, eventually coming to feel at home in this place so removed from her experience. It was through my relationship to my father that I began to see a broader reality of women's lives in Butte. From the time I was fourteen, I worked in my father's laundry alongside women who were often the sole supporters of their families. I felt the contradiction of my own "multiple subject positioning" when I was solicited to join the union ("union sister") and asked not to attend the meetings ("boss's daughter").

So I returned to study a place in which my own history is deeply enmeshed. It is the place where my "dividuated" sense of self was powerfully shaped. My role as daughter and sister opened doors to intimacies that may never have been divulged to an outsider. Beyond giving me access, these identities gave me a sense of security in this curious process of coming home. I found myself turning to my sisterly and daughterly demeanor in conversations and relationships with men in Butte. These kinship ties created a frame of reference in the relationship and a margin of safety for me as a single woman probing the pain of local history. However, throughout the fieldwork experience, I could never shake my uncomfortable sense of being a voyeur. Friendship, kinship, and scholarship make odd bedfellows. The structure and history of my own life in Butte enabled me to reach for the common ground in my community relationships. Yet it was in the very instrumentality of my reason for being in Butte that the questions of knowledge and power became (and remain) problematic. Throughout my fieldwork, I was privy to stories of trust and betrayal that took many forms. As I tell here the stories of the mining community, I am fully implicated in the tensions of trust and betrayal. I have a mandate to tell some stories and guard others.

Upon arrival in Chile in 1992, I lived in Santiago and worked in the national library, reading accounts of Chuquicamata over the years in the company-controlled press. In conversations about Chuquicamata and copper with acquaintances in Santiago, I was struck by the frequent reference to Chuqui as *otro mundo*, a world apart, physically and socially outside the "true" Chilean ethos. Santiago residents often spoke of *los privilegiados* (the privileged ones) of Chuquicamata, members of an elite working class. Many held strong beliefs about the "otherness" of those who mined the copper in that obscure corner of the country. These conversations provided a context for understanding the complicated sense of pride and resentment in the stories about privilege that I later heard in Chuquicamata.

I encountered a curious silence among feminist scholars in Santiago regarding the women of Chuquicamata. There is burgeoning interest in women's studies in Chile in the wake of the transition to democracy. The focus of the work is on women's political participation, the experiences of *campesinas* (peasant women), women in the seasonal agricultural labor sectors, and women activists in the poor and working-class neighborhoods of Chile's urban centers.[46] Women in the *gran minería*, the major mining districts, receive scarce attention.[47]

My search for data took me to the public relations office of

CODELCO in Santiago, the headquarters of the state-run copper mines. Though CODELCO is largely a man's world, the public relations office was staffed by women. I explained my project and asked for assistance in finding relevant materials as well as contact people in Chuquicamata. The staff provided me with publications on the recent history of Chilean copper. One woman showed me a book filled with photos of Chile's mining history. As she thumbed through the book, it dawned on her that there was not a single photo of a woman in the entire collection. She passed the book to her colleagues. As they talked about this absence of women, she made phone calls to women in Chuquicamata. I left the office with an armful of books and the names of women active in COR-MUTRAC (*Corporación de Mujeres Trabajadoras de CODELCO*), the organization of women workers at the Chuquicamata mines.

The twenty-four-hour bus trip from the greenery of Santiago to the austere desert in the north gave me my first impression of the distant isolation of Chuquicamata. It did not prepare me for the harsh climate of incessant wind, sun, and dust that left me feeling like a parched leaf ready to blow away into the desert. I found a room in a small, family-run guest house in Calama. I introduced myself to Chuquicamata by taking the three-hour public tour of the mines. The tour cost one dollar. Our guide informed us that the fees supported *Chuqui Ayuda* (Chuqui Aid), a nonprofit organization for children with serious medical problems, which was housed next door.

After the tour, I visited *Chuqui Ayuda*. I was welcomed by two of the volunteers, who told me the history of the organization. *Chuqui Ayuda* was founded in 1946 by the wives of the Yankee managers of the mines as a service organization that provided aid to "war orphans." In the 1950s, the organization's focus shifted to the needs of poor children in the region who lack access to good medical care. It is currently run by the wives of the Chilean managerial class of Chuquicamata. Women volunteers devote their time to handicrafts, which they sell at an annual Christmas bazaar to fund their efforts. In recent years, they have hired a crew of salaried women workers who make a product line from bedspreads to baby buntings, which they sell year round. My hosts invited me to their homes, offered both friendship and thoughtful reflections on life in Chuquicamata, and encouraged my participation in the organization, should I return for a longer stint.

I became acquainted with the organizer of CORMUTRAC, a woman born and raised in Chuquicamata, who had worked for the mines for more than twenty years. She introduced me to a diverse group of women employed in secretarial, administrative, and ancillary services of the huge mining operation. CORMUTRAC focuses its efforts on women's professional development as well as on family and community concerns that affect the mining region. The organization provided entree into a network of women whose lives were tied to the mines.

I also visited the Calama-based center for PRODEMU (*Promoción y Desarrollo de la Mujer*), part of a national network of organizations that promote women's personal and social development. The local center sponsors a wide range of classes and workshops from ceramics to cosmetology and includes courses in adult basic education and talks on issues such as violence against women. The center's director encouraged my participant observation. I found the center to be a valuable resource for meeting women whose lives were connected to mining.

Perhaps my most profound moment of serendipity, in which I found my life affected by and entwined with the experiences of other women, occurred on October 18, 1992. I had gone to the plaza in the center of Calama that Sunday afternoon as a dutiful fieldworker, waiting for culture to happen. I saw a copper monument dedicated to twenty-six men who had been executed on October 19, 1973, under the Pinochet dictatorship. As I was reading the homage to these men, a small group made up mostly of women passed through the main street. They were carrying placards with photos of these same men and banners calling for truth and justice.

I joined the march and walked with the group to the edge of town, where a bus was waiting. I asked one of the women if I could join them. She invited me on the bus, telling me that she was the widow of one of the executed and this was the annual memorial service organized by *La Agrupación de Familiares de los Ejecutados de Calama* (Organization of Family Members of the Executed of Calama). First, we paid homage to the men at the municipal cemetery. Then we traveled to a site in the desert, several kilometers from Calama, where bone fragments of one of the men had been found a few years earlier. It was a deeply moving moment. I stood hand in hand among strangers in the desert and felt for the first time the depths of violence that penetrated so many lives during the dictatorship.

I became acquainted with women of the *agrupación*. They are a diverse group, some of whose husbands, fathers, brothers, and sons were labor leaders, political activists, mine bosses, or workingmen at the Dupont explosive factory or in the copper mines.[48] Some of these women were far removed from copper mining. Others were intimately attached to mining history. All were bound together through violence and their ongoing struggles for truth and justice. I realized in my epiphanic moment in the desert that I could not understand the history of this place without comprehending the layers of violence and fear that penetrated community life during the years of the dictatorship. Later, I learned that I could not grasp this recent structure of violence without appreciating that which had come before.

In these very distinct settings and in a very short time, I met women whose lives crisscrossed the Chuquicamata mining community. I left Chile in November 1992 and returned to Butte, and over the course of the next year, I corresponded through letters with several women of Chuqui and Calama. In August of 1993, I returned to Chile for several more months of fieldwork. I rekindled ties with the women's organizations and became an active participant, attending classes and workshops, making handicrafts, and talking with other women. I spent many hours in hopeful and tearful conversations with friends from the *agrupación*. An elemental power of connection carried us to and beyond the profound differences in our histories. Their struggles and strength bolstered my faith in people's capacity to transform history.

There are many gaps in this study. My limited knowledge of Chuquicamata does not match my detailed life experience in Butte. However, given the ties to the Chuquicamata community that I established in my first visit, I was able to move readily into participation, observation, and conversations about community with many women. Through some of the women, I was able to meet and hear the stories of their fathers, sons, and partners. In Chuquicamata, I was not daughter, sister, or homegirl. I was the open, educated gringa with a freedom of movement far beyond the imaginings of many of those who opened their homes and lives to me. Though I eagerly accepted the invitations of women, I was hesitant and reserved in approaching the union and company men of Chuquicamata. Some of the silences in this work reflect the unasked questions behind my own silence.

Two opportunities gave me a deeper insight into the current struggles and dilemmas facing the residents of the Chuquicamata mining community. First, purely by happenstance, I arrived in Chuquicamata at a moment when CODELCO was in the midst of a profound reorganization. The reorganization process — known as the "Cultural Transformation of the Labor Force" (yes, that's their name for it . . . every postmodernist's dream) — calls for modernization and streamlining of the mines through the development of Autonomous Work Units (*Unidades*

Autónomas de Administración) and the formation of "polyvalent" workers. Corporate calls for labor participation in the change process have been met with skepticism. Workers are trying to decipher the meaning and power behind this foreign language.

The cultural transformation is a major topic of conversation throughout Chuquicamata and Calama. I did not have to work at gathering data on the subject. Everyone had an opinion, be it on the bus, in a taxi, or in any conversation that lasted more than five minutes with local residents. It did not take an astute cultural anthropologist to see that something was afoot.

I was invited by a newly formed organization of miner's wives to join them while they planned a community meeting to express their concerns about proposed changes in the organization of CODELCO-Chuqui. They were seeking answers from corporate and union leaders regarding the community impact of the changes and looking to mobilize women's participation in the change process. The group invited me to speak about women in Butte and the connections to Chuquicamata at the public meeting. In mid-November 1993, I stood on the stage in Chuqui's grand union hall, a legacy from the Anaconda years. I spoke about women, struggles, and hope in my carefully practiced Spanish. In the days that followed, I encountered women on the streets and in the stores of Chuquicamata who had attended the meeting. They invited me to their homes to talk more about their lives. At that moment, I acknowledged that I was involved not in a study *of* social change but *for* social change.

My second opportunity also came about through my connections to networks of women acting on their personal and political concerns. Nineteen ninety-three was election year in Chile. A friend had invited me to join a gathering of women at her home in support of a forceful (and successful) woman candidate for the national congress. Twenty women talked politics and expressed their concerns about issues of poverty, health, housing, and economy that affected their lives. I was invited to attend another campaign stop: a meeting of a women's neighborhood organization, whose members were heads of households or wives of men employed as low-paid contracted laborers in the national mines. Through these experiences, I came to appreciate deeply the distinction of *dos mundos*, two worlds, in the mining region — worlds that separate the relatively well-compensated employees of the national mines from the contracted laborers, underemployed, and those trying to make a living in the struggling service economy. Fear and uncertainty regarding the social and economic future of the region and the daily struggle of holding body and soul together were palpable in women's talk. These concerns fueled rather than dampened their commitment to action. I came face-to-face with another meaning of *dos mundos*: my privileged position as an educated woman from the United States had given me access to these worlds of pain. I witnessed and felt the political contradictions as I sat among women, strangers, who talked of hunger, illness, and survival.

By the summer of 1994, I had completed a first draft of the dissertation and identified specific gaps in the data. I returned to Chuquicamata for three weeks with specific questions in mind and a few roughly translated chapters in hand. It was a fruitful visit. I had lengthy conversations with men in labor and management posts, whom I had not had access to in earlier fieldwork. I heard detailed accounts of particular strike actions and moments of labor repression. Perhaps most important, I began to see the long-term possibilities and obligations of this project.

Through these kaleidoscopic experiences, I have come to hear, reflect on, and write about the stories of copper and community. Stories create windows into history. They constitute a symbolic shorthand that coalesces politically powerful forces into personally meaningful accounts. The stories we tell provide keys to understanding how we make sense of the structures of our lives. A collection of stories told provides a discursive topography of cultural and political history. The themes and elaborations, fissures and gaps mark the terrain of the thinkable, talkable, and do-able. Throughout this work, I consciously select stories that talk back to and engage with one another, perhaps amplifying some "truths" while obscuring others. I ask you to be mindful of a question: How do we become invested in the truth value of the stories we tell?

The following chapters tell how-to stories of crafts(wo)manship, survival stories of holding body and soul together, and stories of tremendous courage in the face of fear. They are the imaginings of community, its loss and reconstitution. I have changed the names and identifying information of the many storytellers whose voices are heard here. I take responsibility for the structure of this work, which may at best only partially apprehend the meaning and power behind the words.[49] Given the powerful resonance of trust and betrayal throughout this work, the reader will encounter gaps and silences and stories that refuse to be told. In that vague space between scholarship and friendship, I heard many stories of personal and political pain. Though they left their marks on the researcher and the research, few such stories will be committed to print.

This is the case with many intimate experiences of violence, both familial and political. The reader may be frustrated by references and allusions to histories of violence that remain in the shadows, suggested but not defined. In fact, this delicate and at times obtuse treatment of violence mirrors my own fieldwork experience. People spoke cautiously, guardedly, of the physical and emotional scars they carry. A miner's wife, recounting the struggles and losses in her life, said, "You never really learn to live with the pain; you learn to live around it." Out of respect for those intimate spaces that I can neither fully comprehend nor describe, I have chosen to write around them.

TWO

Mining History

A Political Chronology

The dialectics of history, then, are structural throughout. Powered by disconformities between conventional values and intentional values, between intersubjective meanings and subjective interests, between symbolic sense and symbolic reference, the historical process unfolds as a continuous and reciprocal movement between the practice of the structure and the structure of the practice.

Marshall Sahlins 1981

It doesn't matter where you are in the world or how different your life and language and all might be, when you live with something like the Anaconda Company, it shapes your life and you've got common problems.

Butte miner's wife 1993

This chapter explores the cultural politics of copper from a historical perspective.[1] I examine the relationship of the Anaconda Company to its key sites of copper production, Butte and Chuquicamata, in an international political context. By looking at long-term processes, multiple and contested meanings of particular events, and responses of on-the-ground actors, this chapter exposes the complicated interplay of local, state, and corporate interests. It offers a case study in the shifting logics and practices of capitalism, their contradictions and resolutions, and their insinuation in the experiences of daily life from the Andes to the Rockies. It traces the connections between Butte and Chuquicamata and unearths patterns of practice only discernible when those communities' histories are considered in relation to one another and to a larger set of social, economic, and political forces.

In constructing this chronology, I do not pretend to be searching for a single, "true" historical account. Rather, I examine the truths represented in diverse accounts of history and illustrate how these truths are given meaning and power in the personal stories of people's daily lives. The story of a strike as told by the company-owned press constructs a reality distinct from that of the labor press. Neither captures the fear still palpable in the voice of a woman recalling her sleepless night when she thought her husband had been detained by strikebreakers.

ANACONDA:
BIRTH OF A MULTINATIONAL CORPORATION

Butte began as a gold and silver mining camp in the mid-1800s. Vast copper reserves were buried beneath this thin veneer of precious metals. Early miners stripped the top layers and had little interest in the red metal underneath. Copper mining was a labor-intensive process that required extensive capital investment to be profitable. By the late 1800s, the value of copper was recognized. The discovery of the electric current opened a new world of technological possibilities, and copper, an excellent conductor, became an important commodity on the world market.[2]

The recorded history of Butte focuses on the stories of the "Copper Kings," W. A. Clark, Augustus Heinze, and Marcus Daly. These men battled for political and economic domination of the city of Butte, the state of Montana, and the copper industry.[3] Social historians and local residents celebrate the audacity of these Big Men, who wielded their power through ownership of the local press, the flagrant purchase of Senate and judicial seats, and bold maneuverings on the international copper market. From these corporate antagonisms and alliances, the Anaconda Copper Mining Company, started by Marcus Daly and his cadre of financial backers, emerged as the victor at the turn of the twentieth century. The Anaconda Company, or "the company" as it was locally known, became synonymous with Butte.[4]

As the copper industry expanded, so did the need for a permanent labor force. Butte was a magnet for laborers, drawing large numbers of European immigrants in the late 1800s. Some made their way directly to Butte, whereas others followed the mining circuit from Michigan to the Mountain West.[5] The large Irish community gained a stronghold in local politics, and the Catholic Church became a powerful institutional force in the Butte community.[6]

Work in the mines was hard and dangerous, and miners began to organize. Many lives were claimed from mining accidents and "miner's consumption," the popular name for silicosis, a lung disease resulting from inhalation of silica particulate. Miners labored in hot, dangerous conditions in the underground mines and went home to inadequate housing at the end of their shifts.[7] In 1878, the Butte Miner's Union was founded to demand wage increases, shorter work days, and improvements in working conditions. It also established an accident and death benefit fund for miners and their families. Throughout my fieldwork, I was reminded of the harsh realities of mining life as residents talked of losing grandfathers, fathers, and husbands to the mines. "Men in the mines were lucky to live past forty" is a powerful local truism.

Butte became known as the "Gibraltar of Unionism" in the United States. It was the birthplace of the Western Federation of Miners (WFM), with the Butte Miners Union (BMU) becoming the first WFM affiliate in 1893. Unions gained strength while the copper kings were embroiled in their own power struggles in the 1890s. By the early 1900s, however, union organization in Butte was marked by factionalism, corruption, and infiltration by company operatives. The more conservative Irish Democratic leadership of the BMU, many of whom shared a bond of Irish kinship with Anaconda's founder Marcus Daly, found themselves increasingly at odds with the more radical WFM leadership. Ethnic loyalties sometimes undercut a broader working-class identification, thus steering the local union on a conservative course in its dealings with the company.[8]

By 1910, Butte had become a site of organizing efforts by the Industrial Workers of the World (IWW, or Wobblies) and the center of Socialist Party power in the state.[9] The BMU leadership was challenged by more radicalized factions, and struggles over the direction of unionism ensued among the Wobblies, socialists, and "conservatives." Butte's Irish Catholic political machine lost power to the nascent Socialist Party from 1911 to 1914, and party activists gained a foothold in union politics. Anaconda took action against this progressive shift in union organization. In 1912, the company instituted an employment policy known as the "rustling card system," which tightened control on hiring practices and ensured that men with reputations as union agitators were denied work in the mines.[10] Further union conflicts ensued, possibly incited or encouraged by company operatives. The conflicts culminated in the violent destruction of the Miner's Union Hall on June 23, 1914. In August of 1914, after a number of outbreaks of violence and a series of temporary mine shutdowns, Butte was occupied by the National Guard under what would be the first of several periods of martial law. In September, Anaconda announced an open shop and its refusal to recognize any unions (Toole 1972, 138).

CONSOLIDATING POWER

The labor situation in Butte resonated with the national tone of repression in 1914. Fear and hysteria marked the local, state, and national scene at the entry into World War I, when individuals and groups with leftist sympathies were viewed as threats to national security. With the imposition of martial law, the Anaconda Company was not hampered by labor's organizing efforts from 1914 to 1917.[11] However, a disastrous mine fire in 1917 that cost the lives of 164 men resulted in a resurgence of union action. The unsafe conditions of the mines became a rallying point for mass organization.[12]

A strike ensued, accompanied by violence and intimidation of miners on the part of the company's private security forces. Miners joined together to form the Metal Mine Workers Union. Labor organizers were quick to ally themselves with miners in the demand for just wages and safe conditions. Representatives of the American Federation of Labor (AFL), the International Union of Mine Mill and Smelter Workers (IUMMSW, or Mine-Mill), and the IWW courted the affiliation of the Butte miners. The miners also garnered the support of Jeannette Rankin, Montana's pacifist congresswoman, who offered to serve as a mediator of the strike. Though the offer was soundly rejected by Anaconda, it represented a victory for the miners in their struggle to gain government attention to their plight (Calvert 1988, 103–14).

Frank Little, a radical labor organizer, arrived in Butte shortly after the fateful fire to promote the miners' affiliation with the IWW. He was a vocal critic of capitalism in general and the Anaconda Company in particular. Little was lynched in Butte by an "unnamed gang" on August 1, 1917. His dramatic death served as a powerful symbol of the fate that awaited those who challenged corporate power. Although the fledgling Butte union was to affiliate with the Mine-Mill rather than the IWW, Little's death served to crystallize labor solidarity and energize the waning strike effort. Six days after Little's death, Jeannette Rankin spoke to the U.S. House of Representatives, condemning the violence in Butte, supporting workers' rights, and calling for the nationalization of the copper mines. Her stance provoked a strong reaction from Anaconda's president, Con Kelley. Repression against progressive labor and the left continued.[13]

As tensions heightened, the governor of Montana, Samuel Stewart, again ordered a National Guard regiment to Butte and declared a state of emergency. Federal troops were garrisoned in Butte to "maintain order" from August 1917 to January 1921.[14] In 1918, the Montana State Legislature passed the Criminal Sindicalism Act, which outlawed the IWW, and the Montana Sedition Act, which made it a crime to speak against the state. The law bolstered corporate interests. It served as the model for similar revisions in the National Espionage Act crafted the same year.[15]

Labor activism in Butte had been subdued but not completely extinguished. The postwar months dealt a severe blow to the copper industry and the Butte economy. Anaconda responded with layoffs and mine closures. Butte's population total dropped dramatically. Unemployed miners and soldiers roamed the streets of Butte. Anaconda added insult to injury with a wage reduction for the remaining miners. The action provoked a strike and the resurgence of IWW activity, fueled by a nationwide wave of labor activism.

In April 1920, the IWW called on the miners to join them in opposition to corporate greed and initiated a picket line on Anaconda Road, which lead to the entrances of numerous underground mines. The miners joined in, and operations were brought to a halt with a mass picket that filled the road. Four days later, company security forces opened fire on the picketing miners, killing one and wounding sixteen men.[16] The violence squelched the strike and marked the end of IWW influence in the Butte mines. With labor problems in check and copper a key national interest, Anaconda began to expand its empire (Calvert 1988, 115–26; Chaplin 1920, 9).

Anaconda acquired new mining and manufacturing properties and explored foreign copper resources. The company purchased mining interests in Mexico and began extensive exploration work at Potrerillos in Chile.[17] During the postwar slump, with its Butte operations curtailed, Anaconda invested in major development of its subsidiary, Andes Copper Mining Company in Potrerillos, Chile (*Annual Report* 1920). With the copper market still depressed in the United States, Anaconda closed the Butte mines from April 1921 to January 1922. During this time, the company finalized its purchase of the American Brass Company, which spurred its need for more copper supplies.[18] In 1923, after two years of considerable negotiation, the Anaconda Company reached agreement with the New York industrialist Guggenheim family to purchase the Chuquicamata copper mines.[19] With its U.S. labor force subdued and this new acquisition under its belt, Anaconda was in a position to consolidate and expand corporate power (*Annual Report* 1923; Marcosson 1957, 194–203).[20]

ENTRY INTO CHILE

The Chuquicamata region had its own history of labor struggles before
Anaconda's arrival. The incorporation of the Chile Exploration Company by the Guggenheims in 1912 signaled the start of intensive exploitation of the copper deposits and concerted efforts at labor organizing
in Chuquicamata.

Chile has a long history of labor movements, from the miners' rebel-
lions in Chañarcillo in 1834 to the strikes and mobilizations by dock
workers, urban laborers, and coal miners in Valparaíso, Santiago, and
Lota beginning in the 1850s. Scholarly and popular accounts of Chilean
labor history describe the emergent labor movement in the early twentieth century with references to the Valparaíso dockworkers' strike in
1903, and more significant for mining history, the struggles of the
nitrate miners of the desert north.[21] Social historians and labor activists
claim the nitrate region as the *cuna* (cradle) of labor organization in
northern Chile.

Current labor leaders in Chuquicamata tell a scriptlike story of working-class struggles. The history begins with the struggles against deplorable conditions in the nitrate mines. It is crystallized in the massacre of
thousands of nitrate miners, wives, and children by state militia at
Santa Maria de Iquique in 1907. And it speaks to a diaspora of labor
consciousness throughout the northern mining region as the word of
struggles spread and unemployed nitrate miners sought work in the copper mines.[22]

The labor-history script has a mythic quality in the telling, but it is
grounded in fact. For example, Luis Emilio Recabarren, a noted labor
activist, member of the Chilean House of Deputies and founder of the
Chilean Socialist Worker's Party, wrote an editorial in 1913 describing
his trip to Chuquicamata to support the organization of the first miner's
union. His editorial describes the exploitative conditions in which
Chuquicamata's thirteen hundred miners labored and predicts: "A
Miner's Union has been organized that is still small, but I am sure that
it will be a firm base for the future organization that will give the miners the power to put an end to all of the exploitation and tyranny. . . .
The Miner's Union of Chuquicamata will adopt its statutes in form
identical to the labor organization of Iquique."[23] Recabarren's words
resonate with those of current union activists in *Sindicato Dos*, Chuquicamata's oldest labor union. Founded in 1915, the union shares Recabarren's vision of class struggle. Communist party philosophy and direction have been instrumental in the union's history.

Labor unrest surged once again throughout Chile from 1917 to 1920, and fledgling unions gained membership and organizational force.[24] Eulogio Gutiérrez and Marcial Figueroa wrote of the rapid growth of the *federación obrera* (workers' federation) in Chuquicamata and its demise at the hands of the Guggenheims.[25] A significant number of Chuquicamata's miners had joined the *federación*, and in December of 1919, they voted to march in solidarity with striking railworkers in Antofagasta. The company responded by posting notices that any worker who failed to report for work on the afternoon of December 20 (the designated time for the march) would be relieved of his duties and expelled from the camp. The notice sparked indignation among the workers, who risked their jobs, participated in the solidarity action, and paralyzed operations in the mines. Military troops called in at the company's request forced forty *federación* members and their families out of the camp and arrested the union leadership.

By December 23, a state of emergency had been declared, more workers were forced to leave the camp, and nearly six hundred workers had been detained. Though the company accused outside agitators of fomenting dissension, Gutiérrez and Figueroa list the names of sixteen union leaders, showing that all were resident workers, many married with children. These sixteen men were sent to the public prison in Antofagasta. This show of corporate and military force effectively subdued nascent labor action in Chuquicamata for several years.

Anaconda's entry into Chile in 1923 coincided with a period of constitutional reform and demands for social change. Arturo Alessandri Palma, a corporate lawyer turned populist, had been elected president in 1920. His reformist agenda was limited by economic depression, widespread unemployment, and resistance from the Chilean elite. His tenure in office was troubled by growing military tensions and attempted coups. Although Alessandri oversaw the approval of a new constitution that included an extensive new labor code, he resigned in late 1925, claiming unbearable military pressure. He was followed by the rise to power of General Carlos Ibañez del Campo, who, first as minister of the interior and then as president, operated a virtual dictatorship from 1927 to 1931 that was marked by violent repression of communism and nearly all forms of political opposition. He sought to split the communist-led labor movement in the country by sponsoring government-backed unions. Labor reforms were not implemented until 1931.[26]

Anaconda's Chuquicamata-based subsidiary, Chile Exploration Company (CHILEX), was in a good position to establish corporate hegemony with little interference on the part of organized labor. And when labor attempted to organize, the company squelched it with the tried and true methods it had practiced in Butte. Company bosses kept a blacklist of presumed labor activists, which they exchanged with their compatriots in the El Teniente mines, ensuring that workers fired from one mine would not be hired in another.[27]

Ricardo Latcham, a social critic living and writing in Chuquicamata in the 1920s, wrote of a fellow named Oscar Hidalgo, who "earned his salary from Chile Exploration Company, though no one knew what he did." The company moved him around a lot, and in Latcham's observation, he appeared to be a company spy. Hidalgo was assigned to work on the election of the *Federación de Empleados Particulares* (white-collar employees) being formed in 1924. He "had lots of money and resources at his disposal and was fraudulently elected president of the federation, and in his hands it died" (Latcham 1926, 38–39). The union was not to be officially established until 1930, and then only under company control.[28]

According to Latcham, corporate influence extended far beyond local union elections. Anaconda made its influence felt in national politics through payments to politicians for political favors, commission appointments, and intervention in electoral affairs (1926, 40, 42). Prominent lawyers were involved in promoting company interests in the national political scene. However, Latcham argues that "Yankee intervention in politics had been most active in the neighboring town of Calama, where Chile Exploration Company enjoyed virtual control of the municipal government" (1926, 42). In sum, Anaconda entered Chile when copper was surpassing nitrate as the cornerstone of the Chilean economy. The company became a major player in this young democracy. The story that unfolds illustrates the contradictions between state sovereignty and international capitalism. The history is one of a compromised democracy, in which the Chilean government contested and acquiesced to the demands of a powerful corporation that was often backed by U.S. government policy and politics.

INSTITUTIONALIZING CORPORATE-LABOR RELATIONS

The Anaconda Company made major capital investments in Chile during the 1920s. The company reaped benefits of higher copper prices, and the Chilean government developed a taxation system to reclaim some of these corporate profits. The heady times of profit were short-lived, because copper prices crashed in 1929 and the depression took its toll with massive unemployment in Chile and the United States. To promote economic recovery in the United States, a high tariff was imposed on copper imports. The effects of the tariff were hard felt in Chile, where copper production cutbacks resulted in a 66 percent unemployment rate in the Chilean mines in 1931 to 1932 (Corporación Nacional del Cobre 1974, 35).

The 1930s brought expanded government regulation in efforts to support economic recovery. The Chilean Government initiated a series of laws addressing exports, taxation, and control of the sales of natural resources. In the United States, the National Recovery Act supported a broad range of economic and social welfare programs. Both countries initiated important labor legislation. In Chile, a sharp depression had spurred the collapse of the Ibañez regime. The country endured a succession of military coups over the following one and a half years. Chile's labor reforms were enacted in the Labor Code of 1931, with Alessandri returning as president in 1932. Under the code, unions won the right to organize but were brought under state supervision by the setting of legal limits on strikes and the institutionalization of a fragmented labor system that split workers into plant unions and professional unions.[29]

The discourse in La Voz Sindical (The union voice), the "official organ of the unions of Chuquicamata" from 1931 to 1934, reflected both these political changes and the philosophy and intent of the new labor law to build a harmonious partnership among labor, capital, and government and to reject communism. La Voz Sindical praised the "new union orientation":

> In its new form, unionism has lost its communist, revolutionary character, it has ceased being apolitical and antipatriotic in order to become what it truly is and should be in its essence: the organizing force of the society. . . . All social categories should form economic bodies, and should constitute unions: the bosses, the salaried employees, and the laborers. For everyone, unionism is a voice of order, a clear formula, a well-made and healthy orientation. Its end is the legal ordering of the society in the economy; in the occupation of the forces of capital and labor, under the tutelage of the State.[30]

Despite legal recognition, union organizing suffered under the antilabor policies that characterized Alessandri's second presidential term. Massive unemployment throughout the country, and particularly in the troubled nitrate region, created a labor surplus that the mining companies used to their advantage.[31]

In the United States, New Dealers were advocating reform of labor legislation. The Wagner-Connery Bill, introduced in 1934, provided for union recognition, elections for union representation, and a process for regulating labor disputes. Labor unrest and a wave of strikes throughout the country pointed to the urgency of this legislation.[32] Butte was a site of labor's struggle, with a long and at times violent strike in the copper mines that ran from May to September 1934. The company-owned newspapers ranted about unreasonable union demands and gave front-page attention to the "lawless acts of violence and rowdyism by mobs of hoodlums," disrupting their efforts to keep the mines operating.[33] Despite company claims, however, the strike was less violent than earlier labor conflicts, and this time local authorities supported the striking miners, and the governor did not put the National Guard at the company's disposal.[34]

The Eye Opener, a prolabor press, offered contrasting accounts. The paper named "scab" workers who "went behind the fence" to work during the strike and reported on sympathy strikes and boycotts by other Butte unions. It praised the refusal of Butte newsboys to deliver the company-owned newspapers and published the "big salaries" earned by Anaconda "Big Shots" while the people of Butte suffered. Emotional editorials played on and fueled miners' resentments:[35]

> What is the Purpose of the Present Strike? What is the present strike all about? Well, here is just about what it amounts to. The A.C.M. Company, which has done just about everything it could to hold Montana back so it would dominate everything; the A.C.M. Company which maintains a flock of lying newspapers, so as to keep people ignorant; the A.C.M. Company which maintains a bunch of henchmen or fixers to salve legislators; the Company which never does anything for Butte in the way of permanency; the Company which has steadily reduced wages in its mines by cutting the prices per foot on contracts; the Company that washes its hands of its employees as soon as they are incapacitated by that occupational disease known as the Miner's Con; the Company that pays its President Con Kelly [*sic*] from $200,000.00 to nearly half a million dollars a year; the Company that fights compensation cases of its employees to the very last; the Company known the world over for blacklisting those who do not line up with their policies; the Company that has entered into various lines of business, other than mining, in competition with local merchants; the Company that persecutes and invisibly boycotts; the Company that drives its laborers; the Company that now refuses to recognize the demands of its awakened miners.
>
> The miners, who for years have slaved in the hot boxes; the men who made it possible for Con Kelly to grab these enormous amounts of salary; the men, unorganized for years, who were compelled to take what the Company wanted to give; the men whose contract rate was cut and cut and cut; the men who were forced, if they wanted to hold their jobs, to work alone in dangerous places, inhale poisonous gases and deadly dust. These men are

asking to have the "killing contract system" and the one-man machine elim-
inated from the mines and to have a 6-hour day. What fair minded person
would say these miners are not entitled to such demands?

The strike of 1934 remains firmly embedded in the memories of
many older Butte residents. Their stories are marked by the particular
language of strikes, the talk of "scab" labor, and powerful images of
boundaries as men were brought in to work behind the fence. As one
old-timer recalled, "We used to practice our pitchin' arms throwing
rocks at those scabs behind the fence. They'd walk to work with paper
bags over their heads, and we'd run alongside to get a peek at their
faces, but lots of 'em you could recognize just by their shoes." Jack, the
son of a miner, offered this account:

> We lived near The Hill. It used to be all lit up, but during the strike it was all
> pitch-black. All you could see was big spot lights, shooting around like dur-
> ing the war. And they'd have guards, oh, you bet, and when the strike started
> they'd bring in railroad cars, Pullman cars. They'd bring everything in — all
> the food, they'd even bring women in. Everybody behind that fence was well
> taken care of. Scab laborers just stayed there. And the railroad cars would be
> there with all the food and booze and everything.[36]

Political cartoons in *The Eye Opener* during the 1934 strike captured
the contradictions of wealth and poverty, played with representations of
gender, and reflected the company's ever-present threat of force. "Big
Wages for Gunmen" plays on images of corporate greed, class distinctions, and exploitation as it ironizes freedom of the press. Curious gender images are evoked by the company Mama, taking care of her "boys,"
the scabs and gunmen, who do not deserve the status of "real men." The
gunman's response, "He won't play Indian with me," may reveal more
than pervasive local racism at the time. Older miners in Butte say you
could recognize company gunmen by their cowboy hats, which, contrary
to Western fashion of the day, real Butte men did not wear. Thus the message is that no self-respecting Butte miner would be conned into a dangerous game with the company "cowboys" (see figs. 5 and 6).

A brief article appearing in *The Eye Opener* in June 1934 raises the
troubling contradiction that perhaps the strike itself was serving company interests:

> Copper Surplus Big Asset to Company: Who represented the sweaty miners
> at the meetings which lead to the adoption of the present copper code? The
> code was primarily the work of the heads of the various domestic copper
> companies. None of the nine newspapers owned by Anaconda Copper
> Mining Company in Montana published the most important section of the

Big Wages for Gunmen---

No Money for Miners

Figure 5. "Big Wages for Gunmen." *Eye Opener,* 26 July 1934, 1.

copper code as adopted. This highly important section reads as follows: "Any copper mined prior to May 22, 1934, which has been contracted for by any fabricating company will be considered Blue Eagle copper." In plain everyday English this section means that the Anaconda may call on its huge copper surplus as having been duly contracted for by the Anaconda subsidiary known as the American Brass Company. No wonder that the Anaconda has made no effort to arbitrate or make any concessions which might lead to settlement of the strike.[37]

The Anaconda Company stockholders report of 1934 suggests that there was some truth to this concern. The report indicates that copper

Figure 6.   "Don't Cry Dear." *Eye Opener,* 6 June 1934, 1.

surpluses were high and that the company could afford to wait out the union (*Annual Report* 1934). This was a time of domestic recession and climbing foreign markets. Anaconda was in a good position to reap the benefits from the sales of its Chilean copper on the foreign market. When the strike was settled in September, workers had gained raises, concessions in the contract mining system, and union recognition. And in Chuquicamata, copper production increased from 61,000 metric tons in 1933 to 98,000 in 1934, signaling both recovery from economic depression and Anaconda's capacity to strategically balance and exploit its transnational resources (Corporación Nacional del Cobre 1974, 485 table 1; United States Department of Interior 1934 and 1935). While local labor struggles were waged, the news headlines in Butte were dominated by international events, including civil war in Austria and Hitler's rise to power. As conflict brewed in Europe, things began looking up for the copper industry.

The 1930s were also a time of intensive vertical integration for the Anaconda Company. Through its network of subsidiaries, the company became the world's largest producer and consumer of copper (Marcosson 1957, 167–93; Girvan 1974, 117). In spite of its rhetoric, the company did not necessarily want to see high domestic copper prices, because company subsidiaries were its own best customers. We often hear talk of the "copper market" as if it were an abstraction ruled by neutral economic principles. In reality, very little copper was traded on the open market. We can better think of this market as a series of long-standing relationships and obligations between buyers and sellers, based on close ties, anticipated future contracts, and mutual risk avoidance.[38] Chile was interested in keeping copper prices high, because tax revenues generated funds for state operations. There was growing resentment in the country about being a captive producer beholden to foreign corporations. The Chilean government wanted a role in the pricing and marketing of copper but lacked access to networks of market relations. It was the negotiation of these political and economic relationships that shaped corporate practices in the coming decades.

WARS HOT AND COLD

The growing demands for copper during World War II relieved economic tensions and created political ones for Anaconda and the Chilean government. In Chile in 1938, the Popular Front rose to power, constructing a coalition government of radicals, socialists, and communists that won strong working-class support. Following its slogan, "*pan, techo, y abrigo*" (bread, a roof, and clothing), the Popular Front promoted state-sponsored industrialization, social welfare, and public works programs. Revenues from copper taxation were critical for industrial expansion and the service of foreign debt. As historian Thomas Klubock describes, the Popular Front government, under President Pedro Aguirre Cerda (1938–1941), promoted a nationalist discourse that recognized and valorized miners as citizens. The government sought to implement labor reform, at times intervening directly in labor conflicts.[39]

The copper enclave, however, kept tight control of its industry. Caught between its dependence on copper taxes and U.S. government assistance on the one hand and the growing radicalization of the miners on the other, the Popular Front was unable to make good on its commitments to the Chilean working class.[40] And while copper production was at its peak in Chile, contributing to national tax revenues, wartime copper price controls, imposed unilaterally by the U.S. government,

scaled back Chile's earnings from copper taxes and sales, further jeop-
ardizing the Popular Front's precarious position.

Though the Chilean government remained neutral during World War
II, Chuquicamata was a site of U.S. patriotism for the war effort.
Chuquicamata's weekly newspaper, *La Pampa*, published reports of the
Allied efforts and praised patriotic production records.[41] Residents of
Chuquicamata's American Camp (exclusive enclave of Yankee managers
and other foreign professionals) kept their fingers on the Allied pulse as
well, while suffering few wartime privations. As one former American
Camp resident recalled:

> We of course kept up on things with shortwave radio. The Voice of America
> or BBC, we could get that. And then we'd get our magazines and so forth.
> There were some things you could not get, the shipping was disrupted for a
> time. Oh, I can remember the time everybody was out of Corn Flakes. We'd
> get Corn Flakes and peanut butter, and of course Americans have to have
> peanut butter, and the rest of the world could care less. The staples were all
> there, but they would ship in food to a limited extent, and you had rationing,
> for instance on some things, for instance, on those little cookie things. Yeah,
> Ritz Crackers, because they were so good at parties. People would just grab
> them and save them. Well, you would be limited to a couple of boxes when
> a shipment came in. But for all the staples and so forth, we weren't rationed
> on anything. The sugar, tea, anything. There was no shortage of anything.[42]

In Washington, D.C., Anaconda executives maintained close contact
with the Office of Price Administration and the War Production Board.
In Butte, the company and its unions joined together to promote patriotism and production through their Victory Labor-Management Committee (see fig. 7).[43] The committee's wartime publication, *The Copper
Commando*, praised the contributions of miners and their families to the
Allied cause. The promotional posters of the Victory Labor-Management
Committee reflected and promoted national sentiments, praised the
patriotism of a steady workforce, and connected Butte to a world community fighting for democracy. As part of wartime policy, miners' wages
were frozen. When the Mine-Mill protested, they were criticized for their
lack of patriotism. Meanwhile, back in Chile, the Allied cause enjoyed
the support of radical President Juan Antonio Rios (1941–1946) and his
coalition government of radicals, communists, and socialists.

The end of World War II brought another downturn in the copper
industry, with surplus copper and wartime price controls still in effect.
Anaconda rejected the petition for wage increases by the Chuquicamata

Figure 7. ACM Victory Labor-
Management Committee Flyer,
October 1943. Courtesy of
Montana Historical Society
Archives, Anaconda Company
Papers MC 169, 71–75.

unions in 1945, claiming the hoped-for wage increases to be unrealistic
given the current state of the copper industry.[44] This time the miners
were not willing to acquiesce. They went on strike. The Communist
Party had gained strength and built support among the miners, and
unions had gained political space during the Popular Front government
(Klubock 1993, 421–696). The miners had experienced the undemoc-
ratic practices employed to accelerate wartime production in the "fight

for democracy." They now claimed a greater share in corporate profits. The strike ended with government intervention, the arrest of union leadership, and resentments on the part of the miners.

Chile's fragile coalition government fractured as Rios cracked down on communism and labor activism, with the support of foreign corporations (Keen and Wasserman 1988, 347–48).[45] Workers throughout the country responded with a nationwide general strike on January 30, 1946. In February, a six-week strike began, affecting copper (including Anaconda operations), coal, and other industrial sectors. According to *El Siglo*, a Santiago-based prolabor and procommunist paper, the strike was a forced lockout by the industry bosses in reprisal for worker participation in the national strike.[46]

Back in Butte, miners returned home from their patriotic duty only to find limited work and frozen wages. Their anger burned as contract negotiations failed, and in April 1946, they conducted a short but violent strike whose drama remains crystalline in community memory. The company press offered sordid details of the violence that marked the community:

> Mobs wreck dozen Butte homes. Pictures reveal wanton destruction. More than ten homes wrecked by apparently organized gangs of terrorists reveal the unparalleled destruction that resulted when mobs roamed the streets of Butte and vicinity Saturday night and Early Sunday.
>
> Orgy uncontrolled in wild night of terror, lawlessness. Boy Wounded. Houses Wrecked and hacked by roving bands of hoodlums. Windows broken, furniture tossed out. . . . A crowd of more than 3000 witnessed the destruction of a home on Locust Street. Carloads of youthful, husky individuals cruised along the street.
>
> The horror which began Friday night reached a crest after dark Saturday when terrified housewives bombarded the police station and sheriff's office with calls for help. Sheriff Al McLeod said that some of the gangs included women and that women were reportedly the leaders in some instances of house wrecking. . . . Many persons paused en route to church to gaze at the debris.[47]
>
> Mob's cruelty unchecked, witnesses say officers did not stop killing of pets, destruction. . . . It was reported that some of the chambermaids in a local hotel refused to make the beds for families of ACM company maintenance men who had moved to the hotel for safety when the gangs destroyed their homes.
>
> The Shame of Butte: The rest of the nation is looking in horror and apprehension at Butte, where man's home is no longer his castle, where defenseless women and children alone are the targets of despicable actions.[48]

Longtime Butte residents recall the strike of 1946 with a curious mix of bravado and shame. "Piano stories" are told with eyewitness conviction about the baby grand that made its final crescendo from the window of a "scab" home. The year, the setting, and the strike vary with the storyteller, but the piano is firmly fixed in this fusion of memories that have come to stand for "everystrike" (see fig. 8).

The stories are marked with humor and shame over the property destruction, disgust at the participation of women — a clear violation of local norms — and, of course, a vivid memory of the piano, a silenced symbol of privilege and privation in the familiar tune of Butte's labor struggles. The strike lasted nine days, but the resentments lingered as the company press claimed the riots were incited by communist workers.[49]

In Chile, workers were mobilizing throughout the country. Strikes threatened the economic stability of the Popular Front government and revealed its political fault lines. One month after settlement of the Butte conflict, a strike broke out in Chuquicamata, lasting from May 27 to June 30, 1946. Though the Chuquicamata papers offered few details of the strike, *El Siglo* went on the offensive. The paper accused the company of forcing the strikers to pay higher prices in the *pulperías* (company stores), of falsifying production costs, and of colluding with Chilean government and banking interests. Alongside these reports were exposés of copper sales to Hitler and Mussolini, arranged through Argentine and Brazilian operatives during World War II.[50] The strike ended as the Office of Price Administration was lifting wartime price controls; with postwar reconstruction underway, copper was poised for a boom. A series of brief strikes throughout 1946, including the first strike by Chuquicamata's white-collar workers, revealed labor's discontent and ongoing activism.[51] Despite a year of labor troubles, Anaconda's stockholders were pleased to learn that although the company had a 10 percent loss in gross income, it enjoyed a 17 percent gain in net income (*Annual Report* 1946).

Though the economic future of copper on the world market was bright, labor strife continued. The Red Threat fueled political fear from Washington to Santiago, and Anaconda joined the high tide of nationalism defined by and through repression of communism. Gabriel González Videla won the Chilean presidency in 1946 with the support of the communist party. However, with heavy political and economic pressure from capitalist interests, including the mining companies and U.S. government, he quickly moved to the right and denounced his erstwhile communist supporters.[52]

Figure 8.   Remains of the piano thrown from Butte home during 1946 strike.
Photo and headline from *Montana Standard*, 16 April 1946.

El Siglo denounced the obstructionist practices of Anaconda and
Kennecott, but the paper was censored, then shut down by government
order from 1948 to 1952.[53] In 1948, the Chilean congress passed the
Law for the Permanent Defense of Democracy, repressive legislation that
outlawed the communist party and resulted in the mass roundup and
detention of party members and other leftist sympathizers. A detention
camp was set up in the isolated coastal town of Pisagua, a former nitrate
oficina (mining camp), in Chile's desert north (Keen and Wasserman
1988, 348).[54]

La Pampa, a procompany paper in Chuquicamata, offered regular
reports on the ongoing arrests and detention of communists — in general,
labor leaders in the mines.[55] At the same time, *carabineros* (state police)
in Chuquicamata were detaining people who entered the camp looking
for work. The company's tidy town had fallen prey to other influences,
and Anaconda was determined to get back in control. With the voice of
opposition silenced in Santiago, reports on daily life in Chuqui were
reduced to the company-owned or sympathetic press. After the strike in
1946, the following two years were punctuated by growing union
activism, a series of brief strikes, labor conflicts, and detention of presumed communist sympathizers. For many residents of Chuquicamata,

memories of those years blend together, perhaps reflecting the struggles and fears that permeated them. During a conversation with a group of Chuquicamatinas, the talk turned to memories of that era:

> It was the strike of '48, was that when that was? Well, it was a hard and difficult thing. There were soup kitchens, and the women went out in the plaza to protest. It was a violent strike. It was the only one I remember where the women went out in the streets. The women always supported the men however they could, but in general they didn't get involved in public acts, but that strike brought the women out.[56]

I then spoke with a woman who had raised her family in Chuquicamata and asked her about the strike. Her voiced filled with emotion as she recalled:

> We came to Chuqui in '49. Before, we lived in Copiapo, where my husband worked in the mines there. We had heard lots of stories about Chuqui and the violence there. He had relatives that worked in Chuqui and they told us about their experiences there. In '48, the year before we came to Chuqui, there was a terrible, violent strike. It was during the government of Gonzalez Videla. . . . It was terrible. People died and others were sent to Pisagua. I was afraid of the move to Chuqui, but the work offered more opportunity and a better salary for my husband; it was better for the family. . . .
>
>   It was my *comadre* [godmother] in Chuqui who told me about those days. There were lots of arrests during the strike. Union leaders were arrested and a lot of them were sent to Pisagua for one or two years. The women tried to protect the men and hide them out. . . . The women would face the *carabineros* and cover for the men. Sometimes the men had to leave the area in order to avoid arrest. When the men were sent to Pisagua, the women and children were put out of their houses in Chuqui, because [the houses] belonged to the company. My *comadre*, she was from Coquimbo. Her husband was sent to Pisagua and she and her children were sent to Punta Arenas, I don't know how, maybe by train. They had to make their way back to Coquimbo by boat while her husband was imprisoned in Pisagua.[57]

Her story resonates with those of many residents of Chuquicamata whose family members have suffered political repression over the generations, from the days of their grandparents in the nitrate mines, to their parents under Gonzalez Videla, and to themselves under Pinochet. A retired Chuquicamata labor leader recounted both political and personal memories of the late 1940s:

> The government of Gonzalez Videla caused a crisis in labor politics. The communist party had a lot of influence; it was a real force in the country. But there were also a lot of different unions, and we lacked solidarity, and that hurt us. But the unions suffered, especially the copper miners, from the

repression. The trauma of those years left their mark on me. I was just a boy. My uncle disappeared in 1948. We never saw him again. Lots of people got sent to Pisagua. The military put people out of their houses. In '48, there weren't confrontations or violence in the streets, people just disappeared. Especially anyone registered in the communist party. They came to the house in the night and put them out. Lots of people disappeared, and others were relegated to Pisagua. And when they came back to the community, they were ostracized.[58]

The hysteria of the McCarthy era caused a similar wave of repression in the United States. The passage of the Taft-Hartley Act severely limited labor's strike power. Red-baiting became a popular tactic to discredit union leadership (see figs. 9 and 10). In 1950, Butte's powerful Mine-Mill union was ousted from the Congress of Industrial Organizations (CIO) over accusations of communist membership.[59] Serious infighting and power struggles to take over the local union became the center of labor politics in Butte, while fragmented leftist parties vied for loyalties of the copper rank and file in Chuquicamata. A reduction in force in the Chuquicamata mines in 1949 served notice to the miners of their vulnerability.[60] Anaconda was back in control.

The company was now ready to pull back the stick and offer the carrot by financing the construction of a new union hall in Chuquicamata, to replace the "communist mausoleum," and by building a recreational center and sponsoring a housing program for the Butte miners.[61] In keeping with the high tide of nationalism, Anaconda shifted its attention to Butte, investing in expanded underground mining and plans for open-pit mining known as the Greater Butte Project. The company also rewarded the Chilean government for its fight against communism by investing over one hundred million dollars in expansion of operations in Chuquicamata in order to recover copper from sulfide ore (*Annual Report* 1948 and 1949; Klubock 1993, 690).[62]

Though Anaconda was expanding its operations and building production potential, copper prices were still low. The company was still resisting efforts by the Chilean state to play a role in copper pricing and sales. Chile paid the price for Anaconda's political and economic worries: production in Chuquicamata showed a decline each year from 1948 to 1953. By the end of the 1940s, Anaconda had proven itself to be a worthy defender of capitalism and foe of communism. The corporate image as champion of democracy was tarnished, however, when top officials of its wire and cable subsidiary were imprisoned on fraud charges for selling defective materials to the U.S. government during World War II.[63]

Figure 9. "Communism!" Flyer from Butte Miners Union File, Butte-Silver Bow Public Archives. No date.

KOREA, CAT AND MOUSE

U.S. entry into the Korean War was a defining feature of copper politics in 1950. Once again the U.S. government unilaterally fixed copper prices as part of wartime production. Thus the price paid for copper mined by U.S. companies in Chile and sold in the United States was lower than prevailing world market prices. During the Korean War,

Figure 10. "Taft-Hartley." Butte Miners Union File, Butte-Silver Bow Public Archives. No date.

those differences were huge: the price set by the U.S. government was twenty-four and a half cents per pound, whereas the world price was forty to fifty cents per pound (de Vylder 1976, 118–19). This time, the Chilean government was unwilling to accept these one-way decisions. Chile sought markets for its copper and demanded concessions from the United States regarding tariffs and pricing. The situation was a tenuous one, however: although Chile could wrest control of its copper stocks, it lacked access to long-standing market relations.

During 1951, negotiations were underway at many levels in Chile. The fragmented copper unions joined together to form a confederation, through which they could demand equal salaries and benefits and common contract dates throughout the copper industry.[64] The confederation supported the nationalization of the copper mines.

Chilean senators Salvador Ocampo and Elias Lafertte launched a vir-

ulent attack against the history of clandestine dealings between government officials and the copper companies, pointing to the conflicts of
interest that compromised the Chilean state. For example, Chile's minister of economy, one Señor Yrarrazaval, was also an attorney for the
American Smelting and Refining Company, a major copper company in
which Ocampo and Lafertte claimed Anaconda was the majority stock-
holder (Lafertte and Ocampo 1951).[65] In 1951, they proposed a plan to
congress for the nationalization of the copper industry. Though the plan
was not approved, the possibility of nationalization drew widespread
interest. Meanwhile, a Chilean delegation brought the nation's concerns
to Washington and won a three-cent-per-pound increase in the price of
copper sold to the United States and the right to independently sell 20
percent of the country's copper production in "free world" markets (de
Vylder 1976, 119).

In Butte, contract negotiations were underway between the Anaconda Company and the Mine-Mill union. Talks broke down at the end
of August, and the miners went on strike. A court injunction and invocation of the Taft-Hartley Act forced the miners back to work in
September without a contract. In October, the Chilean government and
the copper companies reached agreement on a new taxation and exchange rate. And in late October 1951, Anaconda reached a contract
settlement with the miner's union in Butte.

By 1952, the discontent between Chilean business and political interests and the interests of the mining companies had intensified. In May
1952, the Chilean congress passed a resolution indicating that, although
the country was not yet ready to nationalize the mines, it wanted more
control over its resources. Just days after the Chilean resolution passed,
Anaconda announced plans for massive expansion of its operations in
both Butte and Chuquicamata. But the tensions between corporate and
national sovereignty in Chile did not subside. The more Chile asserted
demands for control of the copper market, the more intransigent were
the foreign companies. When the Korean war ended in 1953, copper
stockpiles were once again a problem, and the Chilean government, copper companies, and U.S. state department were embroiled in conflicts.[66]

El Siglo, back in publication in 1953, was once again on the attack,
with reports of Yankee copper profits from Chile, secret accords between Chile Exploration Company and former president Gonzalez
Videla, and manipulation of the exchange rate by foreign companies. El
Siglo accused Anaconda and Kennecott and the U.S. government of boy-
cotting Chilean copper.[67] Chile had received offers from the Soviet Union

to purchase surplus copper. But U.S. interests blocked the settlement. The U.S. government also refused to purchase Chile's copper stockpile, in spite of the serious economic problems the country was facing.

In short, the copper companies wanted a new deal with the Chilean government — a deal in which they would be assured their autonomy in production and marketing.[68] They were ready to use their strategic powerplays, and when a strike was called in Chuquicamata in October 1953, Chuqui became the pawn in their game. Union leaders cited the company's complete refusal to negotiate a settlement. *El Siglo* charged company intransigence as the reason for the strike: "For [the company,] the strike is a transitory solution to the problems of accumulation."[69] Union leaders accused the company of using the strike to pressure the government for better benefits. In retrospect, labor leaders in Chuqui also claimed that the company was attempting to fracture the newly formed *Confederación Nacional de Trabajadores del Cobre* (National Confederation of Copper Workers, or CTC). In November 1953, U.S. President Dwight Eisenhower sent his brother Milton to Latin America on what the United States press touted as a goodwill mission. *El Siglo* saw Milton's visit as a "Yankee mission to obtain better deals for the North American companies that exploit Chilean workers."[70]

The strike lasted for six weeks, with Chuquicamata as hostage to deep political play. But the strike was not a game to the woman who had arrived in Chuqui with her family in 1949:

> I remember the year 1953 well, because when the strike began I was pregnant with Claudia, and I had three little children at home with me. The strike lasted more than two months. I was so afraid for my husband. One night, he didn't come home all night, and neither did my neighbor's husband. I was so scared because I was thinking about what happened in '48. I was afraid my husband had been arrested, or sent to Pisagua or some other place, or even worse, I was afraid he'd been shot. He didn't come home all that night or the next day, without any information about where he was. I was there in the house, pregnant, with three small children, and filled with a fear I had never experienced in my life. Finally, my husband came home the next day. He and the others had run to the hills outside of Chuqui and hidden there when the strikebreaking began. Then, when it looked like they weren't arresting people, they came home. In that strike, nobody was sent to Pisagua.[71]

While the strike forged painful memories, the copper companies and U.S. government forced Chile to the point of economic crisis. As Anaconda euphemistically described the situation to its stockholders: "The reduced sales and lowered taxable income of the American copper companies operating in Chile, together with the accumulation of stocks of copper, had a material effect on the economy of the Republic of Chile" (*Annual Report* 1953). According to a Chilean source, "Undoubtedly, the United States wanted the stockpile and the consequent penury for Chile to be a lesson for our intentions to freely sell copper" (Corporación Nacional del Cobre 1974, 74). The Chilean government persisted in its right to sell its copper but conceded to some corporate demands. Workers in Chuquicamata returned to work in December 1953. In March of 1954, the Chilean government began to finalize plans for the sale of one hundred thousand tons of surplus copper to the Soviet Union. Within days, the U.S. ambassador to Chile arrived at *La Moneda* (the government palace in Santiago) with an offer from the United States to buy the same one hundred thousand tons of copper (of which sixty-four thousand tons were from Anaconda's operations) (*Annual Report* 1954). And in August 1954, with another contract expired and stockpiles high, the Mine-Mill workers in Butte and across the country were once again on strike for two months.[72]

By the end of 1954, Chile was faced with problems of international debt and national inflation. Copper production rates had fallen to their lowest since before World War II. The Chilean government abandoned efforts at intervening in the copper market and returned instead to a free-market philosophy under the economic policy known as *Nuevo Trato* (the Chilean New Deal). This policy supported the unfettered "rational actions" of foreign investors in the hope that benefits from investments would trickle down to all Chileans (Corporación Nacional del Cobre 1974, 75; Moran 1974, 95). Much like in the early days of Anaconda's international expansion, repressive political practices had cleared the way for promotion of a free-market economy. The copper companies won concessions that included lower tax rates, low base production figures, and free import of equipment. As corporate profits soared and production in Chile escalated, a few benefits trickled down to the workers when Anaconda announced a five-year expansion plan in Chuquicamata that included construction of a hospital and more housing. In this favorable economic climate, Anaconda netted its largest annual income to that time: 111,501,358 dollars in 1956 (*Annual Report* 1956).

The company was in a good position to expand. It implemented plans for a new mine, which it named El Salvador (the Savior), near the depleted Potrerillos mines located about five hundred miles south of Chuquicamata. And in 1956, the Anaconda company and the Mine-

Mill union in Butte signed a three-year labor contract. But with heavy start-up costs at El Salvador, low copper prices, and a low demand for copper, Anaconda curtailed operations in its high-grade underground mines in Butte and reduced workers to a five-day week in 1957, and Chuquicamata endured another strike, which lasted fifty days, in early 1958 (*Annual Report* 1956).[73]

Labor leaders of Chuquicamata describe the late 1950s as a time of recomposition and solidification of union power. They speak of the greater solidarity among the *obreros* and *empleados* (blue-collar and white-collar workers) as they joined forces under the direction of the CTC to address their common concerns.[74] There was growing resentment of the disparities between the living standard of the gringos in the American Camp and that of the Chilean workforce of Chuquicamata. The unions shifted their focus from workplace conditions to the social conditions and living standards in the community. They demanded cost of living allowances, improved housing, and an end to the paternal "ration card" system whereby a portion of their salary was given in the form of a monthly ration of food and clothing at the *pulperías* rather than in cash.[75]

The year 1959 was a critical one. It was a year for contract negotiations in Butte. Anaconda claimed that mining and the Butte community would continue to prosper only as long as the industry was not burdened with additional costs.[76] The union called for 1959 to be the year for substantial wage increases and better pensions. But that call was drowned out by a louder cacophony of voices in the power struggle among the Mine-Mill, Chemical Workers, and United Steelworkers for control of the local unions (see fig. 11).

In the meantime, Anaconda invested millions of dollars to develop the El Salvador mine, which began producing copper in May 1959 (see appendix 2). As the company reported to its stockholders, "We feel that we can conservatively predict that [El Salvador] will be one of the truly great mines of the world and that no lower cost copper will be produced anywhere than from this property when it comes into production in 1959. That will be the year when the first fruits of our present program will be harvested" (*Annual Report* 1957).[77] On the heels of the opening of El Salvador, union-company negotiations ground to a halt in Butte. Rumors of a strike circulated for months. The massive strike began at midnight, August 19, 1959. The night before the strike began, Montana's most devastating earthquake in decades struck, toppling a mountain in Yellowstone Park, 150 miles south of Butte, and jolting the

Figure 11.   Picket line, Butte, 1959. Courtesy of Butte Historical Society, Butte Labor History Project Collection.

already tense community. In local stories, the 1959 strike is often equated with the earthquake, as people remember the "night the mountain fell" and the "strike that broke the backs of the unions."[78]

Gladys, a Butte native, has powerful memories of the 1959 strike:

> I had five kids at home at that time and my husband was out of work. He had to leave town to find work. First, he went to Glasgow and had work there 'til Christmas. We were lucky that he found work, but it was hard managing alone with the kids. And it was quite a time before he got his first paycheck. I didn't know how I was going to keep things going until that paycheck came in. I had family here, but I had my pride too, and I just couldn't ask for help, even though they were always good about it. Finally, he got paid and that eased things a little, but it was hard with him so far away. Then that job ended right around Christmas and he came home. It was a rough time, because there was no end of the strike in sight. The talks had stalemated for so long. And there were rumors that the company was just going to shut things down because the operations in Butte were costing too much and they could get their copper a lot cheaper in South America.[79]

Betsy was in grade school in Butte in 1959. Grown-up worries filled her child's-eye view of the world:

> The '59 strike was awful, really scary. My dad and mom, they always saved money, but . . . And my dad, he'd run around and do whatever work he

could do for somebody else under the table — fix cars, put on a roof, sometimes for free. At that time, he wasn't drinking so much. Some days we'd be eating beans. Christmas was sad, not so much because we didn't have money, but it was the fear. What was it going to be like next Christmas? That strike was real scary. I remember thinking this could be real awful. It could be the end of our families; we might have to go back to Yugoslavia. As a kid, I thought that was sort of neat. My family felt forced by the union. The workers didn't want that strike. I remember the talk in the living room, with names of union men coming up: "So-and-so is just worried about paying off his truck," "The company bought him," "He's a company man." There was terrible suspicion and fear. I was afraid when they'd say things like, "Gonna' burn The Hill."[80]

A Butte union leader captured the sense of frustration and betrayal shared by many miners as negotiations remained at an impasse:

> Anaconda, in indicating the possibility that they might consider negotiating a 6.7 cent package, is in effect saying miners and smeltermen, by accepting [a settlement far below the emerging industry pattern] should subsidize Anaconda in order to keep their jobs. . . . All during the more than 75 years that the company has been in existence and has grown into a worldwide corporation, their prosperity has been made off the backs of Butte miners. All Butte has to show for it today are large graveyards.[81]

The strike lasted for more than six months. The eventual settlement produced few gains for labor, and a series of layoffs and mine closures followed.[82] While the people of Butte suffered half a year of uncertainty, Chuquicamata enjoyed favorite-child status in corporate paternalism. On July 4, 1959, CHILEX President Charles Brinckerhoff initiated construction of a monument dedicated to Chuquicamata's miners with words of praise for the "great family of Anaconda." In October, he claimed Chuquicamata as the "Copper Capital of the World" and announced plans for a Museum of Copper. In November, the new union hall was inaugurated. In December, Brinckerhoff announced plans for social progress and new housing for Chuquicamata. And in April 1960, he praised the miners for their year of record production. In 1959, while Anaconda mined seventy thousand tons of copper in Montana, it produced 350,000 tons in its combined operations of Chuquicamata and El Salvador.[83]

1960s: ALLIANCES AND ANIMOSITIES

By the 1960s, demands for agrarian reform and nationalization of the copper mines were central to Chilean political discourse. In the United

States, fears of a proliferation of socialist revolutions captured the attention of the Kennedy administration. The response was a political agenda for the United States and Latin America known as the Alliance for Progress. In short, the Alliance for Progress was an incentive plan whereby the United States would help jump-start underdeveloped economies in exchange for social and political reform. Though benevolent in theory, the plan was designed to promote capitalist development and expand U.S. trade. Land reform was a key component of the Alliance for Progress and one that seriously challenged the interests of Chile's landed classes. At the same time, the prospect of nationalization of copper threatened the very existence of Anaconda. The stage was set for decades of political and economic tensions to come to a head.[84]

The copper companies and the U.S. government had an interest in maintaining Chile as an ally. They saw the Christian Democratic candidate Eduardo Frei as the strongest supporter of their interests in the Chilean presidential campaign of 1964. The U.S. government and the mining companies contributed generously to Frei's successful campaign.[85] On the national political front in Chile, the failure of *Nuevo Trato* to produce benefits for Chile brought the issue of state intervention in the copper mines back to center stage. As in the 1940s and 1950s, there was a powerful convergence of interest in nationalizing the copper mines. From the socialist perspective, nationalization was part of a broader political project of worker control of the means of production. For the liberals, state management of the mines would generate revenues for state-sponsored economic development and social welfare. For the conservative Chilean entrepreneurs, nationalization would halt the exodus of profits that could be better invested in their capitalist ventures. The elite landowners' support of nationalization was perhaps the most ironic. The Chilean elites held many interests in common with the foreign copper companies. However, they were threatened by the agrarian reform agenda of the Alliance for Progress. They supported nationalization of the mines as a key political bargaining chip. They intended to pressure the foreign companies to pressure the U.S. government to abandon land reform. If landholders lost, so would the copper companies.[86]

Upon election, Frei took a pragmatic approach, orchestrating the Chileanization of the copper industry — that is, the purchase of majority ownership of the copper mines by the Chilean government. Initially, the plans called for a new state-corporate partnership based on increased production, government participation in marketing and exploration, and joint company-government ownership of new mining ventures. Anaconda entered a long-range agreement with Frei's government that called for a more than 50 percent increase in copper production and the expansion of operating facilities between 1965 and 1970.[87] In theory, Anaconda agreed with the plan, telling its stockholders that "the state and the Anaconda company in Chile will become closely associated in purpose, interests, and results" (*Annual Report* 1964, 4).

Though the general terms of the agreement were favorable, Anaconda and the Chilean government disagreed on the specifics.[88] Like the landed classes, the company had a long history of rights and expectations grounded in corporate sovereignty that they were loath to share. Anaconda maintained full control of Chuquicamata and El Salvador and agreed to a partnership with the Chilean government in the development of Exotica, a new mineral deposit, in which they would hold 75 ownership and the government would own the other 25 percent. Despite the promises of a stable, harmonious partnership between the Chilean government and the copper companies advocated in Frei's plan, Anaconda saw nationalization as an inevitable next step. The company responded by initiating a strategy of massive short-term exploitation of its Chilean mines.[89]

In fact, a plan to nationalize Anaconda's operations was agreed to in late 1969.[90] But in the four years prior, the company maximized immediate extraction of high-grade ore. Sources claim that Anaconda put off development plans and the disposal of toxic waste, a policy that resulted in environmental damage as well as damage to equipment and operations that hindered later production at the Chuquicamata plant (Moran 1974; Zapata 1979).[91] However, during this period both the company and the Chilean government reaped short-term gains. Work stoppages would hurt both parties' interests.

Labor activism was on the upsurge in Chile as agrarian and industrial workers mobilized for a better share in Chile's political and economic future. Work in the copper mines was punctuated by frequent strikes and partial work stoppages, which the government and companies called "illegal" and "political." A strike involving all copper miners in the CTC shut down the copper industry for thirty-seven days in late 1965. Workers in Chuquicamata recall the strike as a bitter one that produced a major shift in the miners' benefits. As a result of the strike, miners won the right to own their own homes rather than be forever beholden to assigned company housing. The strike ended in early December, after a state of emergency was declared and military forces occupied Chuquicamata, detaining labor leaders and "guaranteeing the right to work."[92]

In January 1966, miners at Kennecott's El Teniente mine initiated a strike that both symbolized and amplified existing tensions between Chilean labor and foreign capital.[93] By February, the miners at Anaconda's El Salvador mine had joined in a sympathy strike. Government reprisals were swift and forceful. The Ministry of the Interior invoked the Law of Internal State Security, permitting state police to take extreme measures.[94]

El Mercurio (a Santiago-based newspaper chain), the voice of the political right, claimed that the miners of El Salvador had rejected the strike in a secret ballot but were being forced to strike by leftist union leadership. And "because of this, every precaution has been taken to prevent professional agitators from Tocopilla and Antofagasta from entering Chuquicamata, as occurred last November during the strike that affected the whole mining industry."[95] Six union leaders were arrested, as was the secretary of the National Workers Confederation (CUT), who had gone to meet with union leadership in Chuquicamata. As a result of these actions, *El Mercurio* claimed that "everything was back to normal in Chuquicamata" by March 5.

El Siglo portrayed a different reality, describing the militarization of Chuquicamata and claiming the town to be under a state of siege:

> The Chief of the Plaza, Colonel Roberto Viaux, forcefully intervened in the local union, impeding the assembly that was scheduled for yesterday afternoon. The police force was reinforced by two hundred *carabineros* and military troops brought in from Antofagasta. Union leaders are under watch and are threatened with arrest if a solidarity strike is initiated with Braden [El Teniente]. Groups of people are not permitted to pass through the streets. When the LADECO [national airline] flight arrived, the airport was closed by *carabineros* while other police officials demanded identification cards from the passengers."[96]

In her personal account of the 1966 strike, a longtime Chuquicamatina told me that Salvador Allende, then a Socialist Party senator and president of the senate, was among those forbidden to enter Chuquicamata. She spoke with outrage at Anaconda's arrogance and filled with pride as she recalled the impassioned speech that Allende delivered in Calama's central plaza, calling for an end to imperialist control of the copper mines.[97]

The miners of Chuquicamata joined in the solidarity strike for two days beginning on March 6. The response was stringent. *El Siglo* described entire sectors of the town being converted into make-shift detention camps as massive arrests were made, yet *El Mercurio* published reports from local authorities in Chuqui who claimed that the situation remained peaceful and that no violence had broken out that would require "extreme methods." The procompany paper praised the armed forces and *carabineros* for guaranteeing the "freedom to work" in the mining camp.[98]

A Chuquicamata labor activist who participated in the strike committee in 1966 vividly recalled those days:

> There was a state of siege in '66, a military occupation and lots of violence to break the solidarity strike. . . . There was a lot of brutality during that strike. A march started from the *fundación*. By the time they passed *Puerta Uno* [a main entrance to the mine], there must have been two thousand men in the march. There was a terrible confrontation, with lots of violence and arrests. But they kept going in spite of the violence.[99]

While the miners in Chuquicamata returned to work, those in El Salvador continued their solidarity strike amid mounting tensions. On Friday, March 11, government troops opened fire on a large group of miners and their families outside the union hall in El Salvador, killing seven people and injuring dozens. Despite prohibitions against public gatherings, groups had been coming together daily at the union soup kitchen. Some claim that members of this group were defensively arming themselves, whereas others accuse the group of initiating an attack on the "peace keepers." Whatever the initial provocation, the end was a brutal display of official police power. In El Salvador, the price of copper was paid in human lives. For the political left, the deaths became emblematic of the "close association of purpose, interests, and results" between the Chilean government and the Anaconda Company. Anaconda chose not to mention the deaths of the five men and two women in their stockholders report of 1966.[100]

This period of massive extraction of copper in Chile in the face of nationalization occurred at the height of the Vietnam War, when copper supplies were critical. The company maximized its advantage by increasing production without creating a surplus. And in July of 1967, the labor contract affecting operations in Butte expired. The United Steelworkers had taken over for the Mine-Mill as the representative of the Butte miners in May of 1967. In contract negotiations, the union demanded industrywide bargaining and common contract dates, concessions that the big U.S. copper companies were not willing to make. In

July 1967, the largest and longest strike in the history of the U.S. copper industry began.[101]

The strike lasted nine months and affected tens of thousands of workers nationwide. Operations in Butte idled and the local economy was devastated, while production in Chuquicamata peaked. News accounts and political rhetoric criticized the striking miners for "interfering with the war effort." The Anaconda Company sponsored full page ads calling on the miners to return to work by Thanksgiving or Christmas. Yet some miners, in retrospect, have a different perception. As one union man said, "Oh, sure, the company wanted to negotiate with us, they gave us this much room to negotiate," and he showed me the space of an inch between his thumb and forefinger.[102]

Union leaders drew on their own war metaphors in responding to corporate questioning of their national loyalties. A United Steelworker spokesman, addressing an AFL-CIO convention in December 1967, launched a counterattack:

> This resolution notes that for five months nearly 60,000 workers belonging to 26 unions have been engaged in a common struggle against the major copper producers; that the companies are using record-breaking profits to finance a war against their employees; and that they are determined to starve the worker into submission. . . . We charge that the industry has refused to bargain with the union and this precipitated the strike. . . . We charge that the industry is engaged in a conspiracy to raise the price of copper and in cold blood is using this strike to gain this objective. . . . We know that the industry welcomed this strike.[103]

In a telling footnote, the pamphlet containing the written text of this address mentions that support for the striking copper miners included a fifty-dollar donation sent by a South Vietnamese Trade Union.[104]

As in the 1959 strike, Chuquicamata once again reaped the benefits of corporate paternalism to appease the labor force. In June 1967, Anaconda announced plans for a huge new housing construction project in Chuquicamata. In August, the company lavished praise on its Chuquicamata miners for record production and announced plans for renovation and expansion of the *pulperías*. In September, President Frei arrived in Chuquicamata for the inauguration of Exotica, the new joint mining venture, which was to produce one hundred thousand tons of copper in its first year of operation.[105]

By early 1968, the strike was still dragging on. Anaconda was the most recalcitrant of the Big Four U.S. copper producers in reaching a strike settlement. Phelps-Dodge, the only one of the Big Four without foreign holdings, was seen by strike insiders as the most likely to settle. By early March, Kennecott and American Smelting and Refining Company (ASARCO) were showing some movement in their negotiations with United Steelworkers.[106] After intense negotiations before the National Labor Relations Board, Anaconda finally reached a settlement with the union, and the strike in Butte officially ended at midnight, March 30, 1968. And on March 31, 1968, the labor contract expired in Chuquicamata, resulting in a brief strike that was settled quickly.[107]

There seems to be a convergence of forces at work here. Nationalization loomed on the horizon, representing very different meanings for different political interests in Chile. Anaconda saw nationalization as inevitable and hoped to maximize short-term gains and minimize long-term losses. The miners had heard a lot of rhetoric but had experienced little change. Like the miners in Butte, they were a politically diverse group who now enjoyed better wages than the average worker in the country. They saw their unions as sources of both real power and heavy-handed ideology.[108] And they lived the contradictions of the company's tactics for making short-term profit. The miners in Chuquicamata could relate to Pat, a welder in Butte's Berkeley Pit, who offered his workingman's wisdom on those demanding times in Butte when Anaconda wanted copper on the market and intensified production:

> The place was crazy. We ran full shifts twenty-four hours a day, seven days a week. We all signed up on Fridays to work a sixth day. The company didn't even mind paying overtime. I was working in the shop repairing equipment. The bosses, they didn't care. We overloaded the trucks all the time. They were always breaking down, but it didn't matter, all that mattered was repairing them and sending them back out. Now, a good weld takes some time, but a sloppy weld, well it's just going to give way again. But they didn't care about good work, it was all numbers and speed. So the trucks kept breaking down, and we kept repairing them. It got to be that we knew all those trucks by their welds.[109]

When miners of Chuquicamata and their families spoke of the last years of Frei's government and the three years of Allende's Popular Unity government that followed, they often spoke of dissension, conflict, and frequent strikes, with little substantive gains. Nationalization did not necessarily offer them political or economic enfranchisement. For some, it meant a new hope for the future, a major step on *la via chilena*, Chile's peaceful and democratic road to socialism. For others it meant just another boss and some broken-down equipment. For many, it meant loss of a well-ordered and familiar system that had structured the practices of their lives since birth.

In 1970, Salvador Allende, the socialist candidate backed by the leftist Popular Unity coalition, was elected president of Chile by a slim margin, despite CIA and corporate funding of opposition efforts to undermine his inauguration.[110] Allende moved quickly to nationalize the mines, realizing all of Anaconda's worst fears. He introduced legislation to nationalize the mines without further compensation to the foreign companies. He offered both a rationale and financial accounting to argue that the nearly fifty years of lucrative profits had more than compensated for purchase price and capital investments. On July 11, 1971, with unanimous approval of a constitutional amendment, Chile reclaimed its mines from the foreign companies.[111] The headlines of *Oasis* featured powerful images of the newfound freedom from U.S. imperialism as the Chilean government proclaimed July 11 the National Day of Dignity (see fig. 12).[112]

Meanwhile, back in Butte, another strike was underway, but news of the strike was interrupted by news from Chile with headlines that read "Copper Grab Due in Chile" and "Chile Congress Drops Copper Ax."[113] Marie, a miner's wife in Butte, remembers the day well:

> My husband had gone down for the paper and we read the headlines about Chile expropriating the mines. It was pretty disturbing. Nobody knew what was going to happen next, but we knew it was going to have a big impact on the operations in Butte. We couldn't believe they'd just take the mines like that with no compensation after all Anaconda had invested there. It was the beginning of the end for Anaconda, and things never really recovered in Butte after that.[114]

The U.S. government demanded immediate compensation for the U.S. companies in Chile and imposed diplomatic and economic sanctions. The Butte copper strike lasted for months, as did the uncertainty regarding Allende's plans for compensation. On September 28, 1971, in one of his most forceful speeches, Allende accused the U.S. government and companies of breaking the rules of fair play and claimed Chile's freedom from decades of exploitation at the hands of U.S. companies. In the end, Allende concluded that Anaconda owed Chile money for excess profits.[115] The miners in Butte returned to their jobs on October 1, 1971, perhaps a little more optimistic about Butte's central place in the Anaconda operations. As one local put it, "Some of the biggest fans of Salvador Allende live right here in Butte." But as economic and politi-

Figure 12. "Ours!" Chile claims copper and freedom from U.S. imperialism. *Oasis,* 11 July 1971, 1, special edition.

cal sanctions put the squeeze on Allende's troubled government, the loss of two-thirds to three-quarters of corporate profits wreaked havoc with the financial stability of the Anaconda Company.

In retribution for Allende's decision, the Nixon administration announced plans to cut off foreign aid and U.S. exports to Chile.

Critical financiers such as the World Bank and Import Export Bank followed suit, and credit began to dry up from sources such as the U.S. Agency for International Development (USAID). Chile was denied short-term credit essential to international trade. The copper corporations blocked import of parts and machinery needed for copper production. They also called on their long-standing relations to block sales of Chilean copper on the European market.[116] The CIA funded and orchestrated a "destabilization" plan whose fundamental strategy was to provoke and support strikes by trade associations and disgruntled workers. U.S. military intelligence provided technical support to their Chilean counterparts. The U.S. government and companies provided financial support to El Mercurio, their friend for many years, and found political allies among the Chilean right, growing ever more polarized from Allende's socialist movement.[117]

In Chuquicamata, the rapid move to nationalization of the mines was plagued with problems at the operating level. In addition to the Yankee exodus, Chilean men with years of experience were replaced by political appointees as Popular Unity sought to integrate itself in the mine and sell the political value of nationalization.[118] Participation became the buzzword of the new administration, but daily operations did not always match the new discourse. Management turnover, equipment breakdowns, and political struggles over control of the operations left miners in a situation of uncertainty. Gone was the familiar, if paternal power of the past. In its place were confusion, conflicts, and shortages of basic goods.

DARK DAYS AND A LIGHT IN THE TUNNEL

As miners lived with growing uncertainty about their own political and economic future, their support of Allende began to erode. There were a series of wildcat strikes.[119] In 1973, a strike for a cost of living increase began at the El Teniente mines. The miners at Chuquicamata staged a series of solidarity strikes. The opposition forces, with the help of U.S. funds, fanned the flames of social discontent. Some miners joined in support of the truckers strikes of 1973, which crippled the Allende administration and created bitter splits within the labor movement.[120]

On September 11, 1973, Allende's socialist government was toppled by a violent military coup in which Allende died. Chile was controlled by the military dictatorship of Augusto Pinochet until 1990. The military regime's violent repression included attacks on labor leaders and the suspension of union activity. Some union leaders, administrators, and workers from the Chuquicamata mines were among the thousands executed, imprisoned, or "disappeared" as the military regime established control through force and fear. David Silberman, the chief executive officer of the mines appointed by the Popular Unity government, was "disappeared" shortly after the coup. Several other employees of the mines were among those slain by a government death squad who summarily executed political prisoners throughout northern Chile during the "Caravan of Death" in October of 1973.[121]

The dictatorship imposed its own rigid structure and police-state practices on the operation of the mines and on daily life. Curfews, control of the media, censorship, and prohibition of public and private meetings reconfigured the contours of Chilean life. Arbitrary searches, arrests, detentions, and torture shot fear and suspicion through the fabric of everyday experience. Military appointments — from the head of the mines, to the heads of the local sports leagues — created and maintained Chuquicamata's new order. The mines kept producing copper and life continued, under scrutiny and with surreptitious resistance struggling in the shadows (Politzer 1989).[122]

The armed hand of the military dictatorship cleared the way for the invisible hand of the free-market economy. Chile's economic policy under Pinochet was formulated and developed under the mentorship of University of Chicago laissez faire economist Milton Friedman and his protégés known as the "Chicago Boys." Once again, a repressive political climate constituted a friendly environment for capitalist interests.[123] Pinochet knew the value of gentlemen's agreements and negotiated a repayment plan with the Anaconda Company for loss of its Chilean assets. Despite U.S. concern over his record of human rights violations, Pinochet soon found himself back in the good graces of U.S. interests, with dollars and resources flowing once more.[124]

Despite eventual compensation from the Chilean government and the Overseas Private Investment Corporation (OPIC), Anaconda never fully recovered from the loss of its Chilean riches.[125] Company reports, news accounts, and industry analyses of the 1970s portray Anaconda as a company in trouble. The cumulative effects of "unreasonable" union demands, low copper prices, "restrictive" environmental codes, and the "expropriation" of the Chilean mines became the litany to explain Anaconda's fall from grace.[126] In 1977, after multiple corporate maneuverings, the Anaconda Company was sold to Atlantic Richfield (ARCO), a major oil company. Though ARCO's stated plan was to continue operations as usual, labor conflicts persisted and layoffs increased. In 1980, all smelting and underground mining operations in Butte were halted. In 1983, the open-pit mine was shut down, which brought all operations to an end. The people of Butte met the closure of the mines with disbelief. The community had accommodated to a tempo of flux but had not been prepared for the music to stop.[127]

Many former employees waited in hope that the mines would reopen. Others left town in search of work elsewhere, but jobs were few. The closure took an emotional as well as economic toll, as miners described the depression and helplessness they felt at the loss of their livelihoods. Local government and businesses worked hard to attract new industry, with modest success. The Environmental Protection Agency became a major player in the local economy; years of toxic waste accumulation in the mines contributed to Butte's fame as the nation's largest Superfund cleanup project.[128] Lawsuits and counter suits regarding liability for environmental damage opened up lucrative terrain for legal and technical consulting industries.

In 1986, after considerable behind-the-scenes negotiations, mining resumed in Butte. A Montana businessman purchased the entire mining operation for the reported amount of 5.2 million dollars, what one local observer called "less than the value of the scrap metal in a mine yard."[129] His is a modest operation of three hundred workers. Despite its small scale, this new mine has a particularly notable feature: it is nonunion. As such, it signifies a profound shift in the labor practices of a community that historically earned the name of the "Gibraltar of Unionism."

The past twenty years have produced a very different history for the people of Chuquicamata. Wages of the copper miners declined under the dictatorship. The distrust workers harbored toward unions and company was amplified to palpable fear and suspicion. As one woman described the years of the dictatorship:

> Under *pinocho* [Pinocchio, a popular reference to Pinochet], it was like having a drop of water in the forehead every hour, every day. It doesn't sound so bad, but over time it eats away at you, drip, drip, drip. With enough time, a drop of water can even wear through a rock. And after a while, it changes you. You don't trust, you don't think for yourself. Over the years, it produced a collective psychosis.[130]

Despite and because of the fear, the surveillance, and the violence, people began to mobilize. Women took to the streets, demanding answers about the disappearances and detentions of their loved ones. Workers began to organize. In 1978, after five hard years of repression and frozen wages, Chuquicamata's miners mobilized their resistance once again. They began a daily hunger strike, refusing their midshift meal in symbolic rejection of the meager wages they were receiving. The action went on for some time, with the men gathering outside the plants on their breaks. Many men were arrested for their participation in the labor action and sent to a small community in the Atacama Desert that had been converted to a detention camp.[131]

In 1983, the collective power of national work stoppages challenged the brutality and repression of Pinochet's regime.[132] Though the protests were squelched by force, the spirit was not. And in October 1985, men, women, and children of Chuquicamata joined together in a massive march from Chuquicamata to Calama, calling for social and economic justice. They were met at the outskirts of Calama by *carabineros* and the military armed with guns, clubs, and tear gas, but their force in numbers could not be ignored.[133] Movements within the country and growing pressure from human rights groups outside Chile continued their resistance until Pinochet called for a plebiscite in 1988 in which the people of Chile were able to decide whether Pinochet would continue in power for another eight years. The result was a resounding *No*. In 1990, Chile began the transition to recuperation of its fractured democracy.[134]

Despite the formal shift from dictatorship to democracy, little changed in the operations of the Chuquicamata mines. The hierarchy laid in concrete by the Yankees seventy years before retained an autonomy all its own. Chilean politicos replaced gringos, military officers replaced civilians, and the civilians finally returned. But when asked about what has changed in the operation of CODELCO-Chuqui since the years of Allende, the typical response among workers is "Not much." Folks talk of the days when the gringos ran the mines as somehow better, well organized, and more personal, where a man (and sometimes even a woman) could get promoted for doing a good job rather than for his politics or education. Things were chaotic during Allende's years, and after that the hierarchy just got bigger — more bosses, more bureaucracy. Faith in the unions isn't what it used to be. When the military regime lifted the ban on union activity and permitted the existence of a restructured labor organization, it also promoted the foundation of a new union in Chuquicamata, known locally as the "company union." In many ways, the union seems to symbolize the contradictions that have confronted the labor movement in recent years.

Today, while interunion struggles and suspicions constrain the labor movement, the mine management has undertaken a grand plan to reimagine the future of Chuquicamata through the Cultural Transformation of the Labor Force. The powerful discourse condemns the "old order" characterized by rigid authority, dependency, and a lack of efficiency. It valorizes a "new order" based on worker participation in a process of "communication for action." With the language of teams, collaboration, and transparency, the national mines are undertaking a grand "modernization" project.[135] They hope it will render them competitive in a tough world market where copper prices are precarious.

The workers are skeptical. They see layoffs, early retirements, and the upsurge in small, private nonunion mines on all sides. They work side by side with nonunion contracted laborers who earn a fraction of their salaries. They resent these intruders and fear for their jobs. Some see this whole process as nothing but smoke and mirrors to mask union busting and privatization of the national mines. They heard about participation from the Popular Unity government and the military dictatorship, and they were not convinced then. Nor are they convinced now. In the late 1990s, fear, uncertainty and distrust grip the community spirit of Chuquicamata, something of a déjà-vu to Butte in the early 1980s.

I have offered here a plausible account of a particular history, selecting fragments of a past and weaving them together to tell a story. Perhaps I have toyed with the reader, emphasizing some moments such that they become events, relegating others to the footnotes, and merely ignoring the rest. I have constructed this chronology in much the same fashion that "official" stories and perhaps "unofficial" memories are constructed. I have given discursive power to meaningful events and selectively represented the meaning of powerful events in the lives and stories of people in Butte and Chuquicamata. Much like mining itself, it is only through the excavation and assay of multiple layers of history from many samples and sites that a larger picture, full of fissures and veins and impenetrable walls begins to emerge.

The picture that emerges is a complicated one. It details a history of transnational power and suggests the power of transnational history. The tracing of copper connections through time and space is not only illuminating but necessary to grasp the patterns of relationships and practices. This approach has pushed beyond and disrupted boundaries of comparison and tapped the intersecting veins of meaning and power that course through this story of copper, culture, and community in the making.

As this chapter traces the trajectory of a particular corporation, it also illustrates key developments in twentieth century capitalism. David Harvey has discussed the shifting logic of capitalism and the regimes of capitalist accumulation in the twentieth century.[136] He addresses four broad eras. The first marked the beginnings of mass production and mass consumption. It was a transitional time of trying to figure out labor control needed to build a proletarian work force. Surveillance, rewards, and brute force were the methods of choice.

The interwar years constituted the second era. It was a time of struggle, when workers did not simply roll over according to corporate plan. Capitalism needed the right mix of disciplinary strategies and state intervention to survive. The new social and labor legislation enacted in the 1930s served this end. It was in the postwar boom, Harvey argues, that a new capitalist configuration reached maturity. With the support of state intervention, the long postwar boom, and a privileged workforce, this mature configuration, which Harvey refers to as Post-war Fordism, became a total way of life and an international affair.

However, growing political and social unrest accompanied by strike waves through the mid 1960s to early 1970s once again revealed the contradictions inherent in capitalism and the inability of the Fordist regime to contain them. The result, according to Harvey, was another crisis of capitalism and a reconfiguration to a fourth regime, one of flexible accumulation. The hallmarks of this new regime are further global integration and labor control geared to the construction of a flexible workforce. Harvey's abstract overview reads like a summary of Anaconda's concrete history. It suggests that this history may serve as a model for asking critical questions about the larger story in which it is embedded.

An abstract sequencing of eras fails to capture the ways in which terms like *crisis of capitalism* unfold with deeply felt human consequences. This is the history we must not forget. The history I outline here is not only a backdrop to the stories I am about to tell. It is also a felt and lived backdrop that resonates against and penetrates the practice of the present in Butte and Chuquicamata. I turn now to the question of community and its central place in the struggles for meaning and power.

Mining Community

It was called the Richest Hill on Earth, and for some — those who got there first and claimed control of the butte — the riches were easy. For others, for the men and women who came from the east to find a better life, there was hard work, exploitation and early death.

Al Dempsey 1989

On a slope of the Andes in Northern Chile not far from the border of Bolivia stands an impressive monument to Anaconda enterprise. Here, nearly ten thousand feet above sea level, has been reared a productive community in an area once the habitat of Indians. For this is Chuquicamata, site of the world's largest known copper deposit, mightiest bastion in all the domain of red metal. Its transition into a vast open pit operation with a town of 25,000 people enjoying every modern facility, is one of the wonder stories of mining without precedent in the long and adventurous narrative of industrial endeavor.

Isaac Marcosson 1957

The disciplining of labour power to the purposes of capital accumulation — a process I shall generally refer to as "labour control" — is a very intricate affair. It entails, in the first instance, some mix of repression, habituation, co-optation and co-operation, all of which have to be organized not only within the workplace, but throughout the society as a whole.

David Harvey 1989

The making of community is an intricate affair, a complex crafting of place, belonging, and boundaries.[1] Community was both site and subject of struggle as Anaconda's practices of labor control filtered through local experiences and perceptions of we-ness. In this chapter, I explore the strategic community building on the part of the Anaconda Company and its relation to the communities created by the residents of Chuquicamata and Butte.[2] I pay attention to the communities that were made and not made as diverse imaginings of common ground coalesced and collided over time. What was at stake in the making of certain kinds of communities? In the drawing of particular lines of exclusion and difference?

I do not equate community and place.[3] I am interested in ways in which place is deployed in delineating and blurring boundaries of community. The very names "Butte" and "Chuquicamata" stood to residents as powerful symbols, coalescing history, structure, and practice and evoking fierce loyalties to a sense of place. However, when residents looked to connections beyond the bounds of locality, they often found them in ethnic ties and cultural practices rooted in their own histories. Such common bonds mitigated against the imagined community of copper miners of Butte and Chuquicamata, united in solidarity that crossed national, geographic, and cultural boundaries. In contrast, Anaconda took a global view of copper and community, while strategically exploiting a more circumscribed sense of place as it variably constructed communities to suit its labor force needs in Butte and Chuquicamata. The ethnographic data offer insights into the corporate eye for detail in crafting its labor community.

IMAGINING COMMUNITY

As the Anaconda Company was building a steady and reliable workforce, residents of Butte and Chuquicamata were crafting their own sense of belonging. Yet neither their visions of community nor their sense of themselves as members was entirely of their own making. The corporate imagination carved the physical and social contours of community in Butte and Chuquicamata. In the process, it forged forceful images of what it meant to be good workers, citizens, and consumers.[4]

I draw on Benedict Anderson's notion of "imagined communities" as I consider the multiple constructions of community that linked and separated the people of Butte and Chuquicamata (B. Anderson 1991). Anderson applies the notion of "imagined communities" to the question of nations and nationalism. He asks how it is that this amorphous sense of "belonging" to a group that one can at best know very partially can become the basis for such powerful sentimental and political attachment that people are willing to die for it. The concept of "imagined" is crucial here. Anderson does not take the nation to be an imaginary entity. Its power and meaning are intimately grounded in the "imagining" — that is, the active, creative, meaning-giving practices of its members. With an eye on profits, Anaconda imagined, invested in, disciplined, and rewarded its transnational labor community. Likewise, local residents challenged, acquiesced to, and participated in the building of a mining way of life even as they crafted their own visions of belonging in the interstices of the corporate imagination. The meaning and power of (trans)nationalism variably shaped the contested terrain of community.

In two isolated corners of the world, the Anaconda Company promoted larger-than-life images of grandeur — images that were tributes to the challenging terrain and the tough people who took it on. Butte became known as the "Richest Hill on Earth," a name the community stills wears with pride, as if the mere evocation could restore its depleted wealth. Chuquicamata bore the title of the "Best Mining Camp in the World." Over the years, when Anaconda wanted to promote local harmony or to admonish residents who challenged corporate power, the company played on these images through a discourse of greatness and vulnerability.

Anaconda recognized the power of the press in shaping social thought and action. The company owned seven of ten major daily newspapers in Montana's five largest cities until 1959.[5] Anaconda also controlled the press in Chuquicamata. And throughout its tenure in Chile, the company enjoyed laudatory press coverage in the pages of *El Mercurio*, a major Chilean newspaper chain that accounted for over half of the daily newspaper circulation in the country.[6] The newspapers provided a daily forum for crafting the corporate visions of community, ensuring sympathetic coverage of corporate interests and scarce attention to conflict. Anaconda's power of the press did not go unnoticed by its critics. Ricardo Latcham, living and writing in Chuquicamata in 1926, observed:

> During the time we were living in Chuquicamata and paying attention to, among other things, the reports in *El Mercurio de Antofagasta* regarding the management of Chile Exploration Company, all information about the mine was minimized. When there was an accident, publicity was avoided. When a worker died, torn apart by a gun shot or crushed by a cave-in, which happened often, when the *carabineros*, always in the service of the Yankees, detained people without cause, when finally, anything happened that inconvenienced the company, it was kept quiet through the efforts of their mouthpiece, the well-paid gentleman, Sr. Cruzat Lavin, loyal and effective servant of their goals. . . . The Chilean proletariat press is the only one that struggles to speak out against the Chile Exploration Company. (Latcham 1926, 49)

The company press provides a rich data base not only of the corporate images of community, but of the construction of difference as well. These "official" accounts hold clues to the struggles that the company was engaged in and responding to. In Chuquicamata, Anaconda used the local press to construct a model of American free enterprise and capitalism that Chileans should emulate. A message of the U.S. success story as the model for Chilean advancement permeated images of domesticity, education, child rearing, and food and clothing styles, as well as images of a free-market economy. Implicit was a message of difference and inferiority, suggesting that Chile had not yet arrived at the U.S. standard of success. A distinction between "Americans" and "natives" was elaborated through the discourse and practices of corporate paternalism. Though the distinctions often fueled resentment among "native" residents, the spoils of corporate benevolence frequently earned Anaconda high praise. This curious system of resentment and reward structured the community disposition of Chuquicamata for fifty years.[7]

In Butte, many of the struggles between corporate and labor images of community were expressed in the language of patriotism and citizenship, where the meaning of *American* was at stake. Despite their competing claims to national identity, the company and the unions seemed to agree in their construction of the Chilean miners as "other." They were outside the world of "American" miners, who found common ground in their chauvinism. Alongside this nationalism, there was often a parallel discourse of localism, expressed through corporate appeals to "community good" and a sense of "we're all in the same boat" democracy. Community survival was constructed in terms of the local solidarity needed to fend off pernicious outsiders, though the meanings of *local* and *outsider* were constantly shifting. The community identity of Butte, America, was shaped through the fusion of these charged images.[8]

I turn now to a comparative look at the cultural milieus of community and the practices of community building in Butte and Chuquicamata. In keeping with the corporate eye for detail, I look beyond the mines to the practices of daily living and offer a comparative examination of the corporate presence in the ways people lived, ate, played, and celebrated community.

BUILDING BUTTE, AMERICA: DREAMS AND REALITIES

Community building in Butte began as an international affair. First came the miners from Cornwall, both those recruited for their knowledge of copper and those in search of a better future. They were followed by an outpouring from Ireland in the late 1800s. Butte's Irish community established itself as a formidable social and political force, making up one-quarter of the city's population by 1910. The early 1900s also saw the arrival of immigrants from Germany, Italy, Canada, Finland, Scandinavia, Serbia, Croatia, and Montenegro. Distinct ethnic neighborhoods grew around the entrances to the labyrinth of underground mines. Walkerville, Meaderville, Centerville, McQueen, Finntown, East Butte, Hungry Hill, Dublin Gulch, and the Cabbage Patch: the neighborhoods' names marked place, language, loyalty, and history. Local historians claim that at one time, there were forty-two languages spoken in Butte. Butte shifted from transient mining camp to cosmopolitan center of the Mountain West, its industrial base and ethnic diversity an anomaly on the frontier.[9]

The hyperbolic histories told of Butte's florescence celebrate its infamy as a "wide-open town," a thriving mecca for drinking, gambling, and prostitution. Its red-light district was said to rival that of New Orleans.[10] According to local lore, mines were not the only tunnels laced beneath the streets of Butte. Underground passages connecting bars, restaurants, opium dens, and brothels promoted interesting business partnerships and quality customer service. Local storytellers claim that the tunnels were conduits for a ready supply of bootleg liquor during prohibition. Perpetually shrouded in a sulfuric cloud of mine smoke, Butte was a menacing place, where only the iron-willed or the foolhardy could walk the streets without fear. Butte, they say, was not only the "richest hill on earth," it was also the "perch of the devil" (Atherton 1914; Glasscock 1935, 85–87).[11]

Wide-open images and promises of prosperity were tempered by the hard work and harsh realities of mining life. The single men, who arrived first, did not return wealthy to their homelands. They toiled in the mines, saved what they could, and sometimes helped family and friends to join them. Young single women also came to Butte to take advantage of employment opportunities. Though prostitution remained a cornerstone of the service economy, women found "respectable" work in restaurants, hotels, laundries, hospitals, and private homes. The gender balance shifted. The male-dominated mining camp gave way to a city of workingmen and women, marriage, and family. In the process, Anaconda gained a steady, reliable labor force.[12]

There is both humor and hardship in the arrival stories told by and about Butte's early residents. There was Mary Buckley who:

left a life of poverty in Macroom, County Cork, Ireland in the early 1900s, landed in New York harbor amid signs of "Help wanted: Irish need not apply," and died in Butte half a century later. Her realm was a two story frame house at 526 N. Wyoming where, with Irish brogue and iron will, she bore and reared six children and provided room and board to 17 miners and feed for 30 more. . . . Michael [her husband] worked in the mines, Mary the boarding house where most of her boarders were Gaelic-speaking Irishmen. More than one left the homeland bearing the tag, "Ship to 526 N. Wyoming." (McCormick 1980)

Waldemar Kailaya was born in Butte in 1907, son of Finnish immigrants who had met and married in Ironwood, Michigan. They came to Butte in 1904 because the Butte miners had won an eight-hour day, whereas the Ironwood miners were still working ten-hour days. In his memoirs, Kailaya recalls:

There were four Finnish saloons located around Finntown. Two were located on East Broadway and the other two were on East Park. These were a great impact on many families, my own among them. I always had to meet my father at the pay office on pay day. Otherwise he would stop at the saloon and lose his weekly pay. At one time, he had lost his full months wages when I was not there to meet him. That caused a great hardship for a large family like ours.[13]

Butte's new arrivals brought with them their particular histories of oppression, political knowledge, and cultural practices. They established churches, stores, fraternal organizations, and social clubs. Scandia Hall, the Ancient Order of Hibernians, and the Order of Reudenburg, among others, were key sites of ethnic identification for Butte's newcomers and arenas for maintaining cultural symbols and practices over the years. However, the close-knit ethnic communities also defined boundaries of distinction and exclusion. The stories of community building offer an amalgam of melting-pot nostalgia and markers of difference:

I grew up in Walkerville, where everything was intermingled. It was a friendly place, small. I wasn't aware of the difference. Then we moved to McQueen and I became very aware of the difference. I resented it. I was Irish and my husband was Italian . . . and there were all these older Slavish women who were real standoffish. You sort of had to prove yourself to them. They'd say, "Oh, you're Irish." I felt like saying, "No, I'm American." The neighbors were Yugoslavian, well not Yugoslavs, but Slovenes and Croatians. They had a Croatian paper and they talked . . . It's a funny thing when you lived around them. My mother couldn't understand them and I couldn't understand why, because they sounded fine to me. They did talk broken. Down where [my husband] lived, they all talked Italian. He never knew a word of English until first grade.

Holy Savior Church was down around the Franklin school. That's about the division line between Meaderville and McQueen. There was Holy Savior Church and St. Helena's. When I had my first baby, I lived in McQueen, so I called Father P. about baptism He said, "Oh, no, you'll have to call Father S. up to St. Helena's," but didn't say why. So I call Father S. and he says, "Oh, with a name like yours [Italian], you're baptized down here where you belong." That just infuriated me. I felt like saying, "Well, I'm not Italian." But they consider, well, [my husband] was head of the house and his name was Italian and the Italians went to St. Helena's, so that was your church.[14]

●　●　●

My folks bought their home in Meaderville in 1912, the year my father got his citizenship. . . . We liked the Meaderville location. It was close to the mines and mainly comprised of people of Italian and English descent. There was lots of good shopping and eating there. McQueen had lots of Austrians. In Meaderville, there were a few Austrians, but lots of Cornish from the tin mines. At one time, there was quite a Chinese Community in Butte. They were often the cooks in the restaurants and had many restaurants in Chinatown. There was a settlement of Chinese out at Nine Mile. The Chinese farmers would come in from Nine Mile with baskets over their shoulders. My mother bought produce from them. She never hesitated to do business with them because she felt sorry for them. And she liked their fresh produce and they came right up the street by our house, so it was very convenient for her. The Chinese had stores on South Main. My mother went there every Fourth of July for fireworks. They also had laundries. The Chinese followed the California forty-niners. The Chinese would work the low grade ores that the forty-niners abandoned. That's how they first came to Butte. And isn't it ironic that it is a Chinese man up at Tech [local college] who is teaching us how to get the minerals out of the pit? Isn't that an interesting state of progress? They came from such poor roots and now they are leading us. It's a small world.[15]

Even popular Irish toasts played on the distinctions that shaped local culture in Butte:

We do our work for an Englishman
And room with a French Canuck.
We board at a Swedish restaurant
Where a Finnlander cooks our chuck.
We buy our clothes off a German Jew
And our shoes off a Russian Pole
And we trust our hope in a Roman pope
To save our Irish soul.[16]

As noted in chapter 2, the lines of ethnic distinction and solidarity crosscut class relations in the mines and the community at large. As Jerry Calvert observes: "The stratification of jobs also fueled the intraclass ethnic conflict in the mines. The hardest, dirtiest, most unhealthy and most dangerous jobs went to the newest immigrants" (1988, 61). Anaconda's founder, Marcus Daly, had forged a strong bond with Butte's large Irish immigrant workforce. Although he did not recruit workers from Ireland, the results of his sympathies were clear. The burgeoning Irish population dominated the Anaconda Company workforce at the turn of the century. Selective hiring by Irish shift bosses fed the interests of Butte's Irish Catholic political machine and tempered Irish miners' labor activism (Emmons 1989; Calvert 1988). Long after Daly's death in 1900, Irish loyalties served as a counterbalance to class interests.

Butte residents tended to the social and cultural aspects of family and community life while Anaconda focused on shaping Butte and Montana's physical, economic, and political landscape. The company enjoyed the right of eminent domain to exploit mineral resources beneath surface lands. And as the largest property owner in the State of Montana, Anaconda worked hard to ensure that state and local taxation policies favored company interests. As a retired Butte politician recalled with wry humor:

> A map of Butte and Silver Bow County looks just like a hunk of Swiss cheese. There's all these holes in it. Because everywhere there was a mine shaft comin' to the surface, that property was considered out of the city limits. So think about it. Everywhere there was a Gallows Frame, there was a hole in the map, outside the limits. So the City of Butte looks just like Swiss cheese.[17]

It was on this terrain of Swiss cheese that Anaconda negotiated its relations with the Butte community. Perhaps this strategic shaping of the physical boundaries of community provides a useful metaphor for Anaconda's shaping of the social boundaries of community.

Anaconda made few efforts to rein in Butte's wide-open image and practices. A little surface vice took the edge off the hardships of underground mining. Locals say that miners picked up their checks at the company pay offices and cashed them at the uptown bars, where a bottle of beer and a shot of whiskey awaited. And prostitution remained an active part of Butte's service economy until the last of the brothels closed with the last of the mines in the 1980s. Butte miners worked hard and played hard, and that served the company well. In building its Butte labor force, the Anaconda Company maintained an unofficial policy summed up in the words of famed Butte boxer and nightclub owner Sonny O'Day: "It was the policy of the Anaconda Company to keep the miners happy, keep 'em broke and keep 'em working" (M. Murphy 1990, 199).

However, by the 1910s the realities of harsh working and living conditions shattered new arrivals' dreams of prosperity. State investigators documented what Butte residents already knew about deplorable housing and unsafe mining conditions.[18] The chasm between the haves and the have-nots was glaring. A critical mass of miners had crossed the bounds of ethnicity and identified class struggle as their common ground. Socialists were offering alternative visions of what it meant to be a worker, citizen, and consumer through community efforts such as the Young People's Socialist League, which sponsored social and cultural events and citizenship classes.[19] As we have seen, the company and the state responded to this "anti-American" activism with repression in the mines and community. Some residents continued the fight. Others lost their vision of community in the daily struggle to survive. Hopelessness took its toll. During the 1910s, Butte had a suicide rate two and a half times the national average.[20]

Facing the resurgence of labor activism in 1920, Anaconda elaborated its nationalist discourse, making powerful distinctions between rabble-rousing immigrants and the true citizenry of Butte, America. For example, on April 22, 1920, the front-page headlines of the *Anaconda Standard* read: "IWW Pickets Shot in Battle with Officers. Six of Wounded Aren't Citizens of the Country," and "IWW Pickets Beating Boy Routed by Woman's Bluff." The first article notes that eight of the "terrorists" were of foreign birth and that six, "while they have lived in the U.S. for many years, have made no effort to take out citizenship papers." The second reports:

> A dozen burly IWW pickets put to rout by a little, frail, white haired woman, who possesses the courage of her convictions. Heroine is Mrs. Elias Cundy, 60 years old. She saw a number of IWW pickets beating a boy who was on his way to work in one of the mines. "I saw a bunch of those foreigners mauling the poor lad," she said, "and I ran right over. When I got close to them I called them to stop or I would put a gun on them and I put my hand in my pocket. As soon as I reached for my pocket they stopped beating the boy and some of them started to run. . . . I don't see why it is that a bunch of these foreigners can stand there on the hill and tell an American citizen that he can't work."[21]

Through its newspapers, Anaconda promoted a heightened nationalism and xenophobia that fueled fears of domestic radicalism.[22] At the
moment when Anaconda was poised to seek its fortune beyond U.S.
borders, it was forming an "all-American" labor force in Butte: subdued, patriotic, and more interested in consuming Irish whiskey than
Socialist literature. The message must have seemed ironic to the immigrants who made up the bulk of the mining labor force in 1920.
However, they were more likely pondering survival than irony as the
mine shutdown in 1921 resulted in the layoff of sixty-five hundred miners. When the mines reopened in 1922, the company could selectively
choose their labor force. Anaconda favored "family men" whose histories were free of labor activism. The company viewed married men and
those with dependents as more conservative and perhaps more likely to
share the corporate vision of good community members (M. Murphy
1990, 48).

Over the years, the meaning of *American* defined a key point of contention among competing images of community in Butte. During the
Depression, national identity tangled with class struggles in the definitions of common ground. For example, by the mid-1930s, more than
eight thousand people in Butte were unemployed and nearly half of the
families in Butte were receiving state relief. The local collective myth of
Butte's promise of prosperity was once again under siege. *The Eye
Opener*, describing Butte as a "poor city atop the richest hill on earth,"
reported that Butte had the second highest percentage of persons on
relief in the country. The federal government, not copper, was sustaining
the community.[23]

It was time for labor to turn the tables on defining who was
"American." *The Eye Opener* challenged Anaconda's lack of support of
a tariff on copper imports, which was intended to ease the plight of U.S.
miners, and charged: "This company is so entangled with the capitalis-
tic system and with foreign holdings that it does not endorse a movement that would help the domestic copper situation. It is not truly an
American company."[24]

As it criticized company loyalties and ironized the company's nationalism, labor revived its language and practice of class-based solidarity. In
1935, *The Eye Opener* drew connections between the high salaries
earned by Anaconda executives and the low wages paid to company
workers in Poland, Mexico, and Chile. Miners organized a massive May
Day march, where a strong language of class consciousness and struggle
permeated the speeches.[25] At the same time, however, the labor press

criticized Anaconda for providing a progressive social insurance program for its "peons" in the Chilean mines while neglecting its "men" in
Butte: "The great American copper company insured its Chile miners
while the Butte miner places his name on the waiting list to get a chance
to die of silicosis in the state operated sanitarium called Galen."[26]
Curiously, at a moment when labor seemed ready to broaden its vision
of common ground beyond the interests of Butte, America, chauvinist
sentiments and beliefs about difference cut short their view.

The cleavages of class were more readily felt and identified at the
local level, where disparities and distinctions loomed large. To this day,
many Butte people speak of Big Shots and little guys to distinguish those
with power and wealth from the rest.[27] Though a Butte miner might
have trouble seeing the common ground between himself and a Chilean
miner, he could not escape the markers of poverty and affluence that distinguished his world from that of the local Big Shots. The stately mansions on Butte's West Side offered a permanent display of opulence. The
distinctions marked power and triggered resentment, as illustrated in a
1934 commentary in *The Eye Opener*:

> If actions speak louder than words, then mansions also speak with much
> greater voice than shacks. If the Federal Mediator [called in to mediate the
> 1934 strike] wants to get a real comparison of the home life of the Butte
> miner and the overlords who manage Rockefeller's "Richest Hill on Earth,"
> he should first make an extended visit to the north and east side dwellings in
> Butte.
>
> Houses or shacks planked against old mine dumps, front yards of rocks
> and mud, children in tattered clothes and anxious mothers, toil worn, calling
> youngsters back from the dangers of street play.
>
> Then let the federal man run over to Swan Lake where C. F. Kelley, Jim
> Hobbins and others have summer homes that for splendor exceed the palace
> of Caesar. Hundreds of acres of grass and trees, private launches, every mod-
> ern luxury including a corps of gunmen who tell the stranger to keep mov-
> ing. He would at least find some comparison.[28] (see fig. 13)

The language of class struggle and critique of capitalism largely fell
by the wayside after the labor struggles of the 1930s in Butte. Perhaps,
as the Lynds argue in their analysis of Middletown in transition, labor
and capital had reached tacit agreement on the correctness of the capitalist system and hoped to confine their differences to negotiating the
shared fruits of that system (Lynd and Lynd 1937).[29] But the language of
Big Shots and little guys, forged in local experience and imbued with
local knowledge, remains as a reminder of the distinctions that crosscut
this all-American town.

Figure 13.   Butte family, Depression era. Courtesy of Butte Historical
Society, Butte Labor History Project Collection.

While Anaconda was earning record profits from its Chilean mines in
the postwar years, it was promoting a local pride steeped in nationalism
in Butte. Butte miners were depicted as a privileged bunch, partners in
American know-how and free enterprise. They were, in fact, earning a
"family wage" and seeing home ownership as an attainable goal. A
1956 *Time* article touts Butte as a "model" company town that embodies the "social and economic maturity of U.S. industry." "No oldtime
company town in the U.S. better typifies industry's modern attitude than
Butte, Mont.," the article claims. It describes the postwar years as a time
for Anaconda to make up for its neglect of community responsibility by
investing in recreation and education:

> In quick succession Anaconda backed a housing program, that provided
> homes for 650 families, [compared to] 150 houses completed in the previous
> 15 years, invested in a hospital, a civic auditorium and a $400,000 club
> where C.I.O. miners were soon bowling and drinking beer with the once-
> hated "sixth floor boys," i.e., Anaconda executives. The company also coop-
> erated in clamping down on "Venus Alley," helped slash the VD rate west of
> the Mississippi to 3.2 per 1,000 residents. Today, in the town John Gunther
> once called "the only electric lit cemetery in the U.S.," signs in merchants'
> windows proclaim: "Butte is my home, I like it."[30]

A language of community pride and partnership permeated the corporate structuring of community in the postwar years. Company investments in housing, public health, and recreation provided a thoughtful mix of reward and discipline as the company gingerly reined in this wide-open town and claimed it as a model American city. However, when hard times hit during the 1959 strike, the American irony emerged once again. A reporter talking to strikers waiting in line to be certified for surplus foods captured the moment:

> "It doesn't seem like America in 1959," one man said.
> "It doesn't seem like Butte at all," said another.
> "They didn't let Khrushchev see things like this when he was over here," added a third man, with a tinge of bitterness. "He would have had to tell the Russians when he got home."
> "One good thing about it," an oldtimer observed, "we've reached the bottom now. If things change at all, they'll have to get better."
> Irrepressible humor surfaced. One man called to another, "Hey, Joe, see that Okie neighbor of yours and find out for me how to cook corn meal, will you?
> "I can't find time," Joe replied, "I've got to hunt up a Chinaman and learn how to cook rice."[31]

Butte, America, a community constructed in a web of contradictions: "American" miners might challenge corporate patriotism, even as they accepted corporate constructions of "foreigners" and elaborated their own.[32] And in this vision of common ground, Chuquicamata was a threat, not an ally. The ironic bonding between the miners and bosses in Butte and their distinction from the Chilean "other" is best exemplified in the words of a Butte labor leader. Reflecting on the downfall of Anaconda, he said, "You know, the worst thing that ever happened to the Anaconda Company was when those Mexicans in Chile got educated."[33]

CARVING CHUQUICAMATA

It was a mature and politically sophisticated corporation that approached the prospect of community building in Chuquicamata in 1923. Corporate headquarters had abandoned the Richest Hill on Earth and moved to New York City's financial district. Through its expansion efforts, Anaconda had realized its motto, "From Producer to Consumer." The world's largest mining company was poised to encounter the world's largest copper deposit.

Large-scale copper exploitation and community development did not begin in Chuquicamata until 1914, under the Guggenheims, but practices of labor control had been underway for some time. The massive ore deposits of Chuquicamata occupied liminal space both culturally and physically in the Chilean imagination. Until the War of the Pacific (1879–1883), the remote Atacama Region, where Chuquicamata is located, was contested terrain parceled among Bolivia, Peru, and Chile.[34] Because it lacked water, Chuquicamata was a nearly uninhabitable space. The surrounding desert region was dotted with small subsistence farming communities that had grown up around a few precious water sources. Indigenous artisans had engaged in small-scale mining and metalwork, but Chuquicamata's wealth lay dormant for years.[35]

By the 1840s, massive exploitation of other mineral deposits in northern Chile was underway. Aided by new refining technology and infusions of British capital, Chile established itself as the world's largest copper producer by the 1850s. Meanwhile, the nitrate industry of Chile's desert north was undergoing explosive development. Julio Pinto and Luis Ortega describe the expansive northern mining region as the birthplace of Chilean proletarianism (1990, 49–79). The industry needed a workforce, something unavailable in the region. Mining companies wanted workers conditioned to physical and occupational mobility who were willing to abandon their homes and relocate in inhospitable terrain. Though recruitment efforts were made to bring in workers, Pinto and Ortega argue that promise of a salary was the real incentive for Chileans, Argentineans, and Bolivians to emigrate to the mining region.

The rich nitrate reserves being exploited by British-Chilean interests extended into the Bolivian province of Antofagasta and the Peruvian province of Tarapacá. As the companies intensified their mining efforts, they ran into serious conflicts with their Andean neighbors. These conflicts culminated in the War of The Pacific, which pitted Chile against a Bolivian-Peruvian alliance. Chile emerged from the war a political and economic victor, gaining control of the mineral-laden provinces, which included the untold wealth in copper at Chuquicamata.[36] This place beyond the mental map of Chile, pertaining to the physical and cultural space of the altiplano, became marked as an emblem of Chilean nationalism.

It was not until the late 1890s that a number of small Chilean mining interests began working the ore deposits at Chuquicamata (Alvear Urrutia 1975, 68). But these small-scale mines could not compete with large-scale capital. In 1910, Albert Burrage, a Boston capitalist with longtime involvement in copper, conducted a study of the Chuquicamata ore deposit and was convinced of its profit potential. He secured rights to the entire Chuquicamata area from the Chilean government and the British companies that were involved in some of the small operations. He sold the rights to the Guggenheim family, and in 1912 the Chile Exploration Company (CHILEX) was officially incorporated (Marcosson 1957, 196–97). The Guggenheims went to work building their company town. They benefited from the region's established history of labor recruitment: if you offer a wage, they will come.

If the building of rough and tumble Butte was something of an (un)happy accident, the building of Chuquicamata was a study in scientific management. Harry Guggenheim, vice president in charge of operations at CHILEX, outlines the process in a 1920 *Engineering and Mining Journal* article entitled, "Building Mining Cities in South America: A Detailed Account of the Social and Industrial Benefits Flowing from the Human Engineering Work of the Chile Exploration Company and the Braden Copper Company — Organization, Administration, and Conception of the Objects Sought" (Guggenheim 1920, 204).

Guggenheim details the physical construction of Chuquicamata but emphasizes the science of "welfare work" that went into making a successful company town: "[T]hese companies had not only to develop and equip their mines, but they had to build railroads and to establish towns, or if you please, cities, complete, sufficient to house from 10,000 to 15,000 inhabitants, and to supply them with food, water and other necessities, as well as to keep them clean, healthy and content" (204).

Guggenheim divides the welfare problems into "two classes," one for the so-called staff, consisting of "Americans, Chileans and Europeans, and the other for the workmen, who are in the very great majority Chilean and who have had few of the advantages enjoyed by citizens of rich and more industrially and culturally developed American and European countries" (205). The first attempts at welfare work focused on "hygiene and amusement for the Chilean workmen and recreation for the staff." The key to a successful welfare program lay in selection of a competent "welfare expert." Guggenheim favored personal qualities over technical expertise, and put a longtime smelter superintendent in charge of welfare development in the Guggenheim operations. His welfare manager "knew the Latin American laborers through many years experience with them; appreciated their abilities and their weaknesses; and primarily had a real interest in their development and a profound faith in the general proposition that humanity progresses" (205).

The article describes the types of housing that were designed to serve "various classes of employees." They ranged from the "Official Houses — Occupied by heads of departments. One story cottages having six rooms, two baths, and a kitchen. The total floor space in each is 1,500 sq. ft.," to the "Type D Houses — Occupied by native laborers and their families. One story, with either two or three rooms. The floor areas are 242 and 363 sq.ft. respectively." Guggenheim notes that "authority has been granted recently to add shower baths to a certain number of these houses that are occupied by natives that can be classed as permanent employees who have shown more than the usual interest in raising the standard of their homes." The company was willing to promote that interest, offering prizes "to encourage cleanliness in Chilean workmen's homes and beauty in their garden plots" (206).

Guggenheim was well aware that labor control demanded attention far beyond the workplace. He outlined a comprehensive community development plan that included schools, hospitals, social clubs, potable water supplies, sanitation, churches, markets, amusements, and policing. A two-tiered school system ensured separate education for the "American" and the "native" children. He praised the progress of the native youth, "the outward sign of which is an extraordinary improvement in cleanliness and dress." In addition to basic academics, native children also had the opportunities to join the "organized brigades" of boy or girl scouts (208).

Visiting nurses kept tabs on the home conditions and child-rearing practices of Chilean mothers. Their services "included a limited control of the personal habits of the Chilean laborers, who are encouraged to bathe and wash their clothes, and are obliged to be free from parasitic insects." And, as a supplemental home service, "a committee of ladies, experts in household craft and economy, has been formed to both assist customers in purchasing and to give advice on household matters" (208).

The Guggenheims recognized that the Atacama Desert was a foreboding place to call home: "[A]mple and varied diversion is necessary for the employees and their families if they are to be content. Clubs, moving pictures, festivals, bands, games, athletics, and horse races have been provided, and are kept going as actively as possible. They are an offset to the temptations of the various forms of vice which have

appeared just outside the company's properties, especially at Chuquicamata" (209). Meanwhile, the executive staff could recreate in the "very
handsome American Club [that] has been erected in Chuquicamata at a
cost of $128,000. This building contains a large reception hall, a ball-
room with a stage at one end, billiard room, reading room, dining room
and kitchen, a bowling alley and a swimming pool 20 by 50 feet" (207).

As a result of Guggenheim's welfare effort:

> great strides have been made forward. The Chilean laborer, who five years
> ago lived in a hovel in filth, with all the mental degradation that is concomi-
> tant with such surroundings, today lives in a small but comfortable home,
> enjoying the fundamental facilities that modern hygiene affords. Instead of
> the ragged, barefooted, irresponsible laborer of five years ago, there is a well-
> dressed, well-shod workman with a spark of ambition burning within him.
> Great as has been the improvement with the men, it has been even more
> marked with the women and children. The latter, in their school house, com-
> pare favorably in appearance with the children in the public schools of the
> United States. With this social change the Chilean laborers have developed
> great intelligence and adaptability and have advanced greatly in effi-
> ciency. . . . Experiences at these properties has taught that so-called welfare
> work is worth while, not only from the human but from the economic results
> to be achieved. These companies have now a skilled, permanent class of
> employees instead of the roving, unambitious class of laborers from which
> they formerly had to draw. (209–10)

The enlightened paternalism that informed the Guggenheim's imagination of Chuquicamata was grounded in a fundamental divide between
"American" and "native." Neither Chile in particular nor Latin
America in general were included in this myopic view of America from
the north. Over the years, Anaconda elaborated and refined these distinctions. They never disrupted the fundamental order first established
by the Guggenheims. For example, Anaconda's preoccupation with
order in Chuquicamata is revealed in the detailed attention to attendance records of workers in the mines and of their children in school.
Stockholders reports in the 1920s provide annual census data from
Chuquicamata that include the number of pupils in school, the percentage of turnover in the labor force, and the number of workers eligible
for "attendance bonuses."[37] As one Chuquicamatina put it, "Chuqui
wasn't just a class system, it was a caste system and it still is."[38] But these
practices did not go uncontested or unappreciated. The negotiation of
"American" and "native" communities became a fifty-year struggle.

Harry Guggenheim's assessment of Chuquicamata did not pass unnoticed by the "natives." In their 1920 critical history, *Chuquicamata, su*

grandeza y sus dolores, Eulogio Gutiérrez and Marcial Figueroa assert that:

> In his ignorance, Harry Guggenheim doesn't have even a remote idea about our country. He ignores the fact that before Chile Exploration Company and Braden Copper, which are the same thing, we already had colossal riches such as Chañarcillo, Tamaya, and Caracoles, besides the prodigious nitrate industry, unique in the world, and the coal, agricultural, and livestock industries in the central and southern regions.
>
> Before the Yankees arrived, there were already three-hundred miners successfully working these resources. . . . [But now, with the arrival of the Yankees,] life in Chuquicamata, for the native, the negro, as those North American masters of our riches call us, is a problem they don't want to solve. Housing is crowded, unsafe, unhealthy, and inadequate. The work is hard and exhausting. There is hunger in the workers' camp. Many men go begging. Women suffer malnutrition. And children grow up malnourished in squalor. . . .
>
> The comfort, decency, and hygiene of the American Camp has not been made for the blackman, because that Yankee democracy that lynches the negro son of the Union on their soil has established in Chuqui the distinction of classes and races, setting themselves as members of the privileged race and us as the backward, unadapted, indigenous race. The promiscuity, misery, and abandonment in which our people live has generated licentiousness, corruption, and loss of control.
>
> And when they say that Punta de Rieles and Banco Drummond, two nearby shanty towns, are the places where the most repugnant social diseases are contracted, they aren't telling the whole truth, because in CHILEX's own New Camp, forced by the difficult circumstances of misery, lack of food, and clothing, mothers are prostituting themselves. . . . The infant mortality among the blackmen is incredible. See for yourself in the cemetery the large number of graves for children and adults. . . . Pauperism has invaded everything. Misery is painted on the faces of the children in the streets begging a few coins for bread. Families of five or more are living on salaries of seven pesos. The water we drink here is full of salt, sometimes pure brine, whereas the water for the whites, that is, the bosses, is pure and fresh water that comes from Toconce. The Chilean family in the New Camp lives dying. A new generation, impotent, suffering from the pox and tuberculosis, is going to go out of here, without spirit, without vigor in their red blood cells that the rich blood of our fathers has passed down to us from the last generation, healthy, valiant, and strong blood. Chuquicamata at present is the cemetery of the race. (Gutiérrez and Figueroa 1920, 9–11)

This vivid and scathing description of Chuquicamata in the 1920s not only reflects hostility to the Yankee landlords but also reveals a critical consciousness of the classism and racism that underpinned corporate practices. Throughout Gutiérrez and Figueroa's text, there is strong identification with the "blackman" and images of the Yankee colonizer exploiting slave labor. They speak of the hospitable Chilean being duped by the fair-skinned, fair-haired foreigner. They point to labor practices whereby transient Yankees could arrive in their country and get a better job in the mines than the experienced Chilean. They ask why it was that blue eyes and blonde hair were taken as a sign of competence (Gutiérrez and Figueroa 1920, 160–72). Conflicted class and national relations were expressed through and embodied in images of racism.

The meaning of *native* was problematic in its own right, because it was blurred by and elaborated through other ethnic distinctions. As in Butte, Chuquicamata became host to a diverse immigrant workforce. By 1923, Chuquicamata had a population of 12,700 people and a mining workforce of 5,000. Ricardo Latcham claims that there were twenty languages spoken in Chuquicamata in the 1920s (1926, 180). Stereotypical images of ethnic distinctions abound in the early reports of Chuquicamata's ethnic diversity. There are vivid descriptions of the "brutish" Slavs, who numbered nearly 1,200 in 1924, "uncultured" Bolivians who carried their "superstitions and paganistic beliefs" across the border with them, and the "enterprising" Chinese and Japanese who ran the groceries and barber shops.[39]

Despite the colorful depictions of this ethnic kaleidoscope, the relationships within Chuquicamata's ethnically mixed labor force were complicated. On the one hand, early writers suggest that Chuquicamata's ethnic groups blended and mixed, finding common ground in their work and solidarity in their struggles. On the other, these same writers often elaborate and draw on pejorative ethnic distinctions, especially in representations of los bolivianos (Bolivians) as uncultured, malleable, and a threat to the more sophisticated Chilean miner. Images of the distant "blackman" evoke a powerful rhetoric of colonial ruthlessness and social injustice. Representations of the neighboring boliviano suggest a real fear of competition for jobs in the mines. Perhaps that fear fused with a more complicated resentment of los bolivianos. Because of their supposed "passivity, malleability, and lack of culture," Bolivians had lost this precious terrain to the more sophisticated Chileans.[40] Now their very shortcomings were resources to the foreigners who were siphoning Chile's riches out from under it. These distinctions have staying power. References to the racist underpinnings of Yankee labor practices as well as to the Bolivian cultural character still permeate popular accounts of local history. Imelda, a longtime Chuquicamata resident reminded me:

> You gringos were racists, too. Anaconda had some pretty racist ideas. They always preferred to hire *los bolivianos*. They thought they were a more passive race than *chilenos* [Chileans]. And they had less education. And because of this, *los bolivianos* wouldn't take part in union action. They came to Chuqui to look for work in the mine, and without family or community or citizenship in our country, they were the most vulnerable group in the mines. *Los bolivianos* didn't have much culture. And the living and working conditions for those single men from the interior were the worst of all.[41]

Imelda's opinions echo those of Latcham, who observed the situation in 1926: "In the mining region there is a significant population of Bolivian Indians, sorry competitors of the Chileans in the work of extracting copper. But they are content with poor salaries and don't demonstrate many material demands, and for this, they are often preferred by the North American capitalists" (Latcham 1926, 116). Latcham's analysis reflects his own essentialist (and nationalist) views of the Bolivians as "other," qualitatively different from the Chilean laborer. In his view, the difference was fact; the injustice lay in Anaconda's exploitation of it.

The company may have exploited perceived differences, but a discourse of distinction was also a key part of "the peoples'" construction of Chuquicamata. As in Butte, residents spoke of the diversity within the community, the physical distinction of *rostros nortinos* (northern faces), of people carrying their customs with them and preserving them in Chuquicamata:

> You could tell the *nortinos* from the interior by their dress and customs, like carrying their children in packs on their backs. Often, the *bolivianos* came and set up their small businesses. They would sell food and wares on the street corners. I remember one couple, the woman worked one corner and her husband another. Sometimes they kept their inventory in their cart at my grandfather's house. . . . We celebrated all the national holidays here. There would be a big celebration for Bolivian Independence Day. People used to say that's when cats would start disappearing. The cats made a poor substitute for rabbit in the dishes folks prepared for Independence Day.[42]

• • •

> There used to be lots of small businesses run by *bolivianas paisanas* [peasant women] near where the public market is now. Some were really filthy, but not all. One women used to get the less desirable meat, like tongue and tripe, from the markets in Calama and sell them from her house in Chuqui. The smell of the meat was terrible, but sometimes I bought from her. One *boliviana* ran a small store. We became friends, and I handed down clothes from my children to hers. I helped her out as I could. Then, when my husband

died, I was left with nothing and my kids were still small. By then, this woman had her business running well, and she gave me a job. She helped me a lot.[43]

Their stories speak to connection, distinction, and practices of community building in the interstices of the corporate design. Competing claims for community and identity shaped the terrain of Chuquicamata.[44] The fundamental divide between "American" and "native" was obscured at times by other visions of belonging. The divide was also laden in contradiction as residents sometimes joined the Yankees in reaping the benefits of paternalism and sometimes joined together as allies against Yankee imperialism.

LABOR CONTROL: A COMMUNITY AFFAIR

For nearly fifty years, Anaconda elaborated a separate and unequal system of provision and distinction that penetrated virtually every aspect of daily life in Chuquicamata. In Butte, the company was the beneficiary of crescive social changes and could take a more laissez-faire approach to many practices of community building, but Chuquicamata was another matter. Anaconda saw itself as architect and strategist of community structure and practice. Labor control was a community affair that demanded attention to home and family, vice and virtue, and bread and circus. I turn now to a closer look at labor control in Chuquicamata, which served as a prototype of "modern" industrial community building, and offer comparisons to Butte along the way.

HOME AND FAMILY

The fundamental social and physical divide in Chuquicamata was between the New Camp and the American Camp. The New Camp, named for the new construction initiated by the Guggenheims in 1917, housed the Chilean workforce. The American Camp was the secluded enclave of the Yankee bosses. Worker housing in the New Camp was assigned according to one's position in Roll A, B, or C: supervisor, salaried employee, or laborer. Residents did not pay directly for rent or utilities, which were part of the wage package. Workers lived as guests of the company during their tenure of employment. When miners quit or were fired, they lost their home as well. Few were the Chileans who shared a privileged place with the foreigners on the Gold Roll: those who received their salaries in dollars and lived in the American Camp.

While corporate builders sang the praises of life in the modern mining camp, local critics challenged sanitized images and offered an alternative view. As Latcham puts it, "The Yankees say that Chuqui is the best mining camp in the world. Official visitors don't see the deplorable housing, stench, hunger, syphilis, and prostitution" (1926, 80). In 1925, Latcham completed a housing inspection for CHILEX, reporting on the precarious living conditions he encountered. His report plays on the company's concerns for stability in the camp, linking unsafe physical conditions to unsafe moral conditions. In this way, he appeals to the company's desire for a steady, reliable work force and argues that an improvement in physical conditions would promote social harmony:

> The influence of single men, and the lack of special facilities that are provided to set themselves up decorously with wives and families, provokes a wave of corruption that is intensifying day by day. When a worker has a clean, comfortable house, he feels a stronger attraction to home and avoids dangerous company and alcoholism. . . . The same social peace is achieved in the construction of the family. Disruptive and dangerous elements find their greatest cooperation among the single men. In contrast, married men have strong ties that make it impossible for them to join in seditious strikes and movements that disrupt the public tranquility. (Latcham 1926, 131)

It seems that the Anaconda Company shared Latcham's preoccupation with conditions necessary for labor stability, as the practice of attendance bonuses implied. The company also calculated a plan to create the optimum gender, class, and reliability factors that would maximize productivity in Chuquicamata. Correspondence from CHILEX to New York headquarters in 1925 provides graphic documentation of the corporate strategy for ensuring community stability:

> Complying with your request of recent data I am sending you herewith all of the information I can find relative to housing facilities and cost thereof at Chuquicamata. . . . You will note from this that there was a considerable shortage of housing facilities, and also that only 45% of the employees were married men. They have found at Chuquicamata that it is highly desirable to keep at least 60% married men and they are trying to attain conditions where they will have 70% married men as they find that ratio is most satisfactory.
> The married men are, of course, more reliable during labor troubles and are not absent so frequently after payday as the single men. However, they prefer to keep about 30% single men in the camp as these men board with the married men's families, thus bringing in a little more income for the latter and stabilizing conditions to some extent.[45]

However, given the company's interest in minimizing costs rather than maximizing comfort, housing conditions were slow to improve.

Figure 14.   Housing in Chuquicamata, 1994 (author photo).

When the residents of Chuquicamata speak of housing, they speak of
Las Latas, a sector so named for its metal roofs, which gave it the
appearance of a collection of tin cans. *Las Latas* was home to many Roll
C workers and their families until the 1960s, and the conditions showed
little improvement despite years of struggle. The name and place are
infused with symbolic power in the popular memory of Chuquicamata
residents. *Las Latas* stood for and contained the physical evidence of
Chuqui's social inequities. Residents speak of *Las Latas* and the
CHILEX Club, the exclusive playground of the American Camp, when
pointing to concrete distinctions that marked the two worlds of Chuquicamata. The descriptions of *Las Latas* are vivid reminders that living
conditions for Chilean laborers often left much to be desired:

> Things weren't all good here. The were good things and bad things during
> the years of the gringos. The housing for the *obreros* [laborers] was bad,
> awful conditions. *Las Latas* was a housing complex near the Plaza, where
> *Chuqui Ayuda* [Chuqui Aid] is now. There were common bathrooms on the
> corner, and the people didn't have potable water, they didn't have any water
> in their houses. They had to get water from the pump on the corner. There
> was one water pump for every two blocks and one bathroom for the men and
> one for the women for each block. They had to take showers on the corner.
> And many houses didn't have a kitchen and the people had to cook with coal

or wood outside their houses. And the women had to look for fuel in order to cook.[46]

By the 1950s, housing conditions became a rallying point for union organizing in Chuquicamata. The "private" world of domestic life, rendered public each day at the water pumps, toilets, and communal showers, became a political issue. Labor struggles shifted to the community terrain as the unions demanded better living conditions. Some say it was the wives of the miners, the women who hauled water each day and washed clothes on the corner, who made home life a public issue, pushing men to take up the cause.[47] And, with its economic position bolstered by the *Nuevo Trato* (the Chilean New Deal), Anaconda was in a good position to respond positively to these demands for community improvements and temper local activism in the process (see fig. 14).

Anaconda did not neglect the women of Chuquicamata in the process of community building. Perhaps the company had learned the power of women's activism from the Housewives League in Butte. This group, organized in 1919, took to the streets to combat the high cost of living in Butte, developed direct producer to consumer food cooperatives that bypassed middlemen who were inflating prices, and engaged in public vigilance of prices and profits that put local Big Shots on notice.[48] In Chuquicamata, Anaconda sought women's alliance rather than animosity on the subject of community consumption.

The company developed innovative policies and practices to ensure women's support in maintaining family and community stability. Until the 1950s, the company provided employees with both a monthly family allowance, the *asignación familiar*, and an additional supplement that was based on the number of dependents the worker had. Initially, this supplement was redeemable for merchandise in the *pulperías*, the company stores. In the late 1950s, the company changed its compensation system and initiated a monthly payment program popularly known as *la compensación de la mujer* (women's compensation).[49] Under this program, the wives of miners received a monthly subsistence income paid directly to them and based on the number of children they had. This payment was also part of the benefit package paid to workers in Kennecott's El Teniente mines in Rancagua, Chile. But it was only Anaconda who paid the compensation directly to women.[50]

The benefit was frequently a topic of conversation among the women and men of Chuquicamata with whom I spoke during the course of fieldwork. Some say it contributed to the chronic lack of responsibility on the part of men. Others raised an eyebrow as they told me that, with enough children, a woman could earn as much or more than her husband. Many men chuckled about this being women's "productive labor." Women didn't laugh. For many, the compensation was recalled as a progressive innovation on the part of the company to recognize the necessary contribution of women's traditionally unpaid labor as mother, wife, and caretaker, guarding community consumption and teaching community values.

Most women agreed that husbands could not be counted on to use their paychecks for family support. Too many men, so the stories go, squandered their pay on drinking, gambling, and womanizing. Their wives and children never saw a peso. So the company, in its wisdom, decided to pay the women directly for their family and community labors. It wasn't much, but at least they could survive. To this day, most women of Chuquicamata praise Anaconda for its foresight in recognizing and paying for women's work. The practice continued under the Popular Unity government. They speak with resentment of the military dictatorship that dismantled the program in 1973. When community stability meant corporate profits, it was good business to pay women for their labors of love.

There were some women and families, however, who fell outside the range of Anaconda's benevolent vision. The Atacama Desert housed communities intimately connected to yet distinctly separate from the company town. These small villages were composed largely of women and children, who survived on their subsistence agricultural practices in the desert interior near the Bolivian border while their men sought work in the mines. Though Anaconda had constructed an image of a troublesome population of single transient laborers, these men often had family ties outside Chuquicamata.[51] In *Historias Testimoniales de Mujeres del Campo*, women from the Atacama village of Toconce tell their stories of maintaining community while their men looked for work in the mines (Valdez, Montecino, de Leon, and Mack 1983, 21–43). Maria is an *aymara* woman, member of an altiplano indigenous group. She described her life:

> One doesn't need a husband. There are many single women here. All of us are alone here. Papa went to work in Chuquicamata when I was twelve. The work was bad, and it was hard when I was a child. I went to Chuqui to get Papa when Mama was sick. Papa was sick from working in the mines. It began to suck the flesh from his hands. Papa died in the hospital in

Antofagasta five years ago. . . . They're fat, they go to Calama, and they come back skinny. There are many children without fathers. My mother is going to get his pension, the pension that my father left behind. In Chuqui, he was working for the company in the mines, and for this they gave him a pension.

While Anaconda was building its proletarian community of workers, women of Toconce maintained their *campesina* (peasant) community in the desert, materially supporting their children and emotionally supporting their husbands when the mines had used them up. Maria identified herself as *aymara*. In the politics of identification of Chuquicamata, the women of the interior are *nortinas, indias, bolivianas*, and the frequent targets of disparaging critique of their way of life.[52] Curiously, these women with cultural histories deeply rooted in the Atacama region were positioned beyond the bounds of community in both the "American" and "native" imagination of Chuquicamata.

VICE AND VIRTUE

The Butte experience taught Anaconda important lessons about the balancing of virtue and vice. When Anaconda arrived in Chuquicamata, they found their tidy company town living shoulder to shoulder with licentious barrios that beckoned miners with their bawdy nightlife. The barrios were full of:

> bars, gambling, prostitutes, fights, and death. . . . Blood ran often. Any incident whatsoever was reason for fights to break out and knives to flash. No one who came here could be assured of leaving with his life, and even less with his wallet. Even if he won something, he might still pay his debt on the road home. Numerous crosses mark the site of frequent assaults near the barrios. In the solitude of the desert, the cadaver of one victim was found, from an episode so vulgar it scarcely bears repeating. (Alvear Urrutia 1975, 65)

The company seemed to take an ambiguous position regarding these dens of iniquity. On the one hand, the company, gauging family men to be more committed to their jobs and conservative in their union activism, wanted to promote the values of domesticity and sexual morality. On the other hand, as the company knew from Butte, hardworking miners needed their release. The company's welfare efforts did little to interfere with life in the shadows.

Over the years, the illicit barrios were covered by mine tailings, and the *niñas alegres* (prostitutes) moved down the road to Calama, where they still work on the street and in the nightclubs. But prostitution continued to thrive in Chuquicamata. *Los Buques*, the large dormitory-style housing provided for the single men, was infamous for prostitution. Chuquicamatinos tell of the arrangements women made with the single men to rent their quarters while the men were at work, in order to conduct business. *Los Buques* was the site of sexual services, scandals, tragic liaisons, and violence against women.

Men in Chuquicamata tell the story of a strike circa 1960 that was brought on by the company's effort to put an end to prostitution in *Los Buques*. The men revolted and went on strike, demanding the right to maintain the long-standing arrangement. The company conceded to the workers' demands, so the story goes. It instituted a public health service aimed at halting the spread of venereal disease and required the women (not the men) to get regular exams.[53] Anaconda put a Sonny O'Day spin on Guggenheim's advice as they opted to keep 'em clean, keep 'em healthy, and keep 'em content.

It is important to note the apparent interest in public health and the regulation of sexuality on the part of the company in both Butte and Chuquicamata during the postwar years. Though Anaconda continued to ignore the dangerous risk of silicosis for its miners, it engaged in struggles over risks of illicit sexual behavior. Corporate visions of a "model" company town built on shared responsibility called for new forms of discipline and the making of citizens who embodied respectable community values. Such were the cultural markers of capitalism's new-found maturity in the postwar years. Images of the "new, respectable" Butte were posed against a past when "[t]he town was grimy and corrupt, demoralized by frequent shutdowns, cynically proud of its sleazy clip joints."[54] Improved family life and clean entertainment were promoted in lieu of base sexual pleasures. However, as the stories from both towns suggest, Anaconda was at best only partially successful in its postwar respectability campaign: women's bodies became more closely regulated in the fight against venereal disease, and prostitution continued with a bit more discretion.

BREAD AND CIRCUS

Arturo Alessandri, the president of Chile at the time of Anaconda's arrival, ascribed to a simple philosophy on maintaining the masses: give them bread and circus. In this, Alessandri and Anaconda were of one mind. A content workforce needed to eat and play. The *pulperías* fed and clothed Chuquicamata. They were centers of daily social activity and sites of labor struggles. They remain powerful symbols in the discourse of community nostalgia, even though their doors have closed.

Chuquicamata housed three *pulperías chilenas*. Workers were assigned a *pulpería* just as they were assigned housing, based on their status in the labor force. The quality and availability of goods diminished as one moved down the pecking order from Roll A to Roll C. These company stores stood apart from the *pulpería americana*, where the Yankee world shopped among an abundant supply of familiar U.S. labels. The North American store was seldom lacking in the daily necessities of Ritz Crackers and Corn Flakes, or in luxury items such as imported liquors and cigarettes. Some of these food stuffs found their ways to the shelves of the *pulperías chilenas*, just enough to whet appetites for imports. The *pulperías* loom large in the stories of longtime Chuquicamata residents, illustrating both their material and symbolic power in the community.

Elena was born and raised in Chuquicamata. When she talked of the past, she talked of *pulperías*:

> My mother worked in the CHILEX *pulpería*, and she met my father when he was. working there, too. How romantic! Those were good days. We were young and we liked all the gringo things. The toys and clothes and food. We had quite a taste for peanut butter. It was a lovely time with so much activity there. We enjoyed gringo things and celebrations and everything. And the prices in the *pulperías* were good, too. We lived there for years, but it's a different place now.[55]

Her story shows a scriptlike similarity to those told by other Chuquicamata residents. Some, like Alejandro, offer richly elaborated accounts of the material world the *pulpería* contained and represented:

> Each family used to receive a card for their monthly ration of goods. Based on the number of children in the family, you received a ration of rice, beans, potatoes, milk, whatever. It was a generous ration. A family of four would receive forty-five kilos of bread a month. That's a lot of bread. You would bring in the card each day when you made a purchase, and they would deduct your purchase from your monthly ration. At the end of the month, if you had some ration left over, that was the *salva* [savings]. You could apply that as credit to purchase whatever else you needed in the *pulpería*, like shoes or fabric. You could buy shoes for a peso or two. My mother used to buy material by the meter to make handkerchiefs. She would cut them into squares and hem them. We had more handkerchiefs than we knew what to do with. You were well provided for in Chuqui.[56]

The memories are not all rosy. As one Chuquicamatina began to tell
of the women waiting in line each day in front of the *pulperías chilenas*,
her companions joined her in filling in details:

> There were different *pulperías* for the different classes of workers and differ-
> ent lines for whatever thing you needed: clothes, meat, bread, vegetables.
> And there were always lines of women and children. There was a lot of
> bureaucracy in the *pulperías* and lots of waiting, too. Women passed hours
> each day in line at the *pulperías*. There were women with lots of kids in the
> line each day. And the wind was terrible, and the problem of the dust was
> worse than today. . . . The dust was so terrible some of the women of Chuqui
> dressed in pants. Women in other parts of Chile didn't wear pants, but here
> it was a necessity in order to survive the conditions of the mines.[57]

The *pulpería* stories carry symbolic force. The *pulperías* appear as
key elaborating symbols of the complex system of paternalism, privilege, and distinction that characterized daily life in Chuquicamata.[58] As
longtime residents told their stories, the smile of a maple syrup memory
often gave way to indignation at the politics of difference the system
imposed. The *pulperías* represent both access and its limits, a sampling
of Yankee tastes to offset shortages of meat and vegetables. They are
icons of dependence, indices of labor's incremental successes, and contradictory symbols of a past when "things were better in Chuqui."

The people of Butte were not directly beholden to a company store.[59]
For many years, Butte residents and local grocers thrived on interde-
pendence. Merchants often carried mining families on credit during the
weeks or months of a strike, counting on a faithful clientele during good
times. Ann, an old-time Butte resident, recalled:

> When there were strikes, we would just about starve because there was no
> way of getting groceries. What we used to do was charge the groceries. The
> grocers would come to your house and take your order and then deliver it the
> next day. They were independent grocers. They would carry you for maybe
> five or six months, for the duration of the strike. It was such a hardship to
> pay that back. It would take maybe a year or two years to get them back on
> their feet. (Calkins 1982, 57–58)

As the strikes grew longer and the chain groceries came to town, some
families abandoned this neighborly obligation to local grocers, leaving
behind big bills and bad feelings.

But the historic hub of shopping in Butte was the Hennessy's store, a
grand mercantile, started by D. J. Hennessy, a friend of Marcus Daly
and one-time board member of the Anaconda Company. Many fine
stores came and went during Butte's rise and fall, but Hennessy's was the

grandest of them all. The working class and elites rubbed elbows in the aisles of the lower floors, and the upper floors housed the local head-quarters of the Anaconda Company. For the people of Butte, the sixth floor of the Hennessy Building was the center of local power. References to corporate practices and decision making were often given through a shorthand reference to the sixth floor, encoding the power that reigned there. Images of Hennessy's mark memories of Butte's vibrant past, and its closure in 1980 stands for some as a betrayal nearly as tragic as the exodus of Anaconda from those sixth-floor offices.

Beyond the bread, Butte and Chuquicamata enjoyed their circus as well. Bars and brothels shared space with more wholesome diversions. Butte's theaters and nightclubs brought "culture" to the mining city, with plays, orchestras, and the latest in big-name entertainment. And residents supplied their own grassroots entertainment through their smorgasbord of social clubs. Historian Mary Murphy (1990) examines the pairing of community and leisure in Butte during the interwar years. She argues that leisure was the realm where people of Butte enjoyed a broad range of choices beyond corporate dictates. I see a stronger cor-porate penetration in the way people played in Butte than Murphy sug-gests. However, play in Butte resembled a three-ring circus when com-pared to the orchestrated amusements of Chuquicamata.

Chuquicamata had its share of nightlife and culture. The company sponsored an orchestra, and entertainers from other parts of the coun-try were regular guests in the mining town. One of Anaconda's contri-butions to Chuquicamata was the stylish Chile Theater, built in the 1930s. Residents enjoyed a steady diet of first-run John Wayne westerns and an occasional gala night with the likes of the Bolshoi Ballet. In keep-ing with Chuqui's stratified architecture, the seats in the multitiered the-ater corresponded to status in the camp. As I toured the town with Cristina, a native of Chuquicamata, she recounted the story of the theater:

> The theater has three levels. The first, with the best seats, was reserved for the gringos. The second was where the more privileged Chileans sat, and the third was the gallery, the cheap seats. That's where I watched lots of movies from the United States, especially those westerns. And see those big windows up there on the third floor? Well, when we didn't have any money and there was a soccer game in the stadium, we'd climb the stairs up to the third floor and watch the game for free. We had a great view of everything.[60]

Both Butte and Chuquicamata were sports-oriented towns. *Fanatic-ism* is a fair word to describe the devotion to local teams. As company news took a backseat in the corporate press, sports news dominated. Football and soccer champs were the local heroes, and residents came out in force to support their teams. Anaconda sponsored teams, leagues, and sporting events. Professional boxing drew big crowds: audiences in Butte and Chuquicamata witnessed matches between world-class prize fighters.

The company created and subsidized the Mines League Baseball in Butte, seeing the sports field as a place to transform workplace animosities into friendly competition. An *Engineering and Mining Journal* article praises corporate efforts, noting that the "mine manager rubs shoulders with the shoveller and all class distinction is eclipsed by the common desire to have the company's team victorious."[61] Likewise, the bowling leagues at the employees club matched miners and bosses in friendly competition.

North American football gave way to soccer in Chile, but Anaconda managed to cultivate local interest in bowling, basketball, and baseball. Women's sports also gained popularity and support. Chuquicamatinos gathered to watch sporting events in the Anaconda Stadium, built by the company. A larger-than-life copper arrowhead, Anaconda's emblem, graced the entrance, a perpetual reminder of corporate benevolence. As with the rest of the community, sports leagues were distinguished according to Roll.

There were spaces, however, where Chuquicamata's play was less constricted and Butte's was less free. For example, in Chuquicamata, the secluded world of the American Camp did not go unnoticed by the "natives." Through the spy missions of childhood and domestic labors of adult life, Chuquicamatinos kept tabs on Americans. Their habits and practices, from the peculiarities of diet to the silliness of golf games in the desert, provided a steady source of amusement and insight. As Latcham observes: "The social customs in the American Camp have a distinct flavor. The Yankees are big fans of the social life. Their dances last until dawn, and they drink copiously. . . . The Yankees do not distinguish themselves by their correct manners. For them, life is reduced to eating, drinking, and self adulation" (Latcham 1926, 154).

In Butte, the centerpiece of community at play was a place steeped in Anaconda history. Butte's greatest jewel, the Columbia Gardens, was the peoples' playground. Tucked in the folds of the east ridge of the Rocky Mountains, it was a safe distance from the toxic city. This community park, with its lush gardens, elegant dance hall, and carousel of hand-carved wooden horses, was the setting for a collective nostalgia of an innocent past. According to local history, the gardens were a gift to the people of Butte from one of its copper kings, W. A. Clark, whose assets were absorbed by Anaconda.[62] Over the years, the company partially subsidized this community treasure. It was the site of many company-sponsored social events. The Gardens became a site of corporate-community struggle in the 1970s, when Anaconda planned to expand mining to purportedly rich veins of copper that ran beneath this surface treasure. The community mobilized to defend the gardens, but the company pushed ahead with plans. In November 1973, Columbia Gardens mysteriously burned to the ground, writing another blazing chapter in the community saga of trust and betrayal.

CELEBRATING COMMUNITY

The daily mix of repression, habituation, co-optation, and cooperation was punctuated with celebration. Anaconda displayed benevolent paternalism at its finest in its generous orchestration of community spirit at holiday time. The Butte Hill glowed at Christmas with lighted trees perched atop the gallows frames. Nativity scenes graced Chuquicamata's central plaza, glittering lights spelled out holiday greetings on the barren hillsides north of town, and out-of-place snowmen, sleighs, and Santas adorned the downtown streets in the sweltering summer heat. The children of Butte and Chuquicamata enjoyed company-sponsored Christmas and Halloween parties. However, it was in the celebrations of labor and citizenship that corporate power over the meaning of community was most manifest.

June 13, 1878, marked the founding of the Workingman's Union in Butte, predecessor to the Butte Miners Union. The day became the celebrated symbol of Butte's union power. For thirty-six years, Miners Union Day was Butte's most important holiday. In 1914, the celebration turned to violence as interunion conflicts and corporate repression came to a head. By the end of June 1914, the miners union had collapsed, and Miners Union Day was erased from the social calendar of community celebration until 1935.

Miner's Union Day was replaced by Miner's Field Day, a company-orchestrated celebration to promote Anaconda's safety campaign, labor-management harmony, and family life. This company-sponsored tribute to labor was an annual event until the Depression, when goodwill gave way to budget cutting. When Miner's Union Day was revived in 1935, the aura of Miner's Field Day lingered. The company helped sponsor the day's events, which were held at Columbia Gardens and featured safety contests and competitions among the men, who represented their particular underground mines.[63]

During the negotiations to settle the 1967 strike, Anaconda put holidays on the bargaining table and suggested that Miner's Union Day be replaced by a date marking the takeover of the local union by United Steelworkers.[64] The suggestion was a move in a deeper corporate game of community irony, pointing out that Butte's union leadership had handed their local power over to "outsiders from Pittsburgh." Miner's Union Day remained an official holiday in Butte until the closure of the mines. It now passes once again without recognition.

May Day, the first of May, which commemorates the deaths of labor activists in Chicago in 1886, has come to symbolize the struggle and hope of organized labor in many parts of the world. The date has been relegated to the margins of popular consciousness in the United States. It was overshadowed by Miner's Union Day in Butte and did not stand as a symbol of working-class struggle in Chuquicamata, as it did elsewhere in Chile. Under Anaconda's tutelage, the day was transformed into a homage to "steady and reliable" workers: In Chuquicamata, May 1 was the day Anaconda annually awarded gold watches to employees with thirty years of faithful service. Official news of the solemn ceremony praised the lifetime dedication of the thirty-year men. The gold watch stood as an example of corporate commitment to senior employees in many people's accounts of the days when the gringos ran the mines. Now that senior workers face cutbacks and the push to early retirement, it is the gold-watch story that symbolizes the personal side of Anaconda's operations, in contrast to the "cold and impersonal bureaucracy" that characterizes descriptions of the current management.

Longtime employees of the mines told the May Day story in their depiction of the "good old days in Chuquicamata." Hernan's description has a familiar ring to anyone who enjoyed a Miner's Union Day celebration in Butte:

> There was another thing here, *El Día de Trabajo* [Labor Day]. We celebrated May 1 here, but I bet we celebrated it differently than any place else in the world. Labor Day in Chuquicamata was really beautiful. We celebrated it with the full support of the company. There were competitions, parties for the whole family, queen pageants, and teams of miners who competed against each other, and it was really great.
>
> On May 1, the company gave out gold watches for those with thirty years of service. It showed their respect for the worker, for seniority. The watches

were real gold. Anaconda was probably the only company in the world that carried on this tradition over the years.[65]

Saint Patrick's Day in Butte has historically been the town's largest and most boisterous unofficial holiday — a time when Butte's Irish citizenry proclaimed their heritage. The nature of the celebration, however, was subject to Anaconda scrutiny. According to local historian Bob McCarthy, Butte enjoyed grand St. Patrick's Day parades since the 1880s. However, when the parades took a political turn during World War I and later became an embodied expression of Irish nationalism and struggles for independence, the company intervened. McCarthy argues that the Anaconda Company put a halt to Butte's St. Patrick's Day parade in 1923. The parade was not to resume until 1968:

> In lieu of the parade, Anaconda promoted the founding of a new organization, the Friendly Sons of St. Patrick. The sole purpose of this all male group was to throw a party on March 16. They were an ACM organization. They received lots of coverage in the Company press, and they were non-controversial in terms of larger politics. The program from the 1925 dinner offers a nice example. The impeccably set table had one bottle of Irish whiskey for every three men. The whiskey served at Friendly Sons banquets was Jameson, the Republican whiskey. Bushmills, a product of Belfast, was not served. The party was always a stag affair until recent years. The honored guest, toastmaster and speaker list read like an ACM Who's Who, full of officials and pro-company lawyers and judges. ACM had control of the organization and saw to it that there were no parades and no political controversy. There were few miners in the Friendly Sons in those days, though the group was to become more democratic over time. Many a governor attended as guest of the company for the night at a suite in the Finlen Hotel, attending Mass and breakfast the next day.[66]

It was in the evocation of patriotism that Anaconda truly shone. Butte's Fourth of July celebration was grand and extravagant. Community groups strove to outdo each other in building floats for the parade. The Meaderville Fire Department often dominated the competition. The practice of float building began in 1941 but was suspended during the war years. When it resumed in 1947, the Meaderville Fire Department showed its stuff. The one-thousand-dollar construction cost for their prize-winning entry was no problem for the fire crew: they used a purchase order number from the Anaconda Company, and the company wrote off the charges to operating costs.[67] Perhaps this corporate benevolence took the edge off the animosity when Meaderville was targeted for destruction with the building of the open-pit mine in the 1950s.

Chuquicamatinos also enjoyed company-sponsored patriotic events. Youngsters received a new set of clothes in September, in anticipation of September 18, *El Día de la Patria* (Chilean Independence Day). Residents of Chuquicamata were no strangers to Fourth of July celebrations. July 4 was the first in the series of patriotic holidays that included Bolivian Independence day and culminated with Chilean Independence Day. *Oasis* featured laudatory articles on national patriotism to recognize each date. The themes emphasized the merits of capitalism and free enterprise as the hallmarks of any truly independent state. The multiple patriotisms of Chuquicamata were the topic of many conversations during my fieldwork. Perhaps the most telling evidence of the power of the U.S. patriotic message was revealed when a middle-aged Chilean woman, reflecting on childhood memories of the Fourth of July in Chuquicamata, burst forth into a perfect English rendition of the "Star-Spangled Banner" that seemed to surprise even her. Her song bore physical evidence of the habituating power of celebration and the seepage of the "American" distinction into the "native" consciousness.

People of Chuquicamata celebrated community outside the bounds of the corporate imagination as well, especially through religious organizations. Particularly important were the various dance troupes associated with homage to the Virgin of Guadelupe of Ayquina. The dance troupes are mixed-age, kinship, friendship, and parish-based groups who train rigorously and perform intricately choreographed dances at religious festivals throughout the year in the desert north. The dancers' calendar culminates in September with ceremonies and competitions in the village of Ayquina, located in the Atacama Desert east of Chuquicamata. Each year, a group of young people, often the leaders of their particular troupe, walk the seventy-eight kilometers from Calama to Ayquina to fulfill their promise to the Virgin.

The richly detailed accounts of costumes and dances told by young and old alike suggest a separate reality outside the shadow of Anaconda. It is a reality that draws on the cultural histories and practices of the *nortinos*, the inhabitants of this liminal space who preceded its "Chileanization." Resentments are set aside and cultural knowledge appropriated as "natives" in their many guises toy with gringo images while excluding the gringos themselves. The costumes of the dancers reflected a curious borrowing from the images of old westerns, Busbee Berkeley Hollywood classics, and the pages of *National Geographic*.[68] Dancers sported the stereotypical outfits of cowboys and Indians, of Chinese coolies with long black braids, even glittering tutus and head-dresses that rivaled the Radio City Rockettes. And as one local observer pointed out to me, the devil (always present) was represented as a blue-eyed blond. The celebrations powerfully articulate and elaborate difference in its many forms in the making of community. They reconstitute the *mestizaje* (of mixed ancestry) culture of northern Chile from the materials at hand. They vilify the "true" foreigner, the gringo. They craft a folkloric amalgam that stands for the curious we-ness of *el pueblo* (the people). In spite of corporate power, there was more than one way to imagine community.

This chapter illustrates the complicated politics of community in the making: a contested mix of repression, habituation, co-optation, and cooperation. As Anaconda (re)invented and (re)asserted its definition of good workers, citizens, and consumers, residents of Butte and Chuquicamata crafted their own sense of belonging, their images variably colliding and coalescing through time and space. Shifting boundaries of inclusion and exclusion defined and glossed differences, confusing perceptions of power in the process.

We have seen that the relationship between place and community cannot be assumed as given. Residents of Butte and Chuquicamata speak to a physical sense of bounded space, an emotional sense of belonging and commitment, and a political sense of knowing one's place. The Anaconda Company imagined and built a transnational labor pool as it cultivated localized and localizing loyalties. The ties that bound residents to space and place served to constrict visions of commonality while magnifying the differences between Butte and Chuquicamata. The possibility of common struggle perhaps seemed as distant as the thousands of miles that separated (and linked) their rich ore deposits. Anaconda worked to keep it that way.

In Chuquicamata, Anaconda operated directly as architect of a company town, taking an overtly paternal approach to the construction of community. In many ways, the company provided well for its residents, offering workers material benefits and a quality of life better than that of most Chilean laborers. At the same time, the company created and maintained powerful distinctions between the "Americans" and "natives." The company both provided the makings of community needed for a steady, reliable workforce and crafted difference that fed a politics of envy. Ironically, the corporate efforts at community building worked well enough to promote a sense of community solidarity that became the base from which to demand greater corporate accountability.

Today, the relationship between the Anaconda Company and community in Chuquicamata is expressed through a dual discourse of praise and resentment. Throughout my fieldwork, I encountered a chorus of accolades as Chuquicamatinos regaled me with stories of the *muy linda* (very lovely) days of Anaconda. The power of positive memories was both so urgent and pervasive that I could not interpret it merely as a generous response to the gringa visitor.

Even the most vocal critics told stories of the "good old days," when the hard life had its rewards and the community its vitality. Critiques of corporate paternalism and Yankee imperialism were tempered with warm memories of soccer matches, movies, and fiestas. Chuquicama-tinos pointed to the union hall, theater, and hospital as enduring mark-ers of Anaconda's commitment to community. Because the company saw the need for a second generation of miners, it recognized the value of tempering discipline with reward. The result of this concern was a long-term project of community building. These images of the past stand in sharp contrast to characterizations of community in Chuquica-mata today, where paternalism still reigns but the sense of community it once supported has been abandoned, much like the central plaza that once teemed with social life.

The company-community relationship in Butte presents an ironic twist on the "development of underdevelopment" theory.[69] Once Ana-conda had established its preeminence in Chile, the population of Butte and its mining labor force began a gradual decline. Little by little, this corporate father of copper mining was abandoning its Butte family. There was the occasional grand resurgence of interest and investment that stirred community hopes for the future, but from the 1920s on, Butte did not experience "growth." The company turned to images of commonality, drawing on ethnicity, nationalism, and the image of hardy survivors to elicit compromise and sacrifice from the community. Even as the company gradually abandoned Butte, it exploited and promoted the images that "we are all in the same boat." An implicit sense of we-ness grounded in tacit acceptance of the correctness of capitalism came to constitute a broader, uncontested terrain of community in which other struggles played out. Butte now has a small mining operation and a large void where Anaconda once was. Whereas Chuquicamatinos talk a double discourse of privilege and privation, people of Butte reclaim histories of solidarity and survival to fill the pit of uncertainty that is the imagined future of the community.

FOUR

Mining Men and Designing Women

Miners are men's love object. They bring together all the necessary elements of romance. Life itself is endangered, their enemy is the elements, their tragedy derives from forces greater than they, forces of nature and vengeful acts of God. That makes them victim and hero at the same time, which makes them irresistible. They are represented as beautiful, statuesque, shaded men. The miner's body is loved in the literature of men, because of its work and because it works.

Beatrix Campbell 1984

My Madonna

I hauled me a woman from the street
Shameless, but oh so fair!
I bade her sit in the model's seat
And I painted her sitting there.
I hid all traces of her heart unclean
I painted a babe at her breast:
I painted her as she might have been
If the worst had been the best.
She laughed at my picture and went away
Then came a knowing nod
A connoisseur, and I heard him say:
Tis Mary, The Mother of God.

Robert W. Service 1907

Who are the men and women of the mining community?[1] In this chapter, I explore representations of masculinity and femininity that have shaped the construction of social actors and compare the making of class and gendered subjects in Butte and Chuquicamata. I examine the images that filter through mining myth and history. Powerful cultural representations of gender shaped but did not determine the agency of men and women. Drawing from ethnographic data, I illustrate how men and women talk back to these images as they talk of labor, friendship, intimacy, and one another. I look to people in diverse social positions, considering what they do, what they say about themselves, and what others say about them. Their stories reflect the relational power of class and gender and the making of self through engagement with circumstance. I hope to capture some of the complexity in the making of social subjects in Butte and Chuquicamata, while delineating important distinctions between the two.

This account of men and women as works in progress needs to be read through the kaleidoscopic lens of community (as presented in chapter 3). Masculinity, femininity, and class consciousness were shaped by and through the complicated overlaps and exclusions of community in the making. As men and women drew on the cultural materials at hand to create themselves, they worked from their own sense of place and positioned others within these matrices of belonging. In so doing, they staked claims to their position, knowledge, and rights as community members.

MINING MEN

Mining is dirty and dangerous work. The miner has come to represent the prototype of working-class manhood.[2] These masculine images have been variably reinforced and challenged in popular literature, by company bosses, by women, and by miners themselves. In popular accounts, the miner is often depicted as a certain "breed" of man — a depiction that suggests an essentialism about those drawn to the mines. The Butte miner has been the subject of poetry, song, and story.[3] He is the "honest workingman," the "sturdy man who pounds the drill."[4] Miners "shared a brotherhood of possible disaster and grueling hard work" (Dempsey 1989, 15). They are the men with strong backs and weak brains, storytellers in the bars who are rendered mute in the face of intimacy and loss (see fig. 15).[5]

There is pride in the image of the hardworking, hard-drinking man who proved his masculinity each day in the hot, dank tunnels that course thousands of feet beneath the ground. They were the men who worked "collar to collar," a telling reference to their daily entrapment as the hoisting cages carried them from the surface to the shafts below. The

Figure 15.   Miners going on shift, 1945, Butte. Courtesy of Butte Historical Society, Butte Labor History Project Collection.

true miner labored underground, defining his manhood in tonnage of copper pulled from the earth. Even though open-pit mining came to dominate underground operations in Butte, the image of the underground miner remained salient as the real miner. Though miners joked among themselves about the power of brawn over brains, they were quick to anger when the company took them for "dumb workingmen."

In Chile, as in the United States, the miner defines the quintessential workingman. In Chuquicamata, an oversized statue pays homage to the miner, a complex melding of strength and simplicity, whose "strong shoulders bear the weight of Chile's wealth in copper." He is the arrogant man who takes on the challenge of sun, wind, and penetrating cold in his labor for *la patria* (the fatherland).

In the desert north, it is the copper miner that is a peculiar breed, distinguished from the nitrate miner by his devotion to the red metal that represents the country's economic lifeblood. The Chuquicamata miner has taken on Mother Nature at her most unforgiving, proving himself each day in the desert extremes. Though arrogant in the face of nature's forces, the miner is also a "humble and simple man. With the force of his muscles, he is not afraid to defend his country and ideals. He is the champion of sweat and pain."[6] An interesting man, this miner, who meets nature head on but succumbs meekly to culture, his needs and wants simple.

Miners are walking contradictions of wisdom and ignorance, humility and bravado. These complex images have been elaborated and reworked in popular accounts of local histories and in the company press, with particular images reinforced at particular historical moments. The Anaconda Company newspapers, magazines, and promotional literature offer a rich archeological record of the corporate construction of mining men. In Butte during World War II, it was the "steady Butte miner" who won the war for the Allied forces. During long strikes in Butte, the company regularly appealed to the "rank and file" miner, who knew deep down that his family and community needed him in the mines. He was an honest man who knew the difference between hard-rock economics and union politics. The Butte miner was a man much like "Juan Minero" and "El Beño," two characters who shared their musings on mining in the Anaconda Company press in Chuquicamata in the 1950s and 1960s.[7]

El Beño hailed from a village in the Atacama Desert.[8] He left his sweetheart and family behind and went to make a better life for them in the mines. In his weekly letters to his fiancé, El Beño poured his heart out. He was not a political man, and he just couldn't make sense of heavy-handed union politics. And when he broke his arm, he reassured his "sweet Teruquita" that all was well by giving her every detail of the outstanding treatment he had received in Chuquicamata's new, modern hospital, thanks to the company (see fig. 16).[9]

Juan Minero was a more pensive sort. He was born in Chuqui, son of a miner. He was a patriot, a man of the left but, as he said, a reasonable man. He just couldn't see the good in nationalization of the mines. Juan was a man who looked to the future. Mining was his lot in life, but he wanted his children to get ahead, and education, especially the quality education available in Chuquicamata, thanks to the company, was the ticket to a better future (see fig. 17).[10]

El Beño and Juan Minero are graphic representations of the corporate construction of mining men of Chuquicamata. They reflect distinctions among the miners themselves and at the same time symbolize actors in a changing copper economy. In the post–World War II years, Anaconda advanced its technological capacities and reduced the size of its labor force in Chuquicamata. These changes are reflected in the commentaries offered by Juan Minero and El Beño. Both wax philosophical on the values of education. Perhaps, by the 1960s, the company was not looking to reproduce another generation of laborers to take their fathers' place. The company would need a select group with technical know-how. And the rest? They would need an education to help them find work beyond the mines.

As we have seen, images of privilege filtered through corporate and community discourse in Chuquicamata. These images are at the core of controversy over what it means to be a miner in Chuquicamata. Chileans outside of the mining region, as well as those in the region who work in the low-paying jobs outside the mines, identify the Chuquicamata mine workers as *los privilegiados*, the privileged ones.[11] The miners have historically been represented as the country's labor elite, gaining salaries and benefits considerably better than the country's low-paid service, industrial, and agricultural workers. Both the working conditions and the economic rewards have been better than in Chile's nitrate and coal mines. Over the years, the company promoted the image of privilege, especially during labor negotiations.

There is a curious double talk among Chuquicamatinos regarding this identification as a privileged class. Residents often speak with pride of Chuquicamata's reputation as the "best place in the country" to work during the Anaconda era. At the same time, there is deep resentment of the notion of privilege. Chuquicamatinos are quick to defend their salaries gained through hard-fought union battles. They point to the tough conditions of life and work in the desert, where miners paid with their health each day. Privilege is a relative concept, continually compromised by and contingent upon both risk and distinction.

The notion of privilege remains deeply embedded in both popular and corporate depictions of Chuquicamata's labor force. The current management of the national mines has paired the concept of privilege with that of dependency to create a problematic image of the workers of Chuquicamata.[12] As CODELCO attempts to streamline and modernize its mining operations, the company has constructed a discourse of "old" and "new" orders. The old order is characterized by privilege and dependency, inculcated during Anaconda's reign in Chuquicamata, which supposedly bred laziness and inefficiency. The current corporate modernization script has redefined *privilege* as *vice*, a corruptive influence from the old order that must be expunged before it taints the new order.[13]

The new order, say company spokespeople, is characterized by collaboration and efficiency. The company and unions must work together

Cartas a mi Pueblo

Hola mi Teruquita:

¿Como está mi morenita linda?

¿Se acuerda siempre de su huasito que la quiere re tanto?

Yo como siempre mi'hijita me acuerdo de Ud. re toititos los días y más me acordé la noche del 31, pensando que estaba tan re lejos pa darle el abrazo de Año Nuevo, han corrido hartos días del Año Nuevo; pero yo todavía pienso en que la podría h a b e r tenido e n t r e mis brazos y haberla apretao a rabiar, con el gran cariño que le tengo, pero que le vamos a hacer m'hijita la distancia nos separa; pero el amor nos reune, como dice una canción por ahí.

Te contaré que tal como dice el refrán: Año Nuevo, vida nueva, he empezado a modificar mis rumbos. La pega en que estoy trabajando no me convence mucho esa cuestión de ser albañil, la encuentro ahora que no está pa mis gustos, así que he empezado a buscar por ahí otra cuestión mejor, más adelante te contaré como me ha ido.

De las novedades que te puedo contar del mineral mas grande del mundo, ya que vos siempre me preguntai por copuchas a pesar que no conocis por estos lados, es que este Domingo se eligen los Dirigentes Sindicales. Fíjate que la cuestión ésta, es tan importante aquí, como las elecciones de parlamentarios o presidente en otras partes.

Toos los ñatos que se candidatean, que son mas de 20 pa 5 puestos, se hacen propaganda por el diario, con volantes, por la radio, en fin por toos los medios. Tienen sus comités, en fin le dan harto color a la cuestión.

Lo único que falta es que p'al día de la elección manden milicos a controlar el asunto, debe ser harto importante este asunto del Sindicato por too el color que le dan.

Lo único que no me gusta es que está muy re metida la política en el asunto, yo como trabajador asalariao que soy, creo que estas cuestiones gremialistas deberían ser ajenas a too partido político.

En fin, no soy naiden pa criticar, ni tampoco pertenezco al Sindicato, pero me voy a meter a dirigente cualquier día de estos y propugnaré —¿Que tal la palabrita?— por la independencia de los gremios en las luchas de los partidos.

Y como le iba diciendo compañera, bah, perdona Teruquita, me había entusiasmao, no sigo más porque capaz que te haga hasta un discurso y a Ud, mejor que eso, le doy un besito y un abrazo con todo el amor de su novio lejano:

El Beño

Figure 16.   El Beño: "Letters Home." *Pukará* (Chuquicamata), 11 January 1964.

Las Inquietudes de "JUAN MINERO"

Yo soy un minero. Aquí nací, y me crié, y eduqué. Mi padre también lo fue, aunque él llegó de otras tierras. Vino desde el Sur, de la región de Coquimbo. Aún cuando siempre tuvo la esperanza de volver a su pueblo, no lo pudo lograr, porque aquí se casó y formó su hogar. El decía que en ninguna otra parte podría ganar lo que aquí ganaba, y se fue quedando. Pero en sus ojos siempre había una nostalgia de verde.

Con su trabajo pudo educarnos a nosotros; y digo nosotros, porque fuimos cinco hermanos. Mi hermano Pedro también trabaja aquí e igual que yo, está contento de ser un trabajador más de esta enorme empresa. José y Francisco, se fueron hacia el Sur, y Luís se quedó en el puerto.

Cuando yo he ido de vacaciones con mi familia, los he pasado a ver. Siempre se quejan de la situación económica y se lamentan por no haberse quedado en el mineral, donde también, posiblemente, estarían trabajando.

Pero, en fin, cada uno se forja su propio destino.

Mi destino era seguir como mi padre; ser un minero más de Chile. Y aquí estoy, con mis hijos ya grandes y también educándose. Con mi compañera de tantos años.

Mis hijos son tres. Juan, el mayor, se educa en la Universidad Técnica de Antofagasta; tiene 19 años y ya está por recibirse de Técnico-Electricista. El que sigue es Pedro, de 17, y está estudiando en el Liceo, donde cursa el 5º Humanidades, y Ricardo, el benjamín, que apenas tiene 13 años, también estudia en el Liceo, pero de Calama. El, es el único que vive con nosotros, porque los dos mayores están internos en Antofagasta.

Ricardo dice que quiere llegar hasta la Universidad y que le gustaría ser médico. Nosotros también quisiéramos que lo fuera, aunque sabemos que esto costará mucho dinero.

Pero mientras hay vida hay esperanza, y mi esperanza y la de mi mujer es que todos puedan educarse al máximo, para que, cuando nosotros faltemos, ellos tengan como defenderse.

Figure 17. "The Worries of Juan Minero." *Oasis,* 6 June 1964.

to rid the mines and miners of bad habits and wasteful ways. The prototype of the new order is the "polyvalent worker" currently under construction in Chuquicamata. He is flexible and streamlined, able to be independent or a team player on command. These workers are not limited by union rules to a single trade, but are jacks of all, shifting their labors with the company's changing needs. The fat of privilege must be trimmed away to build a lean, healthy, competitive company.

Similarly, in the final years of Anaconda's operations, the image of "lazy union workers" came to define the company's talk about the workingmen of the Butte mines. Disparaging jokes about needing to call in an electrician to change a light bulb or needing five union men for every job, one to work and four to watch, are legion in Butte. Spoiled by privilege, union men had allegedly lost their work ethic. During the years of Anaconda's decline, those stories became a part of popular discourse. Longtime union loyalists spoke of the tail that wagged the union dog; unreasonable labor demands were often touted as a main reason for Anaconda's downfall. As Butte's numerous unions fought the company and among themselves throughout the 1970s, they seemed a far cry from spokesmen for that "special breed of man."

The men of the new Butte mines are a "different breed" as well, their image constructed in opposition to the "lazy union worker." The new miner is a team player with fresh ideas, a partner in production, where everybody works together. They are union free and proud of it. The new Butte miners are the equivalent of the polyvalent workers of Chuquicamata, flexible workers conforming to the shifting demands of capitalism.[14]

The women of Butte and Chuquicamata offered their own perspectives on mining men. When Butte women talked of their mining men, there was often a tone and substance distinct from the corporate images and those of popular literature. Yes, he was still the hardworking man who risked his life each day. And he was also often a boy, one who needed care and protection. He was able to lift hundreds of pounds of ore but could not be counted on to manage his own affairs. He needed his drink to take the edge off his hard labors, but he likely didn't know his own limits. He needed a woman around to keep him in line. In short, they say that Butte boys needed their mothers, and their mothers often obliged, much to the resentment of many wives. This image of women as vigilant mothers and men as irresponsible sons remains as something of a popular truism among many Butte women. It resonates across generations and has outlasted the mining industry itself.

The women of Chuquicamata told similar stories of their mining men. They spoke about the mining men of Chuquicamata as irresponsible, with a penchant for drinking and nightlife. It was up to the women to keep them in line. The women in Chuqui spoke much more than did the women of Butte about rampant infidelity among the men. In their accounts, it appears that salaries and benefits earned by the miners gave them a degree of economic freedom that allowed them to support more than one woman and thus act out their essential, unfaithful, masculine nature.[15]

Other women spoke of their husbands as *"típicos chuquicamatinos."* Such a man, as one woman said, is "macho, egotistical and individualistic. He only thinks of himself. He was born and raised in Chuqui, *típico chuquicamatino*. He thinks the world should revolve around him and that he should be the center of my world."[16] Another woman noted, "He's so self-centered, he drinks too much, and he has these rigid expectations of women, *puro chuquicamatino*." These men, it appears, are the problematic products of privilege. They are second-generation miners, born and bred in a world built around men and mines. Perhaps they have come to see both the risks and rights as given. Yet the same women who spoke of their husbands as *típicios chuquicamatinos* were quick to reject the notion of privilege. With the rejection came a challenge to those "on the outside" to try the life in Chuquicamata for one day, with the sun, wind, dust, unbearable heat from the smelting furnaces, and the smoke that chokes the town, before they dare to talk of privilege.

This image of mining men constructed from a feminine point of view suggests as much about the complicated social positions of miners' wives as it does about the miners. The women of Chuquicamata defended and stood with their husbands along class lines, denouncing the myth of privilege.[17] At the same time, they pointed to the problematic and unequal nature of gender relations on the domestic front. Women carried the burden of family caretaking, suffered the humiliations of infidelity, and lived with a greater degree of economic uncertainty than did their mate.

In her fascinating book *Madres y huachos: Alegorías del mestizaje chileno*, anthropologist Sonia Montecino argues that the constitution of masculinity and femininity in the Chilean cultural ethos must be understood within the cultural frame of *marianismo* — that is, the cultural and historical significance of the Virgin Mary.[18] Montecino asserts that *marianismo* and machismo operate conjointly in the mestizo social order of

Chile. She states that the "*mariano* symbol constitutes a cultural frame that assigns specific qualities to the categories 'feminine' and 'masculine': mother and son, respectively" (1993, 31–32). I return to Montecino's insights later, in considering the construction of femininity. Here, the key point is her assertion that mother-son identities are central to the construction of femininity and masculinity in both historical and contemporary Chilean culture. Curiously, I found that mother-son imagery resonated more clearly through the ethnographic data in Butte than in Chuquicamata.

In short, the image of the miner has been under construction on many fronts. The images have been reworked over time, reflecting historical and political exigencies. The images serve as clues to the nature and power of the social relations between the miners and their many image makers. The mining men of Butte and Chuquicamata did not merely accept these multiple monikers; they constructed, and at times deconstructed, their own identities in relation to their labors and changing labor practices. Miners of Butte and Chuquicamata often spoke of fathers and sons, the importance of generational ties that bound men to mining, and, for some, the sense of loss they experienced as their own sons had to look elsewhere for work. Others, however — especially those among Butte's underground miners — hoped to spare their sons from this grueling labor.

Miners crafted themselves through their work. Pride of craftsmanship resonated through their detailed "how to" stories as men described their labors in the mines. For men in Butte, those stories often pitted workingman's wisdom against incompetent management. Pat, an unemployed boilermaker, described the painstaking process of designing and building a new piece of equipment with only the remnants of the old part as his guide. He had respect for his craft but lamented that no one at Anaconda valued those skills. As he summed up his relationship to his work: "By the end it was all politics and suction."

Pat offered his "shit always rises to the top" theory of boss selection: "The skilled craftsmen always turned down the bossing jobs. So you might get a boss with some skills but no intelligence, no common sense. They weren't smart enough to know what they didn't know." Pat talked of workers saving the day and bosses taking credit. But when it came to the final blow, the closing of the mines, he put the blame back on the workingman: "We were too stupid to see what was coming."[19]

Al, a longtime worker in Butte's Berkeley Pit shared Pat's point of view:

It takes certain people to mine. You have to be a good listener. I had a lot of trouble getting things across to people in upper areas of management. Like the drilling and blasting process. We knew what needed to be done, but we were ignored. We knew they'd come around to see it our way. There was one guy at the concentrator who was pretty sharp. He did a comparative study on drilling and blasting versus not doing it, and sure enough, we were right.[20]

In Chuquicamata, I heard similar stories of workingman's wisdom and "how to" accounts as men described the intricacies of their labors in the production of copper. I was humbled by the knowledgeable, technical questions of workingmen in Butte and Chuquicamata who wanted to know more about the operations in their counterpart communities, and I had no ability to respond. The mining men were building their own images in relation to their skills and in contrast to their bosses. In Chuquicamata, however, there was a different structure to the talk of workingman's wisdom and corporate ignorance. When workingmen spoke of the days when Anaconda ran the mines, they spoke well of the operation and of the gringos who recognized and rewarded skilled labor. Despite the litany of social inequities in the mines and in the community, which these same men often cited, they felt their hard work and know-how earned them both respect and compensation.

In contrast to Marxist representations of the working class, the workingmen of Chuquicamata did not talk of "alienation" from their labor, but of intimacy with and respect for that labor during the Anaconda years.[21] It was later, under Allende, Pinochet and current management — when college degrees and party politics overshadowed workingman's knowledge — that "things began to go downhill." Longtime workers complained about the rapid advancement of young men with college degrees who don't know anything and about the lack of respect for the cumulative knowledge of older workers. The young men countered that age and experience do not necessarily reflect ability and that the mines need new blood and fresh ideas in management. Young and old alike decried the ignorant outsiders coming in from Santiago, having earned a management post as a result of *pituto* (personal and political favors).

As one labor leader in Chuqui summed up the history of Anaconda's exodus and the nationalization of the mines, "The gringos left and the Chilean gringos arrived."[22] His words capture a troubling irony and the distance between the promise and the practice of nationalization. Through their talk of hard work and the good old days, the mining men of Chuquicamata today are constituting themselves as they invert the current corporate story of "old" and "new" orders. Perhaps, as they stake claim to the good old days, they are claiming their value as workers, something many believe Anaconda valued as much as they did. Meanwhile, Butte miners (except for the handful who still work in the mines) reclaim their histories and reconstitute their identities in retirees clubs, barrooms, and nearly abandoned union halls.

BIG SHOTS

Popular images of down-to-earth miners stood in sharp contrast to those of the high rollers who got rich off the miners' labor. Butte has enjoyed a long-term romance with its Copper Kings, the brash men who built the town and bought the state. And the favorite of them all was Marcus Daly, who remembered his roots by tipping a beer and telling a story with the rank and file. Those who came later were no longer kings but Big Shots who were variably revered and reviled. The Big Shots of corporate headquarters in New York City were largely a nameless, faceless lot, generic targets of blame and resentment when things were bad in Butte. As Marie, a miner's wife, put it:

> They say Chile was Anaconda's downfall, but that wasn't the problem; it was the weight in New York. Those retired Big Shots with big pensions and chauffeurs and company houses. There was a glut of them, and they live long. Now, some of the top brass were miners. They worked their way up. But they weren't the ones living so long. Used to be the miners didn't live past forty-five or fifty, even less with the "con" [miner's consumption]. But not those who bought in. They never went in the mines They live long, collecting a big pension. The local brass were pretty okay.[23]

Local Big Shots were the subject of personal scrutiny. Those who won respect were those who followed in the Daly tradition, making themselves small to mix with the common man. Art, a retired miner, reminisced about one of the latter day Big Shots and his popularity among the little guys: "Jimmy R. was a great guy, just a great guy. We used to have some good times with Jimmy. One time there was this 'nigger' piano player down at the Finlen. And he was singin' 'My Mother Came from Ireland.' Well, he got thrown right out of the place. And you know who booted him out? It was Jimmy R. He was quite a guy."[24] A touch of Irish nationalism coupled with unbridled racism carried more weight, so it seems, than fair labor practices in equalizing relations between Big Shots and little guys.

In Chuquicamata, as we have seen, there was little mixing. Yankee power was cultivated through social distance and physical separation in the workplace as well as the community. Chuquicamatinos do not speak of Big Shots but of gringos — a term that embodies the force of capitalist privilege. Residents recall detailed images of the gringo boss who stood apart from his Chilean labor force, distinguishing himself with the formalities of suit, hat, and tie, his presence unflappable in the harsh desert clime. Some speak of Mr. (it is always *Mr.* and *Mrs.* when speaking of gringo bosses and their wives) Brinckerhoff, longtime chief of the Chile Exploration Company, as a sincere and simple man. He was fluent in Spanish. But there are no stories of Brinckerhoff and his men making themselves small, drinking and carousing with the miners. Rather, there are stories of surveillance and the watchful eye of the gringo who took note of a job well done and selectively rewarded the conscientious miner with a bonus or promotion. At a personal level, the Big Men of Anaconda did not appear to play by ethnic and party politics in Chuquicamata, as they often did in Butte.[25] They ran a selective meritocracy through which some Chileans, so the story goes, might gain a larger share in corporate spoils through pure hard work.

In the stories of Chuquicamata's miners, this management style contrasts sharply with present day Big Shots, who maintain distance from their workers through bureaucratic machinations. I encountered unison in the voices of residents of diverse political stripes as they favorably compared the gringo operation to the current situation. Hernan's account is a case in point:

> I've worked in Chuqui for thirty years. I was born here and my father worked with the gringos for twenty-five years. Those were good times, and it meant something to work in Chuqui. The work was good and important, and lots of people wanted to work here. I wanted to follow in my father's footsteps. It was a tradition among men. If the father worked in Chuqui, the son wanted to work here, too. The work had value. I had six or seven years with the gringos before the mines were nationalized. When the gringos left, things went downhill. The gringos were demanding and hardworking and they paid well. You had to work, but it was good. It was better when the gringos ran the mines. The gringos knew copper. They wanted to get copper out of the ground at any price. So they built a good life here and paid well. You got rewarded for a job well done. We had good houses and good salaries and everything. I grew up in that era; it was important in my life. You had to live with them, and we lived well. For me, personally, it worked well. I have a lot of respect for the gringos. There was baseball and basketball, and the gringos were big boxing fans. They promoted boxing here. I'm still a baseball and basketball fan, because those were the sports that I grew up with. We lived in the body of the king. We had everything during the gringo

years. . . . My mother worked for the gringos, too. She worked for Dr. Bradford at the hospital. We lived in *Las Normas*, the best houses here. The houses were good, but *Las Normas* were the best. . . .

The gringo bosses respected the workers, not like now. The gringos recognized the workers as individuals. There were *chilenos* that earned responsible positions because of their abilities. The operation was personal and direct. The bosses knew who the valuable workers were. Degrees weren't important; skills, discipline, and capacity to do the work counted for everything.

The gringos respected the value of a job well done more than formal education. Now, lots of people have formal education, but they don't have knowledge of the work, and when they get jobs as supervisors, the workers don't have confidence in them. The gringos, they watched the operations carefully and knew who was capable and had the talent and skill to advance in the company.[26]

In Hernan's recollections of the Anaconda days, praise wins out over resentment. I could give several meanings to his adulation of Anaconda. First, his family enjoyed Roll B status and its benefits. Second, Hernan seems to have his own theories about people nosing into Chile's recent past. As he spoke to me, he spoke against a view of history where Anaconda was the demon and Allende the hero. He made it clear that he had no use for communists in general nor the Popular Unity government in particular. If he had his way, Anaconda would still be running the mines, and things wouldn't be in the shape they're in today.

Hernan's comments were also part of a broader discourse, suggesting more than his personal experience and political beliefs. In many peoples' stories, seemingly contradictory accounts of hardships and the good life fuse together. It appears that the gringos crafted a transparent system of privation and privilege. Distinctions and rewards were not disguised but elaborated. Peoples' stories reflect the complicated practice of living as beneficiaries and victims of corporate largesse and exploitation. They tell "both-and" stories not "either-or" stories of pain and possibility.

Then-versus-now comparison is at the heart of these stories. Both the good and the bad of the Anaconda days need to be read against the current discourse and practice that vilifies both the old order and its participants. The gringo bosses left a material legacy on this harsh desert terrain: a state-of-the-art hospital, theater, library, stadium, and plaza. Those architectural markers now mark the stories told about the days of the gringos and offer grim comparison to the current state of affairs. Movies no longer play in the Chile Theater; no Sunday concerts fill the plaza with life. The hospital has gone downhill and is under threat of demolition to make way for expansion of the open-pit mine. Calama is now the place for soccer games. And the library closed its doors in 1995. For many Chuquicamatinos, the departure of the gringo bosses marked the breakdown of community as they had come to know it.

The Big Shots constructed themselves as they built images of their workforce. Paternalism permeated the corporate image as community benefactor. Corporate fathers knew what was best for the great Anaconda family. Company loyalty was the key expectation of its managers; they sought to instill loyalty in the rank and file as well with the rewards for longtime service. Company management invariably portrayed themselves as fair and reasonable men, devoted to the preservation of order, free enterprise, and the right to work. The Anaconda Big Shots did not portray themselves as "team players" with their workingmen. They were the bosses, and they intended to keep it that way. Perhaps their transparent image as paternal power holders made the unequal relations between labor and management more palatable than those practices in Chuquicamata today, where management promotes a discourse of collaboration that contradicts its practices of inequality. Those practices currently fuel worker criticism of the Chilean manager who, to borrow a verse from Pablo Neruda, "dresses like a gringo, spits like a gringo, dances like a gringo, and moves up."[27]

THE MEN IN THE MIDDLE

Mining was more than a system of miners and Big Shots. It was a complex and contradictory system of allegiances and animosities as men strove for personal and shared visions of getting ahead. Unions symbolized the collective struggle of the workingman to better his wages and working conditions and to provide his family with more than he had known as a boy. But the structure and practice of labor relations in Butte and Chuquicamata placed some men in what Erik Olin Wright terms "contradictory class locations," straddling the line between labor and capital (Wright 1989, 4–5; Giddens and Held 1982, 112–29).

The lines between union and company men were often blurred in Butte. Many Butte men made the difficult transition from union man to company boss. These men followed the cultural script for getting ahead, abandoning their formal union affiliation in hope of a better future for their families. Seldom did their move give them access to upper echelons of corporate power or a more affluent lifestyle. They walked a fine line between loyalty to the company and to their men.

The problems and promises confronting the men in the middle are illustrated in the stories told in Butte. Elaine, the wife of a former mining boss, recalled:

> My husband was a strong union man, and he eventually took a bossing job. He cared too much for his men, and if something wasn't working right, he would jump in and help, but that was not what ACM wanted in a boss. He eventually gave it up. But to this day, the men who worked for him love and respect him. Whenever we go out, we always run into men who insist on buying him a drink and reminiscing about what a great boss he was.[28]

Shirley, the widow of a shift boss, remembered her husband's stand in refusing to enforce company policies that he didn't believe in: "There was a time when the company made the shift bosses inspect the men's lunch buckets before they left shift. There was lots of talk of stuff being stolen from the mine, so the company made this lunch box inspection rule. But my husband refused to do it. He said he wouldn't degrade his men with such a thing."[29] More than one miner must have breathed a sigh of relief as his shift boss looked the other way, selectively ignoring corporate rules. As Vic, a miner's son told the story: "I remember my Dad telling about the men coming out of the mines with their lunch boxes heavier than when they left for work. They stuffed everything they could get in to those lunch boxes, tools, pipe, anything. Half the houses in Butte were built with company supplies that they took out of the mines."[30]

Were these men in the middle located in "contradictory class locations," as Wright would argue? In the sense of Ortner's definition of structural contradictions as conflicting discourses and conflicting patterns of practice that recurrently pose problems for actors, perhaps the answer is yes. Work as they will, they are not making much progress toward the cultural script of getting ahead. In Marx's (political economic) or Bateson's (psychological) sense of an absolute "damned if you do, damned if you don't" double bind, the answer is no (Bateson 1972, 271–78). These men did not succumb to schizophrenia, or other paralysis of agency, as a result of embodying the incompatibilities between the forces and relations of production.[31] Instead, men in the middle sought to resolve their lack of fit by creatively inventing what it meant to be a boss. And in so doing, they toyed with the imbalance of power.

An important way in which the men in the middle resolved the problem of their awkward fit was through this play in which miners could steal from under the noses of the company. This play gave the little guys something much more valuable than supplies the size of a lunch box. It gave them a "get even" script. Almost every miner, miner's wife, and miner's child can tell a version of how "half the houses in Butte were built with company supplies." The stories encode the mutual pride and common ground of the little guys and the men in the middle as they talked back to corporate power. They may not have gotten ahead, but sometimes they got more than they bargained for, while the company got screwed. In these stories, getting even carried more weight than getting ahead.

Longtime residents of Chuquicamata reported little upward mobility in the quasi-caste system of Rolls A, B, and C. Nonetheless, it was possible that the man who stood out, his work a notch above that of his union brothers, might be promoted. With his move came a marked shift in quality of life; a move from Roll C to Roll B brought concomitant privileges of a larger house and a better stocked *pulpería*, powerful incentives for trying to get ahead. But there is more to the story.

Through its corporate propaganda, Anaconda promoted the values of the American Way: competition, free enterprise, and getting ahead. However, it seems that this discourse was conflated with that of "having arrived." Anaconda had structured both its labor force and community in Chuquicamata around the notion of privilege, of having arrived. Like any other privileged class, the workers of Chuquicamata had arrived. This was as good as it got within a larger state system that had *not* yet arrived at the "American" ideal of free enterprise. With salaries and benefits a cut above the rest of their compatriots, getting ahead was not to be the issue for Chuquicamata's miners.

But these miners had arrived in this remote corner of the world only to live alongside their gringo bosses in a dual system of privilege. Despite their talk of free enterprise and opportunity, the gringos had nearly succeeded in building a closed system of class distinctions. Some, like Hernan, found satisfaction with their place in the system. Others did, in fact, get ahead, by taking advantage of education, developing political prowess, and strengthening their labor organizations. Labor activists built alliances across the boundaries of ethnicity and Roll, defining common ground as workers and challenging the rules of order in Chuquicamata. By the 1950s, the white- and blue-collar unions joined forces and created the base for a newfound sense of solidarity, a community working together to claim their rights to the American Way. They joined together to get ahead. And yet these men in the middle became the target for attack. Under the Popular Unity government,

Chuquicamata's miners were criticized for their lack of class consciousness and commitment to Chilean democratic socialism. Under Pinochet,
they were criticized for lack of patriotic commitment to "national recuperation." And currently they are under fire for their wasteful ways, a
by-product of privilege inculcated by Anaconda. Selfishness, say their
critics, has blocked their vision of the common good.

    An area that deserves more thorough consideration than I can give it
here is the place of race and color in the constructions of masculine identities and their distinctions along class lines. Montecino, in her analysis
of el mestizaje chileno (Chilean mixed ancestry), discusses the powerful
valuing of whiteness within Chilean cultural identity, the concomitant
sense of superiority of Spanish over indigenous roots, and the interplay
of cultural and religious ethos and social practices that served to maintain and justify a social hierarchy of class and color distinctions
(Montecino 1993). This color-coded social order appears well entrenched in Chuquicamata today. In my conversations with men in
Chuqui, I seldom heard direct references to the privileging of whiteness
or to the workingman as the "black man," in the earlier style of Eulogio
Gutiérrez and Marcial Figueroa. Rather, it was the language of indio,
nortino, and moreno that often encoded not only distinction but also
devaluation along color lines. At a more pervasive level, the upper ech-
elon of mine management and social life in Chuquicamata is dominated
by "white" men, whose physical features and class backgrounds have
combined to promote their access to education and social and economic
power. I lack data to examine the meaning and power of whiteness in
the daily negotiation of relations among Chilean workers and their
gringo bosses during the Anaconda days in Chuquicamata. Perhaps, in
the complicated politics of identification, color served as a highly
nuanced resource or liability for negotiating one's position vis-à-vis the
company. It is a question that merits further examination, especially in
order to understand the mobility of men in the middle.

    In Butte, a complicated politics of race and color unfolded as well,
despite the city's acclaimed identity as a cultural melting pot. As noted
earlier, Butte's ethnic mix was not without tension, and tolerance
extended only to particular definitions of whiteness, though even there
the boundaries were fuzzy. Butte's significant Chinese population was
the target of virulent racism, and Chinese workers were effectively
excluded from the mines. Mexican and Native American workers,
although not excluded, were often the targets of racist humor and
assigned to the dirtiest jobs. But the superiority of whiteness as a bond

among Anaconda's mining men was vividly illustrated in negotiations between management and union leaders regarding the labor force shortage at the smelter during World War II. In his fascinating thesis, Matthew Basso uses records of these meetings to document the negotiations and resulting agreement to hire local women rather than nonlocal black or Mexican men as replacement workers (Basso 1996).[32] Despite complicated class-based antagonisms, Butte's Big Shots and little guys found comfort and common ground in their white masculinity.

DESIGNING WOMEN

Though women have usually been assigned cameo roles in mining history, feminine imagery abounds. Both Chuquicamata and Butte have been given feminine identities in popular discourse. In Spanish, the word *mina* (mine) is a rather disparaging euphemism for women. Numerous old mines around Chuquicamata, as in Butte, bear women's names — perhaps, as Alvear Urrutia suggests, warning of "insecurity, capriciousness, betrayal, hopes and fears, habitual characteristics of the relations between us and them, distant, inaccessible, and coveted" (1975, 65–66).

In the analysis of masculinity, I present a rather tidy portrayal of men in relation to their labor: miners, Big Shots, and men in the middle. In analyzing femininity, I find myself struggling for a way to frame the discussion. Perhaps this struggle is a result of my resistance to reducing myself and the many women I have come to care about to mere images. Moreover, my ethnographic data, more heavily weighted toward women's lives, are not easily categorized. More fundamentally, it may be that women have historically straddled more complex matrices of social relations vis-à-vis gender, labor, and class. Women's social practice is the focus of the next chapter. In this section, I address constructions of womanhood in key cultural symbols, in popular literature, and in the company press. Although these images themselves reflect a masculine angle of vision on femininity, I look specifically at examples of men's construction of womanhood in Butte and Chuquicamata. I then turn to the practices through which women crafted themselves, in relation to men and to other women, a theme that is developed in chapter 5.

A key image of womanhood, that of the Virgin Mary, needs to be addressed at the outset to set the broader cultural and social context in which other feminine representations are embedded. Catholicism has been a powerful cultural influence in both Butte and Chuquicamata. A critical analysis of Catholicism is beyond the scope of this work. Suffice it to say that in both the Irish Catholicism, as manifested in Butte, and the Chilean *mestizo* Catholicism, as manifested in Chuquicamata, the symbol of the Virgin Mary played a key role in religious practice and in defining ideal womanhood.[33] She is the embodiment of the ultimate feminine contradiction: virgin and mother.

The image represents a sanctified fusion of incompatibilities. The women of Butte and Chuquicamata were not faced with the simple "virgin-prostitute" dichotomy, something of a classic in feminist literature, as the masculine ideal of womanhood. Rather, they were to embody the contradictory trinity of virgin, mother, and prostitute, those feminine ideals that have a special place in the hearts of men. These representations have shaped the meaning of womanhood for all women, regardless of class position. The discussion that follows needs to be contextualized in relation to this deeply embedded cultural image of womanhood.

In the historic fiction and popular stories of Butte, the matron of the boarding house and the madam of the bordello stand as key representations of womanhood. They are the big-hearted women who generously meet the needs of mining men. Brothels and *borracheras* (bars) are the scourge of *la blanca viuda de Punta de Rieles*, the mythical widow who put fear in the hearts of Chuquicamata's miners on dark, windy nights, as she searched for her husband who died in a barroom brawl (Alvear Urrutia 1975, 65–66). Anaconda buried Punta de Rieles under the slag heaps, but not the myths. Contradictory images of womanhood embody the force and counterforce of mining, the mystery and risk of penetrable depths, the givers of pleasure and protection.

But the force of the mines often prevailed over women's protective counterforce. In dimensions larger than myth, widowhood came to define the lives of many women of Butte and Chuquicamata who lost their husbands to mine accidents and silicosis. Their numbers attest to the harsh realities behind the heroic images. The beloved matrons of Butte's boardinghouses were often widows, dependent on the contributions of their boarders to make ends meet. In Butte, stories of mother-son relationships resonate with women's desire to protect young men from the fate of their fathers and grandfathers and the reality that the mines were often the only opportunity for economic survival. One woman told me with relief that "none of her men had to go underground." A retired miner told his story of lying about his age in order to get a job in the mines at fourteen. His father had died in a mining accident, and as oldest son, he had to help support the family. His mother, with six younger children at home, needed the money, even if that meant risking her son in the mines that had claimed her husband. In Chuquicamata, the company had a protection plan for miners' widows, offering them work as cleaning women in the communal bathrooms. However, because there were more widows than cleaning jobs, some women scraped out a living as vendors and domestic workers or through continued subsistence labor in the desert interior that had bolstered family survival all along. More recently, during Chile's seventeen years of dictatorship, widowhood became symbolic of the profound social tragedy that stemmed from state violence. Women throughout Chile, in groups such as the *Agrupación de Familiares de los Ejecutados de Calama*, publicly proclaimed their widowhood in a politics of identification that challenged the dictatorship.

Over the years in the company press in Butte, women were constructed as conservers of culture and caretakers of family and community. The society page regularly featured the social and charitable practices of middle- and upper-class women and in general ignored the labors of working-class women. The Big Shots' wives were constructed in terms of sociality, not sexuality; their graciousness as hostess and philanthropist was the measure of their worth. It was in the moments where powerful cultural scripts were violated, such as in the strike of 1946, that working-class women received publicity. And it was usually bad press, which admonished them for shirking their moral and social obligations.[34]

In the company press of Chuquicamata, an image of middle-class Yankee womanhood was promoted each week in *La Página Feminina*.[35] In much the same way as other images of free-market America were sold as the measure of success to the local readership, so was thoroughly modern womanhood formed around U.S.-made images of grooming, mothering, and hostessing. The tips on hair styling represented a classic example of the anglo-American standard of beauty held up for emulation by Chilean women. Not only do the models' features appear "foreign," their hairdos would not last long in the incessant wind of Chuquicamata (see fig. 18).

While women talked of the boy in the man, men in Butte and Chuquicamata talked of the mother in the woman, as evidenced in a Butte writer's praise of motherhood:

It is estimated that as high as 25 men died monthly because of injuries or diseases from the mine. Because of this, just imagine the widows that were left, often with large families. Families that may have had as many as twelve or

fifteen children at a time when there was not the type of welfare we have
today. Or for that matter hardly any of the means of sustenance we have
today. And yet these widows did an amazing job of raising their children. . . .
When you think of Mother's Day and motherhood nothing could equal the
greatness of those women and the sacrifice they made in bringing up their
children. . . . In all of Butte's history — and it is a very interesting and startling
one — there should be no other aspect that we should be more proud of than
the mothers who raised such great children on such limited means. They are
the real heroes of our history. They are greater than Clark, Daly and Heinze
will ever think of being. (Lynch 1979, 38)[36]

Alvear Urrutia writes of the watchful wife, standing guard over her
husband in the pay line at Chuquicamata. She was ready to pounce on
the paycheck before he frittered it away and left the family destitute
(Alvear Urrutia 1975, 51). These images construct women not only as
guardians of the moral order, but of the financial stability of the household and community as well. The images were reinforced through practices such as the women's compensation.

It is the Virgin Mother who has reigned as the ultimate guardian of
community moral and social order. In Butte, this key symbol of womanhood was finally set in concrete when, in 1985, "Our Lady of the
Rockies" was erected atop the Continental Divide, overlooking Butte,
"in honor of all women, especially mothers." The story of her construction, documented in a promotional film, book, and numerous news
accounts offers an intriguing mythology that pits man against nature
(and government bureaucracy), and faith against doubt.[37] Our Lady
began as the vague recipient of the prayers of a man concerned for his
wife's health. He sought the counsel of a friend at work, a man of
Mexican heritage with a strong Catholic faith. The friend suggested that
he pray to Our Lady of Guadelupe. The man's prayers were answered
when his wife recovered from a serious illness. In gratitude, he enlisted
the support of a few friends to help him build a small statue in honor of
Our Lady of Guadelupe.

When the project captured the attention of a local businessman and
promoter, it took on a life beyond its creator's imaginings. Through an
amalgam of devotion, machismo, and salesmanship, plans for the
statue grew from lawn ornament size to a woman of mythic dimensions: ninety feet of reinforced steel weighing sixty tons. In the process,
a new identity, Our Lady of the Rockies, emerged. Our Lady's main
promoter and first financial backer saw marketing potential but had his
reservations:

PROPORCIÓN ES BELLEZA

ROSTRO FORMA DE CORAZÓN

ROSTRO OVALADO

ROSTRO ALARGADO

ROSTRO CUADRADO

Figure 18. "Proportion Is Beauty." *Oasis*, 7 March 1964. Accompanying text included makeup and hairstyling tips.

Can you imagine what kind of tourist attraction a beautiful large statue maybe 60 feet tall of Our Lady would be up on the mountain? You could see it from anywhere in Butte and it would attract people from all over the world. I think it's just a great idea. However, one thing that worries me is the statue might be associated with the Catholic Church. I believe that would pose a danger for the whole project. Even though I'm Catholic, I believe it's important that we include all religions and faiths because we will need them all to finish this project. The statue has to be nondenominational to work successfully. . . . If we do this right it would be a Mecca and bring people here from all over the world just to see Our Lady up there on that mountain-top. . . . From a promotional standpoint, we need to develop our own name. . . . My idea is to call it "Our Lady of the Rockies." (Kearney 1990, 25) (see fig. 19)

And so, in this predominantly Catholic community, a key symbol of Catholicism and womanhood became the focus of men's dreams, desires, and craftsmanship and found herself transformed in the process. In this fascinating fusion of capitalism and cosmology, Our Lady was destined to become a powerful community icon, intimately grounded in a sense of place, and a popular tourist attraction as well.

The story of the five-year process of Our Lady's construction is an emotional one. Except for Our Lady herself, the key actors in the narrative and the video productions were men. The story is a celebration of manual labor, featuring the triumph of uneducated laborers over outside experts. The project overcame the ridicule and opposition of skeptics to become a community rallying point. Her construction created a community of men once again bound by the intimacy of doing. Her creators once again appropriated materials from the company for their purposes, taking something back for all they had given. (Her fingers are the exhaust pipes of dump trucks from the mines). And once again, the company was silent partner in the building of community even as it planned the final betrayal, the closure of the mines.[38]

In the final two years of construction, the project was very visible, with Our Lady's head and shoulders resting prominently in an equipment yard adjacent to the interstate highway that crosscuts Butte. Financial support began to pour in as this economically depressed community rallied behind the project. Local stories credit both divine intervention and Machiavellian politicking for the success in getting Our Lady solidly mounted on her base. Through threats by Montana's congressional representatives to filibuster a defense bill and appeals to then-President Reagan, the work crew and their friends in high places managed to appropriate a national guard helicopter to lift Our Lady in

Figure 19.   Our Lady of the Rockies. Photo by Tony Difronzo, Rainbow Photo, Butte.

five multi-ton chunks to the mountain top. The city stood breathlessly by, watching this ultimate challenge of men and faith. The tension of the airlift was heightened by near-catastrophe at one point as the helicopter spun out of control. But after four trying days, Butte residents joined in celebration on December 20, 1985, when the project was complete and Our Lady began her permanent vigilance over Butte. Less than two months later, a Montana businessman announced plans to resurrect mining in Butte.

Our Lady is a complex entity. She stands as a lasting tribute to crafts-manship. She is the product of the collective struggle of a community of men. For some, she symbolizes community hope; for the more skeptical, she represents the feminizing of Butte's labor force.[39] Perhaps she embodies a struggle for a sense of order, an enduring presence in a time of uncertainty, an immutable representation of motherhood. It was Butte men, unemployed miners and entrepreneurs, who envisioned and built the statue, perhaps constructing themselves as sons in the process. Butte now lives under the constant surveillance of Our Lady, a power-ful symbol of faith, doubt, and contradiction that shapes the imagina-tion of womanhood, manhood, and community.

Chuquicamata has its own cultural elaborations of devotion to the

Virgin Mary, as illustrated in the discussion of the Virgin of Guadelupe of Ayquina in chapter 3. Throughout the year in Chile's desert north, dancers take to the streets and young girls dressed in white march in tribute to the Virgin Mary, reflecting and reinforcing images of the good woman. The power of these images remains strong in community practice (see fig. 20).

I was in Chuquicamata and Calama for the feast of the Immaculate Conception on December 8, 1993. The day is an official holiday, and all of the mine offices were closed. People filled the streets for the grand procession honoring the Virgin Mary.[40] Dancers in elaborate costumes and masks led the way, flanking the group who carried a statue of the Virgin above their shoulders for all to see. They were followed by hundreds of schoolgirls and women. Many were dressed in white with veils, and others in ordinary dress joined the march from the sidelines. They walked solemnly while praying the rosary, led by a male voice booming over the loudspeaker in a pickup truck. Perhaps here, where ritual practices of devotion served to publicly reconstitute and reaffirm this image of enduring womanhood, the Virgin Mary does not need to be set in concrete in order to fortify her cultural staying power.

A less dramatic but perhaps no less telling image of womanhood has been under construction during the current Cultural Transformation of the Labor Force underway in Chuquicamata. In 1993, the chief executive of CODELCO-Chuqui initiated a new practice in the change process, a series of "Letters to the Women of Chuquicamata." The letters appear about once a month in Oasis, which is distributed to all employees.[41] Replete with the language of mother, God, and country, these letters call on women to join in and support their husbands through participation in the change process. The cultural transformation is described in metaphoric language as the need to "clean the house" and "do the laundry." Although the mines and their ancillary services employ hundreds of women and large numbers of women have salaried jobs outside the mines, the letters speak to women as housewives and mothers, discounting the broader realities of their lives.

Static and traditional images of womanhood inform these letters. She is the conserver of community culture and the only one concerned with health, education, children, and the integrity of the family. It appears that one thing the company does not want to change throughout this cultural transformation is the traditional role of women. Rather, women are to maintain their undervalued position and continue the practices associated with that position.

Figure 20.   Celebrating the Feast of the Immaculate Conception, Ayquina,
Chile, 1993 (author photo).

The letters offer an "open invitation" for women's participation in the change process, but that invitation is limited by the masculine perspectives of women's capacities and contributions. While new forms of polyvalence are being constructed for men, the long-term polyvalence of women's work goes unrecognized. But the letters are not necessarily convincing. As one member of the organization of miner's wives told me, "I quit reading those letters because they don't mean anything to me. It's like reading a foreign language."[42]

Though powerful cultural images have shaped the meaning of womanhood in Butte and Chuquicamata, the women of the mining community actively engaged in crafting themselves. Women created their own identities in relation to labor, family, men, and one another. Women often spoke not of "I" but of "we," creating themselves not as mothers or wives, but as friends, defined in relationship to other women. The image of homebound wives and mothers belies the fact of women's paid and unpaid labors as community caretakers in Butte and Chuquicamata. Women continue to provide the low-wage labor in hospitals, hotels, restaurants, and private homes. Single mothers, whether by death, desertion, or design, often struggle with economic needs and household responsibilities as they work triple shifts, emptying bed pans, cleaning toilets, raising children, taking in laundry, and selling pasties and empanadas to make ends meet.[43]

Through their labors, women's lives crisscrossed class lines, creating opportunities for both building support and negotiating power. During strikes in Butte, the lines of distinction between union and company wives were at times clearly drawn. There are stories told of store clerks and maids in Butte who refused service to management wives during the 1959 strike. There are also the stories of women in the middle, who used their own relationships to management to support other women. For example, Shirley's husband moved from a mining job to a management job. She felt guilty about having an income during the 1959 strike, when those she knew so well were struggling to get by. She had bags of groceries delivered to families she knew to help out. She did not forget the struggles to make ends meet and the important support of friends and family she had received when her husband was on strike (see fig. 21).

Kate was working as a nursing supervisor at the hospital during the 1967 strike. Her husband was a salaried worker in Anaconda's business office. At the time, the hospital had a policy of forbidding women to work during pregnancy. Kate remembers a young nurse, wife of a miner, who found out she was pregnant shortly after the strike began. Kate

Figure 21. Butte, a study in contrasts. Courtesy of Butte Historical Society, Butte Labor History Project Collection.

kept the young woman working, agreeing not to notice her condition. As the strike and the pregnancy wore on, Kate's superiors got suspicious. Kate argued the young woman's case. Rather than changing hospital policy, the administration tacitly agreed to Kate's practice of ignoring the pregnancy and letting the woman work.[44]

The *CHILEX Weekly*, Chuquicamata's English language paper that catered to the social needs of the American Camp, offered graphic examples of the ways in which the gringas crafted themselves in relation to their Chilean maids. During the 1950s and 1960s, the newspaper was edited by women of the American Camp. They occasionally featured helpful Spanish lessons for Yankee wives. They were practical lessons, structured with the special interests of the gringas in mind. There were phrases for the hairdresser and the butcher, and an extensive and revealing lesson entitled, "When Talking to Your Maid." The lesson includes key phrases such as "Wash the dishes carefully with plenty of hot water and soap; wash the clothes in the washing machine; and you cannot go to the cinema tonight because we are going out to dinner." The phrases not only reflect the gringas' lifestyle but also reveal the assumptions the gringas made about their "native" domestic help.[45]

Some women of Chuquicamata have fond recollections of their work in the American Camp. As one former maid put it, "The gringos were less formal, more personal. You were like family and could eat at the table with the family, not by yourself in the kitchen, after everyone else, the way it is with the Chileans. Lots of times there was more of a friendship."[46] Her companion, Cecilia, who had also worked as a maid had a different recollection:

> The gringos were fair but very demanding, everything had to be just so. Everyday I had to make flower arrangements for my employer. She had to have fresh flowers on the table every day. I had never arranged flowers before in my life; we didn't have flowers like those here. She was so critical, it had to be perfect. And my hands would shake, I would be so nervous trying to get it right.[47]

Despite her less than pleasant memories of the job, Cecilia insisted it was worth it:

> I quit that job two weeks after my brother began to work in the mines. That's why I had gone to work there in the first place. Jobs in the mines were hard to come by. You had to know someone. I knew my brother would not have much of a chance on his own. So I went to work for the gringos. It wasn't bad, and I got to know them. They knew I was a hard worker, and I could tell them about my brother, who was a good worker, too. I worked there a year or so before my brother got hired in the mines. They were disappointed and wanted me to stay, but I was about to get married.

Every day, domestic workers penetrated the private world of the American Camp, observing and absorbing the contradictions. It was not the gringas who came to know the intimacies of working women's worlds. Though much of working women's life was public — waiting in *pulpería* lines, gathering cooking fuel, or filling water jugs — they retained a private world as well, as private as their unspoken thoughts about the separate reality they entered everyday through their labors. Like their husbands in the mines, the working women of Butte and Chuquicamata lived the contradictions of capitalism. Unlike their husbands, women lived the contradictions that often permeated the intimate powerplays of family life as well. I develop this theme in the following section.

Given my close ties to women's lives during fieldwork, I was privy to more intimate glimpses of the place of whiteness and color in the constructions of social identities and positioning among women than among men. In Butte, most of my conversations were with women who identified with their white ethnic backgrounds. Their accounts of local history were punctuated with ethnic pride and recognition of difference. Some women recalled with sadness the racist treatment of Butte's Chinese community and the exclusion of blacks from the mines. They seemed to construe the exclusions as exceptional flaws in Butte's history of tolerance. Yet even as they spoke, it was clear that they saw those groups as separate from the Butte community defined by its ethnic whiteness. For the most part, whiteness was implicitly assumed and not part of the discourse among women as they located themselves in relation to one another. That assumption of whiteness was often a source of pain and frustration for Butte's "women of color" — African American, Native American, Mexican, and Asian. For them, Butte's melting pot was a European mix, and they were often marked as outsiders.

In Chuquicamata, color was encoded in many registers of conversation and social relations. Among friends and family, darker-skinned women may be affectionately labeled as *la morena* or *la negra* (dark-skinned or black woman). In my conversations with "working-class" women, their references to self or others were often made in physically descriptive terms that mixed color, culture, and class identities: *negra, india, nortina, campesina,* or *morena.* When speaking of their children or grandchildren, women often described them in terms of color, offering a brief genealogy to trace their resemblance. Many working-class families I came to know had one member referred to as *el moreno* or *la morena,* making dark skin a powerful marker of identity.

Over time and in response to my queries, a few of my women friends in Chuquicamata began to educate me about the power of whiteness. They spoke of the importance of whiteness as a marker of status among the women of Chuquicamata's management class. Executives wives, they said, were preoccupied with whiteness and resorted not only to regular bleaching of their hair, but also to bleaching of their skin. They spoke of witnessing the painful exclusions of dark-skinned children, especially girls, born into upper-class families. These youngsters not only faced rejection by peers but often subtle rejection from their parents and extended families. Given the valuing of beauty over brains for young women, dark skin could prove a serious detriment to their social mobility. My friends' insights were validated in my own experiences among some of the women of Chuquicamata's management class with whom I did volunteer work. The accomplishments and plans of their children were frequent topics of conversation during our sewing groups. As women passed around pictures of their teenage daughters, others commented freely on their light-skinned beauty, or conversely, with sadness and empathy for *las morenas*. Their sons, however, were discussed in terms of academic accomplishments and athletic prowess. Once the pictures were tucked away, the conversation frequently shifted to difficulties with domestic help, where *india, morena, nortina, boliviana*, and *campesina* marked their essentialist criticisms of their employees, even as they masked the power of antagonistic class relations among women. Complicated meanings of whiteness have shaped women's lives in both communities. I have only scratched the surface of this key facet of social identification. It is a subject that deserves further critical attention.

GENDER, INTIMACY, AND DANGEROUS LIAISONS

I have explored constructions of masculinity and femininity, but what of the gendered spaces and relations where men and women come together, building a life because and in spite of mining? I shift the focus here to relations among women and men through which they variably reinforced, challenged, and talked back to these cultural images.

Popular accounts of liaisons and infidelities have added spice to mining history in Butte and Chuquicamata. The songs and lore of the Butte miners are replete with allusions to men's distrust of their women, who remained on the surface while the men were trapped in their work underground.[48] The mines ran twenty-four hours a day, and the lore warns husbands that men from other shifts were taking their place in the bedroom while they were underground. One story claims that the warning whistle blew when there was an accident in the mines, not to alert women of the crisis, but to alert marital interlopers that men were leaving the mines ahead of schedule.

In Chuquicamata, so the story goes, all the houses were built with two doors. This way, when the husband came home through the front door, the lover could slip out the back. The story, in its various forms, is accompanied by a "true fact account" of rampant infidelity in Chuquicamata, a place where men earned enough to support more than one woman, and where women, starved for intimacy, turned to lovers. There is a strong, if unspoken, class dimension to these stories. It was the workingman and his woman who played with the rules of respectability, but it was the company that built the house and blew the whistle, surreptitiously condoning marital infidelity if it served the "keep 'em happy, keep 'em broke, keep 'em working" policy.

The personal stories told by women and men in Butte and Chuquicamata offer a much more poignant glimpse at gender and intimacy. Marie talked of men's worlds and women's worlds in Butte:

> They had different concerns than we did. It was just sort of separate. The men used to go to the bar to plot and plan and piece together their information about the strikes, while the women took care of keeping things going at home. It was probably a good thing they had that time at the bar, because they needed it. And it probably made things a little easier when they were at home, since they could leave some of that behind. They should have just held their union meetings in the bar, because that's where they did most of their union business anyway.[49]

Lil recalled an old truism in Butte:

> "Men brought home to the mines and they brought mining home." This tells you what men talk about and where. They say women are gossips, but we can't hold a candle to men. Those mines shafts held many family secrets, and the underground walls burned with the stories of home life. On the other hand, men brought the mines and the union business home and took their frustrations out on the wife and kids.[50]

For some families, the bars may have served as a buffer between the mines and home. For others, alcohol fueled the frustrations, and wives and children suffered the consequences. Many women of Chuquicamata would appreciate the Butte truism, as they spoke of the numbing and distorting effects of alcohol that flowed through so many lives. A woman friend in Chuquicamata talked often of her concern for the "alcohol problem" in Chuqui and the violence that often accompanied it. It was only after we had been acquainted for months, sharing our firsthand knowledge of our community concerns, that she spoke of her father's slow death from miner's consumption and alcoholism.

Iliana, a lifelong resident of Chuquicamata and union activist in the mines, spoke of domestic violence, child abuse, and alcoholism as common and deeply rooted problems in the community:

> Women carry a sense of blame and shame, and they lack opportunities to create alternatives. Women don't have opportunities to talk about their problems, nor the possibilities for broader participation. And lots of people resist any kind of participation, because they don't like politics that's heavy-handed and ideological. It's hard to get women to participate because they accept violence and alcoholism as normal. They've experienced it for generations, and they don't believe they can change it. It's hard to change this mentality.[51]

Elaine, the wife of a Butte miner, helped me understand why this "mentality" might be so hard to change:

Mining was dangerous. My grandfather died in the mines. My mother and grandmother used to tell me, "Never let your husband leave for work mad." No matter how angry you were, no matter what had happened, you had to put it behind you and tell him that you loved him and kiss him goodbye because you never knew but what it might be the last time you saw him. No problem or fight should ever be so big as to stop you from kissing him good-bye and telling him you loved him. Because no woman wants to live with the guilt of having seen her husband for the last time when she was filled with anger. Don't miss the chance to make amends.[52]

Her words capture the intimate power that kept many women bound to sometimes loving, sometimes violent relations. For some families, the home was a crucible where the painful tensions of outside lives erupted in intimate violence. I am reminded of Robert Lynd and Helen Lynd's poignant description of working-class life in *Middletown*, where hus-bands and wives did not see one another as individuals but as foci of problems and fears (1929, 133). The Lynd's is an apt depiction of many accounts of family life in Butte and Chuquicamata. This description was not limited to working-class families of the mining community: daugh-ters of company men in Butte talked of the insidious alcoholism that invaded family life, and women of Chuquicamata spoke of the "dirty secrets" behind the doors of management homes where corporate images covered a world of hurt.

For other mining families, the home was a work in progress, a place where men and women shared a partnership in building a life together. Elsie, wife of a carpenter in the Butte mines, showed me around her modest home while giving me detailed descriptions of the structural transformation of the house over the years of remodeling. Her husband worked on the house during the strikes. He was forced to retire when the mines closed, but he hasn't given up remodeling: "We've had a keg of nails in the front room for years. He's afraid to finish for fear he will die. He just has to keep extending every project, because what would it mean if he ever finished, what would be his purpose in life?"[53] Elsie's stories echo those of many women of Butte who shared an intimate partnership with their husbands through *doing*, respecting one another's labor as they built a home together. For many, the home-improvement stories were spiced with truths and lies about putting one over on the company as the houses of Butte (not theirs, of course) were built with the company contraband smuggled out over the years in weighty lunch buckets.

These homebound stories of pride in craftsmanship as a space of men's and women's shared intimacies seemed peculiar to Butte. Among Chuquicamatinos, talk of homebound intimacy came through in the stories of family events. It was not the space of the home that shaped the story, but the gathering of family and friends in the celebrations of baptisms, birthdays, and first communions. The home was merely a stage, on loan from the company, for a busy calendar of social events that bound families together in a life outside the mines.

But the mines were a powerful force in shaping intimacy among women and men. In the next chapter, I explore women's community-based intimacy and action. For the men of Butte and Chuquicamata, the terrain of male intimacy seemed to be tightly circumscribed in the space of mines and bars. In the catacombs beneath Butte, men forged intimate bonds. Underground miners worked side by side as partners, often for years, sharing labor, confidences, and fear, trusting one another with their lives, and suffering the losses. Jake and Marty were partners for years, good friends underground and on the surface. Their families got together on Sundays for picnics, the wives and kids eating and playing, while Jake and Marty split a six-pack. Jake told the story of losing Marty:

> We were working together the night it happened. We were working at the 'Con. I helped bring Marty out. I'd helped him get the job just a few months before. Marty had left after the '59 strike and was working out of town. He came back and needed a job. I knew he was a good worker, so I put in a good word for him and we got back as partners again. Then the accident happened right before Christmas and Marty got killed. He hadn't even been back on the job but barely a couple months. I had to go and tell his wife with the coroner. The coroner kept sayin', "Your husband's been hurt," and she kept sayin', "How bad?" and I had to tell her, "Marty's dead."

Jake's wife, Dot, broke in, "Jake didn't want to go back to work after that. He just stayed drunk for three days, right through the funeral. He hated to go back there but he had to. And the day he went back they hadn't even cleaned it out." Jake continued: "Yeah, they were supposed to clean it out with lime, but the smell of death was still in there. And there was all the blood still there and they hadn't touched it. I couldn't work with the smell of death everywhere. I went back up and told them I couldn't work there, so they transferred me to a different level. I never went back there." Dot concluded: "It was such a sudden thing. A fall of ground struck Marty on the head and he was gone. It was so hard to have Jake go back in there, but what else could you do? You just have to live with it."[54]

Lucille saw her husband, Ray, through the strikes and supported him during the dark days after the mines closed in Butte. She was just glad he came out of it with his health after twenty years as an underground miner. He was philosophical about losing his job in 1983, telling Lucille, "Maybe they're doing me a favor." Unlike his longtime partner, Ray came out alive. Through all the tough times, the day that sticks out in Lucille's mind is the day Ray's partner died:

> His partner was killed in a mine blast, and they brought Ray home. He had been hurt a lot of times, a piece of metal in the eye, cuts, things like that, but nothing serious. They had to get him out of there this time. He was like a wild man. The shift boss brought him home. He wanted tea and wanted me to sit with him. They had been partners for nine, ten years. That day is fixed in my mind. Ray couldn't sleep after that, he just kept reliving the moment and the blast and frantically digging, trying to get to his partner. But he made himself go right back to work. He knew he had to go back. He told me it was like being in a car accident, and if you didn't start driving again right away, the fear would paralyze you. It was dangerous work, and lots of times I was scared. If the phone rang late at night, I'd have that fear that something happened in the mines. But his belief was "If the Good Lord wants you, that's it.' He knew the dangers of the mines. We talked about it, and we prepared for the contingencies. But the loss he had that day, that stands out more than anything. After that, I used to talk to him about leaving, but he would say, "Well, the Lord didn't want me, he chose Dan."[55]

Mining men in Butte found intimacy among themselves in their shared stake in daily survival. They sought intimacy with women who comforted them in times of loss.

In Chuquicamata, the dangers of labor activism and political violence often overshadowed the risks of mining itself. The long history of repression suffered by workers, labor leaders, and their families forged powerful bonds of solidarity among men and women. Marta was the widow of a Chuquicamata labor leader executed in 1973. She spoke of the many years of struggle and solidarity she shared with her partner before his death. In 1948, he was arrested during the purge of communist and socialist labor leadership. In 1953, he had to leave Chuquicamata to avoid arrest. In 1966, during the solidarity strike with El Teniente, he was among the labor leaders detained and held in custody for the duration of the strike. After having returned to a union leadership post under the Popular Unity government, he was arrested and executed in the early weeks of the Pinochet dictatorship. A few weeks later, Marta was arrested on false charges while at work in Chuquicamata. She vividly recalled the terror of those years. "They were taking people during the night from their homes. Each morning that I awoke in my bed, I thanked God I was there, I thanked God I was alive. So many people disappeared and died in the night."[56] The deep love she shared with her partner was inseparable from their political commitment. Politics forged their intimacy and mutual respect; that intimacy and respect now fuel Marta's political struggles for truth and justice.

In moments of community crisis in Chuquicamata, gender relations took ironic turns. The working-class men and women of Chuquicamata played with cultural representations of gender that promoted class solidarity and personal safety. Men and women alike tell the story of strikes, scabs, and the rage of women. During strikes where the company hired scab workers, groups of women would surround and overpower the illicit workers. The women dressed these men in women's clothing, with makeup and the works. They paraded these men-dressed-as-women through the town, making a public spectacle of their lack of manhood in their failure to support the strike. They say that the men were so humiliated that they left their jobs and never found work in the mines again.[57]

But a feminine facade could have its benefits for a man. A union leader recalled the state of emergency declared during a strike in the 1960s. The order was given to detain all of the union leaders, and the *carabineros* surrounded the union hall and the mine's huge processing plant. There appeared to be no way out of Chuquicamata for the union men. So what did they do? "We dressed as women to get out. With makeup and everything. We walked out arm in arm with other men, right under the noses of the *pacos* [cops]. And we got out of Chuqui."[58]

This chapter illustrates the dynamics of actors making themselves as they were being made in a complex politics of identification. Their sense of gender and self was not fixed by the time they toddled off to kindergarten, as some theories of development would have us believe. Rather, the formation of gendered consciousness and relations were continually shaped through daily practices of and negotiations with the mining life. Raymond Williams develops the concept of "structure of feeling" to depict the emergent yet inarticulate shaping of self and sentiment through engagement with a myriad of determining social forces. Throughout this chapter, we have seen the seepage of myth and image into gendered consciousness like silica into the lungs of a miner. We have also seen the contestation and negotiation, as women and men talked back to myth and image and crafted their own identities from the cultural materials at hand.

In general, men defined themselves and were defined in relation to their labor, grounded in class-based distinctions. Dominant images of womanhood, bound to cultural ideals of motherhood, have a classlessness about them. Thus the labors of working-class women were often undervalued by their male counterparts, and the very practice of labor distanced them from the images of ideal womanhood. Both class and gender images posed problems for working-class women. Their social practice in the face of these problems is the subject of chapter 5.

Overall, the ethnographic data suggest more commonality than difference in the construction of social actors in Butte and Chuquicamata. However, there is one important difference I want to draw out here. Popular thinking, cultural literature, and to some degree, the ethnographic data here suggest that there is a greater disparity between culturally proscribed gender roles in Chile than in the United States. There is a common perception that a more powerful machismo dominates gender relations. Thus cultural and economic contingencies restrict women in Chile to greater passivity and dependency than is the case in the United States. What I find both curious and important in the ethnographic data is that these cultural representations of gender were mobilized by both men and women as important resources for working-class action in Chuquicamata. Women humiliated men by turning them into women. Men outsmarted men by posing as women. Working-class men and women together promoted working-class power and solidarity by inverting and politicizing the gender images that had carved a fundamental cleavage between them. Their gender play may not have been practiced so dramatically once the moment of crisis had passed. But in that moment, they opened up the possibility that the meaning of gender was malleable and the transformation of gender relations was a politically powerful act.

Crafting the Everyday

Don't you wonder why we ever
Left our job to go and feather
a nest for two (or so we thought)
That old bullshit's a lot of rot.
If I had any sense I'd have
Stayed on the hill
And worked for the cops
Til they invented the pill.
But it's too late now,
It's all in the past,
The damage is done,
The die is cast.

From the "Collected Poems of Sam and Lou," Butte

Sometimes I think of the *pampa* as a woman, the other woman. My husband is with her now and I cannot get him back. Someday I am going to write a poem and call it "Celosa de la Pampa" [Jealous of the pampa].

Member of the Agrupación *of Calama.*

This chapter explores and contrasts women's social practice in Butte and Chuquicamata.[1] I consider how corporate practices shaped the spatial and temporal contours of women's lives and how women crafted community and critical consciousness as they conformed to and reconfigured those contours. Women's many forms of paid and unpaid labor were not "outside" of capitalism, they were at once intrinsic to capitalism and a source of challenge and resistance. Working from the ethnographic data, this chapter focuses on the personal accounts of women in Butte and Chuquicamata from the post–World War II years until the nationalization of the Chilean copper mines and Anaconda's downfall in the 1970s. I then consider shifting forms of women's social practice in light of changes over the past two decades.

This chapter emphasizes the stories of wives and daughters of miners, "working-class women," in an attempt to address the complex interplay of class and gender from women's points of view. The ethnographic data illustrate how the "experience of class, even if shared and fully recognized . . . does not necessarily produce a shared and even consciousness" (Alexander 1994, 276).[2] Women expressed different concerns than men, suggestive of a different relationship to their class position. At times, the class politics of men created problems for women and the practices of women created problems for men.

There is a distinct character to the cultural stories told by the working-class women of Butte and Chuquicamata. Their stories are different from those of working-class men. In turn, they are distinct from the cultural story told by middle- and upper-class women. And, importantly, the stories of working-class women in Butte and Chuquicamata are differently scripted yet complementary, reflecting and challenging their particular relations to men and mining. In their stories are lessons of agency and community building.

A convergence of paternal, patriarchal, and capitalist forces structured women's maternal place and practice as guardians of social reproduction and stewards of community consumption. These cultural representations and corporate practices shaped but did not determine women's consciousness and action. Women were critical actors in their own right, who proved to be much more than strategists seeking personal gain. A better metaphor is that of artisans, creatively engaged with available schemas and resources in life projects of being, doing,. and becoming.[3] Working-class women of Butte and Chuquicamata used their positionalities actively and creatively as bases for constituting meaning and claiming power.[4] They positioned themselves in the ambiguous spaces among competing cultural images of femininity. Women staked claims to the cultural schema of motherhood and mobilized maternal identifications. They transformed the ambiguities of their positioning into resources for creative action and in the process politicized concerns of family, community, and consumption.[5]

I build from aspects of William Sewell's work on structure and agency in my effort to address the "how" of women's agency here.[6] Sewell describes structures as "mutually sustaining schemas and resources that empower and constrain social action and that tend to be reproduced by that social action," though reproduction is never automatic (1992, 19). Following Bourdieu, Sewell holds that human subjects are "endowed with the capacity to engage in highly *autonomous, dis-*

cerning and *strategic* actions" (1992, 15; emphasis mine).[7] He describes agency as the capacity to mobilize resources and transpose and extend the schema of one's particular milieu into new contexts. I draw from the ethnographic data to illustrate how these mobilizations, transpositions, and extensions are imagined and put to practice. I argue that the women of Butte and Chuquicamata crafted self and circumstance through engagement in collective, convergent, and reclamatory actions. Their agency is grounded in and crafted from the schemas and resources available to them as women making a mining way of life. They spoke and acted from their positionality as working-class women to make claims that challenged and at times changed their circumstances.

RHYTHMS OF LIFE

In Butte, thousands of lives were structured around the shifts in the mines and each day was punctuated by the dynamite blast in the Berkeley Pit. As Gladys, a miner's wife told it, the little things made a difference:

> Like the whistles that blew at the mines, the "hooters" my kids used to call them. The hooters blew every day at eight o'clock, noon, four o'clock, and midnight, at the shift changes. And when there was a strike, there'd be that silence, without the hooters that you got used to measuring time by. And you just geared your life around the shift work. When his shift would change, the whole family schedule would change with it. It was hard sometimes to accommodate to graveyard. But you did it.[8]

Strikes were a fact of life for mining families in Butte. In women's stories, it was the memory of the personal and the particular that often served as the mnemonic device for speaking of strikes. Marie, the widow of a miner and mother of five children, recalled strikes in terms of key events in her children's lives: "There were so many strikes, the dates kind of blend together. The only way I remember them is with the kids. Michael was born during a strike; Colleen made her first communion during a strike. Tim graduated from eighth grade. Those kinds of things, those are what you remember about the strikes, . . . those and the tight purse strings."[9]

Strikes signaled a marked change from the noise and bustle of community life during times of employment. Rose grew up in a close-knit neighborhood near the Mountain Con mine. She fondly recalled playing on ore dumps behind her house and remembered the strikes:

One thing I always remember about the strikes, when I was a kid, I thought it was just great because for that length of time there was a strike, this is to a child's mind, it was so peaceful and quiet. Because the damn fans were off. They hummed constantly and you could hear them, they were really loud, they were this noisy, continuous MMMMM all the time. So when there was a strike, oh God, it was so nice and quiet.[10]

But for women like Lil, with her husband out of work and six children at home, the silence was nearly unbearable. Lil talked of a visitor asking how she ever stood it living so near the mines with all the noise of the engines and bells. She replied, "It never bothered us. The only time they ever bothered us was when they stopped. Nobody could sleep. It was horrible. Funny how it shapes your life."[11] The powerful sensory awareness of absence and silence was not tied to dates of a single strike, but to the form and contours of a way of life.

From the early 1950s, union contracts in Butte were negotiated every three years. Life plans were made in three-year increments. Miners' wives built their stories of personal and community life around the tempo of union-company contracts. This cycle can be thought of as a constant rhythm for mining families and merely a recognizable beat for community members whose lives were not directly tied to mining.[12]

Women accommodated to this modulation of life through their vigilance, maintaining a state of readiness and mobilizing their resources when men were out of work. To minimize the uncertainty, women planned and prepared for the possibility of a strike, but the strikes still took a material and emotional toll. Elaine and her friend Dorothy grew up in mining families, and both married miners. Elaine recalled:

It was kind of a way of life. You'd save and save and save. If something came up, you never bought anything you couldn't pay for in three years. You figured there was another contract in three years. So you figured, every three years either a strike or a layoff. You knew, don't buy anything big you can't pay for in three years. You didn't want to get too far in debt.[13]

Dorothy concurred:

I have always worked, just about always had part-time jobs. You really had to, you know; there was that three years. You did fine for three years, and then there was a contract come up. You did the best you could and didn't buy anything big. You got by with what you had. You learn to plan and put a little away. We planned things, you know. That was hard, you know, to have a man around the house every hour of the day. They didn't know what to do with themselves after the first three or four weeks. So little jobs, like painting, didn't cost much, and you could put a little money away for it. We finished the back bedroom one year during the strike. We'd talk about it, "Looks like it's going to go again." We made all these plans, put a little money away. Little things like painting, putting up a fence, those kinds of things. It was after the first couple of months, when money ran out and the little jobs ran out. That's when everybody's nerves started to get jangled.[14]

Women's social practice intensified during strike time as they mobilized networks of kinship and friendship to support family and community through the crisis. While men were idle, women worked overtime, sometimes earning the respect, sometimes the resentment of their partners. Women spoke of their daily negotiations with grocers, bankers, landlords, and utility companies to make minimal payments and hold off debts. For some women, the difficult memories of strikes mingled with fond recollections of the generosity of those who offered material and emotional support. In Louise's memory, it was the anonymity of the giving that she treasured:

> One time the ladies from the women's organization at the church, I belonged to it for years, but I didn't at the time . . . but there was a knock at the door. It was just around the holidays, around Christmas. I went to the door, there wasn't anybody there, but there was a box, a big box. I brought it in and opened it up. There was a canned ham, and all those goodies, you know, for dinner and a little toy for each one of the kids, and that was the most precious . . . I never forgot that. I never did forget that. It wasn't anything big, no big toys or big feast, but it was the thought behind it, to think they were so thoughtful, and I didn't even belong. I was real thrilled . . . I never knew who sent it until years later when I was a member.[15]

The struggles to make ends meet and the importance of family and neighborhood support were themes of several women's accounts: "We had support from my brother-in-law. Like at Christmas time, they'd buy the kids a big gift. One year it was watches. And they invited us to dinner a lot. They'd just make it an invitation, 'Come for dinner,' but it was really to help us out."[16]

The stories of giving without obligation and anonymous generosity show both a concern for individual dignity and a commitment to a community connected in common struggle. Some women talked of support coming from many sources, which often crisscrossed class lines and corporate loyalties, and summarized the situation as "We were all in the same boat." But this vision of a supportive community of little people aligned against the power of the Big Shots is simplistic. For many women, family survival during strike time came down to their dogged and often degrading labors, which clarified both their resentment and their commitment to struggle rather than broadened their visions of a benevolent community. Mary Lou's story is a case in point:

> I remember the tough times during the strikes. And I'm only fifty-six, so I don't know the worst of it like some of the older folks. I don't really know how we got by; you just tried to make it day by day with coupons and strike funds and turning to your neighbors and family for help. You counted on your grocer to carry you. That was called a signover. You would just sign over your check to them once you started working again, and you never saw the paycheck. You spent your time after the strike getting caught up on what you owed. I worked cleaning apartments during the strikes. I never saw a paycheck. It just went toward rent payments. It was hard work; I cleaned apartments in exchange for rent. You would never see a payday. I worked for [a realty company.] They had apartments all over town. . . . There was tons of people in and out of those apartments. . . . It was hard work, and I didn't like it. They would give me a list of apartments to be cleaned, and I would work until I was through. Sometimes I went by myself and sometimes I took the kids, depending on what the situation was. And I never seen a payday. It was just something you had to do. Now, women today work out of the home because they want to and they get a paycheck. But there was so much that women did behind the scenes. And it was not because I wanted to but because I had to in order to survive. I don't think the men really knew.[17]

Many women sought paid work outside the home or, like Mary Lou, traded their labor for the essentials of food and housing. Some who returned to work during a strike kept working beyond the settlement, despite the protests of their husbands, claiming their paid labors as a responsibility of motherhood. Others joined together in an informal economy of exchange of goods and services to ease the burdens of strike time. Informal women's clubs and groups of friends who met regularly for companionship and conversation over the years were key to women's emotional support and became conduits for material support during hard times.

As many Butte women made their transition from miner's daughter to miner's wife, they formed clubs, small groups of old schoolmates and new neighbors. Through their club meetings, women set aside time and space away from their obligations as wives and mothers. In the intimacy of friendship, they sewed, danced, compared notes, and developed critical theories. Jeanne remembers her mother's "club ladies" as an important resource during the strikes:

> My mother, during the strikes she would do a lot of sewing. She made a lot of dance costumes. It was funny, too, she charged according to income or whether she liked you. If you lived on the Westside, you got charged way

more. She took in ironing. I remember my mom mostly sewing, wedding dresses, bridesmaid dresses, that kind of thing, mostly for friends. She never did that for strangers other than during the strike years. She never advertised; it was through her club ladies. . . . That's where a lot of the sewing came from. They would know people and say, well, my mother could use the work. She was a pretty handy person.[18]

Patricia, a miner's wife, also counted on her neighborhood-based group of women friends for support:

It was people recognizing the needs and helping one another. I knew that I could go to my friends and say, "I'm out of this, can I have some of this." We traded and borrowed and handed down clothing. We had a lot of heartaches with it, and we had a lot of fun, too, and it was just something you did. . . . We had so many good times. Getting older, we don't get together so much. Raising families, we didn't have all that much money to go here and go there. So we'd go for coffee. At least once a week we'd get together for coffee, and in the summertime we'd walk every evening. The kids would be ready for bed, and all the women would take off for a stroll. Those were special times. . . . That's far from union work, but it's all part of it. Maybe if we hadn't done those things, we wouldn't have been so close. Now, see, there's a few women whose husbands weren't involved in the strikes, and they were good people to lean on. It made a close-knit bunch, the bunch of us.[19]

Ladies club stories are often richly detailed, mixing memories of illicit poker games and nightclub stops with how-to accounts of craftswomanship: how to make a Martian costume out of old nylons and green food coloring; how to make a Christmas centerpiece out of a bleached Thanksgiving turkey carcass; and how to remake everyday trials and tribulations into poetry. Women carved out spaces and moments outside of their responsibilities as wives and mothers. They came together as women, crafting friendship and mutual support in the time and space apart from the obligations that structured their lives. They drew on their pooled emotional and material resources as they redoubled their efforts to ensure community and family survival during the strikes.

For union men, strikes meant picket lines, odd jobs, and heated discussions of labor politics to fend off the uncertainty of their future. Strike time also offered a reprieve from their hard labors in the mines. George worked for years as a carpenter in the mines and offered his thoughts on work time and strike time:

I could always find good work during the strikes, sometimes out of town. Sometimes I made better money away from The Hill than while I was there. The company usually wanted the strikes, but in the long run they didn't do much good for anybody. The men didn't always mind the strikes, because it gave them a break from the work. So being out of work for a while wasn't such a bad thing. Usually you found some way to get by, like we did.[20]

For women, "getting by" often meant hard work behind the scenes in an effort to maintain routines and create security in a time of crisis. Patricia summed it up well:

> Women played a big role in the background, of saying, "Oh well, maybe tomorrow," and not letting your kids feel you were worried, you know, about tomorrow. I don't think the strikes were done on a whim. It took a big risk, but then you have to take a risk to gain something, don't you? I think where women played a big role was behind the scenes. We'd keep things going at home, keep a routine, keep it just, you know, a way of life.[21]

Women crafted a sense of the ordinary to hold family and community together during the strike. They used their material and emotional resources to create a sense of the possible. They were *artesanas*, craftswomen, reworking the tools and supplies at hand to create new meanings and purpose.[22] They struggled to transform a situation of apparent powerlessness into one in which they exerted control as caretakers. In the face of crisis, women of Butte crafted the everyday.

Patricia's assessment does not suggest naïveté, but thoughtful strategy. Women worked creatively and collaboratively to maintain the daily rituals, the gestures of comfort and safety that might assuage the sense of crisis. Working-class women mediated community conflict during the strikes and modulated rhythms of daily life by accommodating to the cycles of certain uncertainty. They responded with strategic actions and long-term projects grounded in their collective concern for family and community and informed by their grasp of everyday politics.

Perhaps women's practice can be seen as servitude to company interests. I have put forth the argument that strikes served Anaconda's needs when stockpiles were high and copper prices low. Perhaps working-class women and corporate power holders were bound together in an ironic partnership, as women's labor served to alleviate the sense of urgency needed to spur settlement of a strike. But there is more to the story.

After the 1934 strike, the Butte unions and the Anaconda Company reached an agreement that allowed union workers to maintain the mines for the duration of future strikes. Through this structuring of corporate-labor relations, the company protected itself against losses from damage to equipment and operations, and the unions hoped to protect against the company's ever-present threat to abandon Butte. It seems that both unions and company were partners in another critical, if unspoken, maintenance contract: that of community maintenance. The efforts of working-class women ensured the maintenance of community for the duration of the strikes. While union and company men were embroiled in institutionalized powerplays, women were multiply burdened with their responsibilities as caregivers, laborers, and stewards of community.

Women mobilized to preserve family and community life in the short run. In the long run, their efforts served to bolster the structure of corporate-community relations that both devalued and exploited them. Just as the mine maintenance agreements benefited capital over labor, so, too, women's work benefited the company. When stockpiles were high, when prices were low, and when foreign labor forces could be mobilized, women's practices of crafting the everyday served the company well. These practices both defended women's imagined communities and merged with the corporate imagination.

But the story is not so simple. Women were not drones, silently acquiescing to the determined machinations of capital. Another part of women's practice was their talk. Women questioned the rules of the company-union political game. They spoke the unspeakable among themselves and, at times, to their husbands. Working-class women of Butte expressed and honed their critical consciousness as they spoke of men, labor, and power. Though they expressed strong philosophical agreement with the need for and purpose of unions, they often expressed equally strong criticism of union structures and practices. Marie shifted from the talk of strikes to that of unions:

> They got a lot of things through those strikes, lots of benefits that they never would have had, and the unions were strong. But there was one bad thing, one of the worst things about it was that the tail began to wag the dog. Unions were there to control the company, and then the unions were so strong, and . . . it just didn't seem like it was the smartest thing to do.[23]

Louise took a historic perspective in trying to understand union power:

> That's where unions really came in handy. The first number one local, the first Miner's Union in the country, was in Butte. And I've read about it. There were so many bad things they had to do. These men came from all over, and a lot of them could not speak English. Most couldn't read or write. . . . If one or two were told to go into the hole and they knew it was a bad hole, they had to go. What else could they do? So they'd go in, and a lot of them got killed. . . . They were at the mercy of the company. Then, as people got educated and unions got to be more of a big business than a help to the men, it was all a power struggle toward the last. Unions against the company with the worker caught in the middle.[24]

Women offered critical analyses of the contentious relations between union men and company men. Over kitchen tables and fence posts, while changing hotel and hospital beds, women talked about unions, the company, and the blind spots of men. Some of their critiques were harsh: "The unions would control the men. It wasn't a case of the men controlling the unions or the unions helping the men. The unions more or less told them what was going to happen and how to vote. So we [the women] were not real happy about this. . . . We could see the situation from a different point of view."[25] And together, the women examined the situation:

> My neighbor and I, we'd get together, and her sister and my sister, we'd all get together. My sister had the same problems I had. If you mentioned anything against the unions, my brother-in-law had a flying fit. You could see it was a dictatorship, you know. "You do this and you do that." On the other hand, it was the company saying, "You do this and you do that." They were kind of squeezed in the middle. But it took the women to see what was happening. But the men wouldn't listen to us, of course.[26]

Nell summarized more than forty years of discussion about the unions and the company:

> My husband was a fanatic. My dear, if I dare say, "Oh, the unions don't do anything for you," he'd have a worm! He held small offices, a union man through and through. And if I'd start saying the union doesn't do a darn thing for you or you should fight for this or that, he'd say, "Well, the heads of the union know; we go by what they tell us. They know what they're doing." . . . Now, unions are fine, and I don't say unions didn't do a lot for the men in years gone by. The company used to make slaves out of people. But, you know, like anything else, whoever has the monopoly goes nuts with it. You've noticed that . . . whosoever has got the monopoly.
>
> Oh, I agree with unions. They got us better wages, but when you had a grievance, they'd never fight for you. That is, the union I belonged to. And I really don't think the unions worked hard enough for the men on The Hill either. They could have done a lot more for them. Better conditions, better working conditions. Of course, my husband didn't have it all that bad, but when he was underground, it was no party for him either. The unions did an awful lot. Many years ago when my father was a young man, they didn't even have a good place to change clothes. They came out all wet. They didn't make conditions good for them until the men got organized and really fought for their rights. Then, in later years, it was all dollar signs, all they wanted was a paycheck.
>
> That's what I could see. I'd always say to my husband, "It may be true they need this or that, but why don't they fight for conditions and never mind an increase [in wages], because you lose it the first time you go shopping."

They don't even consider the small stuff and it adds up and eats them alive. Without the unions, the men in the old times, if they hadn't been organized, they'd be the same as slaves. But when capital has the reins in their hands, they go nuts with it, and when labor has the reins, they go nuts with it. It's the power, you see.

My husband used to say to me, "Oh, you just don't have any faith in the unions," and I'd say, "No, I don't," see. "I'm not that close to it. I'm further back than you are." His union, or any union on The Hill, they were too close to it to see what was happening. If you stood back and saw what was happening, that's where I got my ideas. He'd say, "Oh, don't be running down the unions." And I'd clam up then. What's the use of saying anything? One time I said to him, "Union men are like a bunch of sheep. One guy leads them and they just follow along." That's what sheep do, you know, you get two or three sheep going and they're all off and going! And he didn't like being classified as a sheep![27]

Women built their critical consciousness from childhood onward, as the rhythms of mining life shaped their youthful views of gender, labor, and power. Kay was the daughter of a mechanic who worked in the Berkeley Pit. She identified the roots of her own political activism in her childhood exposure to labor struggles. She described the heated union discussions in her home among her father and uncles. Kay would take up her strategic spot on the dining room floor, inconspicuous with her book for cover, her attention riveted on the men's talk in the front room. She recalled the tension and fear that would burst forth in angry accusations from the men as they pieced together rumors about strikes and layoffs. As tensions built in the front room, Kay would move to the kitchen, where the women gathered:

The women were busy, and they were working and resentful and angry and scared. So when this stuff started coming down, what I remember about the women is them being real secretive, whispering a lot. The men would be in the front room and the women in the kitchen, and they'd be whispering, and even when they talked to the kids it would be in whispering tones. We had to be quiet so we wouldn't irritate any of the men. It was like walking on egg shells, and it got worse and worse before the strikes. And then once the strike happened, that meant they drank a lot and there was no money, and the woman was angry and the guy was angry and it was an ugly cycle.[28]

As women talked back to unions and company, they offered an alternative vision, a different "common sense" regarding the gendered structures and practices of power. Though they spoke astutely of the contradictions that left their men "squeezed in the middle," it appears they only partially grasped the contradictions in which their own lives as working-class women were embedded.[29] In their stories, women positioned themselves outside the concerns of labor and capital that dominated the men's world of mining. Yet women's social practice was critical to the maintenance of that world. Their redoubled efforts enabled a union-company stand-off, and many women suffered the violent consequences of men's frustrations on the homefront.

At the same time, women played with those contradictions and ambiguities. They drew on "naturalized" images of womanhood and motherhood as they mobilized efforts for family and community survival. As "good mothers," they transposed the schemas of womanhood, claiming greater space in the labor market and recognizing caregiving as a collective concern. They also challenged the defining cultural schema of motherhood as they crafted the separate spaces of feminine intimacy. Together they claimed their positionality as women and honed their consciousness of the politics of production and consumption.

WOMEN'S SPACE

A different structure shaped the contours of women's lives in Chuquicamata. Chuquicamata's social stratification was carved into the physical landscape. As we have seen, during Anaconda's reign in Chile, workers were divided into Rolls A, B, and C, and housing was assigned according to one's Roll. The difficult conditions of *Las Latas*, the worker housing discussed in chapter 3, represented the rule rather than the exception for Roll C families. The *Dos Miles* was another typical family neighborhood for Chuquicamata's working class. The 160 compact units housed upwards of eight hundred people. A common bath and shower facility served the entire neighborhood. A communal faucet supplied water for washing clothes and dishes. Many women gathered *yareta*, a natural fuel source found in the desert, to use with makeshift stoves set on their small patios. In the women's words: "There was a water pump on the corner, and we'd carry water to do the washing. There'd be women at the water pumps at all hours of the day, women in their crooked, broken-down shoes, from standing all day. Women's work was very hard." "We came to Chuquicamata in 1956. We lived in *Los Adobes*. There were baths and showers on the corner, with a canal running underneath that carried the water downhill. The women's showers were above and the men's below. The women would go down together to the shower and watch out for one another."

When we first got married, we lived in a single room in Calama. Then my husband got on with the mines, and we got a one-room apartment in Chuquicamata, with bath and shower on the corner. . . . We had the two little ones in this one room for four years. Then we got a one-bedroom apartment. My husband plumbed in a makeshift sink, so I could do the wash at home. Our house was the most popular place in the neighborhood because we were the only ones with running water.[30]

The working-class women of Chuquicamata tell a distinctly structured story of personal and community history during the Anaconda Company years. Their stories resonate with the double discourse of praise and resentment. They describe the era as *muy linda* (very lovely), a time of community solidarity, culture, and streets teeming with people. Women also speak of the harsh climate, "even worse than now," with wind, sun, and dust that pocked the skin. Central to every woman's story are the daily lines at the *pulperías* to secure supplies for their families. This is a story not told by mining men, nor by management wives.

For the wives of Chuquicamata's miners, waiting was women's work. Given the scarcity of basic goods available in the company stores, women had the full-time job of waiting in line each day in order to feed and clothe their families. The unions had won price concessions, and thus the *pulperías* offered a better deal than the public markets of Calama. But basic goods were rationed, and shortages were a chronic condition. The structure of life during the Anaconda years forged powerful memories for many Chuquicamatinas. As I was taking photos of the abandoned remains of *Dos Miles*, an older woman stopped and told me her story, which echoed those told by other women of Chuquicamata, capturing hardship and reward in the same breath:

I came to Chuquicamata in 1936. Before, it was a wonderful place, full of life, not like now. The wind was awful, the dirt and rocks would go right through your skin. . . . Over there was the *pulpería*, and we would wait in line for hours. Word would travel fast when new things arrived, like shoes for the children. You could buy shoes for almost nothing, a couple of pesos, but you had to get there early. So there we'd be, waiting in line in the middle of the night to get shoes, or whatever. It was quite a time. And at Christmas, Chile Exploration Company had big parties for all the children. Each child got a gift. For *dieciocho* [September 18, Chilean Independence Day], each child could get a new set of clothes at the *pulpería*. Chuqui was a different place in those days.[31]

Clarita, now in her forties, was born and raised in Chuquicamata. As the oldest daughter, she spent many hours waiting in line:

There were always lines, lines of women and children every day. And sometimes there would be fights between women over a place in line. It was com-
ical, women hitting each other and pulling hair. But there was support, too,
and lots of conversation and trading of places in line. What I remember most
is the women knitting. Almost every one arrived in line with her knitting, and
there'd be the clicking of knitting needles up and down the line. There were
lines for everything. It started at dawn and lasted all day long. In order to buy
the better stuff, you had to be in line real early. I remember that they'd arrive
early in the morning and then sell the place in line. That was a business for
some of the older kids. I used to do that sometimes to get extra money. But
most of the time, the older girls had to take care of the little kids at home
while their mothers waited in line. There are a lot of women around my age
that had a lot of responsibilities at home during those days. And because of
their experiences, they're really responsible, especially those who were the
oldest in their families.[32]

Mrs. Morales, the widow of a miner and mother of five grown children, worked her daily shift waiting in line:

Each day I had to leave the house before dawn. I would go at five o'clock in
the morning to wait in the lines at the *pulpería*. There was a line for milk, and
one for bread, meat, clothes, everything. The only way to get the things my
family needed was to wait in the lines. Lots of times it was a bad situation,
with spoiled food, like the rotten meat brought in from Mexico. Sometimes
we had to eat buffalo. But at the same time, it was the only thing available
for the family, and you had to eat what you could get at the *pulpería*. And the
pulperías corresponded to the Rolls in the company. The gringos always got
the best of everything. But in the worker's *pulperías*, we got what was left. It
was short on quality and quantity, and for this I had to arrive early every day
and wait. Every day the streets were filled with women and children in line.
Sometimes the older children would look after the younger ones at home.
    My brother lived with us for a while. He couldn't find work in the mines,
and so he helped out with the family income by working in the line. Each day
he'd get to the *pulpería* at dawn and sell his place in line. There was a lot of
support among the women in the lines. We saved spaces for one another.
There was lots of conversations about family troubles and such. And we'd
exchange recipes. There was solidarity among the women in the line. It was
the same thing with the *ollas comunes* [soup kitchens] during the strikes.
Sometimes, my older kids would sell places in line, too. In those days, the climate in Chuqui was even worse, because the dust was so bad. And the
women would be in line every day with the dust and the sun and the wind for
hours, to get whatever their family needed. But there were good times, too.
Like when the whole family was working together. I would make sopaipillas
and empanadas and things like that, and my older children would sell them
on the street and in the line.[33]

Mrs. Morales's talk of politics was closely tied to her daily experience of waiting in line. She told me that things got better when Frei was president (1964–1970): "The food improved and the lines got shorter. Frei was a good man." It was also during the late 1960s, after serious labor conflicts, that workers of Chuquicamata won the right to own their own homes and secured corporate concessions to significantly improve company housing.

For miners' wives, waiting was a full-time obligation and a measure of the good mother. Their experiences were distinct from the structures of privilege that defined the daily practices of "homemaking" for management wives. Esperanza, who worked for years in the *pulpería americana*, offered her insights into the structure of privilege:

> I got a job in the *reparto americano*, that was the part of the *pulpería* where we took grocery orders by telephone from the gringa ladies. Most of them didn't speak much Spanish, so I took their order by phone, then wrote them down in Spanish for the other employees. There was one woman, from Argentina, who was more gringa than the gringas, real uppity. When the other girls received her calls, she would only talk to them in English, even though her English was bad and the girls couldn't understand anything. But when she spoke to me, she spoke in Spanish, because she knew I could speak English.
>
> The grocery delivery operation was big. We took the orders by phone and then we had a schedule each day to go door-to-door with deliveries of fresh bread, milk, and eggs. Lots of times, the gringas didn't advise us when they were going to be out of town. And we'd go with the delivery and find yesterday's bread or milk at the door, spoiled. Some of them were real good about it, but others acted like it was our fault and refused to pay for it.[34]

The women of the American Camp did not define their womanhood by waiting in lines, nor did they have to witness the daily ritual of Chilean working-class women for whom waiting was part of their unpaid labors.

Lines structured the social space of working-class women's daily practice through which they maintained community ties. At the water pumps, showers, and *pulperías*, women built solidarity through their public practice of domesticity.[35] The lines are elaborating symbols in the stories told by women of Chuquicamata.[36] They define both the stage and experience in which women were publicly "positioned" and through which they positioned themselves as community players. Women transformed the lines into economic resources and sources for social support. As they were being together, doing "what working-class women do," they were becoming critically conscious actors.

Their stories speak to the rawness of the desert clime that penetrated their flesh and to their daily witness to the markers of difference. The lines graphically symbolize the locally situated inscription of class-based womanhood in Chuquicamata. Working-class women came together in the lines to fulfill their obligations as wives and mothers. Their legs bore the weight of waiting in broken-down shoes. Women of Chuquicamata were well aware that waiting in line was not a "natural" condition of womanhood but a product of historical, political, and economic circumstance. Through their daily experience of distinction and convergence in the lines, women recognized the disparities between the cultural images and the social realities of womanhood. They claimed the resource potential of this ambiguous space and transformed their positionality into a "weapon of the weak."[37]

Strikes in Chuquicamata were shorter and more frequent than in Butte.[38] They do not modulate the stories of community life in the same manner as in Butte. In Chuquicamata, women and men alike spoke of the key importance of women's behind-the-scenes support for the duration of the strikes. As in Butte, most claimed that women did not involve themselves "directly" in labor actions. However, the anecdotal stories suggest otherwise. During strikes in Chuquicamata, women moved from the *pulpería* lines to the *ollas comunes* and thus extended their responsibility for consumption from the family to the community: they gathered food and organized soup kitchens in their neighborhoods and at the union hall and, in so doing, transformed their stewardship of family and community into a political practice.

Just as women positioned themselves each day in lines and at water pumps, during strikes they positioned themselves between their men and violence or as aggressors in defense of men's labor. When Mrs. Morales spoke of the violence and repression in Chuquicamata in the late 1940s, she also spoke of women's protective role: "The women tried to protect the men and hide them out. And when the police came to the door, it was the women who would meet them and cover for the men. Sometimes the men had to leave the area to avoid arrest."[39] Likewise, Clarita recalled a moment during one of the strikes in Chuquicamata that vividly captured her belief in the strength and activism of the women of Chuquicamata: "During one strike in Chuqui there was a big march. The women positioned themselves at the front, rear, and sides of the marchers, sandwiching the men in the middle. The women were protecting the men from the *pacos* [cops]."[40]

As we have seen in chapter 4, at times women went on the offensive for their mining men as they surrounded and attacked scab workers and dressed them as women. In moments of forceful, class-based alliance with their men, women of Chuquicamata appropriated masculine power and humiliated their enemy by feminizing him. In critical moments, women came out from behind the scenes and placed themselves on the front lines in solidarity with and protection of mining men.

Like the women in Butte, the women of Chuquicamata formed their own critical consciousness, talking among themselves at the water pumps and in the lines. Despite the vivid images of class-based solidarity described previously, women's talk revealed their skepticism of power and their alternative visions of community concerns:

> You know, there were a lot of strikes during the years of the gringos. But I don't think they served the workers very well. In their petitions, they always asked for more money, or other benefits. And if the company didn't agree with them, there would be a strike for sixty days, the legal limit. It was like a fiesta, with the *ollas comunes* and a spirit of community. Usually the women didn't take part in the strikes, but they managed the *ollas comunes* at the union hall, and everybody would gather there. And there was always a man from the union outside peeling potatoes. There was a lot of support during the strikes, lots of camaraderie, but things didn't change. What bothered me most was the housing conditions, like *Las Latas*. . . . Sometimes I would complain to Mrs. Johnson [gringa for whom she worked] about the bad conditions there, and she would tell me, "It's your own fault. If the unions asked for better houses instead of money in the petitions, they could change the bad situation in *Las Latas*." You know, she was right, but it took a long time to change things. In the last years of the gringos, they built houses in Calama, good, solid houses.[41]

Sometimes, the women of Chuquicamata and Butte spoke virtually in unison: "The women always saw the need for improvement in living conditions rather than higher wages. The women in Chuquicamata didn't concern themselves much with the strikes. They had other concerns."[42]

As in Butte, some women spoke of forming their critical consciousness through their childhood experiences:

> I've lived in Chuqui and Calama more than thirty years, but my strongest memories were formed earlier, when my family was living and working in the nitrate mines. . . . I remember one strike there, where there was a big people's march, with women and children, too, and they surrounded the boss's office. The working and living conditions were terrible. There was a long history of *ollas comunes* and strong solidarity. When I was thirteen, I started looking for work to help support the family. Then we came to Chuquicamata, and my father worked in one of the offices. He didn't receive a very good salary, but the situation was better than the nitrate mines, and the *pulpería* had good

prices and whatever we needed, so my family lived better here. But Chuqui
was different from the tough life in Iquique. People here were accustomed to
another lifestyle. They were more materialistic. They could buy whatever
they needed at good prices, and there was a lot of waste. People here didn't
keep the leftovers from one meal to the next. I had never had the luxury of
extravagance, and I didn't like it. I had learned hard lessons at a young age
about the value of food and clothing and the experience of hunger, and I
couldn't go along with this way of life.[43]

For some, those early lessons were tied to a critical understanding of
corporate and state power:

I remember finding this drawing; it was a map of Chile with a giant
Anaconda wrapped all around it. The head of the Anaconda was in the
north, and it was eating Chuqui. I didn't understand it and showed it to my
father. He explained it to me. I'll never forget that image. Then another time
I found this cartoon; it was of your Uncle Sam carrying away something like
a sack full of copper, and he had a baby in his arms, and the baby was Chile.
I used to talk to my dad about those things, and I learned a lot about politics
from him.[44]

There was another register in women's discourse in Chuquicamata
that pointed to an additional facet of their "in-betweenness" as working-class women. The women of Chuquicamata were beholden both to
corporate paternalism and to their often precarious marriages to mining
men. Working-class women of Chuquicamata were a miner away from
poverty. In many ways, the Anaconda Company played "responsible
father," positioning working-class women as responsible mothers and
their mates as irresponsible sons. The *compensación de la mujer*
rewarded women for mothering and provided a financial safety net
against the errant ways of their men. Likewise, the *pulperías*, the
Christmas gifts and fiestas, and the new clothes at holiday time bound
women as mothers to corporate benevolence. In short, Anaconda was a
more reliable provider than many a husband. But the husband provided
the necessary connection to corporate resources, both material and
"cultural." Women's stories often suggest their awkward position in
between vulnerability and power:

I was widowed in 1959 and went to work as a janitress in the school in
Chuqui. I worked there until 1974, and then everything changed. Lots of
widows worked as janitresses, or cleaning the public bathrooms, things like
that. It was humble work, but we earned salaries equal to the men. The company was good that way. A widow could get by. But you only had work as
long as you were in Chuqui.[45]

• • •

We came to Chuqui in 1956. It was a hard life here, but Chuqui was a wonderful place then, with the orchestras and the dances in springtime and the
celebrations for May Day. . . . Then my husband left me with three small
children. It was a very hard time. When my husband left me and left his job,
we couldn't stay in our home in Chuqui. I went to Calama with my children.
I worked all day every day doing whatever work I could find to support my
family. I did washing, ironing, worked as a maid. I still don't know how we
survived.[46]

Women of Chuquicamata shared their burdens as women within the
contours of a paternalistic, quasi-caste system. Anaconda crafted a community that put women in their place. Yet, at the same time that the
company was crafting its stratified community, it was also engendering
a power base of women. Women were willing to claim their rights and
obligations as women and mothers. They were willing to stand with,
perhaps in front of, their men to fulfill their obligations as protectors
and conservers of community life. As protective mothers, they
attempted to keep their sons from danger when the corporate father of
the "great Anaconda family" turned malevolent.

WOMEN AND ACTION

Crafting the everyday was a key social practice for women of the mining communities, one that points to commonality and illustrates important differences in the structures of women's lives. Whereas Butte
women came together in temporal rhythms, women of Chuquicamata
built solidarity through the spatial structures of their lives. Through the
gendered spatial and temporal structurings of their lives, they both
responded to and challenged the problems they confronted as working-
class women. The women of Butte mobilized efforts in order to modulate community life, maintaining the rhythms of daily life when the
crises of a strike threatened community survival. In so doing, they
expanded their positions as laborers, caregivers, and community
builders. The women of Chuquicamata responded to and challenged
their subject positionings by positioning themselves as protectors. They
claimed the public space of their domesticity as political space and social
space. As the women of both communities mobilized their "feminine"
positions as conservers of family and community integrity in support of

working-class men, they broadened their own claims as women to a greater share of social, political, and economic power.

By 1971, the spatial and temporal structuring of women's lives was encountering fissures and arrhythmia. The year marks a critical juncture in this story of transnational capitalism. The interlocking history of Butte and Chuquicamata was about to be severed. Nationalization of the mines was imminent. Allende's election in 1970 spurred an exodus of Yankee managers from Chuquicamata. In Chuquicamata, the Popular Unity government was incorporating into its political discourse women's social practice as conservers of community. Party representatives called on women's political engagement in housewives' committees and *pulpería* committees to address problems of management and shortages. On the eve of nationalization of the mines in July of 1971, Chuquicamata was struggling with shortages and looking to women to position themselves between scarcity and need. But the paternal provider had abandoned the women of Chuquicamata and taken the resources with him.

In Butte, workers faced another strike and new uncertainties as Anaconda's Chilean wealth and corporate future were called into question. Women's long-standing practices of forging normalcy in the face of crisis would not be enough to maintain the familiar rhythms of community life. Two stories in particular offer intimately connected examples of women's social action at this key moment. These stories embody the traces of their histories in Butte and Chuquicamata and point to their tellers' skills as craftswomen, creating new forms of practice in the face of new kinds of problems.

The moment is July 1971, days prior to the nationalization of the mines. While reading news accounts of this moment in Butte, I came across a front-page article and photo of women picketing the community hospital as an angry doctor protested the picket line. The accompanying article reported that the women were angry because the hospital had announced it would accept striking Anaconda Company employees only on an emergency basis. One of those women was Mary Lou. Twenty years after the fact, I called on her and asked to hear the story of the picket. She replied, "I just did what I had to do. People were on strike and families were hurting and it was just plain wrong for the hospital to refuse service to anyone. I got my stubborn Irish up and decided I wasn't just going to stand by. I even surprised my husband." Mary Lou got some cardboard, sat at her kitchen table, made posters, called friends, and started a picket in front of the hospital. "And boy were some of those doctors mad. Dr. C, boy was he mad. He was yelling at me and shaking his fist and telling me to go home. I stood my ground, and I was just shaking inside, and my knees were weak, but I knew I just had to stick it out. It was hard to do, but we won."[47]

Through perseverance, Mary Lou and the women who joined her won the reluctant support of the men's unions and got the hospital to change its policy. Mary Lou's move from behind-the-scenes labor to public protest was informed by her personal struggles during previous strikes. Her life had been profoundly shaped by the three-year cycles of life in Butte and her unpaid labors that kept her family housed during the long months of those strikes. Mary Lou had learned that her dogged labors were no longer enough to protect what she held sacred: the health and safety of her family. Speaking from their positions as mothers and caregivers, Mary Lou and her supporters crafted a strategy drawn from the resources and schema of "masculine" labor struggles in Butte as they claimed the community's right to care as a political issue.

I was thinking of Mary Lou and her work to politicize women's concerns as conservers of family and community while reviewing news accounts of this key political moment in Chuquicamata's newspaper, *Oasis*. I came across the story of Berta, a community activist who organized a housewives' committee to address skyrocketing food prices in Chuquicamata in July of 1971. Berta talked of arriving in Chuquicamata with her family at the age of fourteen and going to work as a maid. She recalled the frequent food shortages, waiting in long lines in the *pulperías*, and the times that the residents had to eat buffalo. She credited the concerted, tireless work on the part of workers and housewives with improving the situation.[48]

Berta was no stranger to struggle. She recalled a strike in the 1960s when she joined with other women to take action. It was during a solidarity strike with the miners of El Teniente, when the community of Chuquicamata was in crisis. Berta joined with seven other women to start a women's movement. They went door-to-door during the night, calling on other women to join the movement. The women began a march from the *pulpería americana* and were driven back by police forces. Berta's clothes were ripped from her, and when she kept going, clad only in her slip, a police officer struck her so hard that he broke her tooth. But she and the other women persevered with their struggle and gained concessions from the company that alleviated the crisis. The experience fueled her commitment to struggle for women and workers.

Now, in 1971, the community faced another food crisis with accelerating inflation and a cost of living that impoverished miners and their families. Clearly, Berta was a supporter of the Allende government and the process of nationalization, even though the community was suffering the results of economic pressures on the government. Much as the Anaconda Company had strategically used the press to serve its interests, the Popular Unity party used Berta's testimony in the newspaper now under its editorial control to serve its political interests. But an important shift had occurred. Berta was doing more than voicing the party line à la Juan Minero. She directly criticized the shortcomings of the current government, made a political issue out of the *pulpería* lines and food shortages, and called for women's participation in a political process. Berta spoke as a working-class woman from the position of her public domesticity to claim her rights as a political actor.

So in early July of 1971, as Mary Lou stood on the picket line in front of St. James Hospital, Berta went door-to-door, organizing women to combat rising food prices. Both women crafted new forms of political action for and through their practice of the preservation of family and community life.[49] They both accommodated to the conditions of their lives and mobilized to change those conditions, strategically and creatively reworking the materials at hand.

In crafting the everyday, the women of Butte and Chuquicamata also crafted themselves as critical actors and carved out a broader space for women's social and political action. The practice of crafting the everyday was not merely something women did by virtue of their sex. It was hard work that demanded daily physical labor and critical analysis. It was a vigilant practice through which one builds consciousness of power, vulnerability, and possibility through careful action and reflection. Arbitrary constraints and demands on women's experiences were never naturalized. Rather, they fueled the formation of critical consciousness and the search for novel resources and possibilities for action. Just as mining men wrested copper from the ground, women extracted and forged the resources of community from the raw materials at hand. Women positioned themselves in the social world, spoke from their perspectives as women, and used that knowledge as the motive force for repositioning themselves and challenging their circumstances.

Let me return to the questions of agency raised earlier in this chapter. First, agency is realized through *artesanía* (craftswomanship), a situated process of working from the constraints and possibilities of positionality and creatively defining and mobilizing the resource potential of the situation. The selves envisioned and created by the women of Butte and

Chuquicamata are not autonomous individuals in search of personal interests. They are both social and "dividuated" selves, complex and creative works in progress. They lived the contradictions of mining life, forged facets of their "dividuality" in the interstices of that life, and crafted their agency through relationships and collective concern.

Second, Sewell's notion of discerning actions places the emphasis on analytic capacity. These women's stories speak more to convergence. Critical consciousness developed as women made connections among the cultural and corporate forces that shaped their lives. They spoke to the connections of union and company power and to the interpenetration of capitalism and patriarchy (though not in so many words). As women lived with these convergences that structured time and space arrangements, they built a critique that challenged the naturalization of the arbitrary, even as that critique was limited by their very positionality.

Third, as women developed and carried out short-term strategies, they engaged in reclamatory action. Their strategies were part of larger life projects through which women made claims as women, mobilized and challenged cultural schema of womanhood, and broadened the bases from which to stake future claims in the process. Through their practice, women made claims about the meaning of community, the rights and needs of their families, and the politics of consumption. Their critical engagement with the relations of consumption was a long-term, collective project, one that illustrated the craft, politics, and possibility of human agency.

STRUGGLES ON SHIFTING GROUND

Over the past twenty years, Butte and Chuquicamata have weathered profound changes, with powerful impacts on women's lives. *Comparison* strikes me as far too pale and inadequate a word to use in sketching the changes occurring in Chuquicamata and Butte during the 1970s and 1980s. The violent repression of the dictatorship constituted another magnitude of difference from the social and economic dislocations experienced in Butte. Yet the relationship between capitalism and community was shifting dramatically under dictatorship and democracy, as were women's experiences and actions. At the risk of gross oversimplification, I offer glimpses into this critical era.

From the early 1970s until the closure of the mines, Butte experienced a phenomenon of loss that many have described as a "collective depression." One cannot read the local news of the 1970s without feeling that depression's weight as labor force cutbacks and rumors of Anaconda's precarious stability chipped away at community integrity. There were plans to relocate Uptown Butte, the heart of the city, to make room for more mining. The company's threat to pull out if the community did not make concessions forced the hands of local decisionmakers. Fear and uncertainty kept churning as news of more layoffs became a monthly event. Then the music stopped.

Despite a decade of slow and painful fadeout of mining in Butte, few were prepared for the silence. People in Butte spoke of the shock they felt when the mines finally closed. Mining men waited in the hopes that the mines would reopen, or tried to find work elsewhere. Many men spoke frankly about the depression they suffered at the loss of their livelihoods. Many women became both the emotional and financial caretakers of family and community. And some suffered the blows as men's pain erupted in intimate violence. While Butte men left their families in search of work — often temporary labor in construction or in other mines — women stayed behind, maintaining family and community on limited means, single parents by default rather than choice, in this respect not unlike the women of Toconce.

During this time of community crisis, a group of women joined together to address violence against women and to create a safe space in the community. They built an "underground" network of women and founded a shelter, naming it, fittingly, Safe Space. Women made connections between life in the mines and women's struggles where the dangers and fears in both mining and massive unemployment manifested themselves in family violence.

Rather than retreating behind the scenes once a crisis has been weathered, women now stake permanent claims to the political and economic space of community. The rhythm of community life has shifted, and with it, so have women's claims to community. Women are building economic bases and organizational competence to promote and sustain small businesses and to support and train others entering the formal labor market. Women are working to reclaim and document women's labor history in Butte. Newcomers are joining with longtime residents to spearhead important community development projects, with women's interests in mind. Many continue their behind-the-scenes efforts, whereas others have moved to the public arena, winning posts in city and county government. Working-class women of Butte have left a rich legacy of community action and support. But just as the rhythms of life that modulated their action have faded, so too has the class-based experience of female consciousness grown more diffuse. A sense of middle-class professionalism now dominates the image of women's practice. Critical lessons of community building are embedded in the stories of working-class women. This chapter constitutes an initial reclamation project of working-class women's stories, documenting the meaning and power of their craftswomanship.

The military coup and ensuing years of the dictatorship produced deeply felt ruptures in the social fabric of Chile — ruptures with profound implications for women's social practice. I grapple with ways to write about the numerous accounts I heard that described relentless assaults on the daily lives of so many people.

My own introduction to Chile's desert north was profoundly impacted by my encounter and subsequent friendships with members of the *Agrupación de Familiares de los Ejecutados*, who have been in the vanguard of struggles for social justice from the moment their histories were fused through state violence. Our conversations took us directly to the heart of their pain and struggle. In conversations with women in other circles, our talk of the years of the dictatorship was often obtuse and indirect, the reflections growing more intimate with our relationship over time.

Some women talked of shock and disbelief, of crying every day and being unable to eat, the world as they had known it gone, and new people, new rules invading community life. Others told of the arbitrary arrests and detentions, as remote desert villages were transformed into makeshift detention camps. Some heard the screams of the tortured in police headquarters, and others heard and saw nothing at all. Daily life for many became a relentless series of intrusions as state surveillance penetrated the home. For others, life went on, and they slept better, knowing that order was being restored.

Many say that you didn't know whom you could trust. Parents practiced censorship in the home and coached their children on what could and could not be said. Some took direct action, with varying degrees of success. Others learned new forms of vigilance. Families were split apart through their knowledge, action, and silence. It was the "drop of water, every hour, every day, eating away the rock, drip, drip, drip." It was the "loss of our ability to think for ourselves, the loss of our creativity." And as more than one person summarized those seventeen years, "We suffered from a collective psychosis, and in many ways we still do." Many blame the dictatorship for the erosion of the community solidarity that characterized Chuquicamata during the Anaconda years.

Though fear penetrated daily life, women and men made delicate movements around the edges of the talkable and do-able. In spite and because of curfews, censorship, and sanctions against public and private gatherings, some came together in twos and threes, perhaps to do ironing or care for a sick friend. Cautious encounters in taxis provided time and space for cryptic exchange of news. Through these fragile networks, they fortified their vigilance and strategized direct action. The mass mobilizations that eventually wore down the dictatorship were not spontaneously generated but the results of a myriad of practices, of vigilance more relentless than the surveillance to which it responded, the crafting of trust in the face of unspeakable betrayals.

Some women were direct targets of state violence. Others learned to practice unrelenting vigilance as they searched for family members and struggled to stay alive. They sought out spaces in the shadows where they could give voice to their fear, outrage, and claims for justice. Others, both because and in spite of their fear, risked everything to position themselves between their loved ones — the *detenidos, desaparecidos*, and *ejecutados* (detained, disappeared, and executed) — and the violence of the military state.

Through many nights of tear-filled conversations, a friend and member of the *agrupación* told me her stories of suffering, struggle, and action. She is a widow of Calama: her husband was among the twenty-six men executed in Calama on October 19, 1973, by an elite military squad authorized by the dictatorship. Their men's bodies were rumored to have been buried in the desert. My friend recounted her first trip to the desert, to publicly acknowledge the deaths and begin searching for the bodies, an open challenge to the dictatorship:

> There was a small group of us that went to the edge of town. Others were too afraid. I was so filled with fear, I could hardly move. I thought, "What if they kill me? What if my children lose their mother, too?" But I couldn't not go. In spite of our fears, I took my friend's hand and the two of us set out for the desert. We had to act. We had to say, "We are here, and we will be here." Little by little, others joined us. And then there were five women in the desert. We didn't know what would happen, but we began to dig. We had a couple of shovels with us, and we started the search. Among those who joined us was a photographer, who managed to take a few photos without getting caught. Those photos were published in newspapers everywhere; they circled the world.
>
> We got to Topater [the site in the desert] around three o'clock, and more people joined us. When the afternoon shifts changed, miners from Chuqui came and joined us, and so did the folks from CUT [*Central única de tra-*

bajadores, national labor confederation]. By early evening, there must have been one hundred people or more. By dark, they encircled the area with their cars and trucks, their headlights lighting up the spot where we were digging. It was a sight to behold. After that we returned every day. We never knew if we would be arrested or what. We took turns, working shifts in the search.[50]

That day in 1985 is also engraved in the memory of her friend who led that first walk to the desert. In the ambiance of our afternoon conversations, amid coffee and cigarettes, she recounted the moment as if it were yesterday:

It was April 7, 1985. There was going to be a meeting of the women's organization of Chuquicamata that night. I had been elected president of the group, though I'm not sure why! That was the same day we began to search in the desert. The meeting started at eight o'clock that night. So I went to the meeting, all dirty from digging in the desert. I was sick and exhausted, it had been such a day. But I had to speak. So I talked about the only thing I could talk about, our first day of digging for the bodies in the desert. The auditorium in Chuquicamata was full. There I was with my hair and clothes covered with dirt. I told them a little of the history of the *agrupación*. There were men and women crying in the audience. And people began to give their own testimonials.

The meeting went late. After the meeting, we marched out to the plaza in Chuqui. And people shared more testimonials. . . . And the *pacos* came and started breaking up the meeting. But the women, they were so filled with rage, they went after the *pacos*. Women got in their vehicles and went after the *pacos*. They scared off the *pacos*. The men, they had come along to support the women, but they were left behind on the sidelines, just watching the women![51]

The efforts and outrage of these women helped to fuel a new wave of resistance that culminated in a massive march from Chuquicamata to Calama on October 9, 1985, in protest of the dictatorship's repression and the economic plight of the miners. More than five thousand women, men, and children joined in the march from the union hall in Chuqui. They walked ten miles through the desert to Calama, planning to rally in Calama's central plaza. The military forces did not intervene in Chuquicamata but attacked the marchers as they entered Calama. Participants described the air thick with tear gas, the beatings, and the detentions that resulted. Some participants lost their jobs or were threatened with firing and subjected to police interrogations.

The climate of repression intensified. But the cracks in the power base of the dictatorship had widened. Women had risked everything to position themselves directly in the face of brutality, because the power and meaning of survival dictated that they could not do otherwise. As my friend summed up her actions in the face of fear, "We women have changed the course of history in the country" (see fig. 22).[52]

I strive but fail to put an analytic frame around these profound moments of women's action. The women's stories, their continuing struggle for truth and justice, and most simply, our friendships, have touched me deeply. Perhaps I could write of their move to publicly position themselves as women, mothers, and widows in the face of the masculine brutality of the dictatorship. But it sounds too pat and simple. It smacks of smug understanding on my part of daily life under a dictatorship, when in fact the stories I tell and images I present are my effort to reconstruct the poignant moments and conversations that penetrated and challenged my ignorance. I am only able to write out of love and respect for these women and their courage. I hope that these glimpses bear some trace of the meaning and power of their acts, standing together in the desert, exposed and vulnerable, publicly claiming the truth, tragedy, and injustice of their losses.

Women's social practice in Chuqui has outlived the dictatorship. Although many women lament the breakdown in community solidarity and the lack of women's social participation, others are taking action. Networks of women in the forefront and behind the scenes continue to work for the preservation of family and community in Chuquicamata. In the spring of 1993, in Chuquicamata, I had the privilege of joining a group of miners' wives who organized to demand answers from CODELCO regarding the community impact of the Cultural Transformation of the Labor Force. The women had concerns about the meaning behind the words in the company propaganda. And they had grown frustrated with their husbands' passive, if disgruntled acceptance of the changes. They organized a public meeting for the women of Chuquicamata in the union hall, invited heads of the corporation and the unions, and asked the hard questions. They invited other women to join them in demanding a voice in the decisions that affected their lives.

It was in their behind-the-scenes planning that I saw familiar practices. Talking around the kitchen table, the women shared their fears of public speaking and helped one another prepare their presentations. They listened to each other's family problems and helped find practical solutions. They recalled the days of the *ollas comunes* and the secretive strategies they had used for organizing during the years of the dictatorship. They talked about what worked and built their action plan. They

Figure 22. Memorial to men of Calama executed October 19, 1973, Calama municipal cemetery (author photo).

drew on knowledge accumulated over the years and shaped by their collective life experiences. They used their status as women to claim their
right to participate in the corporate change process. Once again, women
were positioning themselves in the face of male power to politicize issues
of family and community life. But is women's social practice ever
enough? Or is it eventually consumed by forces bigger than we are? I
turn to this question in the following chapter.

SIX

Miner's Consumption

Once Butte was one of the wildest, richest boom towns in the West. But now there is an atmosphere of age and tiredness about the place, a feeling that the very earth you walk on is worn out from too much mining, that the air you breathe has gone stale from too much steam and ore dust, and that even the people are running low on energy . . .

I arrived in Butte in the middle of a "wildcat" strike that shut down the hill for three days. Groups of men in dirty work clothes stood around on downtown street corners or sat at the long wooden bars of the city's myriad taverns, drinking 10-cent beers and looking bored and depressed and very much like stage versions of surly, out-of-work Irishmen.

Hunter S. Thompson 1964

Chuqui is a different place now. There is no community anymore. People lack conscience and responsibility. Lots of people are seriously in debt. Everything used to be the responsibility of the company — water, electricity, health — everything. They lived a dependent life. Now people have to take responsibility for themselves and can't manage. They're in debt, and get credit on the black market. Everybody is competing with their neighbors to see who has the newest car and the fanciest clothes.

Chuquicamata miner's wife 1994

The depreciation of the human world progresses in direct proportion to the increase in value of the world of things.

Karl Marx 1844

Miner's consumption is the popular name for silicosis among miners in the United States. Silicosis is a prolonged and often fatal illness caused by the inhalation of silica particles, or mine dust.[1] It is death by slowly wasting away. Consumption is also a powerful metaphor for the ways in which political and economic forces have affected peoples' daily lives.[2] In this chapter, I examine miner's consumption both literally and figuratively. First, I consider the illness itself in the context of the dangerous world of hard-rock mining. Then I explore the many and varied manifestations of symbolic consumption in the stories of Butte and Chuquicamata. Consumption is a key theme in the body politics and cultural contradictions that have historically confronted social actors in the mining community. Miners' bodies have been both site of the structural contradictions of capitalism and a measure of exploitation as their lungs were eaten up by their labors. Women told different stories of consumption that reflected both their relations to men and their experience of class.

Residents of Butte have witnessed the consumption of the space they called community, and Chuquicamatinos spoke of the consumption of community solidarity. At present, a dominant discourse in both communities is that of the consumption of community values and the loss of their mode of life. This chapter links ethnographic data to fundamental predicaments of consumption in which gender and class relations are embedded. As Ann Stoler notes in *Capitalism and Confrontation in Sumatra*, the language of consumption is used to express numerous asymmetrical relations (1985, 197). It is a powerful idiom that links meanings, feelings, and material conditions. Attention to the cultural politics of consumption in its many guises sheds light on the noneconomic aspects of exploitation and helps us get inside the "feeling of structures," those embodied, felt, and lived realities of a toxic way of life.

MINING AND RISK

Accidents, from infamous fires and explosions that claimed many men to the litany of daily casualties that stole single lives and limbs, have long been a familiar part of mining history. According to Barbara Kingsolver, between 1961 and 1973, more than half a million disabling injuries occurred in mines in the United States, nearly twice as many as occurred among U.S. soldiers in the Vietnam War (1989, 4). Throughout these chapters, I have illustrated the losses and the concomitant fear and bravado that define the mining "way of life." The violence of the mines has mixed with family, barroom, street, and state violence in crafting a context of danger and defiance. Community histories have been punctuated by tragedies of material and human force, but miners and their families have been victims of a slower, more insidious form of wasting: consumption (see fig. 23).

Miner's consumption was the biggest killer in the mines, yet the

Figure 23.   First aid competition, Miners Union Day, Butte, 1952. Courtesy of Butte Historical Society, Butte Labor History Project Collection.

Anaconda Company refused to acknowledge it as an occupational disease until the 1940s (M. Murphy 1990, 10–11). Thousands of men died young as a result of "the con," the colloquial term for consumption in Butte. Others lived out their years, dying slowly from the disease in hospitals and asylums. In Chuquicamata, many people I spoke with volunteered an unsolicited story about losing a father, grandfather, or uncle to silicosis. Their talk of the illness indicated that the weight of its tragedy is still felt in the community.

In Butte, the stories of miner's consumption filter through family histories and have been documented in public health and welfare records. In a 1921 public health survey of Butte miners, 42 percent of the study's volunteers were found to have miner's consumption (Brown 1979, 23). From the 1940s to the 1960s, the Montana State Welfare Department, not the Anaconda Company, shouldered the burden of pensions for the state's "silicotics." In 1942, of 267 active reported cases of silicosis in Montana's fifty-six counties, 173 were from Butte (Silver Bow County).[3] The sufferers received thirty dollars in monthly aid from the state. By 1960, there were 722 cases in the state of Montana, 552 of them from Butte. The labor press *Mine-Mill Butte Miner* took the company to task over the issue in 1956: "Public welfare benefits are running nearly half a million dollars a year. September public welfare records show 604 silicotics. Of those, 436 reside in their home county of Silver Bow. ACM's profits are at an all time high. It's time the company paid the bill for silicosis."[4] Anaconda responded that the numbers were high because the county was adjacent to a state treatment center for tuberculosis and other chronic respiratory illness, thus the figures for the region were merely inflated. But the thousands of miners who gave their lungs to the mines knew differently.

Numbers do not tell the story of men's wasting. The stories are told by their families as they recall witnessing virile men eaten up by their work. As they say in Chuquicamata, the pay was good, but you paid with your health to work there. Dot, a retired nurse's aid in Butte, would agree. She met her husband when she was working in the hospital in Butte and he had been hospitalized for a mine-related injury. She worked on the miners' ward, which was always full. She recalled seeing sights from the mines that she will never forget. There were always young men on the ward who had been injured, and there were always older silicotics. Some of them had been there for as many as five years, just waiting to die (see fig. 24).

Dot's recollections echo those of women in Chuquicamata. Geromina, the miner's wife from Toconce in the Atacama Desert, spoke of her husband's illness from the mines: "We went to Chuquicamata and my husband worked in the mines for ten years or so. Then we came back here because he was sick. He came out of the mines with green teeth. Later he had to drink wine to wash his stomach out. He was always, always sick and he couldn't work anymore. He died in Antofagasta" (Valdez, Montecino, de Leon, and Mack 1983, 57). Her account speaks to the physical wasting of mining men that need not bear the name "consumption" to capture its corrosive force. The exploitative nature of mining was located in the bodies of men: the greater the production and profit, the more men were consumed. As Marie astutely observed in her critique of corporate greed, the length of an Anaconda Company man's life stood in inverse relation to his physical and social distance from the mines.[5]

At times, men's bodies were politicized as consumption shifted from illness to issue. Consumption became a political concern when the 1954 strike took up the issue of smoke and dust in the mines caused by indiscriminate blasting. In 1959, men's lungs became the site of another form of union-company struggle. In this instance, the Butte unions had an ambiguous position regarding the health risks of men in the mines, as

Figure 24.   Miner's consumption, Butte. Courtesy of
Butte Historical Society, Butte Labor History Project
Collection.

revealed in an article in the *Butte Miner's Voice* on "blackspotting."[6]
There was considerable strife among union men regarding a company
decision that senior miners receive X-rays to determine the condition of
their lungs. Those whose X-rays showed "black spots" would be dismissed from their jobs, supposedly for health reasons. The union interpreted this as a company ploy to get rid of senior employees, who cost
them more in wages and benefits. In dismissing such men, the company
would also ensure that they retired before they were eligible for a full
pension. The men, knowing they would fail the health exams, wanted to
refuse the X-rays so that they could continue working. The union's challenge in this case was a boycott of the mandatory X-rays so that the men
and the company would not know who had "black spots" and the com-

pany could not discriminate against senior workers. The report on the issue indicates that it would be rare for an older worker *not* to fail the exam. It is ironic that the refusal of diagnosis of a chronic illness or health risk would be turned into a union victory. The union won the right for men to risk their lives in unsafe conditions so that they might get a full pension should they live long enough to retire.

The bodies of Chuquicamata's miners were also the sites of struggles between unions and the company. Correspondence from 1949 in the Anaconda Company records discusses complaints of dental, eye, stomach, skin, and respiratory problems brought against the company as the result of working conditions in the mine's processing plants in Chile. The company dismissed the complaints, stating that "the condition of the mouths and teeth of these men is no worse than that of any other group of workmen in Chile, and we do not believe that it is in any way attributable to the atmosphere in which they work."[7]

It is important to note that although such cases are part of the historical record, they were not often the subject of fieldwork conversations in Chuquicamata. People tended to speak of and accept such illnesses as part of the nature of mining. Many praised the excellent health services available at Anaconda's Roy Glover Hospital in Chuquicamata, which was known throughout Latin America for its top-quality medical facilities. When residents leveled criticism against the company regarding mine-related illnesses and health care, they spoke against the current operation of the mines. Many claimed that the health care they received "during the good old days" was superior to that which they receive at present. Despite historical records of claims against the Anaconda Company, its image appears unblemished at present when compared to the "new order" in the mines.[8]

CONSUMING WOMEN

One of Butte's copper kings once claimed that the "measure of arsenic in the smoke [from the mines] gave Butte women their beautiful, pale complexions."[9] Butte women, however, were not so readily charmed by the benefits of their toxic way of life. They spoke not only of the mine dust that sucked the life from their men, but also of more subtle forms of wasting. Many recalled the consumption of worry as they struggled to hold body and soul together. Lenore, a Butte miner's daughter, spoke of her mother's struggles:

It's ironic, here after all these years in the mines, my father is a trim and healthy man and it's my mother who suffers from health problems. The stress and the worry of the years show in her body; they've consumed her health. She was the one who had to do all the worrying and make sure the family got by. If it weren't for the women in Butte, like my mother, the men would never have survived. My mother, like most the women here, took care of everyone else's needs first, and her own needs always came last. She just got what was left at the end, and sometimes that was very little. My father was a typical miner. His word was final, he worked hard and drank hard. But things changed dramatically when he walked away from a dynamite blast that should have killed him. It changed his life. He found religion and quit drinking and smoking. He was sort of a different person after that. . . . My mother went to work nights in a restaurant. My father wasn't happy about it, but mother was a determined woman. She wasn't about to face the financial problems they had been through during some of the strikes again. After all, she knew what it had been like. She had been the one to swallow her pride and stand in line for the welfare checks. The men would never go for the welfare. It was the women who were always swallowing their pride because you can't feed children on pride and they would not let their families go hungry.[10]

The women of Chuquicamata spoke of being consumed with worries, but in a context of the powerful consumptive force of the desert climate itself. It was the incessant wind, dust, and sun that created the backdrop for women's stories of their labors and lives. It was the altitude that took its toll over time on the lungs, leaving people unfit to leave and live elsewhere. Some spoke not of changes, but of continuity over the years. The gringos have come and gone, and Chileans are now in charge. But the physical and social consumptive forces of life and labor in the desert remain a troubling constant. Sylvia, a longtime resident of Chuquicamata, offered her critical feminist perspective on this way of life:

This harsh and isolated terrain presents a challenge to people who arrive here from other parts of the country. Among women, there's a high incidence of depression, alcoholism, and other forms of stress and emotional problems. There are high rates of domestic violence, too. But the big cultural lie among the upper class here is their denial of the reality of these problems in their own lives. There is a lot of pressure by the company to demonstrate marital harmony and stability among its executives. A single or divorced person isn't going to advance very far in the corporation. The social life of the executives and their wives, they are 99 percent men, is important as another representation of power, and it's important to show the happiness and stability of this power as the natural order in the community. So there is no recognition of the serious problems in these families with alcoholism, depression, violence. All that remains in the shadows, a dirty secret. The big lie is to say that only the lower-class people, those without culture, are the people who suffer these problems, as if it were a symptom of their ordinary status, their inability to comport themselves correctly. Then it's important for the upper class not to manifest these symptoms. Its like the emperor's new clothes: nobody is able to say that he is naked, they just live the lie. And it's a lie that causes women lots of suffering. They are the victims and participants in a system of servitude to maintain the masculine power on which mining was built. . . .

In every part of Chuqui, there are problems with physical and emotional health and without adequate resources to deal with them. . . . Here the practice is to ignore the problems. There are health problems that affect the whole area, but the company doesn't recognize them. The silicosis is obvious, but there are other problems, like high rates of petit mal epilepsy among the children and psychological problems, lung disease, arsenic poisoning. Every aspect of life is hard. The people who live at this altitude for many years have lung problems when they return to sea level. They are accustomed to the altitude, but the fibers of their lungs have become rigid. So in climates at lower altitude with more humidity, they get sick. Many people have to return here to survive. And then the people from other parts of the country talk about Chuquicamatinos as *los privilegiados*. They have no idea of the reality of life here. It's a life so demanding and difficult, a life that consumes the people and absorbs all their energy and demands all their energy in order to survive. Nobody would live here by choice; people live here because the riches of the country are here. Without the mines, nobody would submit themselves to this artificial life created just to exploit copper. The image of privilege is a lie.[11]

Other women of Chuquicamata spoke more personally of being consumed by the desert and by their isolation in this men's world of mining. Many of the women I met had come to Chuquicamata with their husbands from other parts of the country. In some respects, this isolated mountain desert was as foreign to them as it was to the Yankee women who arrived over the years. Miners' wives carved out spaces of sociality in this hostile terrain as they waited in line each day. Management wives defended themselves against the consumptive force of the mines by carving out spaces of friendship and sociality with other women through the creation of formal women's organizations. As previously mentioned, *Chuqui Ayuda* is a women's voluntary service organization that assists children with disabilities. In its fifty years of continuous operation, the organization has provided a service to the community and a means through which middle- and upper-class women could craft their own gendered social space in spite and because of the mines.[12]

Volunteers at *Chuqui Ayuda* spoke of their sense of dislocation and isolation upon arrival in Chuquicamata from other parts of the country. Their emotional survival depended on their determined efforts to build a life outside of the mines, to carve a sense of themselves on this bleak terrain before it consumed them. Some women spoke of the power of those consumptive forces in spite of their best efforts at resistance as the desert sucked away their health and fertility. Women shared their intimate stories of miscarriages, their inability to support life in this unforgiving place that consumed their life-giving capacity. In one touching account, my companion talked of the fetus itself not having the "will to live" and simply giving up on her. She had to get tougher, grow stronger, to nurture a life capable of surviving in the desert. In Chuquicamata, the socialization to a toxic way of life begins in utero.

CHILD'S PLAY: DANGER AND DEFIANCE

Miners faced their dangerous work with an air of bravado that masked their fears. That bravado was cultivated from early on as the youngsters of Butte and Chuquicamata, risk-takers extraordinaire, claimed slag heaps as their playgrounds. Young and old alike speak with fondness of those days of digging in the silty yellow-brown soil that left them stained to their skin. While guiding me on a tour through Chuquicamata, a third-generation Chuquicamatino stopped at the base of the *ripios*, the steep flat-topped hills of mine tailings, and told me a story:

> That was our favorite playground. The game was to toss a tin can as high up the hill as you could, then run up the steep slopes to retrieve it. The company didn't like us up there. They used to water the *ripios* to keep us off, but it didn't work. The train ran right along the top, above the *ripios*. The kids would grab stuff that fell by the wayside. Sometimes, when the ore [in the train] was really rich, these bright blue streaks of copper water would run down the *ripios*, and it looked just like a watercolor painting.[13]

Slag heaps were child's play. Older youth preferred to up the ante in their derring-do. Women and men alike in Butte talk tough about their gritty amusements, with a mix of humor and pride in their capacity for survival. Francie, a witty, assertive professional woman in Butte, told her stories of risk-taking:

> And you know, when we were kids, up above our house in the back, in between Anaconda Road and the Belle Diamond [mine], was the copper ponds, and we used to go swimming. And then my mother used to get so angry because my brother, the only thing left on his jeans were the brass little pieces of buttons, and the pants just got eaten alive, and the tennis shoes. Back then the kids wore the black canvas tennis shoes, and the eyelets would rot out of them. And they didn't last three weeks. But I didn't see a lot of the copper ponds. We went over to the cement ponds that were on Anaconda Road. That's where the company had its own cement company. And they

went up and emptied their trucks out, and it was wonderful because it ran downhill. And when they flushed the trucks out the cement that wasn't used eventually made a wonderful cement pond. So then we would go up after that shift closed down, and we would turn the hoses on and fill that with water, and that's where we swam. And so I was telling my kids about it. . . . And my oldest says, "Well gee, that wouldn't have been as bad as swimming in the copper ponds." And I said I guess it all depends on how you look at it. Because the cement ponds were full of lime. So whether it was the copper eating away at your clothing or the cement pond, one or the other, that's just what we did.[14]

For youngsters in Chuquicamata, the escapade more daring than their play on the *ripios* was clandestine entry into the American Camp under cover of darkness. This private world of the Yankees was more prohibitive and thus more alluring than the mine itself. Many a story is told of reconnaissance missions to see how these foreigners lived in their private world.

Schools may have launched children on their long, forced march to their place in the working world. But their makeshift playgrounds gave them early lessons in danger and defiance, inculcating the risk-taking spirit demanded of hardy survivors in the mining community. And yet, adult stories of youthful bravado are tempered by sober talk of the risks mining has posed to the health and safety of children and adults. These risks are current topics of concern in both communities. Given the data available on Butte, their concerns are well founded. A health survey that assessed mortality rates in Butte relative to the 480 largest U.S. cities found that Butte had the highest mortality rate for all diseases in 1949 to 1951 and in 1959 to 1961; Butte ranked fifth in 1969 to 1971. In diseases other than heart and kidney, Butte ranked third in 1949 to 1951 and first in 1959 to 1961 and 1969 to 1971. Butte's rates of cancer were significantly higher than the national average — especially cancer of the lung, trachea, and bronchus among both men and women during 1970 to 1979 (Moore and Luoma 1990, 179–83).[15] Anecdotal data from local health reports suggest that Butte's children may also suffer from higher-than-average rates of respiratory illness, neuromuscular disorders, and cancers. I have no corresponding health data from Chuquicamata. However, the concerns and suspicions voiced by community residents echo those expressed in Butte.

Women of Chuquicamata talk of the high rates of cancer, seizures, minimal brain damage, and other health problems among their children. They say that everyone knows that the problems are related to the mines. They criticize CODELCO for failing to take responsibility. Many speak skeptically about the health care they receive in Chuqui, claiming that the physicians are under pressure to avoid diagnoses of illnesses that are costly to treat. There is a common belief that the company avoids responsibility for health risks posed by the mine for its residents. Likewise, in Butte, though the health department continues to document the high levels of heavy metals in the bodies of children near the town's most toxic sites, corporate players prolong their legal wars over culpability. Each resident has her story of unexplained cysts, the presence of inexplicable forms of cancer, and as she talks, she looks knowingly to the mines for the cause. The shadows of doubt have been broadly cast over the bravado of Butte and Chuquicamata, now that the copper has been consumed and residents are left to pick up the pieces of their lives among the toxic residues. And many continue to do as Geromina's husband: they wash out the toxins with alcohol. As one Butte woman put it, "Mining and drinking always went hand in hand. The mining stopped, but the drinking hasn't."[16] Throughout the mining history in Butte and Chuquicamata, alcohol consumption has both numbed and concentrated the damages of a toxic way of life.

LUNCHBOX MEMORIES:
FROM NOSTALGIA TO PRIVATION

Consumption in a very concrete sense played out in the recollections of mining families. I was struck by the meaty litany of lunchbox stories I heard from longtime residents of Butte and Chuquicamata as their memories took them back to tender moments with their fathers who worked in the mines. Colleen told the "poke pasty story" of the miner who was the envy of his friends. Every day at lunch, he had a nice fat pasty, and there was always a big chunk of beef poking out the end. While his companions ate their pasties filled with potatoes and onions and just a hint of beef that made them crave more, this miner munched on a pasty so full the meat was falling out the seams. They didn't know that the tasty morsel was the only beef in the whole pasty, carefully tucked in at the last by his wife. If you can't have the meat for flavor, at least you can have it for show.

Maggie recalled the poignant lunchbox stories of her father's childhood. He would meet his father after shift each day, and the two walked home together. It was always a treat to find a morsel left in his father's

lunch bucket. He would search for a piece of cake or other sweet that
had been in the lunch bucket all day long. It would be covered with the
soot and grime of the mines, but that didn't matter. He would just brush
off the black and eat it anyway.

Lenore and Francie got around to their own lunch bucket reminisc-
ing as they talked of their fathers:

LENORE: "My father always brought me something out of his lunch
            bucket, always saved something."

FRANCIE: "Yeah, it was wonderful, wasn't it?"

LENORE: "And it might be half a Twinkie, a piece of an orange slice, it
            didn't matter."

FRANCIE: "And as soon as he came in the door and put the bucket down,
            I would be there to see what I got."

LENORE: "And we used to fight because the first one there would be the
            one who got it."

FRANCIE: "Now, see, I didn't have to [fight], because my brother wasn't
            there with his eye on the bucket like I was."

LENORE: "I can remember with my Dad, we could just walk right down to
            the mine yard and wait for him. We'd walk to the street where
            the dries [changing rooms] were and wait for him to come out of
            the dries."[17]

Their stories were echoed a continent away as the women of
Chuquicamata talked of fathers and food. Cristina and Iliana, both
daughters of miners, and Iliana's husband talked about growing up in
Chuquicamata during the gringo years:

CRISTINA: "My father worked for CHILEX. We were poor but had a good
            life here. I especially remember when my father had to work the
            night shift. He got these packets of North American cookies in
            his lunch, and he would bring them home with him. They were
            a special treat for us."

ILIANA: "Yeah, I remember those cookies, too. As kids, we didn't have
            much of an idea about our father's work, but I remember those
            cookies. I can still see the package and the brand name."

HUSBAND: "Yeah, lots of things have changed. When the gringos ran the
            mines and you worked night shift, you got *onces* [teatime meal],
            a good lunch with tea and dessert, a whole meal. Now when I
            work night shift I get a sandwich and that's it."[18]

Lunchbox nostalgia is closely tied to distinction and deprivation in
the accounts of community consumption. Stories of the token treats in
the workingman's lunch in Chuquicamata often led to recounting of the

vast array of Yankee products readily available in the American Camp, in contrast to those available to the locals, who got just enough to pique their appetites and make them crave more. In Butte, folks recalled that the Big Shots did not go hungry during the strikes. Food stories in their many forms point to the prominent place of consumption in making and maintaining the distinctions of cultural and material capital.[19] Residents' stories of hard times reveal how fine a line there is between a politics of envy and a politics of survival.

For many women, the lunchbox nostalgia of childhood helped to counterbalance the more painful memories of privation that came later in life. Much like the *pulpería* stories of Chuquicamata, where quality and availability of food was a daily reminder of one's place, the stories of strike time in Butte bring back poignant memories. Stories of family and neighborly generosity are interspersed with those of scarcity. Statewide union efforts brought in food for distribution through the local halls. Some men turned to hunting and fishing to supplement the family diet. Many families received commodities distributed through the union and in more recent years were eligible for food stamps. As Butte women tell it:

> Kids today don't know what it was like to go through strikes and stand in line for food even dogs wouldn't eat. And to get coupons from the union to buy your food. It's true, we would stand in line to exchange [coupons] for food, and we had this little dog, and even the dog would not eat the canned meat we were given.

• • •

> We used to get commodities, corn meal and rice. So we'd use a little bit of corn meal and a little bit of rice and put the rest in the basement. I used to pray every night that it wouldn't rain because the whole house woulda rose! And the powdered eggs, which you couldn't eat, only used them for baking. I remember one time we had a dog, a big black lab. And we weren't buying any dog food because we were barely buying our own food. So we gave the dog corn meal. He ate corn meal and powdered eggs for a while. Even the dog hated to see a strike coming.

• • •

> Now my husband's family . . . they had six kids. He remembers eating powdered eggs and leaving the table hungry. There were so many of them you didn't want to eat too much, especially with your younger brothers and sis-

ters. He ate a lot of cornmeal. He still likes cornmeal, but never did care much for eggs. . . . There was no income coming in and just government surplus to feed the family.[20]

Throughout the histories of these mining communities, from the housewives' leagues in Butte to the *ollas comunes* in Chuquicamata, women have mobilized action around issues of consumption. In their roles as stewards of family and community life, women shouldered the responsibility for consumption. Working-class women were closest to the realities of food and hunger and made relations of consumption a public issue. Though relations of production were challenged, negotiated, and suspended, issues of consumption could only be attenuated for so long without dire consequences. It was through women's vigilance, support, and mobilization that practices of consumption were maintained even when production was not.[21]

In a material sense, the working-class women of Butte and Chuquicamata might grasp their deepest understanding and experience of class relations through their relations to the means of consumption. Miners' wives were the ones who went without as they tried to "maintain the routines" and "keep things going at home." They crafted cornmeal in its many guises and went hungry when commodities ran low. They stirred the pots in the soup kitchens and were last in line to eat. Whereas the bodies of men were consumed by the mines, the bodies of women were consumed by worry as they straddled the competing demands of production, consumption, and reproduction.

I recall a conversation with a former union leader in Butte. I asked him what happened during the long strikes in Butte. How did the community survive? He told me of pickets and marches and the actions of men. Then I asked him, "But tell, me, how did you survive day by day for nine months without a salary?" After a moment of silence, he said, "Well, I guess you'd have to ask my wife." And therein lies the crux of gender distinctions that cannot be grasped by treating relations to the means of production as the defining feature of class conflict. For it is in and through relations to the means of consumption that working-class women often lived the contradictions of capitalism even as they worked to protect their loved ones from its impact. The responsibilities of preserving family and community life involved a stewardship of consumption. Working-class women struggled with the material realities of that stewardship in ways that neither their partners nor middle- and upper-class women had to experience.

COMMUNITY CONSUMPTION

The consumption of community has taken many forms. By its very nature, the production of copper is an exercise in consumption on a grand scale. The ever-widening open-pit mines stood to community residents as icons, indices, and symbols of consumption. In its twenty-five years of operation, Butte's Berkeley Pit consumed a number of neighborhoods that had been three times that long in the making. Thousands of residents were forced to relocate and suffer the loss of their sense of place. The company's right of eminent domain left residents with few options but to accept the price offered for their homes and to resettle. For many, the sense of loss ran deeper than displacement from houses and the disruption of neighborhood ties. As former residents of East Butte and McQueen, two Butte neighborhoods, described:

> From East Butte to Meaderville and McQueen, they are part of the Pit now. Other people get displaced by renewal projects or whatever, but at least they can go back to the physical place. They can say, "This used to be my home." Even if it's a different building, they can still stand on the spot. But not Butte, it's eaten up. The ground isn't there anymore. It's hard to orient yourself to where things used to be. Those moves were hard on people.[22]
>
> Butte lost three parishes to the Berkeley Pit. The loss of St. Helena's, Holy Savior, and Sacred Heart were the greatest travesties and tragedies of the company's actions. Those parishes had bound people together, and then they were displaced from so much more than their homes. They were displaced from the neighborhood, community, and parish that linked them all together. I know a man who went to Sacred Heart church, and he still blesses himself when he passes by the area where the church used to be. To him that was a sacred spot and always will be, but the company had no respect for those sacred places.[23]

Throughout the 1970s, as Anaconda scrambled to recoup its Chilean losses, the people of Butte lived with growing uncertainty regarding copper production and community consumption. The language of consumption was a key metaphor in the daily news. In 1970, Anaconda claimed the Berkeley Pit as Butte's "bread and butter." The company announced plans to expand the open-pit mine westward, encroaching on the Uptown Butte business district, and eastward, in the direction of the Columbia Gardens. Company spokesmen emphatically stated that "the Continental Program would not involve the picturesque Columbia Gardens itself" and that there were "no plans for the pit to gobble the mining city."[24]

Those plans changed. The company did not expand westward. By

1974, several underground mines were closed and the company initiated its new open-pit mine to the east, swallowing up the charred remains of Columbia Gardens in its path. The sense of betrayal runs deep in local accounts of the loss of this community treasure:

> What happened with Columbia Gardens is a good example of the company not caring about people. That place was a natural wonder. I used to fix picnic lunches and go up to the Gardens with my husband after work. We'd sit under the trees and watch the kids play. It was a special place, and we had a lot of fun there. The fire was a terrible thing. I don't believe for a minute that those horses [from the carousel] burned. Nobody ever saw them. I've heard they were taken out of there and sold to places on the coast, and maybe Denver and down in Florida. And then they didn't even mine there for more than a year, and the project was abandoned. But there is no replacing the Gardens.[25]

• • •

> The worst thing the company ever did to Butte was destroy the Columbia Gardens. It meant so much to people. I remember going with my mother to the courthouse to see the page in the record book where W. A. Clark deeded the property to the people of Butte. Then when push came to shove and the company wanted that land for mining, that page mysteriously disappeared. And there was no proof that the land had been deeded to the city. You know, all those horses and biplanes and stuff weren't destroyed in that fire. They were out of there and into the hands of people with power and money before that place ever burned. I think most of them went back east to New York where the Anaconda Company had connections. There are people who know what happened to those horses, and they were worth something. There was a fellow, one of the electricians called up there after the fire. The word had been given that the fire started from a faulty transformer. He had inspected all the transformers, and none were faulty. His conclusion was that the fire had been set. I went up there with my sister the last weekend the Gardens was open. That was the Labor Day weekend in 1973. They had plowed out all around there and there were big trucks and equipment. You couldn't sit anywhere because they had taken out the benches. But in an area that had been leveled, I saw one of the poppies growing, just the one. I figured it had been part of that beautiful butterfly. I told my sister I was going to have at least some part of the Gardens that would survive. So I got down and dug it up and was going to take it home and plant it. Then this guard comes up to me and wouldn't let me take it out of the ground. What was the sense? They were just going to destroy it. But he said no, I couldn't remove anything from the grounds. And that's my last memory of the Gardens.[26]

The loss of Columbia Gardens stood to the community as a powerful symbol of corporate consumption, imbued with the familiar pain of trust and betrayal. With an intensity stronger than when speaking of loss of parishes, people of Butte spoke with a deep resentment of having lost a sacred place when the Gardens were consumed first by fire and then by the open-pit mine. Columbia Gardens symbolized community, a shared space of sentiment, attachment, and celebration, a place where public and private memories were made on the common ground of life outside of mining. With its destruction, many came to the troubling conclusion that nothing was sacred: not even the very survival of the community was safe from corporate consumption.

People of Chuquicamata talk a different language of consumption. Only recently has the open-pit mine graphically gnawed away at the substance of community as it did in Butte. As a company town, Chuquicamata has been at the direct mercy of the corporate landlords, be that Anaconda or the state. The built world of Chuquicamata has not served as a site of struggle over company and community interests in the same sense as in Butte. Conversely, as the substance of community was being consumed in Butte, community was under construction in Chuquicamata. Chileans joined Yankees as consumers of culture in the Chile Theater. Bit by bit, residents saw community improvements, including the well-built, durable houses constructed in 1967 and 1968 as a result of union victories.

The stories of community consumption in Chuquicamata begin after Anaconda's departure. Some stories speak of a community consumed by disorder and confusion during the Popular Unity government. Many speak of a community consumed by fear during the dictatorship. Consumption took other forms as well. For example, the production of copper directly feeds Chile's military machine. In the early years of the dictatorship, legislation was passed whereby 10 percent of the country's earnings from copper production would go directly to support the armed forces. The all-consuming force of the military was fed on the labors of Chuquicamatinos. Gains for the military were made at serious costs to workers. As one Chuquicamatina described, "The years of the dictatorship didn't serve CODELCO well, but CODELCO served the dictatorship well with its copper. The operations of CODELCO went downhill during the years of the dictatorship from the workers' point of view. They didn't gain anything, and they lost status and power. The unions don't have the power they had in the past."[27] The copper tariff that benefits the military remains in place, much to the resentment of many residents who would rather see their labors support health, education, and economic development.

Some Chuquicamatinos spoke with anger and frustration over the consolidation of power in the mining hierarchy during the years of the dictatorship.[28] The bureaucracy became more entrenched. A military base was built near the entrance to the mines. New forms of surveillance infiltrated all aspects of community life. The language of consumption in local stories is one of the consumption of community trust and solidarity:

> The people have little faith in the process of change. It's hard to get people to participate in the community. Now, after the dictatorship, there is no sense of solidarity in the community like there was in the past. Solidarity didn't serve the dictatorship. Even now, people are afraid and maintain their privacy. Neighbors might greet one another, but there aren't relations between neighbors like before. During the years of *pinocho*[Pinochet] it was a dangerous thing to associate with others. And the young people don't know anything of life before. Over the years, they learned the importance of silence outside the home. There might be jokes or whatever conversation at home, but parents made sure that their kids didn't talk outside the house, in school or wherever. Those were important lessons in distrust. Even sports were affected. Sports are so important here. But with the dictatorship, everything changed. People couldn't form their own teams and leagues. Everything was assigned. There wasn't freedom or spontaneity or friendship in sports; it was something else. And now there is this strong sense of individualism here, a lack of communal ties.[29]

Whereas Butte experienced the consumption of key material symbols of community, Chuquicamata experienced a profound loss of solidarity, the emotional glue of community. And worse, the residents were denied the right to acknowledge and mourn this and the many other losses that remained as painful reminders of those years. Further complicating this painful history, the people of Chuquicamata are now witnessing the deterioration and demise of the very structures that long symbolized their privileged place in the Anaconda family. The Chile Theater stands in disrepair, and the *pulperías* have been abandoned, replaced by a national supermarket chain. Meanwhile, the Executives' Club, with its indoor pool and gracious copper fountain, surrounded by garden space and protected by a manicured wall of greenery, has been well maintained and updated over the years. Talk of plans to demolish the Roy Glover Hospital in order to expand the open-pit mine has provoked outrage and frustration among residents of Chuquicamata. One woman confided that she did not believe that CODELCO intended to expand the mine. Rather, she believed that the company merely wanted to be rid of the hospital and "all it stood for" — that is, the Anaconda legacy.

People of Chuquicamata contrast the current situation with that of the days of the gringos, when unions had power and the community had solidarity. Corporate-community relations served a curious double purpose, sometimes joining residents as consumers of Yankee privilege, sometimes serving as a rallying point for social action against Yankee imperialists.

Residents of both communities spoke sadly of the ultimate consumption of their copper reserves and the concomitant loss of a familiar way of life. As copper was tapped out in Butte and the mines closed, many feared the final chapter on community consumption had been written. Residents spoke of the profound depression that leveled the community as a whole. As one woman recalled, "It was a time of mourning for people. People were talking in quiet voices; there was a feeling of mournfulness in the whole community."[30]

Residents of Chuquicamata now face the depletion of copper reserves and the growing threat posed by the proliferation of nonunion mining operations in the region. They are struggling with their own fears of a way of life being consumed. They have weathered the loss of solidarity and the struggles of the dictatorship, and now they face the loss of jobs. As one Chuquicamatino put it, "Chuqui is going to go the way of the nitrate mines. It's going to be a thing of the past. Already there are plans to develop other copper deposits like Mansa Mina and El Abra and others. The costs of getting the copper out of the ground at Chuqui are high, with the transportation and the low percentage of copper. There is no future for Chuqui."[31]

For Hernan, this vision of the future was cause for fear and uncertainty as he struggled to imagine life beyond copper:

> Now, there isn't the solidarity like we had in the past. Now, people are envious, and there's competition among neighbors. Now, during a strike or whatever, those who have, have and those who have not go hungry. Before, things were tougher. Now, there is more change, more education, more professionals, and they all want more. They want nice cars and pretty women and beautiful houses and a perfect climate. They want the life of Santiago with good women and a mild climate. They don't want to live here anymore.
>
> To me, Chuquicamata is beautiful, the best place in the world. The best mine, but it's dying. Chuquicamata doesn't have a future, maybe a few years, but it's dying. It hurts me to think that I have to leave Chuqui, my home. I am Chuquicamatino, and I don't want to leave, but I'll have to leave. I am accustomed here. How could I live in the south with all the rain? I've never owned an umbrella in my life. I'd die there. Or Santiago, oh sure, I'll go to Santiago and buy a house there, with all the people running all the time. I

couldn't do it. We live peacefully here. I couldn't live there and the southern air would kill me.[32]

There is fear behind the humor of Hernan's words, fear of a breakdown of the myriad practices that have structured his life, and fear of the unknown that might replace them. Whatever the violations of the dictatorship, for many people the daily routines of work in the mines may have created the sense of normalcy, the anchor to a familiar world in the face of crisis and fear. Now, residents of Chuquicamata face the possible loss of that anchor and an unmoored future filled with doubts.

In the stories from Butte and Chuquicamata, talk of the consumption of mining life is paired with talk of a loss of values. People speak of a concomitant consumption of solidarity and neighborliness, of their shared stake in survival, and of the political consciousness on which union power was built. The common generational discourse of "kids these days" is marked by a sadness of the specific loss of values among young people regarding the things that mattered in mining life. Many folks in Butte bemoan the lack of consciousness among their children who have not had to struggle as they did. They talk of solidarity grounded in past struggles. There is irony in their stories of wanting to give their children a "better life" than they had. They fear that one of the outcomes of giving them that better life was a failure to inculcate in their children the values that guided their own struggles. Like copper, those too have been consumed.

FROM CONSUMPTION TO *CONSUMISMO*

The Spanish word *consumismo* means both "consumption" and "consumerism." It is a popular buzzword in Chuquicamata, used when people speak of the breakdown in traditional values and their replacement with competition, materialism, individualism, and a "lack of consciousness." There is a virtual *consumismo* script in which Chuquicamatinos speak of envy, the need to have more than your neighbor, flagrant and irresponsible buying on credit, and the ever-present threat of indebtedness. In effect, there is concern that folks are living the life of *los privilegiados* without the material resources to support it.

There are two important aspects to the *consumismo* script. First, people in diverse sectors of the community offered me their own unsolicited version. Cab drivers, waiters, mine workers, and homemakers bemoaned the current state of affairs, where "Everyone is out for himself, . . . the rich get richer, and the poor go hungry." Second, CODELCO has capitalized on the script, making it part of the "official story." In nearly every recent issue of *Oasis* and in every conversation I had with management personnel, there was talk of the rampant *consumismo* that plagued the community. A key feature of the corporate version, however, is that the Anaconda Company is to blame for this pathological *consumismo*.

The story told by CODELCO locates the roots of *consumismo* in the dependency fostered during the days of the gringos, when people grew accustomed to corporate paternalism. The company provided housing, electricity, water, *pulperías*, education and medical care. Residents were not citizen participants in community building; they were passive recipients of corporate goods and services. The management of CODELCO hopes to break down this mindset of dependency and replace it with a spirit of collaboration through the Cultural Transformation of the Labor Force.[33] Official management spokespersons limit their criticism to the classist paternalism of the Anaconda Company era. They do not speak to the effects that a seventeen-year dictatorship had on the operation of the mines and the "culture" of the community.

There are those on the political left who agree in part with the corporate version of the *consumismo* script. They argue that many Chuquicamatinos eschewed the call to participate under Allende because they had grown complacent with their dependent position and did not want to risk losing their comforts and privileges. Yet these members of the left join people of different political persuasions in talking back to the official silence and criticizing the dictatorship. For seventeen years, economic dependency was coupled with political dependency, stripping the last vestiges of autonomy from a largely helpless populace. Now, the community, especially the young people, live for the moment. Socialized to dependency, lacking the skills and experience to be critical actors, they succumb to a life of consumption.

The script, in its various forms, is powerful and ironic. It constructs *consumismo* as a personal problem, one of dependency and irresponsibility. It speaks to the erasure of political consciousness under the dictatorship (or, as in the case of the CODELCO version, erases the dictatorship altogether). At the same time, the script itself erases the long history of action on the part of working-class women and men to build and maintain both autonomy and solidarity within the structures of corporate and military paternalism.[34]

The script is devoid of a larger critique of "neoliberalism" and the

consequent moves to privatization on many fronts that have characterized Chilean political and economic policies since the mid 1970s.[35] The
country's social contract has been in retreat with the privatization of the
social security system and shrinking resources to public health and education. At the same time, ready access to consumer credit is being
broadly promoted throughout the country, and levels of personal debt
are on the rise. These trends have exacerbated the social, economic, and
emotional vulnerability of Chile's working classes. As Duncan Green
notes in his study of market economics in Latin America: "In Chile, the
neo-liberal tiger, a labour force once accustomed to secure, unionised
jobs had been turned into a nation of anxious individualists. According
to a recent World Health Organisation survey, over half of all visits to
Chile's public health system involve psychological ailments, mainly
depression" (Green 1995, 96).[36] Yet critical analyses of the consumptive
force of these "structural adjustments" fall outside the bounds of
Chuquicamata's *consumismo* script, which is rooted in a truncated
genealogy of dependency.

Butte residents have crafted their own version of the *consumismo*
script. It is intimately linked to the closure of the mines and breakdown
of the unions in the 1980s. Some praise and others decry the proliferation of nonunion fast-food restaurants that have sprung up on Butte's
commercial strip since the decline of union power. The arrival of
McDonald's marked a shift to new forms of consumption in the Mining
City. Many claim it was the unions' own voracious hunger for more
power and money that caused their downfall and made way for
nonunion consumption.

The discount and fast-food stores do a brisk business, even as many
residents mourn the loss of union power. Many union sympathizers
lament the lack of a political consciousness among the young who now
live paycheck to paycheck without a commitment to securing their
future. Parents whose veins course with union blood wonder where they
have gone wrong as their children go off to work in nonunion jobs.
They talk of the cycles of unionism, the swing of the pendulum, and the
need for things to get worse for their children before they will join in solidarity to demand changes.

There is an ironic thread that runs through these stories and gives
another level of significance to the phrase "We eat the mines, and the
mines eat us."[37] Over the years, the mines have consumed lives, health,
homes, and the very substance of community. Those who have lived off
the mines have been encouraged to consume the good life before the

hard life eats them up. In the process, they stand accused of having consumed the sacred values that bound them as a community of survivors.

These local consumption scripts parallel broader cultural discourses of consumption. They resonate with the often esoteric analyses of postmodern writers who speak of the marketplace of fluid, ungrounded symbols and simulacra as symptoms of shifting and diffuse forms of capitalism.[38] But this global talk doesn't mean much to local residents. They are concerned with *consumismo* as a community problem. It is in the context of the sentiments and politics of place that they have witnessed and experienced a breakdown in community values. A defining feature of the breakdown is a loss of a sense of history and future and a concomitant loss of the political consciousness that connected them. In their place is a frenetic practice of the present and an insatiable hunger for immediate gratification.

GENDER, POWER, AND CONSUMPTION

There is a strong gendered subtext to consumption. In general, consumption has been popularly constructed as a feminine practice. For example, in Chuquicamata, at the same time that CODELCO warns of the dangers of *consumismo*, it sings the praises of the supermarket and department store that replaced the *pulperías* in 1993. In promoting these new market opportunities, it bills women as the "consummate consumers."

Women and children have been constructed as dependents who consume the productive labors of men. The mines themselves have a feminine mystique, representing "insecurity, capriciousness, betrayal, hopes and fears, habitual characteristics of the relations between us and them, distant, inaccessible, coveted" (Alvear Urrutia 1975, 65–66). Men are surrounded on all sides by feminine forces that consume them, drive their production, and fuel their resentments and fears. The images fit with broadly writ cultural scripts of the consumptive and dangerous force of women's sexuality, perhaps the ultimate consumption of male power. Women are more than "loci of problems and fears." They embody the cultural contradictions of consumption. Women are expected to be the conservers of community life, the stewards of men's consumption, and the consumers that drive the motor of the market economy. It appears that the invisible hand of the market has a firm grip on womanhood, contorting feminine practice to the demands of production and blaming her when she fails to (re)produce.

As we have seen in chapter 5, working-class women are particularly burdened as they straddle the competing demands of production, consumption, and reproduction. They become the targets of blame for their failure to resolve this treble bind in which contradictory images, expectations, and realities collide. When conflicts reign and "traditional" values break down, it is taken as a sign that women have failed in their culturally assigned roles as conservers and inculcators of those values. When men walk away from their families or turn to drink and violence, they have succumbed to the relentless suction of feminine forces consuming them. When children go hungry, women have failed in their vigilance. When women go hungry, few take notice. As Beatrix Campbell notes, women's hunger is too often a well-kept secret, which protects men from the shame of their participation in women's poverty (Campbell 1984, 57).

The power assigned to feminine imagery masks and distorts the relative physical, material, and political powerlessness that constrains women's lives. Like Our Lady of the Rockies herself, larger-than-life images of feminine power cast their shadows over the vulnerabilities and possibilities of women's lived experience. Women often find themselves under siege in their struggles to transform the relations of consumption. Their transformative practices threaten deeply ingrained beliefs about what it means to be a man, woman, worker, and provider in the mining community. Yet in their attention to the relations of consumption, women are cultivating the seeds of an alternative cultural politics. Is there hope in crafting a new politics of consumption, or will it succumb to the weight of distrust and betrayal that has burdened mining history?

Trust, Betrayal, and Transformation

Who knows what to believe? Only if God himself came down and said, "This is the truth," would I believe it. And even then I wouldn't be too sure.

Mick, retired Butte mine worker, 1991

And they say we are a democracy now, but it's a false democracy. There is no trust, no solidarity. In the "new order" there's no respect for old workers. Nobody knows who are friends and who are enemies anymore.

Jorge, Chuquicamata mine worker, 1994

The theme of trust and betrayal has reverberated throughout the histories of Butte and Chuquicamata.[1] In this chapter, I explore the ways in which this theme manifested itself in labor-company relations, in gender imagery and relations, and in political promises made and broken. Trust and betrayal are critical to understanding the disintegration of union power and the shape of current conflicts in Butte. In Chuquicamata, the theme has coursed through the history of labor relations. It acquired a new intensity under the dictatorship. In intricate and symbolically loaded ways, trust and betrayal have been encoded in social consciousness and practice. This theme also underpins workers' resistance to calls for participation in new forms of labor discipline. Ironically, their very resistance may be a necessary part of the process of retooling workers for their transient positions in twenty-first-century capitalism. But residents of the mining community are engaged in another form of social practice as well: reclamation. In this chapter I explore trust, betrayal, and social transformations. I address the complicated politics of reclamation currently in play in Butte and Chuquicamata as people stake their claims to competing versions of history and future possibility.

BUTTE: TRUST AND BETRAYAL

The stories of workingmen's wisdom in Butte are steeped in trust and betrayal.[2] Anaconda Company practices were shrouded in secrecy, leaving a huge void to be filled by myths and rumors, truths and lies. Miners learned to question surface appearances. Butte's early history is remembered in vivid stories of union infiltration by company spies and blatant political corruption. Butte men looked for the markers of distinction that might suggest someone was on the company payroll. Maybe it was the car he drove, or the house he bought, or the cowboy hat he wore. Workingmen were on the alert for the signs that a union man had sold out solidarity for personal gain. Those who crossed a picket line were singled out for personal harassment and public humiliation, their names posted on "scab" rosters, their homes painted with *scab* in large bold letters. Many remember a prominent union boss of the 1950s and 1960s. His critics say that his spending didn't seem to match his salary. Even his sympathizers admit it was poor form for him to buy a new house in the middle of the 1967 strike. The less sympathetic remember him as the only union man for whom the Anaconda Company threw a retirement party.

Though miners' distrust was aimed at the company, it often landed in the union. It was among their union brothers that miners felt the personal threat of betrayal. Company dollars might have paid for the betrayal, but your fellow worker would carry it out. A man had to be on the alert for the "company plant." It seems that grand-scale political machinations on the part of the company were expected as the modus operandi of capitalism. Men were often more infatuated than infuriated with the powerplays of the Big Shots. It was at the personal level, where you needed to watch your back, that men talked bitterly of betrayal.

Butte men tell stories of sellouts, collusion, and the unions coming to mirror corporate power. As one man summarized these suspicions, "The unions and the company had the same boss." The tensions of trust and betrayal were deeply rooted in the conflicts between the Butte Miner's Union and the Mine-Mill in the mid 1950s, when Mine-Mill leadership was discredited for its communist domination and ousted from the CIO. The local union leadership went on the offensive, distancing themselves from the Mine-Mill and suggesting that the Mine-Mill leaders were on the company payroll. The Anaconda Company played on interunion conflicts and suspicions. For example, in the 1959 strike, the Anaconda Company exploited the theme of trust and betrayal by challenging the union to call for a secret strike ballot. When the union refused to hold a secret vote, Anaconda fueled miners' distrust of their union bosses with an open attack on the unions in the press.[3] And throughout Butte's labor history there were news reports on graft, corruption, and the misuse of union funds on the part of union leaders.

Mining men in Butte spoke indignantly about the ways the little guys "got screwed by the union and the company." As Mick, a former mine worker, recalled:

> Back during the '67 strike a rep from the United Steelworkers comes to Butte for this big strike rally. Everybody was standing and applauding, but I refused to stand up and applaud. This guy was wearing shoes that cost more than I was going to earn through the entire strike to support my family. Then in '71, this international rep comes to Butte, telling us how hard he had it during the '67 strike with all that time away from his family while Butte guys just sat on their butts. He got thrown out of the union hall.[4]

Mick and his friend Andy offered a careful analysis of the practices through which union means came to serve company ends in a betrayal of men's labor. The irony in this account suggests more pain than their stories of kickbacks and corruption. Mick put forth the "arm and hand" theory:

> When the Butte workforce was made up of diverse ethnic groups, lots of men were unskilled and many didn't speak English. Each man was assigned a specific job. The company wanted it that way. It was their preference, not the union's. So that became the practice, each man with a specific task, and the unions trying to protect him. Then thirty years later, the company wants to turn it around on them, claiming that the unions locked the company into these jobs. Then you get all these stories about how many workers it takes to change a light bulb. But it was the company that set it up that way when it benefited them. Then thirty years later, you have people locked into specialties and they can't do other jobs.[5]

Mick operated the same machine for thirty years, and that's all he could do. He never had an opportunity to learn anything else. He said, "It's like if I were a baker and could only bake cakes, not pies or rolls or anything."[6]

According to Mick and Andy, workingmen in Butte became pawns in a power game. They were systematically deskilled through specialization. Their account contrasts with the stories of other men who strongly identified with their crafts and resented corporate devaluation of their labors. These contrasting perspectives of alienation and identification suggest contradictions and divisions among union men themselves. In the end, changing labor and corporate practices spelled devastation for both craftsmen and underskilled workers. Their solidarity was as diffuse and fragmented as their daily practice of labor. Through the politics of identification as "specialists," Butte's workers experienced the fission of their identities as mining men and of their union solidarity. The root of the problem was located in the union, not the company.

Andy's voice filled with anger when he talked about the way blame got turned around and placed on the union. He is the first to admit the unions were not blameless. But the power relations are lost when the contradictions are reduced to a union problem. Andy thought about copper and power with a poststructuralist's flair for discourse analysis. (Though he would roll his eyes at that academic description.) He pulled apart the surface language and exposed the betrayals beneath the words. He said nobody uses the word *scab* now; they talk about "replacement workers." And it is not a "nonunion" operation, but a "union-free" one. Even the men themselves talk about their good "company pension," not their "union-negotiated pension." Those words make a difference. They obscure the contradictions that confronted the miners and locate the problems of corporate-union practices in the structure of unions and the bodies of men.

In the late 1970s, Anaconda was purchased by Atlantic Richfield Corporation (ARCO). The budding hopes of a new lease on mining life were quickly overshadowed by cutbacks, layoffs, and increasingly troubled times. But miners claimed they made good faith efforts to work with the new company toward an equitable solution. Andy recalled: "I felt like a real sucker. Here we had pooled all our knowledge together, formed a citizens committee, and were working on this quality circle concept. We poured our hearts into it. Then they closed the mines. The unions even kept trying to negotiate after they closed the mines. We had a flexibility plan all worked out." Mick talked of the devastation of the closure, especially among men with many years of employment but not enough for pensions:

> There was a real personal impact, a feeling of worthlessness. Everybody felt it in a different way. People were asking, "What the hell am I living for?" There were men with twenty-five-years experience out doing lawn work, or flagging on a road crew, two weeks here, two weeks there. We had the retraining programs, and at least they gave people a focus and some sense of worth. But it was kind of ridiculous. They were training electricians to be plumbers and plumbers to be machinists and machinists to be electricians, and there weren't jobs for any of them, so what was the point?[7]

Their talk turned to plans for reopening the mines in 1986. The unions worked with the new owner, helping him get "all his ducks in a row."

But the unions were the "last slice of the pie." Once it came down to negotiating with the unions, the new operation had everything it needed. It didn't need unions. As Andy said, "The sad part was the deception. We'd have worked with them if they'd been up front, but they had to deceive." Once again, the mining men of Butte felt duped in the long saga of trust and betrayal.

These stories are filled with complexities. They suggest that workingmen suffered the consequences for their good faith efforts at collaboration. In short, they were unable to unmask the contradictions inherent in labor-capital relations. Unlike their fathers, who played with the contradictions, these men were trapped, unable to resolve the fundamental problems posed by conflicting discourses and patterns of practice. In retrospect, some mining men believe they were "damned if they did, damned if they didn't" when it came to labor participation. As their wives observed, they were "squeezed in the middle." In some ways, the retrospective stories told by working-class men in Butte reflect concerns expressed by their women counterparts. However, it seems that men's and women's beliefs about one another, perhaps also rooted in fears of trust and betrayal, often rendered them silent, unable or unwilling to voice their fears to each other.

Some people describe the years when the mines in Butte were closed as a "collective depression." They vividly recall the day in April 1982 when the Berkeley Pit closed and the water pumps in the mines were shut down. From that moment, the open-pit mine began to fill with toxic waters, its seepage a graphic reminder of community bitterness and hopelessness. For three years, Butte experienced an exodus. Those who remained carried the weight of the collective sadness. One man described the community as a "mouth full of broken teeth." After a while, any work, not union work was the measure of community survival. When the mines reopened, union-free, many residents found cause to celebrate. The more cynical pointed out that this "miraculous" return of mining was accompanied by more mundane corporate enticements such as a three-year tax break and reduction of power and freight costs (Dobb 1996, 45). Some union men formed a picket line at the new mine, whereas others crossed the line, averting their eyes as they went to their new jobs. This time it was the picketers, not the "scabs," who met with heckling and jeers from passersby.[8] Butte had indeed experienced a profound transformation. And in the process, the concept of worker participation had become polluted.

The long history of trust and betrayal is evident in the local theories that abound regarding the new ownership of the Butte mines. There are those who claim that the deal was made for a single dollar—a token exchange of cash that symbolized the unchanging power behind the scenes. Some say that the new owner is a "front man" for the old Anaconda players. They believe that local wealth is still being siphoned away to the pockets of nameless, faceless Big Shots back east. Others have theories about the hiring practices of the nonunion mines. They claim that psychological tests are given to prospective employees to weed out workers with union sympathies. The mines may be new, but the beliefs about them are enmeshed in old suspicions.

In recent years, mining operations have given way to environmental cleanup as a cornerstone of the community economy. The small population influx in recent years has been of white-collar, professional-class experts in new technology. There is a flurry of activity among legal and technical experts involving plans to clean up America's largest toxic waste site, the result of one hundred years of mining activity. In the center of this site is the Berkeley Pit, whose huge crater now holds twenty-eight billion gallons of toxic water and is filling at a rate of three million gallons a day, with no end in sight (Dobb 1996, 40). There have been efforts, such as the formation of the Citizen's Technical Environmental Committee (CTEC), to educate the community about the cleanup process and to create a forum for dialogue among community members and technical experts. The results, however, have been only marginally successful.

I attended several meetings of CTEC in 1993 and 1994. Discussions were often characterized by two distinct levels of discourse. First, there was the techno-talk of experts giving detailed, complicated, and "reasonable" explanations of the various cleanup alternatives. Then there was the local talk, which probed the politics behind the expertise. For example, at one meeting a chemist gave a highly technical presentation on a process he was developing for extracting and purifying water from the pit. He spoke in terms of liters, milliliters, and shorthand references to chemical compounds and seemed oblivious to the audience members stirring in their seats. Finally, a voice from the back of the room shouted, "Hey, would you mind telling us what that means in English? We're talking billions of gallons here, how does that compute?" Another voice called out, "So, what are we going to do with the tons of dry waste once you suck all the water out of it?" The speaker had no answers. Another series of discussions centered around the risk of groundwater contamination from the rising pit water. Again, a panel of experts spoke of their knowledge of area geology and their reasonable efforts to monitor water in a number of strategically placed wells. Old-time mining men shook their heads in disbelief. They argued that the more than 2,500 miles of tunnels that run beneath Butte's surface have forever disrupted any sense of natural geology and have undermined the experts' theories. As toxic water makes its way through this labyrinth, they say, there is no telling where it will surface.

Community residents routinely posed challenging questions that bypassed the technical mumbo jumbo and got to the point: With all this expertise in town, why is the pit still filling up with water? When are you going to *do* something about it? How many years has the EPA been paying you guys to do another study? You can just *look* at the Pit and see we've got a problem on our hands! And finally, the ultimate question: What would happen if we had an earthquake? The experts give their predictions on the likelihood of seismic events and the overall stability of the ground around the pit. But Butte residents have not forgotten the "night the mountain fell" in the earthquake of 1959. They look to the pit and the wall of slag that forms a dam between the pit and the small lake behind it. They can readily envision a toxic tidal wave washing twenty-eight billion gallons of murky red water over them. The Berkeley Pit, longtime icon of the mining industry, now stands to the community as the icon, index, and symbol of promises made and promises broken and the chasm between expert and local knowledge.

Over the past few years, as environmental damage lawsuits move grudgingly forward, Butte residents have been the audience to widely contested accounts of what constitutes "risk" and how extensive the cleanup process should be. ARCO has launched an extensive public relations campaign that presents the company as a good neighbor and partner in environmental stewardship. Environmental groups have cried foul, arguing that corporate efforts are cosmetic at best and have not gone nearly far enough to address historic damage and current risks. Some environmentalists accuse Butte residents of complicity with the company in this history of environmental degradation and of passivity and ignorance in their willingness to continue to live alongside this sprawling toxic-waste site. Such criticisms do not endear many Butte residents to the environmental movement, nor do they reflect any depth of understanding about the complexities of mining life.[9]

On a November day in 1995, a flock of snow geese heading south for the winter stopped for a rest and a drink at the shimmering waters of the Berkeley Pit. In the days that followed, the bodies of 342 geese were found floating in the toxic lake or washed up on the shores. A few of their bodies were recovered and sent to a university lab for autopsy reports. Butte residents were unanimous in assuming the birds had been poisoned by the pit, but an ARCO spokesperson asserted that the birds died as a result of eating wheat fungus. The autopsy report supported local knowledge, documenting that the birds had been eaten alive by the caustic waters. The snow geese were publicly mourned by concerned environmental groups. Their deaths have become symbolic of the palpable risks that Butte people face each day. And, once again, as contradictory discourses and patterns of practice fan their fears, the people of Butte do not know who to trust.

CHUQUICAMATA: *CONFIANZA Y TRAICIÓN* (TRUST AND BETRAYAL)

As we have seen, Chuquicamata's early social critics and Chile's prolabor press relentlessly attacked the political machinations of the Anaconda Company. But among those I spoke with in Chuquicamata, there was less talk of the larger politics in which Anaconda operations were embedded. They praised the perks and denounced the inequalities built into the mining way of life. Yet their stories of the Anaconda Company do not resonate with the deeply rooted sense of betrayal that echoes through the words of many Butte storytellers. And their stories suggest more than a nostalgic whitewashing of the past. They speak to the transparency of corporate power, where distinctions were directly supported, not denied. Anaconda made no effort to hide their corporate agenda of profit making. They offered concessions along the way to those who toiled in the desert.

Over time, and as my ability to ask the right questions improved, I heard Chilean stories of Anaconda company intrigues. For example, there was widespread belief that Anaconda systematically smuggled untold wealth in gold out of Chile in its copper concentrate, destined for refineries in the United States. I was privy to a rich array of secondhand "eyewitness" accounts that detailed the ways in which bars of copper were hollowed out and their centers filled with pure gold that would thus leave the country undetected. Others told stories of the "gold train" running to Antofagasta. Copper was regularly shipped by train from the smelter to the port city of Antofagasta. Every once in a while, the train would be crawling with armed guards. Of course the cargo *looked* like copper, but with all those guards on board, you *knew* they were protecting something much more precious. Others told stories of Anaconda strategically managing its copper reserves for production and price control. Several people recounted the company's change in production methods during World War II — a change that doubled the rate of copper production — and the company's subsequent reversion to traditional methods when the war, and the financial incentives, ended. Yet none of these accounts were charged with the personal sense of betrayal that permeates the stories told by mining men in Butte.

It was in their stories of the Popular Unity government, the dictatorship, and the current management of the mines that Chuquicamatinos talked of trust and betrayal. In sharp contrast to the stories of the gringo years, these stories carry the emotional load found in the Butte betrayal stories. With nationalization imminent in 1971, there was a mass exodus from Chuquicamata of both North American and Chilean managers and technical experts. But Chuquicamata's workingmen, with their years of experienced-based knowledge, were not the ones called upon to take over the vacant posts. Positions were filled by an influx of managers and technicians "from the south," Chilean men as foreign to Chuquicamatinos as the gringos they replaced. Chuquicamatinos spoke with resentment about experienced men who were replaced or passed over when the Popular Unity appointees came to town. It seems that betrayal at the hands of one's own compatriots is a much more bitter pill to swallow than betrayal by gringos.

From 1970 to 1973, *Oasis* was filled with articles promoting nationalization. The Popular Unity government called on workers to show their support for their country by participating in the social transformation. Rallies were held claiming that "copper belongs to Chile and all Chilenos."[10] The Popular Unity government declared that nationalization would guarantee, respect, and amplify the rights of the copper miners.[11] A campaign urged workers to donate a day of their salary "for Chile," and *Oasis* featured testimonials of workers who took up the cause.[12] Workers were called upon to join volunteer crews for housing and road construction in the interest of local and national solidarity (see fig. 25).

The press controlled by Popular Unity repeatedly attacked the "old order" of Anaconda for its paternalism, profiteering, and pilfering of national resources. In place of the old order was a patriotic program to build the economic foundation of a new national solidarity. Workers were urged to increase production, because the "salary of Chile was in their hands."[13] The messages were both hopeful and heavy-handed. The paper praised the technical efficiency of the new Chilean management but also reported frequent turnover in staff. The shift from old to new order did not proceed smoothly. Chronic food shortages wreaked havoc at the *pulperías*, as residents faced a situation worse than what they had grown accustomed to during the days of the gringos. Operations in the mines were plagued with dozens of work stoppages. In April of 1972, a general union assembly sharply criticized the mine management. The meaning and power of participation became a contested issue in labor-management relations.[14]

In June of 1972, management of Cobre-Chuqui (the name of the newly nationalized mine) proposed a plan to promote production and worker participation known as the Commitment to Action (*Compromiso de Acción*).[15] But the unions rejected the plan. In news reports about the plan, union leaders and members recognized its merit but noted that, ironically, management had not involved workers in the plan's development. Where was management's commitment to the participatory process? Management's words did not match its actions, and miners were skeptical.

In July 1972, *Oasis* published an open letter from the general manager of Cobre-Chuqui, David Silberman, that responded to workers' skepticism about the promise of nationalization. He spoke of the deleterious effect of the work stoppages and promoted the process of participation. He claimed that the problem was the mentality of egoism among Chuquicamata's workers, the result of fifty years of domination of the working class by capitalist interests. Thus the miners thought only of their immediate earnings and lacked identification with the "great masses of Chilean workers." He criticized the limited vision of unionism, through which immediate personal or party interests obscured general long-term interests. He praised the "honest, patriotic, and efficient efforts of the Chilean professionals and technicians" who had successfully replaced the North American administration: "In spite of the extreme youth of the highest level technicians, with only an average age of thirty-one years, they are capable of good and improved management of this complex mining operation."[16] Despite the kernels of truth in Silberman's analysis, his words were a slap in the face to many workers, whose life experience was reduced to contamination by the capitalist order that made them pollutants of the new order. His defense of the new young managers was a negation of many Chuquicamatinos' years of knowledge and experience that had been valued by the old order. He

Figure 25.   "Copper belongs to all Chileans — S. Allende." Wall in Calama,
1994 (author photo).

failed to acknowledge the party politics behind the hiring practices of
the new management class of the mines, something that the miners of
Chuquicamata were acutely aware of.

During the course of archival research in Santiago, I came across a
thesis in social work entitled "Worker Participation in the Production
Committees of Cobre-Chuqui" (Araya Carro et al. 1973). The thesis,
written by five women, was the product of several months of fieldwork
in Chuquicamata in 1972, during which the authors conducted extensive
interviews among workers and managers and participated in the newly
organized production committees. The work contains a strong Marxist
language of class conflict, critical of capitalism and dependency. It calls
for the proletariat to "conquer the political hegemony in order to create
structural change." The authors define participation as a political problem, point to the need for workers to be involved in all levels of decision
making, and criticize lack of executive interest and worker capacity necessary for meaningful participation. They challenge the bureaucracy of
the national mines as a barrier to meaningful worker participation.

Two aspects of their analysis are relevant here. First, they offer a sound political critique of traditional social work, with its emphasis on adjustment and adaptation, as a servant of capitalism. They call for a politicized and participatory redefinition of social-work practice through which workers aligned themselves with the working classes. They seek to make the discourse of participation a meaningful reality, grounded in critical reflection and action. Their critique mirrors my own critical writings in social work and my beliefs about the politics of knowledge and action for social change (Finn 1994, 25–42).

Second, they repeatedly address the alienation and lack of critical consciousness among the workers of Chuquicamata as a result of their years of servitude to exploitative capitalists. They argue that "the mine workers had achieved economic advantages and had lost their revolutionary force" (Araya Carro et al. 1973, 68). The change in ownership had not yet resulted in a concomitant change in the "mentality, attitude, comportment, and social values of the workers, which are still oriented to the capitalist scheme" (Araya Carro et al. 1973, 74). They contend that Chuquicamatinos had been "mystified" by the dominant class and lacked their own popular culture. It seems to me that the authors' political and ideological position obscured their view of the nuances of a life built because and in spite of fifty years of capitalist domination. Their analysis is a haunting lesson as I wonder about the many nuances I have been unable to see because of my own politics and the passion that I bring to this project.

The authors make practical recommendations in support of meaningful worker participation in the workplace transformations that must accompany the nationalization of the mines. They argue that workers need incentives and call for a more active role of the unions in providing motivation for participation. They call for the incorporation of social workers in the production committees to facilitate the change process. And they demand accountability from management to reduce bureaucratic barriers and promote full worker participation. Their raw interview data are equally telling. Whereas some workers praised the new political direction, others complained that the participation was fictitious, limited, or nonexistent.

In summary, the brief years of the Popular Unity government were marked by hope, chaos, and conflict. Workers of Chuquicamata heard talk of participation but saw few concrete results. They found themselves the target of blame because of their longtime capitalist indoctrination. They watched young, often less experienced men take over, and they suffered privations at work and at home. National political rhetoric made little headway at the level of family and community. As global, national, and local forces collided, Popular Unity fell to the dictatorship, and the meaning and power of participation were transformed once again.

Under the dictatorship, the years of Popular Unity became the "old order," or disorder as the case may be, and the military regime rang in the "new order." *Oasis*, out of publication for a week after the coup, returned in late September 1973 with volume one, number one, erasing all that had gone before. News articles and editorials called for citizen participation in the "national restoration."[17] The new management called on the workers to increase production and criticized the lack of labor discipline that allowed chaos to reign under the old order. They described the "ideal union" as the fruitful mix of labor discipline and well-managed equipment. Workers were expected to participate in the national reconstruction, but that participation was tightly circumscribed within the top-down operations of the military rule. There was no political space for opposition. Workers lived under the constant threat of job cancellation, detention, or worse should they attempt to mobilize a collective challenge to wages and working conditions. Some workers lost their jobs for their participation in labor mobilization efforts in the late 1970s and mid 1980s. Others were threatened with firing if they did not cooperate with the military management and name the "communists" who instigated the labor action.

With the arrival of the democratic transition government in 1990, the copper miners of Chuquicamata became the audience to a new discourse of participation, that of the Cultural Transformation of the Labor Force.[18] In language similar to that used during the years of Popular Unity, the workers are now being asked to join in a participatory process of "communication for action."[19] This time, however, the language has been stripped of its critique of the unequal power relations between labor and capital. The corporate discourse speaks to the problematic labor culture that exists in Chuquicamata, characterized by rigid authority, conflict, dependency, and inefficiency. There is concern for the preoccupation with *consumismo* and the lack of discipline and critical consciousness among workers and community members. Chuquicamata is at risk of being consumed not by capitalist exploitation but by its own vices. The proposed transformation calls for changes in the mentality and practice of the community to yet another new order, with yet another new form of labor discipline.

This new corporate discourse, like that of the Popular Unity government, locates the problem in the dependency cultivated through the years of paternalism under Anaconda. The Anaconda Company is the fall guy in the official story of Chuquicamata's community and labor problems. The story was elaborated even further in the unofficial accounts told to me by corporate executives. I listened to several versions of the corporate story about Anaconda's years of mismanagement, its failure to fully exploit Chuqui's resources, and its inculcation of laziness and poor work habits among its Yankee management and Chilean laborers. The stories contrasted sharply with those told by Chilean workers of the Anaconda years. There was an absolute silence on the part of the managers regarding the effects of the dictatorship on the "mentality" and conditions of the labor force.[20] Likewise, there was no acknowledgment that Chilean elites had fit quite neatly into the class structure set in concrete in Chuquicamata since 1912. The structure had complemented rather than challenged the larger class system in the country.

A basic aspect of the cultural transformation is the restructuring of relations between workers and bosses — a restructuring purportedly based on mutual respect and equality. The corporate designers of the transformation have proposed new organizational structures, the Autonomous Administrative Units, to facilitate the development of new workplace relations. The units are purportedly designed to promote teamwork, efficiency, and the participation of each worker in the management of the company. They sing the praises of the *transparencia* (transparency) of the new order. However, in my conversations with workers in the mines, this new organizational structure is the source of considerable skepticism and concern. Employees are well aware of the reality of power relations that are masked by a language of equality in "communication for action." To them *transparencia* has an ironic ring.

The new discourse of participation proposes a change in language from "boss and subordinate" to "leader and collaborator." But employees understand that conversations among bosses and subordinates do not occur in a context of equal power. They have heard the language of collaboration in many contexts and have witnessed practices over the years that exposed the contradictions between words and actions. Many doubt that substantive change in the structure and practice of the mining operation will result from this process. Some express concern that, as usual, the workers will bear the burden of the changes while those with power will grow more secure in their positions. Many fear that the reorganization process is little more than an effort to debilitate union

Figure 26.   "Chuquicamata unions say no to privatization." 11 July 1994
(author photo).

power and privatize the mining operations. They see the restructuring
into autonomous work units as a divisive strategy that undercuts union
organization. In addition, each of these new autonomous units may then
be spun off from the parent organization to nonunion contracted services. Folks joke about how the main social activities in Chuqui are
retirement parties for union workers being replaced by union-free labor.
Skepticism is pervasive in local opinions about the change process.
Though many agree that change is necessary, they see little value in participation. Their past experience has confirmed that calls for participation are part of larger, well-orchestrated schemes that preserve and reinforce the existing structure rather than transform it. The outcome, they
believe, is inevitable: a greater burden on workers and greater benefits
to bosses (see fig. 26).[21]

Many Chuquicamatinos cited the supposed elimination of the Roll
system as a classic example of the axiom "The more things change, the
more they remain the same." The formal distinction of Rolls A, B, and
C was reduced to two rolls, A and B, during the years of the dictatorship. More recently, the formal system of distinctions has been, techni-
cally speaking, abandoned. This move, part of the cultural transformation, was a symbolic act of expunging the old order of rigid authority

that structured labor and community relations for seventy years. But community members are quick to tell you that the change of language did not mean a change in practice. Under the new, "equitable," distinction-free system, there are no status rules that restrict use of community facilities. Roll B workers are free to swim and dine at Club CHILEX. Of course, few Roll B workers can afford the entrance fees or price of a meal, so the practical distinctions remain.

Some claim that the distinctions are even more powerful in their insidious form. One woman who grew up in Chuquicamata told me that during the days of the gringos, the distinctions had not stopped children of Roll A, B, and C from playing together. Now, she said, the distinction carries a stronger stigma: "To be Roll B is to lack culture and education. And the parents perpetuate the stigma among children. The Roll A people no longer ask children their Roll directly; now they say, 'Oh, and what does your father do?'" She spoke of the racism that permeates the distinctions in Chuquicamata, where light skin and light hair, once the markers of gringos, continue to be the markers of status and prestige (and the devil). Although formally abandoned, this deeply rooted system of distinctions remains carved into the social and physical terrain, harboring divisiveness and distrust. Shades of the old order continue to bleed through the new discourse, challenging both form and substance of the transformation.

The current climate of uncertainty is also grounded in a distrust of union leadership that echoes the concerns of workers in Butte. During the time I was in Chuquicamata, there were frequent headlines in *El Mercurio de Calama* about union corruption and mismanagement of union pension funds. Union credibility and interunion conflicts were the topics of numerous conversations. There were those who had little faith in the "company union" established during the years of the dictatorship. In 1993 contract negotiations, this union won a better settlement than the two large unions more closely identified with laborers. For some people, this was further proof of the union's co-optation by management. And, like the stories from Butte, there were a litany of stories in Chuquicamata about union bosses who bear the markers of distinction that suggest they have sold out. Folks talked of union representatives who drive fine cars, whose wives enjoy regular shopping sprees in Santiago, and whose sons have tickets to the big-league soccer games. Though folks wanted to see change, they feared that nothing was really going to change in this process because people with power don't give it up.

Other community members spoke of the overshadowing of the laborer's place in the unions by the influx of professionals. The largest union in the mines now is the voice of the emergent professional class of college-educated technicians. For many longtime laborers, this shift in the complexion of the union signals a further devaluation of working-man's wisdom. Some feel betrayed by unions, which they see as arms of management rather than advocates of the little guys.

Generational conflict is strong in the commentaries on labor-management relations. Younger workers with more education question the merit of seniority clauses. They speak of older workers and their union philosophies as antiquated, a deterrent to progressive change. Older men resent these youngsters who threaten their livelihoods and tell them what to do rather than learn through apprenticeship. They have seen this youthful arrogance before and believe it to be the downfall of the organization. Their mutual distrust plays out in turf protection and an informal policy of every man for himself. Like Mick and Andy, the workers of Chuquicamata "don't know who to trust."

As this discussion indirectly illustrates, union concerns remain largely on masculine terrain. Despite the fact that more than six hundred women work in Chuquicamata's mining operation and the majority of those are union members, women have historically been relegated to the margins of union action. This, however, is shifting. In July 1994, women gained three of nine leadership posts in Chuquicamata's largest union. They retained two of those posts in the 1996 election. Women leaders struggle for credibility as they attempt to establish themselves in the face of heavily gendered challenges to their abilities. Though the women have bases of support, their critics have questioned their marital status, sexuality, and dedication to motherhood and family, charges seldom leveled against their male counterparts.

Let's take a closer look at the labor transformations of Butte and Chuquicamata. In Butte, the fundamental shift from a union-based to union-free labor force in the mines and other economic sectors followed a time of union fragmentation and economic browbeating of the community. In spite of a long history of distrust, unionists took their chances in a nominally participatory process. They worked in good faith with management to reopen the mines. Management reneged, and once again they felt betrayed. As Mick and Andy's stories suggest, they believed that they were duped by their own failure to see the powerplays obscured by the participatory veil. They let their guard down and lost. A new labor structure and practice emerged, employing only a few hundred polyvalent workers in its streamlined operation. Union loyalists continue in their struggle to make their voices heard but find few listeners.

In Chuquicamata, workers are caught in the midst of a nominally participatory process, but many resist. They have heard this line before and have witnessed the results, or lack thereof. For them, *participation* is a problematic word, loaded with the meaning and power of history. As several women noted, the men of Chuquicamata sit in silence through the endless meetings and forums arranged to promote the Cultural Transformation of the Labor Force. One observer said that the bosses take the silence as agreement, when in reality it is fear and distrust. They have witnessed the exodus of two thousand coworkers since the transformation began, and they fear for their jobs. She added that people learned through the experience of the dictatorship not to speak up. Outside the meeting room, people speak skeptically among themselves, questioning both the process and product of the proposed changes. Many challenge the truth value of the cultural transformation by refusing to participate in the process.

As I try to come to terms with the questions of participation and resistance, I am reminded of Paul Willis's work on learning to labor (1981, 119–93). Willis argues that working-class youth, through their resistance to the class structure of the British educational system were, in effect, preparing themselves for their place on the factory floor. Their "partial penetration" of the power relations in education and their refusal to buy into the system served to shape the alienated consciousness necessary for routine factory work. Perhaps a similar process is at work here as workingman's skepticism is transformed into an essential element of the discipline for new, transient forms of labor. The mining industry has claimed that its labor needs are changing. No longer is the emphasis on a long-term, multigenerational community of labor. Corporate players want the timely exploitation of particular mineral reserves, with the flexibility to abandon those works and move on in the strategic pursuit of economic and political advantage. Companies are constructing a transient labor force of polyvalent workers. The workforce is minimal, and automation is maximized. Corporations play high-stakes games in the metals futures market, hedging their bets on a mobile and malleable workforce rather than a stable community. They do not want to invest in seniority, because the energy and flexibility of youth, with the arrogance of expertise and without the baggage of history, provide a more readily exploitable corporate resource. Corporate interests are better served by a new type of worker: adaptable, apolitical and shortsighted, a good consumer willing to live and spend for the moment. This is the "new corporate structure" that the workingmen of Butte and Chuquicamata confront in their acquiescence and resistance to participation.

Men in Butte talk of their skills being eroded and of distrust permeating every aspect of their labor experience. With their emotional and material strength sapped, they gave participation one last shot as they cooperated in the development plans of the new ownership, only to find themselves written out of the plans in the end. Humiliated and embittered, they were sidelined by the union-free labor force. Perhaps what the men failed to appreciate was the fundamentally contradictory nature of the participatory process that they had entered into.

I turn to the concept of "deep play" in an effort to elucidate the contradictions of participation. Jeremy Bentham coined the term in reference to gambling as play in which the stakes are so high that it is, from a utilitarian point of view, irrational for people to play at all. Anthropologist Clifford Geertz took the concept to another level, arguing that one can be bound to a high-stakes game because the stakes of not playing, such as honor, dignity, and respect, are even higher (Geertz 1973, 412–53). This notion of deep play, a game one seemingly cannot win but can't not play, captures the practical essence of the problems posed to workers by the capitalist contradiction. If one accepts a fundamental contradiction between labor and capital, then the process of negotiating the power relations is one of deep play, one that workers seemingly cannot win but can't not play. At times, by their very engagement with the contradiction, they have been able to transform the rules of the game in the process.

As Butte men talked of "heartfelt participation," "giving their all," and "quality circles," it seems that they had not defined the encounter as one of deep play. The workers of Butte chose to play, believing they could win. When one believes in the possibility of winning, one accepts the rules of the game as given, perhaps forfeiting the opportunity of transforming them. The union men in Butte were attending to the moves, the players, and the strategies of the game, but the corporate players were realigning the game's rules. Unionists lost because the rules of participation were stacked against them. Many workers, burned by the failures of past efforts, now opt for nonparticipation.

In Chuquicamata, similar practices are confronting laborers. Young workers are pitted against old. Workingman's wisdom has given way to technical expertise. Workers don't know who to trust. The trumpet call for participation is met with skepticism. Though many workers agree that change is needed, they don't believe that the current process will result in a fundamental reordering of corporate power. Many have given in to the inevitability of the process, opting for nonparticipation and a passive if disaffected acceptance of the process in the works and its outcomes. They don't want to be duped like the Butte boys. They have looked around the corner of the discourse, found it not transparent but vacant, and opted not to play. Yet their very resistance to participation may be an essential element in the success of the new labor discipline for a changing copper industry. This new discipline is producing transient, polyvalent workers whose labor is reduced to a practice of the present, with no sense of history or future security. By refusing to participate in the change process, perhaps they have forfeited their chance at deep play. They have defined the game as one that they cannot win but have failed to define it as one they can't not play. By forfeiting play, they give up their chance to transform the rules of the game and perhaps realize fundamental changes. The workers of Butte and those of Chuquicamata have penetrated opposite sides of the deep-play contradiction but have failed to confront the contradiction itself.

Some of labor's important successes have occurred when the little guys challenged and changed the rules of the game, engaging directly in the contradictions of deep play. For sixty years, labor's power in both Chile and the United States has been constrained by institutionalized rules that made claims on the legitimacy of labor actions. Corporate players have been able to appropriate the rules of the games to their political and economic advantage. The truth value of the phrase "The company never had a strike it didn't want" may be debatable. But the evidence laid out in this work certainly suggests that the company had few strikes it minded. In those few strikes were moments where women and men transgressed the gendered boundaries of participation and joined together in forging new possibilities for collective action. This history is marked by instances where people risked their work and lives, broke the rules of the game, and at times won by the force of their collective deep play. Women formed picket lines to protect family and community interests. Men dressed as women to dodge arrest. Women protected men from the blows of the militia. Men and women marched collectively, ten miles through a desert, thousands strong, to say no to a dictatorship. Deep play, then, is the process of confronting and engaging with the contradictions, broadening the terrain of the thinkable, talkable, and do-able, and challenging and changing the rules of the game.

WOMEN AND TRANSFORMATION

Gender relations have also been infused with the theme of trust and betrayal. The images of capriciousness, the suspicions of infidelity, and the burdens of moral responsibility have variably shaped the constructions of womanhood in Butte and Chuquicamata. Women have talked back to those images. Women have borne the burden of the politics of consumption in their stewardship of family and community. Their bodies have been the sites of contradiction as global politics translated to local pain. Now, once again, women are poised in a contradictory relationship vis-à-vis the structure and practice of transformations that have laid their impress on community life.

During the years when the Butte mines were closed, many women took over as the sole material and social supporters of their families. Women's income from work in the low-paid service economy sustained many Butte families. Women spoke of the delicate balance they struggled to maintain as breadwinner, caregiver, and emotional supporter of an unemployed spouse who had been stripped not only of his labor but also of his identity. As Lenore recalled:

> My ex-husband lost his job when the company shut down in '83. He just drifted on unemployment for a long time. Fortunately, I was working. Those were critical times for men and women. The men were used to being the boss, the kings of their castles. And now they were the ones at home. And the wives were out working. The wives would come home and say, "Why didn't you get anything done around here?" The wash needed to be done and the house cleaned and something fixed for dinner. It was an important time for women to show what they were capable of. But there was lots of abuse and drinking during those years. And lots of divorces. My husband and I split up. I can't tell you how many of my friends got divorced. The men had lost so much, and the women were holding everything together. It was really a time for women to show what we were made of. You know, I have to credit my mother for being such a model of strength and determination. I learned a lot of skills from her on how to get through a bad situation. I've tried to instill them in my own daughters.

Nan, the widow of a Butte miner, also recalled the strain and support of those times:

> My husband had been a contract miner and was working at the Pit when the mines closed. I remember the day he was laid off. He came home and said, "Well I finally got my slip. I don't know if what they aren't doing me a favor." At least he came out of it with his health after twenty years as a contract miner. He didn't know whether to be happy or sad. It was a difficult time for him. His work had been very important to him, and it was hard for him to

be around the house while I was the full-time breadwinner. He had always helped out. I tried to humor him to ease the pain. I'd tell him how much I liked coming home to a home-cooked meal after a hard day's work. After about a year of feeling depressed and at loose ends, and with no possibility of mining in the future, he decided to get involved [in political activity].[22]

Other women experienced the multiple duties of maintaining family, home, and community while their husbands left Butte in search of work elsewhere. Women adjusted to a way of life as single parents and sole decision makers. For some, their husbands' visits were times of tensions and conflicts. As men tried to reassert their authority, women resisted. Women joked about battles over the children's activities and the television's remote control. Some talked of the excitement of new seduction that accompanied each return. Another lamented, "He just can't understand how after a long day's work I really prefer a good book." Though their material resources were greater, the emotional patternings of many Butte women's lives came to resemble those of the women of Toconce, with their fifty-year history of maintaining community while their husbands labored at a distance.

In this moment when women's social practice was expanding and diversifying in new directions in Butte, Our Lady of the Rockies was under construction. This timeless, immutable image of womanhood overlooked the shifting terrain of women's practice below. I look to Our Lady and think of the ironies that surround enduring cultural symbols. The grand pyramids, statuary, and temples were often built at the times of social crisis. They were not reflections of stability but formidable efforts to create a sense of immutability in the moments of profound transformation. It is curious that in a community where women have historically positioned themselves as mediators between crisis and normalcy, Our Lady, in her serenity and stability, would be positioned before the community, perhaps to assuage the ultimate community crisis.

It was the men of Butte who put Our Lady on the mountain, perhaps constructing their own image of enduring womanhood in the process. Some people credit her with Butte's redemption, the reopening of the mines. For others, she is the target of caustic humor. Her construction paralleled a time of shifting gender relations, as women expanded their economic stewardship of community and men suffered loss of their paid labor and workingman's identity. For those engaged in the construction of Our Lady, the practice was a daily celebration of their craftsmanship and the triumph of little guys over big obstacles. The product of their labors was a certain and enduring tribute to "all women, especially mothers," a tribute to deeply rooted and respected images of womanhood and manhood, images that were faltering on this crumbling earth on which they now stood.

Women of Chuquicamata are deeply concerned about the implications of the cultural transformation for women's works and lives. Some women who work for the national mines in ancillary services such as health care and human resources have concerns about job security. They see the possibility of privatization in their work sectors and worry about the implications. Others hope to strengthen the ties between women workers and unions, such that men and women work together rather than against each other as they look to the future.

These women and I talked together about the historic "polyvalence" of women's work — those diffuse, undervalued, and endless practices of maintenance and caregiving. Our conversations resonated with a curious irony noted by Beatrix Campbell in her study of mining families in England: "Most men grieve for the loss of their skills, but don't notice the de-skilling of women in their own communities through marriage to themselves and then motherhood" (1984, 117). Perhaps men should think twice and talk to their wives before acquiescing to the pressures for polyvalent labor. It may be a euphemism for the "feminization" of their labor — that is, its expansion, diffusion, and ultimate devaluation.[23]

The organization of miner's wives in Chuquicamata is questioning the meaning of transformation, polyvalence, and autonomous work units and the implications for women. Through their questions, public forums, and calls for women's participation, they have chosen to politicize their stewardship of family and community. In order to enter the arena where the meaning and power of participation could be negotiated, the members of the organization accepted the invitation to participate offered in the "Letters to the Women of Chuquicamata" issued by the general manager for CODELCO-Chuqui. Perhaps the general manager's invitation to the women of Chuquicamata may be seen as an opportunity to engage in deep play. The women accepted the invitation, meanwhile strategizing to change the rules of the game through their participation and to demand answers and accountability in the process. But these groups of activists are small and somewhat fragmented. They are struggling to position themselves in the public space of community and engage as the community conscience in conversations with both the company and the unions. Should they continue with their efforts and fail, their experience may serve to reinforce the skepticism that is the motive force of the new labor discipline. For the moment, however, they are opening important spaces of indeterminacy and possibility.

While women in Chuquicamata seek to integrate themselves in the process of cultural transformation, women in the *poblaciones* (poor neighborhoods) of Calama are organizing around issues of survival. These single heads of households and wives of poorly paid contracted laborers have not received an invitation to participate in the change process. They are outside the bounds of community and womanhood as identified and circumscribed by the management of the national mines. Here the issues of family and community stewardship are based in the immediacy of basic needs for food, water, and housing. Whereas residents of Chuquicamata struggle to maintain hard-won salaries and benefits, these women demand the right to a livable minimum wage so that they don't go hungry each month, and they continue to face contradictory choices between food and shelter in their struggle for survival.

Many of these women and children have been abandoned by the men in their lives, the daily confrontation with their loci of problems and fear becoming too much for the men to bear. So women are coming together, pooling meager resources in their efforts to survive. In one *población* of Calama, women have jointly formed a community bakery, soup kitchen, and popular education center for children. They look to Chuquicamata with frustration and resentment as they point to the two worlds that separate the haves and the have-nots of the mining region.

There is a strong divide between the direct employees of the national mines and the contracted laborers. As we have seen, people of Chuquicamata spoke of the insidious distinction of Rolls A and B that remain embedded in community life. It appears that the distinction of Roll C, the lowest rung on the social ladder, also still exists in practice. It has come to define the status of contracted laborers and their families. If women and children represent loci of problems and fears for men, the presence of contracted laborers and their families are the loci for the Roll B workers in Chuquicamata. My queries about the possible participation of *los contratistas* (nonunion contracted laborers) in community action plans were usually met with silence or discomfort. The *contratistas* are marginalized members of the community. They are viewed not as potential partners but as a potential threat. Chuquicamatinos maintain their social and emotional distance from the *poblaciones*, and in so doing accept the circumscribed terrain of participation drawn by the company, which, in the end, may serve to realize their worst fears. In effect, this local distinction between union workers and contracted laborers that divides Chuquicamata and Calama into two worlds mirrors the historic divide that separated the two worlds of Butte and Chuquicamata.

RECLAMATION

Histories of trust and betrayal have both informed and limited social practice. In the preceding discussion, I have argued that the skepticism honed by distrust may in effect serve as a limiting force in the process of social transformation. However, people of Butte and Chuquicamata are also talking back, drawing on their skeptic's knowledge, and challenging the politics of identification behind the "new orders." They are staking claims to their histories and to the future possibilities of their imagined communities. They do not speak with one voice. Rather, the cultural politics of reclamation in Butte and Chuquicamata constitute another contested terrain in the making and mining of community.

Reclamation is the environmental buzzword of the mining industry these days. Yet reparation of the land is only one of many complicated reclamatory projects underway. As Butte and Chuquicamata face the loss or change of a familiar way of life, residents struggle to reclaim and assert their histories, their dignity, and their identification with community. In both locales, diverse and at times competing claims to history are being made in the interest of present and future community survival.

Butte is a town of storytellers, of amateur historians who regale visitors with tales of their colorful past. For many years, those stories were rich with pride and bravado. When the mines closed, their once-boisterous voices fell painfully silent. In the midst of that silence, one group began to talk back publicly to the social and economic desperation gripping the community. That group was the Butte Community Union (BCU), a grassroots organization concerned with jobs, justice, and the empowerment of low-income people. Its members — men and women, some long-term welfare recipients, some recently unemployed miners, and some committed social activists — had to struggle among themselves to forge common ground. BCU built its organization through dialogue and broad-based participation among its diverse members. The group conducted surveys that documented the economic vulnerability of many Butte residents. They made claims to their rights and dignity as workers and citizens and pointed to the language in the Montana state constitution that protected those rights. They publicized the irony that the community that had produced untold wealth for so many would now have one of the highest rates of poverty and unemployment in the state. And they took on the state in several lawsuits regarding the rights of the poor. In one of their most challenging and successful legal battles, the BCU stopped the State of Montana from dismantling its General Assistance Program for unemployed persons living in poverty. I had the opportunity to testify on behalf of BCU during the court proceedings in 1984 and to witness the commitment of this scrappy, bare-bones group as they talked back to the powers that be and won significant victories in the process. The constant uphill battle that BCU faced took its toll over the years. Internal tensions sapped the group's energies, and by the early 1990s it had disbanded. Yet through its nearly decade-long run, BCU asserted its reclamatory power, produced tangible changes, and demonstrated both the possibility and tenuousness of new forms of community alliance.

In recent years, a number of groups have made concerted efforts to keep Butte's mining history alive. Volunteers meet weekly at the World Museum of Mining to document and catalog photos and memorabilia from Butte's glory days. The Mai Wah Society dedicates itself to recovering the cultural history of Butte's Chinese community. Some look to mine history by making Butte the mecca for the curious who want to see, taste, and touch America's ethnic working-class roots. New partnerships are emerging among old-time storytellers, economic developers, and professionals in cultural and historic preservation. They are investing in the reclamation of Butte's past in the hope of creating a stable economic future for the community.

Work is underway on a series of community-based labor history projects such as the commemorative marking of the Granite Mountain and Speculator Mines, site of the infamous 1917 fire, in an effort to keep both labor consciousness and the local economy alive. There is contention regarding how history and landscape should be reclaimed. For some, reclamation is a technical chore of attempting to restore health and balance to a damaged natural environment. For others, reclamation also entails the claiming of a tough, gritty history. They do not want a sanitized landscape devoid of the stark reminders of Butte's past. Instead, the gallows frames and mine yards and scarred hillsides must stand as icons of historical consciousness, marking struggles that we cannot afford to forget. Some are seeing the need to locate women in that history and future. Scholars and activists have been reclaiming the legacies of Butte women such as the flamboyant feminist writer Mary MacLean and the formidable organizers of the Women's Protective Union. And as I attempt to show in this work, there is much to be learned when the voices of women are taken seriously in the discourses of history.

In Chuquicamata, the nostalgia stories of the Anaconda days pose a powerful counternarrative to the corporate call for a new order. As long-time residents defend the Anaconda days, they are defending and reaffirming the value of their own histories. Together, they built community against the odds. The Yankee and Chilean visions of community were often disparate, but they sought common ground in their shared stake in physical and cultural survival on the desert terrain.

Workingmen and workingwomen of Chuquicamata enjoyed some of the spoils of corporate paternalism. They fought hard for other rights. They crafted practical consciousness and political organizations, which they drew on to change the conditions of their lives. To label Anaconda as the "old order" that instilled dependency through paternalism is to negate and erase the history, dignity and identity of those women and men. Anaconda did not simply "lay its impress" on Chuquicamata. Rather, the company was engaged in a fifty-year effort to construct and contain its mining community, a process that variably met with support, acquiescence, and resistance.

At present in Chuquicamata, a struggle is underway for hegemonic control over versions of history. There is a double-talk in the local back talk to the "official" story being told by corporate actors. Chuquicamatinos both agree with and challenge the past images of paternalism and dependency. In their challenges, they remind themselves and the corporate storytellers that the people of Chuquicamata were and are critical actors who endeavored to preserve community and to change the conditions of their lives. They are not willing to shoulder all the blame for current political and economic problems facing the mine. And in this struggle, there is uncertainty and the possibility of transformation: new discourses, practices, and structural arrangements.

One important struggle underway in Chuquicamata links directly to the Anaconda legacy and the nationalization of the mines. In recent years, nationalization has been narrowly interpreted to include only the four major ore deposits that were previously under the ownership of Anaconda and Kennecott. A number of new mining projects have been joint ventures with foreign investors or entirely controlled by foreign partnerships. There are currently plans to develop a large ore deposit north of Chuquicamata. The management of CODELCO and their foreign investors contend that this deposit is an entity separate from Chuquicamata, to be developed independently, under the "new" labor

Figure 27.   "Water is life for agriculture. The Loa River is the inheritance of our children. What would happen with 5000 farmers without water." Protest by Atacama Farmers, Calama. 1993 (author photo).

discipline. Union activists in Chuquicamata are challenging the claim; they argue that the ore body is part of the Chuquicamata deposit and as such should be extracted by Chuquicamata's union labor. They are staking claim to the authority of geological surveys conducted by Anaconda decades ago in their attempt to trace the veins that connect this vast deposit of copper.

Water rights define another contested terrain in Chile's desert north. For more than eighty years, the Chuquicamata mine has maintained operations by siphoning scarce water that trickles down from the Andes. The mine's insatiable thirst has taken its toll on the subsistence farming communities of the Atacama Desert. Farmers have taken their protest to the streets of Calama, demanding the right to preserve a way of life deeply rooted in the altiplano. Their future is uncertain, however, and the mine is not their only competitor for scarce resources. The Atacama Desert is currently undergoing explosive development in tourism, with the daily arrival of outdoor enthusiasts seeking adventure, global travelers in pursuit of cultural authenticity, and New Age believers in search of truth. And with each tourist comes the demand for more water (see fig. 27).

These practices of reclamation reflect the meaning of the Spanish word *reclamar*: to claim, demand, or protest. This meaning captures the power behind the local back talk. People are making claims about their histories. They are demanding that the terrain of the talkable be broadened. Some protest an official story that has dichotomized their lives into a past and present, an "old" and "new" order, and has represented them as victims or villains. Others demand their rights to a way of life in danger of being sucked dry. Men are making claims to the validity of their workingmen's wisdom and their rights to meaningful participation in the decisions that affect their lives. Women are making claims for greater social and political space and are transforming the politics of consumption in the process. As these struggles unfold, boundaries of community and exclusion are demarcated and transgressed.

Through their words and actions, people of Butte and Chuquicamata are reclaiming their pasts and the relations and emotions that link them to people and place. It is in their stories and their practices of reclamation that cultural knowledge of community building is encoded. Their stories are filled with how-to lessons, with knowledge of support and resistance. They speak to the consciousness that informed social action and to the actions that shaped consciousness.

Often, women and men have not been encouraged to see the value and validity of their memories and histories. In my work with women of the mining community, I cannot count the times that a conversation began with my companion saying, "Well, I don't really have anything to tell you." Yet in her words was knowledge of practice and in the telling was possibility, perhaps the impetus to listeners to ask more questions, perhaps an invitation to mine the resources of women's histories and memories as we build futures beyond copper.

The process of reclamation offers lessons in critical practice for social change. Through documentation and support of local knowledge about crafts(wo)manship, vigilance, and mobilization, the efforts of less powerful groups may be strengthened and their claims to community heard. Though community may be obsolete to the corporate powerplayers, it remains as the site and subject of action for its members. The challenge is to engage in the process of reclamation with new imaginings of and claims for communities of connection and concern.

Food for Thought and Action

There is nothing outside of the text.
Jacques Derrida 1976

con—clude' v.t. [M.E. *concluden* to conclude; L *concludere*, to shut up closely, enclose; *con-* together and *claudere*, to shut]
  1. to shut up; to enclose [Obs]
  2. to include; to comprehend [Obs]
  3. to arrive at by reasoning; to infer; to deduce
  4. to decide; to determine; to make a final determination concerning
  5. to bring to a close; to end to finish
  6. to stop or restrain, or, as in law, to estop from further argument or proceedings; to oblige or bind, as by authority or by one's own argument or concession
  7. to settle or arrange finally; to come to an agreement about
con—clude' i.t.
  1. to settle an opinion; to come to an agreement; to form a final judgment
  2. to come to a close; to end; to terminate
      Webster's Unabridged Dictionary 1983

"So, what are your conclusions?"
      Most frequently asked question on the topic of research

On a bleak December day in Missoula, Montana, I set out for the umpteenth time to conclude this work.[1] Being well-versed in the rigors of academia, I understand the power of conclusion to give authority to one's work. But I resist. This odyssey does not lend itself to a list of smartly packaged, cogent insights. The odyssey refuses to end. It pushes and pulls me in new directions, rendering me both obligated and impassioned. I write surrounded by piles of books, boxes of reports, bundles of field notes, reams of transcripts. They, like the histories, voices, struggles, and hopes contained within them, refuse to be neatly tied up. They demand openness, not closure.

There is so much that lies outside of this text, so many stories, so many spaces filled with tears, touch, and laughter. There are the vivid memories of my overwhelming sense of inadequacy to do justice to this project. And there are the friendships, love, and commitments that made this so much more than an intellectual journey. If I were to offer one conclusion it is this: this work has transformed my life. It has brought me face-to-face with the depths of human brutality and the well-spring of human courage, hope, and possibility. The practice of research has sparked passion tempered with tolerance and humility. It has constantly confronted me with the partiality of my knowledge and the need to draw on all the emotional and material resources at hand in order to grasp and challenge that partiality.

As I try to come to terms with the unsettled and uncertain subtext that lies beneath these neatly bound pages, my thoughts drift to another December day in Montana several years ago. I was skiing across a snow-covered lake, enjoying the rhythmic kick and glide along the (seemingly) frozen surface. I stopped to take in the view and looked behind to see the blue-gray traces of glacial water seeping through my snow tracks, a silent reminder of my vulnerable position. In that moment, the situation changed as I became acutely aware of my presence, weight, and movements — all which had seemed "natural" a moment before. Haltingly, I began to make my way under conditions not of my own making, searching for solid ground rather than assuming its existence. This story has no dramatic ending. Within minutes I was safely at the shoreline. But I was left with a lingering sensation of that moment when "all that was solid melted into air," when old certainties did not stand up to new circumstances.

This sensation crept over me many times throughout the research process. In part, it was a sense of being where I didn't belong, being out of place. I was the transgressor, crossing over, tunneling under, and blurring boundaries. Perhaps it was the constant struggle to reach beyond the limitations of my knowledge and grasp the complicated politics and histories that infuse present truths and lies. I was the uneasy voyeur of my own history in Butte. I was a curious mix of informant and observer as I uncovered and created intimacies that belied the foreignness of Chuquicamata. I have tried to craft a map of this vast and deep terrain riddled with veins and tunnels as I gingerly picked my way across it. I have told a story that spans one century and two continents. But my rendering remains a thin representation of the thick complexities that confronted the makers of this mining history.

I have not finished with this project, nor has the project finished with me. I now live straddling two continents, moving back and forth between them both emotionally and physically. I am an uncomfortable resident of the United States, no longer able to constrict my view of "America" to its borders. I am a privileged visitor in Chile, who, despite accent, moves chameleonlike across multiple boundaries. Whatever certainties I once held about home, community, and citizenship have been disturbed. I consider new possibilities previously beyond my reach of the thinkable, talkable, or do-able. I am grateful for the gift of becoming that the contributors to this project have given me. I owe them not an ending but an affirmation of openness and connection. This is the spirit of the trialectic: to move beyond dialectical interplay and to respect the power of indeterminacy, of new imaginings that push against and expand the partiality of our knowledge. In lieu of a conclusion, I offer a pastiche of reflections and possibilities.

REFLECTIONS ON A THEORY OF PRACTICE

In this work, I refer variably to a "theory of practice" and a "practice perspective." The notion of a theory of practice does not fit neatly into the dominant discourse of social theory as an explanation for why change occurs. The very nature of practice theory throws into question the notion of an objective, omniscient perspective making claims about the process of social change. If reality is socially constructed through the interplay of structure and practice, then the theorist herself is intimately implicated in the process of constructing her reality and that of her field of research. She is at best struggling to systematically guide her efforts at apprehending and representing complex social phenomena.

A *theory* of practice suggests that social change is both an objective and socially constructed phenomena, grounded in a particular historical moment by particular historical contingencies. Social change is the result of actions carried out in a context of unequal power. Actors are making change and making themselves at the same time as they are being made through a myriad of structures and practices that constitute the social and cultural contouring, resources, and modes of action historically possible and available. Structures gain meaning and power only through their practice. And in that practice is the possibility of error, creativity, and change.

This theoretical statement leaves me overwhelmed yet unable to reduce or simplify it. I find it more productive to think in terms of a practice perspective. By this, I mean a set of conceptual lenses and questions that guide inquiry about the social world from the positions of a grounded actor who is part of that world. The terms *structure* and *practice* are separable for analytic purposes. The perspective, however, places critical emphasis on their mutually constituting relationship and the indeterminacy of that relationship. The perspective asserts rather than empirically questions the centrality and inequality of power. In this sense, the perspective is not neutral but critical and political. Questions of history demand attention to questions of location, possibility, and patterns and trajectories of change. Perhaps the word *histories* serves us better than *history* in recognizing the meaning and power of multiple constructions of past and present.

The attention to actors is both theoretically and politically important. Given the heavy weight of cultural determinism, the practice perspective poses hopeful questions of how and when people find the courage, creativity, and power to act at all. The results may not often match the intent as actors struggle to think and act critically within the confines of their social and cultural circumstances. But the truly remarkable fact remains that they find the wherewithal to act at all. Perhaps most change, in the end, occurs more by accident than by design. But people continue to make themselves as they attempt to make their histories in spite and because of all the forces that are making them. For recognition of this alone, a practice perspective deserves consideration, not only as a means for understanding complex social phenomena, but also as a guide for engaging in the process of social change.

I want to elaborate further on the "human" in agency and subjectivity addressed here. The notion of an intentional human subject has been soundly trounced in the poststructural and postmodern moves to discursively constructed subjectivities and fragmented identities. Ethnography, however, calls for careful listening to the ways in which people find and make meaning, embody and express feelings, and negotiate their way in the world. As I listened to a wealth of stories, I became more convinced of the power of humanness, the search for meaning, and the desire to render coherence in the face of contradiction. Stories are not mere patterns of discourse. They ground us to our histories and

experiences in the world. They inscribe and validate our human inten-
tionality and capacity to find, make, and communicate meaning. As
Peter McLaren argues, "Human subjectivity is never reduced to a hypo-
thetical or abstract bundle of signs. Consequently, social agents never
lose their capacity for suffering or their resoluteness for effecting social
transformation" (1994, 200).[2] It is this sense of being human — having
emotion, desire, and the "sense of project," in spite and because of the
weight of determining social forces — that resonates through the stories
I relate here. A theory of social practice, then, must not disconnect the
human from agency and subjectivity; it must look to the many ways in
which people make that connection meaningful in the face of powerful
fragmenting forces.

As I state in chapter 1, I have come to see this work as a political project, a study for social transformation. It represents a bridging of practice and feminist perspectives and illustrates their mutually informing
potential in a number of ways. First, though practice theorists have, to
varying degrees, attended to questions of power and inequality, there
has been less attention to their own positionalities as researchers and the
constraints and possibilities they face in coming to know their subjects
of study. Feminist theorists have made rich contributions to our understanding of subject positioning, the implications for knowledge development, and the need for reflexivity in the practice of research.
Throughout this work, I attempt to locate myself in the story as I, like
the residents of Butte and Chuquicamata, faced the confusions and possibilities of mining life. I appreciate the parallel processes at work in our
mutual efforts to partially apprehend the meaning and power of complex social relations and conditions. Second, drawing from feminist
insights, I take gender as an issue not a given. The practice perspective
provides an organizing frame for examining the dynamics of gender
relations and the making of gendered consciousness under very particular historical conditions. It is through the illumination of these micro-
processes that we grasp a deeper understanding of how particular forms
of inequality are maintained and justified, how they map on to other
axes of difference, and how they might be challenged and transformed
into resources for change. Third, the on-the-ground analyses of working
class women's social practice offer alternative ways of conceptualizing
agency that push against and broaden the boundaries of current practice
theory. Hopefully, this study contributes to the possibilities for pursuing
what Ortner has termed "subaltern practice theory," which attends to

slippages, disorder, and disruption as well as to the forces of social reproduction (Ortner 1996, 17).

BEYOND COMPARISON

This project has opened up for me a whole new meaning of the word *practice*. I became an engaged practitioner in the fullest sense of the word. There is a world of difference between abstract theorizing about practice and the concrete practice of transnational research. It was through the tacking back and forth, the questioning of presumed boundaries, and the excavating of multiple histories that I began to see beyond a comparative lens. I both employed a comparative strategy and challenged the notion of comparison. The comparisons highlighted distinctions in corporate practices of community building, articulation of class interests, and forms of women's social practice. A comparative approach was informative but insufficient. An exploration of the relationship between these two communities, and of their enmeshment in complex webs of power and significance, was key to understanding the processes of community, class, and gender in the making.

The refusal to be bound to comparison is itself a disruptive act. It challenges ingrained beliefs about we and they, north and south, and male and female. Transgression of the comparative divide has unsettling effects. In both formal presentations and casual conversations in the United States about my research, I am frequently asked to describe the "differences" I found. When I reply, "Differences in what sense?" the questioner often raises a skeptical eyebrow, wondering about my skill as a researcher. I begin to elaborate the relationships that challenge assumptions about comparative categories, pointing instead to the communities' struggles over shifting boundaries of inclusion and exclusion. I seduce my listeners with a larger story of the patterns that connect, sprinkling in comparison along the way. When all is said and done, I often find the initial question still waiting for me, "But what were the major differences you found between Butte and Chuquicamata?" The question is reminiscent of the Butte miners' views of their Chilean counterparts. Difference is taken as a social fact; what we want are the ethnographic details of how different *we* are from *them*. Perhaps the details of commonality pose uncomfortable challenges to the security of assumed boundaries.

I have given presentations on my research to university classes and social action organizations in Chile. Listeners often assume that Butte is a microcosm of the United States, whose bold images of wealth, power, and consumption wage a constant assault on the Chilean populace. Radio, television, billboards, fast-food chains, foreign aid, and the ubiquitous English on secondhand T-shirts deliver an incessant message of having it all in the United States of America. Stories of strikes, shutdowns, bravado, and betrayal carry with them connections that defy the gilt-edged picture that the U.S. markets abroad. In its place is a more complicated picture of internal contradictions and precarious third worlds superimposed on the image of U.S. privilege. I have encountered both surprise and perhaps satisfaction from Chilean audiences in seeing flaws in the image and tracing the patterns that connect. As we recognize and expose the vulnerable underbelly of the United States, we may discover resources and schema for imagining and crafting new visions of common ground. By rethinking assumed axes of difference, we open spaces for the appreciation of multiple distinctions and identifications and the possibilities for crafting connections among them.

REFLECTIONS ON THE THEMES OF PRACTICE

MINING FEELINGS

Raymond Williams writes of "structure of feeling," Michel Foucault of "discourse," and Pierre Bourdieu of "habitus."[3] In their distinct languages and formulations, they grapple with the "internalization of the external" and the "naturalization of the arbitrary." They point to the relations of power that shape interior and exterior terrains of feeling and meaning. Yet the range and depth of emotion engendered by class position have been largely unaddressed. This work tries to move beyond the abstractions and offer an ethnographic encounter with the structure of feeling. The stories of men and women trying to make sense of the confusions of mining life speak to the emotional complexities that shape the intersection of gender and class.

The people of Butte and Chuquicamata lived a confounded reality as a powerful company gave with one hand while it took with the other. Their accounts speak to the internal struggles engendered as competing external forces collided in lived experience. Notions of "class interest," "class consciousness," and "gender relations" fail to grasp the depth of fear, betrayal, bravado, confusion, and aspiration that resonate through these stories. I have come to see this work as an ethnography of emotion and economy. It is not what I had set out to study. But as I learned to listen more closely to the emotional tone of the words, I encountered new languages of class, gender, and community in stories that embodied sentiment, resentment, and (re)sentiment.

Fear and violence penetrate the very fabric of this history. Linda Green, in her important essay on fear as a way of life, describes the internalization of fear and violence that became second nature among people living in the context of state terrorism. Green writes that "fear thrives on ambiguities" (1994, 227). In many ways, fear has been internalized as a way of life among people in Butte and Chuquicamata. The inculcation of fear that defies description grips the stories of torture, terror, and death under the dictatorship. Yet insidious histories of fear and violence run as deep as the veins of copper themselves. Danger filled the very air that miners breathed. The economics of survival taught miners to mask their fears with bravado as they entered the depths of the earth each day. Mining women lived with fears of impending widowhood. Their marriages, too, were often emotionally and economically volatile, offering no safe haven from violence and danger. Bravado could only go so far in masking the fears of death, arrest, hunger, betrayal, and loss of a way of life.

Fear has infiltrated this history, thriving on the ambiguities of mining life. As residents carried the emotional weight of these ambiguities, they crafted their own forms of resistance and (re)sentiment. It is in this sense that I engage with the meaning and power of contradiction here. I present contradiction as lived experience: internal struggles forged through the confusing push and pull of conflicting discourses and patterns of practice. As their bodies bore the weight of intersecting contradictions, women and men of the mining community both resisted and engaged with those contradictions. They challenged the truth value of competing discourses, their skepticism fueling their resistance. They physically stood their ground, engendering class-based solidarity to resist exploitation. They stood together and apart as competing contradictions forged complicated alliances and animosities of power and intimacy. They gave voice to their resentments as they talked back to the tensions of this confusing history. Perhaps the practice of reclamation, of staking claim to one's history and dignity, is also a process of (re)sentiment. They spoke and are speaking to and beyond fear as they claim a range and depth of emotion and experience. Their claims contradict the forces that constrain, distort, and devalue the politics and sentiments of mining life.

GENDERED PRACTICE

Examination of working-class women's practice of crafting the everyday takes us inside the tensions of structure and agency and of emotion and economy. As women lived the contradictions of their class and gender positions, they engaged in critical practice that transformed deprivation into determination. They crafted self and circumstance in and through the ambiguous spaces of their working-class womanhood. As they identified, extended, and transposed the resources and schema available to them, they challenged the certainties of class and gender relations. Women crafted normalcy in the face of crisis. They moved through and beyond fear to find resources and possibility in ambiguities. They stood their ground and suffered the recriminations of men. Perhaps women's very engagement with ambiguity at times rendered them "dangerous" in the eyes of men. As they both mobilized and challenged the images of womanhood, women transformed their subordinated positions into weapons of the weak.

Mining men variably responded with rage, resentment, and reluctant acquiescence as they masked their fears. Doubt has been cast on their deeply held beliefs about work and women, leaving mining men unsure about where to stake their claims to identity. Perhaps it is that uncertainty that now binds them to skepticism of and resistance to the new disciplinary practices for a flexible labor force. With the solidity of enduring truths melting into air, perhaps betrayal is the one certainty that remains for mining men. It is much more familiar and predictable than engagement with ambiguity. In this sense, perhaps the working-class women of Butte and Chuquicamata are more practiced at deep play than are their mining men.

As they crafted the everyday, women honed their skills as critical actors engaged in community building. Students and practitioners of social change could benefit from apprenticeship with these master craftswomen. These women crafted social and dividuated selves that posed challenges to notions of autonomous individualism and interest as the motive force of human agency. In so doing, they taught the importance of maintenance: it is hard to mobilize collective action if the relational infrastructure of those collectivities is neglected. The women of Butte and Chuquicamata remind us of the intrinsic importance of relationships and their need for ongoing nurturance, not merely as means to an end but as ends in themselves, the process and product of humanity.

Crafting the everyday demands hard work and vigilance. Women crafted a sense of rhythm and place from the temporal and spatial structurings of their lives and learned to modulate vigilance and mobilization in the process. They seized the moments of deep play and exploited the potential of their vague and vulnerable positionality as working-class women.

Men have important lessons to learn from women's histories. Polyvalent workers are in demand in the retooled labor market of twenty-first century capitalism. But the history of women's labor is a history of polyvalent labor: diffused and devalued. Without an alternative common sense and political base, the women and men of Butte and Chuquicamata risk a fragmentation of their labor, identity, and solidarity as diffuse as new forms of capitalism.

TOWARD A POLITICS OF CONSUMPTION?

In the Marxist tradition of the critique of political economy, relations of production have enjoyed theoretical and practical pride of place. As feminists have critically engaged with Marxist theory, they have shifted the focus to questions of reproduction. Relations of consumption have been relegated to third tier in this trinity of social relations. However, in the stories of women from Butte and Chuquicamata, concerns of consumption, of food and housing, and of family and community well-being drive their political consciousness and action. Their concerns echo those of women in disparate historical and cultural locations.[4] Their accounts challenge the primacy of production and place consumption at the center of an alternative political discourse and practice.

Temma Kaplan (1982), Caroline Moser (1987), and others address the dynamic formation of "female consciousness" grounded in responsibilities for preserving human life. Kaplan suggests that women with "female consciousness" accept the gendered division of labor of their society. In fulfilling their gendered obligations, women have politicized issues of family and community. Moser documents the daily struggles of women to fulfill their obligations for preserving life in an urban squatter settlement in Guayaquil, Ecuador: getting food and water, laying boards to build walkways between shelters, and waiting in long bread lines. She suggests that women build a common critical consciousness through these practices, such that the daily tasks of preserving family life become political tasks and promote a process of political development. Similarly, Helen Safa, in a recent overview of women's movements in Latin America, writes that concerns for human rights and collective consumption are those around which women are organizing (1990, 354). June Nash has become convinced that the motivations for the great social movements of Bolivian mining communities were the life concerns of the family and community (1994, 9).

These accounts, like the narratives included in this work, speak to consumption as central to the practical politics of daily life, the politics of survival. They speak to social, collective responsibility. Poor and working-class women engage daily with the politics of consumption. They are developing consciousness, commitment, and political efficacy through their practice. In effect, they pose a fundamental challenge to the tenets of liberalism. Their knowledge and practice disrupts the certainties of autonomy, rights, and freedom. They know that without maintenance of basic subsistence needs, the struggles over control of the factory floor become moot.

June Nash returns to the work of Flora Tristan and Rosa Luxemburg in thinking through the centrality of relations of consumption. She reminds us that the consumption concerns they addressed were seen as counterproductive to the struggles directed at seizing the means of production (Nash 1994, 9). But consumption concerns are central to the struggles of women whose daily labors are devoted to the preservation of life. The struggles take different forms, given the emotional and material resources at hand. But what of the radical and transformative potential of a politics of consumption? If relations of consumption were the central organizing frame for a critical theory and practice of social change, how might we challenge limits of the thinkable, talkable, and do-able? As we disrupt the certainties of liberalism, what new configurations of the self, the state, and the social might emerge? Can we imagine a political time and space constructed around an ethics of care rather than rights, as Carol Gilligan (1982) suggests? Perhaps, through attention to the cultural politics of consumption, we can craft a "language of critique and possibility" that talks back to forces of fragmentation and breathes life into new social movements.[5]

There may be more forces that separate than connect women and men in their struggles across borders. But basic survival is at stake for too many to simply dismiss the possibility. As June Nash asks, "Once we reject the false opposition of First and Third Worlds, can we grasp the commonalities in the welfare problems faced by women trying to feed their families and keep their children alive, whether they live in drug war-infested inner cities of industrialized countries or in militarized countries where conflicts are exacerbated by U.S. arms shipments?" (1994, 9). I do not offer simple solutions. Perhaps by imagining a politics of consumption, we will generate food for thought and action.

ON COMMUNITY AND TRANSNATIONALISM

In this postmodern moment of unanchored signs, fluid space, and compressed temporality, a notion of community seems curiously anachronistic. There are those naysayers of the postmodern who claim the end of locality. Life is a simulation and the local a mere abstraction. There are those who dismiss any notion of community with disdain. Images of the "little community" à la Redfield are conjured, mocked for their utopian naïveté, and summarily rejected. Yet this complicated sense of belonging, a practiced commitment to one's place in its many senses, is too central to the stories here to be buried in the ashes of tradition or modernity. The complicated imaginings and practices of community merit sustained attention, not dismissal. How do people carve out spaces of we-ness amidst the chaos and uncertainty of this postmodern moment marked by global integration and brutal inequalities? How permeable are the lines of inclusion and exclusion as old truths and new hopes are disrupted and reinvented?

We have seen a rich rekindling of interest in the community question and its relation to transnationalism in recent years. Drawing on narratives of migrant workers moving between Northern California and central Mexico, Roger Rouse (1991) reenvisions community as a transnational circuit of movement among multiple sites of attachment and economy that profoundly shapes social life. Leo Chavez (1994) challenges this notion of community as a circuit of movement, suggesting instead that people carry and construct multiple imaginings of community with them that transcend bounds of locality as they face the exigencies of a transnational labor market. Some writers document the construction of tightly circumscribed base communities as sites of action in response to repressive politics and economics. Others point to the need for local level studies that examine linkages between macro-level policy changes and local economies.[6] These issues indicate the salience of community for cultural scholars and actors alike. They also point to the need for critical research and action regarding the impact of global forces on local survival.

This work offers a theoretical and practical model for approaching the relationship between capitalism and community. It calls for exposing the veins of power, appreciating historical and cultural possibilities, and engaging with the transformative potential of this knowledge. As capitalism plants its shallow roots within and beyond the bounds of ubiquitous "free-trade zones," more and more communities will find themselves linked as intimate strangers, unwitting victims of their own "local knowledge" that may limit their view of the patterns that connect. The outlook is grim but not hopeless. It gives me pause to reflect on possibilities for community practice in the context of transnationalism.

First, something that struck me in this research was how powerfully this history resonated with both domestic and imperial civilizing projects and disciplinary practices. My lack of comparative attention to this literature is a shortcoming of the project. Certainly, a careful consideration of corporate and imperial "community building" is beyond the scope of this work. However, there is a rich historic and ethnographic base for documenting the making of workers, citizens, consumers, and community members from the rubber plantations of Sumatra to the coffee fields of Brazil, and from the tin mines of Bolivia to the auto assembly plants of Detroit. Those histories tell us not only about forms of power, but also about forms of struggle. As I reflect on the interplay of emotion and economy and on the challenges of contradiction, I want to return to those histories and engage with them. How might a reclamation project that connected local knowledge across industrial and imperial borders enrich our grasp of the historically possible and inform a politics of transformation? How might it expand thinking about current patterns and practices that are linking and separating the displaced auto workers of the U.S. rust belt, the women laboring fifteen-hour days in *maquiladoras* (assembly plants) on the U.S.-Mexico border, and service workers from Punta Arenas to Port Angeles who eke out a living catering to the whims of transnational travelers?

Second, this project has bolstered my faith in the possibilities of connecting local and global concerns. As Elspeth Probyn argues, "Instead of collapsing the local, we have to open it up" (1990, 186). We must challenge the naturalization of "local" and totalizing images of community that suppress difference. In so doing, we must not forget the power of local acts and events to resist, challenge, and transform the global. Local actors are making cosmopolitan connections as they challenge and resist the devastating consequences of global integration. From sister-city projects to peace and justice solidarity groups, local people are building long-term relationships and crafting possibilities for discovering and building common ground. Labor organizations have instigated moves toward social-movement unionism that encompass broad community needs and promote broad-based participation. New alliances for environmental and economic justice are forming to challenge discourses of "jobs versus environment." Organizations such as the Border Committee of Women Workers have formed to foster solidarity among U.S. and Mexican workers.[7] As Richard Falk puts it in "The Making of Global Citizenship," popular organizations need to counter "globalization from above" by expanding "globalization from below" (1993, 39–50).

Finally, a cautionary word. I am concerned about the counterrevolutionary implications of those who espouse the end of locality. It is curious that the death of the local is being proclaimed at the very moment when we are witnessing an intensity of local activity for transformational change. Much of that activity is women's work, politicizing relations of consumption, staking claims for family and community survival, and challenging the foundations of liberalism. Perhaps the local is more dangerous than obsolete.

SPEAKING TO THE FUTURE

During my dissertation defense, Barry Checkoway, a mentor and member of my doctoral committee, posed an important question and challenge: If you were to write the *next* chapter of this history, a chapter of the future, and include yourself as an actor in that next chapter, what would it be? I responded at the time with reflections on myself as an actor in this study, shaped by and shaping the story I tell. I spoke of the possibilities of new relationships and practices that would help us to better see common human struggles amid the fog of distinctions. I talked of the skills involved in crafting the everyday that might enable us to more successfully engage with struggle and contradiction. How might we come to recognize, value, and impart these skills? And I spoke of my responsibility for reclaiming the stories of those who have been silenced and dis(re)membered in mining history. I, too, must talk back and tell the stories, committing my voice to an alternative discourse.

As I have had time to reflect further on the question, I have come to realize that I have been engaged in writing the next chapter from the moment I began the project. I have been articulating the connections as I have been making them, wondering aloud, in public, about the hidden intimacies of Butte and Chuquicamata and learning from the connections and distinctions made by others. Writing the next chapter has become a personal and political practice of telling the story as I live it. I have taken the stories of women, copper, and community to audiences large and small, from international social welfare conferences, to social justice groups, women's organizations, and the local Butte Historical Society. I have seen the glimmer of tears in the eyes of Butte women as I tell the stories of crafting the everyday in Chuquicamata. I have witnessed the anger of Anaconda Company loyalists who have a different story to tell of corporate history. These encounters are part of my commitment to reclamation, to opening up the discussion and situating myself within it. I am uneasy with the sound of my voice on the radio, or my name and photo in the paper as a bearer of "expert knowledge." But I have had the privilege of listening to stories long silenced. I now have a responsibility to make them heard.

Before I wax too sentimental on storytelling, I must return to sobering issues of authorship and appropriation and to the question I raise in chapter 1: How do we become invested in the truth value of the stories we tell? Through months of editing, questioning, and revisiting, I have come to tell a story that I care about and believe. That story is shaped around a familiar beginning-to-end format. But that format is not so much a literary choice as it is the result of my own style of detective work. There was so very much I did not know. I taught myself as I researched and wrote, asking "What else was going on?" or, perhaps, more in line with the childlike sense of curiosity and awe this project provoked in me, "So *then* what happened?" Despite my efforts to represent the seepage of past into presence and vice versa, I have told a story that seems too tidy. Even as I resist the closure of a conclusion, I believe I have erred on the side of containment in my effort to convince.

Storytelling is part substance and part seduction. I want to pull you in to the power of consumption, leave you looking over your shoulder, and render you skeptical of skepticism. I want you to practice your own *artesanía*. I want to register both the urgency and possibility of a politics of transformation writ local and global. I am making claims as both author and activist. In so doing, I am appropriating the stories from histories of social change to legitimize a history for social change. And what themes might emerge, what stories might feed my passions and politics, when I revisit and rethink the data five, ten, twenty years from now?

I am both appropriator and appropriated in writing to the future. As I reclaim silenced histories, others stake claims to my words. For example, in 1994, the human resources and public relations director of the Chuquicamata mine arranged an extensive visit to their operations for me. I spent two days riding around in a company truck, wearing a hard hat, and chatting with personnel handpicked by management. I was accompanied by a reporter for *Oasis*, who gave me a running commentary on Chuquicamata as he chauffeured me from meeting to meeting. In something of a quid pro quo, I agreed to be interviewed by the reporter before leaving Chuquicamata. I gave him essays I had written in Spanish and talked with him at length about my project. Even as I spoke, I was acutely aware of the silences within my own story. Themes of trust and betrayal echoed through my carefully chosen words. I felt an affinity to the reporter, but knew he, too, was bound to craft certain truths and elide others. Joined in an unspoken complicity of intimacy and (dis)trust, we crafted a contested version of mining history.

Some time later, I was presented with "Del Splendor a la Agonía," which is part engaging melodrama of Butte's history and part morality play on the future of Chuquicamata. This article, which graced the pages of *Oasis* in August of 1994, was a curious joint venture whose historical "authority" rested on the insights of a gringa anthropologist, and whose literary authority rested on the fine craftsmanship of a "native" journalist. And the lessons to Chuquicamatinos? Take heed of Butte's conflicted history: collaborate or lose. My words, along with my status as Butte girl and cultural scholar, had been appropriated in support of the "new order." I felt the violation of my words, partialized, depoliticized, and repoliticized. I wonder who might feel the same as they read this book.

Close encounters with the politics of authority remind me that, in the words of Paulo Freire, "Dialogue is not a chaste event." Neither is silence. Part of a practice for social change is to speak to the silences and against histories that mute so many voices. Knowledge is built not only from convergence but also from counterpattern.[8] The disruption of smooth and seamless truths with kaleidoscopic counterpatterns is a political act. Less powerful voices are discounted and distorted by the dominant discourse. But their back talk mocks and challenges, poking holes and exposing the force of power and the fissures of vulnerability. This project has taught me to listen for the silences and the back talk and to search for counterpatterns that go against the dominant grain. I hope it is a lesson I take to heart, not only as a researcher but as a teacher, writer, and activist.

Through this journey, I have learned important lessons in the politics of possibility. The stories of courageous men and women speak to the possibility of transforming positions of oppression into resources for making political claims. They also point to the need for imagining new forms of community in order to confront the challenges posed by the shifting forces of global capitalism. Perhaps, as we practice transgression and trace connections, we can craft future projects and movements informed by the critical lessons of history. We need to claim spaces of ambiguity and transform them into places of solidarity, pooling and reworking the cultural and material resources at hand. As the global economy splits further into haves and have-nots, those committed to a more just image of the world community need to engage in deep play with the forces that maintain and exacerbate inequities. It is a game we seemingly cannot win, but can't not play.

Copper Production, 1920-1972

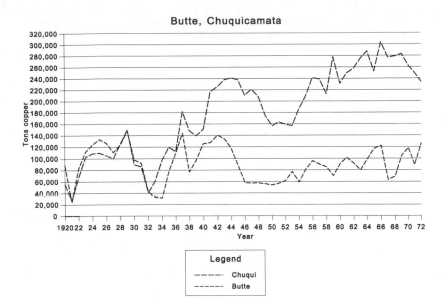

Butte, Chuquicamata

SOURCES: *Mineral Resources of the United States, Part I, Metals.* United States Department of Interior (Department of Commerce, 1930–1932) (Washington, D.C.: U.S. Government Printing Office, 1923, 1927, 1930–1932, 1934–1958). Corporación Nacional del Cobre, *El Cobre Chileno* (Santiago: CODELCO, 1975), 491; Anaconda Company, *Annual Reports,* 1920–1926, 1956–1973.

Copper Production, 1934-1972

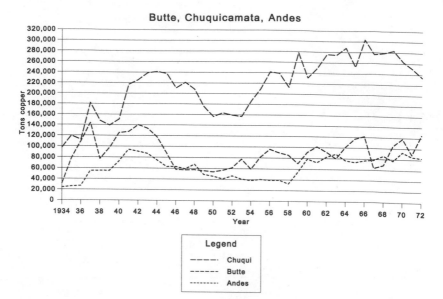

SOURCES: *Minerals Year Book*, U.S. Department of Interior (Washington, D.C.: U.S. Government Printing Office, 1934–1958); Corporación Nacional del Cobre, *El Cobre Chileno* (Santiago: CODELCO, 1975), 490; Anaconda Company, *Annual Reports*, 1958–1973. *Andes* refers to Andes Copper Company, the Anaconda Subsidiary at Potrerillos-El Salvador.

Notes

1. TRACING THE VEINS

1. The chapter's epigraph is from the cover page introduction to Isaac Marcosson's laudatory history of the Anaconda Company, *Anaconda* (1957); reprinted 1976, North Stratford, N.H.: Ayer Co. Publishers. Permission to quote courtesy of Ayer Co. Publishers.

The Anaconda Copper Mining Company was incorporated in 1895 in Montana. The corporate name was changed to The Anaconda Company in 1955, to better represent its diversification beyond copper. Throughout this work I use various references, including Anaconda, the Anaconda Company, or simply the company, as did my informants. The company controlled the mines of Chuquicamata from 1923 to 1971. Atlantic Richfield Corporation purchased the Anaconda Company in 1977.

2. William Roseberry (1991) argues the case for linking anthropology and history, especially in the context of understanding the Americas.

3. On women's social action in North American labor movements, see, for example, Kingsolver (1989), Briskin and Yanz (1985), and Milkman (1985).

4. The 1953 documentary film *Salt of the Earth* powerfully depicts the positioning of women in worker struggles during a strike at a New Mexico zinc mine. For insightful analyses into gender, labor, and forms of social action, see Baron (1991), Faue (1991), Frank (1985; 1991a; 1991b), Kaplan (1982), and Susser (1988).

5. Barbara Kingsolver found a similar pattern and discourse among Arizona women involved in the 1983 strike at the Phelps Dodge copper mine (1989, 17–18).

6. I borrow this expression from Lillian Rubin's title, *Worlds of Pain: Life in the Working-Class Family* (1978).

7. Anaconda had mining, smelting, and refining operations in other parts of Montana, Utah, Nevada, and New Mexico, processing and fabrication plants in a number of states, silver and copper mines in Mexico and Peru, and a lead plant in Poland. Copper, however, was the centerpiece of corporate operations, and

the resources of Chuquicamata and Butte provided the lion's share over the years. The Greene Cananea subsidiary in the state of Sonora, Mexico, was a source of roughly thirty to forty thousand tons of copper annually from the 1920s to 1971. The Andes Mining Company subsidiary at Potrerillos-El Salvador in Chile became increasingly important, with production rates greater than Butte's by the 1960s. An examination of corporate-community relations in these locales is beyond the scope of this work but merits future study.

8. Butte has long been known as the "Richest Hill on Earth" in local lore and history. Recently it has earned the more dubious distinction of being the Environmental Protection Agency's geographically largest "Superfund" cleanup site, a legacy of mining history. See Baum and Knox (1992).

9. I refer here to the notion of subject positioning whereby one's "selves" are constructed through and grounded in particular contexts. As Linda Alcoff argues, subjectivity is "positionality within a context" (1994, 117).

10. Chile's first democratic elections after the military coup of 1973 were held in December 1989. Patricio Aylwin, the successful Christian Democratic presidential candidate, assumed office in March, 1990.

11. Clifford Geertz places meaning at the center of cultural knowledge and practice and develops a textual metaphor to represent the process through which cultural actors construe experience (1973; 1983). Returning to and drawing from the work of Antonio Gramsci, Raymond Williams develops the linkages of culture and power and argues that culture is not only meaningful but political (1977; 1980). Michel Foucault's insights on power as relational are central to my analysis (1990, 93–95). Power is both repressive and productive; it is constructed through a field of social relations and exercised through discursive and nondiscursive practices of definition, domination, reward, and resistance. For an excellent overview of meaning and power as key issues in cultural theory, see Dirks, Eley, and Ortner (1994, 4–34). For further discussion of the centrality of meaning and power in cultural analysis, see R. Rosaldo (1989, 91–108) and Roseberry (1991, 30–54). Excellent ethnographies that address the connection of meaning and power include Sidney Mintz, *Sweetness and Power* (1985), Jose Limón, "*Carne, Carnales*, and the Carnivalesque" (1989, 471–486), and Paul Willis, *Learning to Labor* (1981).

12. Census data in the 1916 Butte City Directory reports the city's population at 93,000. Census data shows a population decline in Butte each decade since 1920.

13. The Plaza, along with the rest of Chuquicamata, was built by the company. Residents claimed the plaza both as social space and political base. In many residents' stories, the Plaza is the setting for social gatherings and a place for launching protests.

14. See "Companies: An Ex-Banker Treats Copper's Sickest Giant" (1972) for a discussion of the aftermath of nationalization of copper mining in Chile. The article notes that the Anaconda Company's Chilean mines supplied two-thirds of the company's primary copper output and 75 percent of its earnings.

15. Early retirements, encouraged by *Corporación Nacional del Cobre* (CODELCO), the Chilean national mining operation, account for a major part of the workforce reduction. Unofficial figures from a company spokesperson indicate that as of 1995, there are approximately seven thousand union and three thousand nonunion contracted laborers employed in the Chuquicamata operations.

16. On nationalizing the copper industry, see "El Presidente Allende habla

acerca del cobre," *Oasis* (Chuquicamata), 10 July 1974, 6; "Nacionalización," *Oasis*, 10 July 1971, 14–16; and "Chuquicamata ya es totalmente de Chile," *Oasis*, 24 July 1971, 3.

17. On Anaconda's economic woes and the labor conflicts, layoffs, and closure of the mines in Butte, see "Private Recession That Plagues Anaconda" (1975), "Companies: An Ex-Banker Treats Copper's Sickest Giant" (1975), Malone (1985), and "La caída de Anaconda," *Oasis*, 4 March 1972, 3, 10.

18. On the overthrow of Chile's Popular Unity government and brutality under the Pinochet dictatorship, see de Vylder (1978), Sigmund (1977), and Verdugo (1989).

19. Patricia Politzer wrote that Chile's largest copper miners' union promoted the first national work stoppage under the dictatorship in 1983 (1989, 101). Though the stoppage was not realized, mass protests were. For a personal account by a Chilean union activist, see "Copper: Boom, Strike, and Unemployment: Victor Lopez Rivera," in Politzer (1989, 100–116). See also Valdés and Weinstein (1993, 81) on the key role of the *Confederación de Trabajadores del Cobre* (CTC) in organizing the first national protest on May 11, 1983.

20. At the time I began this project in 1991, copper prices were low, generally under eighty cents per pound. Prices have risen since then. However, the state-run mining operation is under constant criticism from the opposition forces for its presumed lack of efficiency and need to privatize. The flames of criticism were fueled in 1994 when a futures trader employed by CODELCO lost over two hundred million dollars in state funds through questionable trades.

21. Three terms, *privatización*, *reprivatización*, and *desnacionalización*, are part of this discourse. Their distinct inflections suggest differing interpretations of the practices.

22. Critical writings toward a theory of practice include works by Bourdieu (1977), Giddens (1979), and Sahlins (1981). In "Theory in Anthropology Since the Sixties" (1984), Sherry Ortner addresses the theoretical and political lineage leading to a practice approach and discusses the key concepts and challenges of practice. Ortner applies the theory in *High Religion* (1989), a political and cultural study of continuity and change in Sherpa Buddhism, where she puts forth four key words — *history, structure, practice,* and *actor* — as the organizing frame. She further explores and critiques the intersections of practice and gender in *Making Gender* (1996). I have drawn on her theoretical organization in both the research and writing of this project.

23. Ortner describes current practice work as "an interpenetration, almost a merger between Marxist and Weberian frameworks" (1984, 145). A practice approach challenges notions of "base" and "superstructure," looking instead to ways in which the meaningful and material are articulated through one another in lived experience.

24. For further discussion of practice, see Ortner (1984; 1989, 11–18, 193–202) and Dirks, Eley, and Ortner (1994, 11–17).

25. Anthony Kelly and Sandra Sewell (1988) move from a dialectic to a trialectic model in an effort to grasp the openness and indeterminacy inherent in the relations of structure and practice. The trialectic image is helpful in grasping the conundrum of social reality posed by Peter Berger and Thomas Luckman in *The Social Construction of Reality* (1966, 67): "Society is a human product. Society is an objective reality. Man is a social product." This paradox is at the heart of a theory of practice.

26. For a critical overview of the concept of transnationalism, see Rouse (1995).

27. For studies of Butte history, see Calvert (1988), Connelly (1938), Emmons (1989), Glasscock (1935), Gutfeld (1979), Malone (1981), Murphy (1990; 1997), and Toole (1954). For studies of Chuquicamata, see Alvear Urrutia (1975), Gutiérrez and Figueroa (1920), Latcham (1926), Alvarez Vargas (1988), and Barros Garces (1986).

28. See Brown (1979) and Rosenblum (1995). I would also argue that Butte and Chuquicamata share common features with other enclaves of production, such as the coal, petroleum, rubber, and forest industries. I do not wish to argue the "uniqueness" of the copper industry here. Rather, I see this approach to research as potentially informative in exploring the connections among a variety of colonial, imperial, and industrial projects.

29. I borrow this notion of partial understanding and earnest practice from Robert and Helen Lynd's depiction of working-class life in *Middletown* (1929).

30. "Conflicting discourses and patterns of practice" is Ortner's definition of *contradiction* (1989, 14).

31. Marxist theory points to a fundamental structural contradiction inherent in capitalism: Owners of the means of production profit as a result of the exploitation and immiserization of labor. Anthony Giddens posed the primary capitalist contradiction as that between private appropriation and social production, with a secondary contradiction being the hegemony of the nation-state and the internationalization of capital (1979, 143).

32. Stewart further develops her notion of back talk in her recent book *A Space on the Side of the Road* (1996, 4, 12, 161).

33. This is the view of social actors presented by Pierre Bourdieu (1977). Ortner (1984) critiques this view as essentially individualistic. She contrasts interest theory with strain theory as suggested by Geertz (1973). She sees both as limited and calls for a more complicated grasp of actors as "becoming" rather than "getting."

34. Questions of identity, subjectivity, and subject positions have been the topic of broad theoretical discussion. Lacan's "decentered" subject challenges fixed notions of identity. Foucault's focus on the power relations inherent in construction of the individual undermines neutral premises of role theory. Teresa de Lauretis addresses the construction of gendered subjectivity and identity as a continuous process of personal engagement with external forces (1984, 9). Chantal Mouffe addresses subjectivity and subject positioning in linking personhood and political economy (1988). Kamala Visweswaran depicts the making of subjectivity as a complex "politics of identification" (1988). Renato Rosaldo argues that actors are constructed through their participation in a "plurality of partially disjunctive, partially overlapping communities" (1989, 168–95). I draw on these insights in developing a more complicated view of actors.

35. Marilyn Strathern proposes the concept of "dividuality" in *The Gender of the Gift* (1988, 13).

36. E. P. Thompson (1966) argues that class needs to be understood as a process, not a thinglike structure. I argue that gender and community are also better conceptualized in processual terms, constructed through a relational field of power inequality.

37. An explication of community theory is beyond the scope of this book. For an overview of community theory, see Bender (1982), Stoneall (1983), Bell and Newby (1972), Hawley (1950), and Warren (1978).

38. Dirks, Eley, and Ortner use the image of class and gender linking up and repelling one another (1995, 33). I find the image provocative in thinking about this force field of inequality in which subjectivity is constructed.

39. Williams (1977; 1980) builds on the work of Gramsci in addressing the interpenetration of cultural and economic production.

40. This passing acknowledgment certainly does not do justice to the rich and diverse body of feminist scholarship that has shaped my intellectual course and informed this work. For "classics" of feminist anthropology, see for example *Toward an Anthropology of Women* (1975), edited by Rayna Reiter, and Michelle Zimbalist Rosaldo and Louise Lamphere's groundbreaking edited collection, *Woman, Culture, and Society* (1974). The contributors bring gender to the fore with critical questions regarding gendered social inequality, familial power structures, socialization processes, the relationship between public and private spheres, and the political economy of sexual systems. Karen Sacks (1975) returns to Engels to address the relationship between gender and class structure. In a later work, "Toward a Unified Theory of Class, Race, and Gender" (1989), Sacks elaborates the theoretical connections between the three. Sustained analyses of the interpenetration of class and gender are addressed in works such as Patricia Zavella's *"Mujeres* in Factories" (1991), Lourdes Benería and Martha Roldán's *The Crossroads of Class and Gender* (1987), and June Nash and María Patricia Fernández-Kelly's edited volume, *Women, Men, and the International Division of Labor* (1983). See also Sherry Ortner and Harriet Whitehead's *Sexual Meanings* (1981) for a rich collection of essays that create a more complicated picture of gender as relational, processual, and contextual. For an insightful overview of the historical trajectory of feminist anthropology, see Micaela di Leonardo's introductory chapter, "Gender, Culture, and Political Economy: Feminist Anthropology in Historical Perspective," in *Gender at the Crossroads of Knowledge* (1991, 1–48). See also Eva Baron's excellent introduction, "Gender and Labor History: Learning from the Past, Looking to the Future," in *Work Engendered* (1991, 1–46).

41. On the complex interplay of class and gender, see Gordon (1995, 379) and Ginsberg and Tsing (1990). Beatrix Campbell's *Wigan Pier Revisited* (1984) offers a powerful commentary on working-class gender relations. Though critical of sociopolitical structures and practices pushing the English working class to desperate poverty, Campbell also holds men accountable for the practices of private patriarchy that exacerbate women's vulnerability.

42. The prescient ethnographic analyses of consumption and exploitation offered by Sidney Mintz in *Sweetness and Power* (1985) and June Nash in *We Eat the Mines and the Mines Eat Us* (1979) provide rich food for thought in approaching the cultural significance of consumption. In "Global Integration and Subsistence Insecurity," Nash addresses the theme of local consumption in the context of global integration (1994, 8–9). On women's organizing around issues of consumption, see Blee (1985), Kaplan (1982), Frank (1991a; 1991b), and Weinbaum and Bridges (1979). Campbell vividly illustrates the place of food and privation in the talk among working-class women in Britain (1984, 68–71). I return to relations of consumption in chapters 6 and 8.

43. On the trialectic process of being, doing and becoming, see Kelly and Sewell (1988, 22–29).

44. I use Foucault's term in recognizing the internal relation of power and knowledge (1979, 27–28).

45. Raymond Williams describes "structures of feeling" as "social experi-

ences in solution" — that is, belief systems, meanings, and values as they are lived and felt (1977, 133).

46. S For studies of women, labor, and social participation in Chile, see, for example, Valdés and Weinstein (1993), Frohman and Valdés (1993), Gallardo (1985), Arteaga (1989), Rodo and Hevia (1991), and Valdez, Montecino, de Leon, and Mack (1983).

47. A group of women historians at the University of Chile, under the guidance of Diana Veneros, are currently focusing on women's history in Chile's coal and nitrate regions.

48. Not all of the men executed in Calama on October 19, 1973, were mine or factory workers. Some had other ties to the community. One was an eighteen-year-old high school student.

49. While in Butte, I tape-recorded the majority of my conversations with community members. The stories from Butte are direct quotes taken from transcriptions of those interviews. I chose not to tape-record interviews while working in Chuquicamata. The accounts presented here are my reconstructions from notes taken in Spanish during and after interviews with community residents. Unless otherwise noted, English translations from Spanish texts are mine.

2. MINING HISTORY: A POLITICAL CHRONOLOGY

1. The chapter epigraphs are from Sahlins (1981, 72) and from a personal interview, Butte, 1993.

2. For overviews of early mining and corporate history in Butte, see Marcosson (1957, 1–10), Toole (1954, 10–154), and the Anaconda Company Papers, MC 169, Montana Historical Society Archives (MHSA), "Introduction."

3. Glasscock (1935), Toole (1954), and Malone (1981) offer insightful analyses of early copper politics in Butte and Montana. Toole notes that in 1903, 75 percent of the wage earners of Montana worked directly or indirectly for the Anaconda Company (1954, 147). He refers to Montana as a one-company state and uses a colonialist model in addressing state-corporate relations.

4. I offer here an admittedly sketchy overview of Butte's intriguing history at the turn of the century. The political and economic complexities have been addressed by a number of writers. The works of Toole (1954), Malone (1981), and Glasscock (1935) are particularly rich sources of data regarding the struggles for consolidation and control of Butte's latent wealth, the corporate consolidation (and dissolution) with Standard Oil Trust, implications of the 1872 Mining Act, and shady political and judicial dealings on the part of the warring copper kings.

5. Development of Butte's ethnic communities is addressed in detail in chapter 3.

6. For a concise overview of ethnic history, see Calkins (1982, introduction). The work contains a rich sampling of oral histories told by Butte residents. For examination of ethnic, class, religious, and political alliances and distinctions, see Calvert (1988, 57–70). Emmons (1989) provides an insightful view into the political and cultural history of the Irish community.

7. Silver Bow County Board of Health, "Report on Sanitary Conditions in the Mines and Community, Silver Bow County, December 1908 — April 1912," Typescript, MHSA; "Report Showing Results of Inspections of Dwellings, Hotels, Rooming Houses and Boarding Houses and Their Surroundings,"

Typescript, MHSA; Butte-Silver Bow County Coroner's Reports, 1921 — 1934, Butte-Silver Bow Public Archives (BSBPA).

8. In this discussion of early labor history in Butte, I have drawn extensively from Calvert (1988), Toole (1954; 1972), and Emmons (1989). This condensed presentation does not do justice to their detailed analyses. See also Foster (1914).

9. For detailed analysis of socialism and labor activism in Butte in the early 1900s, see Calvert (1988, 3–35). *Rebel Voices: An IWW Anthology* (Kornbluh 1988, 290–315) contains a collection of writings related to IWW activity and mining in Butte; see also Haywood (1914) and Varney (1919).

10. For discussion of the rustling card system, see Calvert (1988, 78, 104), M. Murphy (1997, 24–25), and Toole (1972, 132). There were a number of mining companies in Butte at this time, of which Anaconda dominated. The companies joined forces in establishing the rustling card system.

11. For critical examinations of wartime labor and political tensions, anti-German sentiments, and the role of the Montana Council of Defense in labor repression, see Gutfeld (1979, 37–48), Calvert (1988, 93–126), and Toole (1954, 175–90). See also Fisher (1923, 20–22).

12. For overview of the Speculator Disaster in 1917, see Gutfeld (1969). Jerry Calvert puts the death toll at 164 (1988, 104). Edwin Dobb states there were 168 deaths in the fire (1996, 47).

13. For details on Little's death and Rankin's actions in support of the Butte miners, see Calvert (1988, 103–14), Gutfeld (1978), and the Jeannette Rankin Papers, MC 147, Box 1, MHSA.

14. Calvert states that federal troops were garrisoned in Butte from August 17, 1917, to January, 1921 (1988, 113).

15. Jeanette Prodgers describes the passage of the Montana Sedition Act on February 22, 1918. She notes that "Montana Senator Henry Meyers introduced a similar bill to the U.S. Congress. At first the U.S. Judiciary Committee ignored the bill, but as patriotic hysteria heightened throughout the country, Montana Senators Thomas Welch and Meyers reintroduced the sedition bill in Congress and it passed May 16, 1918" (1991, 12).

16. For details of the incident in April 1920, see Calvert (1988, 115).

17. See Anaconda Copper Mining Company, *Annual Report*, 1910, 1914, 1915, 1916, Montana Tech of the University of Montana, Butte, Montana. This source is hereafter referenced parenthetically and in notes as *Annual Report*.

18. *Annual Report* 1921 reports the purchase date as February 10, 1922; Marcosson (1957, 167–83).

19. The Guggenheims began developing the Chuquicamata site in 1914. Anaconda purchased 51 percent ownership for seventy-seven million dollars, with an agreement to purchase the remainder by 1929.

20. For a comparative look at Anaconda copper production, see appendix 1. For background on the Guggenheim interests in copper and nitrate in Chile, see O'Brien (1989). For background on Chile's copper industry prior to the entry of Anaconda, see Culver and Reinhart (1989).

21. See, for example, Ramirez Necochea (1956, 58–78) and Angell (1972).

22. Thomas Klubock (1993) addresses a similar discourse of "mining tradition" among the miners of El Teniente in Chile. I am indebted to Klubock's fine-grained analysis of the history of El Teniente for helping me critically examine and clarify themes that I encountered in Chuquicamata. In December 1907, tens of thousands of nitrate miners joined a massive strike action, coming with their

families to the northern coastal town of Iquique. Their attempts to negotiate better working conditions were rejected. When they refused to abandon the grounds of the Santa Maria de Iquique school that served as their base, the state militia opened fire. For details of the massacre at Santa Maria de Iquique in 1907 and its importance in the history of the Chilean labor movement, see Pizarro (1986, 5–6, 33–56).

23. Cruzat and Deves (1986, 201–2). Recabarren's Socialist Worker's Party became the Communist Party in 1922.

24. See Pizarro (1986, 33–76). The post–World War I era saw the collapse of the nitrate industry and nitrates' replacement with synthetic fertilizers. This resulted in a severe blow to the Chilean economy in the early 1920s, provoking crises of unemployment in the mining regions and urban centers. Patricio Frias notes that Federación Obrera de Chile (FOCH, Chilean Workers Federation) was founded in 1909 and consolidated through its conventions of 1917, 1919, and 1921 (1989, 20). FOCH was closely tied to the Socialist Workers' Party.

25. This discussion is drawn directly from my translation of the events as told by Gutiérrez and Figueroa (1920, 172–79).

26. For overview of early twentieth-century political history in Chile, see Keen and Wasserman (1988, 338–57), Gil (1966), and Loveman (1979). *La Voz Sindical*, a Chuquicamata-based labor newspaper, asserted that the labor law was not actualized until 1931. See "La Ley 4057," 15 March 1931, 1.

27. Klubock cites correspondence between executives of CHILEX and Braden copper companies regarding the blacklist (1993, 80).

28. Dates vary in oral histories regarding the founding of the unions in Chuquicamata. In *Bodas de oro: órgano oficial del sindicato profesional único de empleados particulares, CODELCO-Chile*, Chuquicamata (May 1980, 1), the date of the founding of the *empleados* union is given as February 16, 1930. Klubock describes the miner's unions as being under company control until the late 1930s (1993, 93).

29. Jorge Alvear Urrutia notes that the 1931 Labor Code established a process for labor negotiations, a labor tribunal, and standards for occupational safety (1975, 110–12). *Ley* 4057 allowed for the organization of unions. Alvear Urrutia states that the mine, plant, and *empleados* unions were established in Chuquicamata in 1931. Over the years, separate groups such as machinists, electricians, and truck drivers established their own unions. By the 1940s, there were at least eight unions in Chuquicamata.

30. "Las nuevas orientaciones del sindicalismo," *La Voz Sindical*, 15 February 1934, 4, 7.

31. For discussion of labor and copper politics in the 1930s, see Klubock (1993, 426), Pizarro (1986, 93–100), and Drake (1978).

32. For discussion of the U.S. labor scene in 1934, see Zinn (1980, 390–397), Kinney (1934, 86, 99, 386–87), and Millis and Brown (1950, 3–27).

33. "Strike Pickets Hurl Rocks at Watchmen," *Butte Daily Post*, 19 June 1934, 1.

34. Historian Janet Ore (1996) notes this shift.

35. "A Scab Is a Scab," *The Eye Opener*, 16 May 1934, 1; "Full Boycott Ordered," *The Eye Opener*, 14 June 1934, 1; "Miners Pay Huge Salaries," *The Eye Opener*, 6 June 1934. The editorial, "What Is the Purpose of Present Strike?" appeared in *The Eye Opener*, 24 May 1934, 1, 2.

36. Personal interview, Butte, 1991.

37. "Copper Surplus Big Asset to Company," *The Eye Opener*, 28 June

1934, 1, 2. The "present copper code" referred to in the quote is the Code of Fair Competition approved by the Roosevelt administration in April 1934 as part of the National Recovery Act, which set minimum prices purportedly to avoid price cutting, keep mines operating, and protect jobs. The "Blue Eagle" with its accompanying slogan, "NRA Member — We Do Our Part," was a symbol of compliance with the National Industrial Recovery Act. The article is noting the irony that Anaconda's fabricating plants were operating without interruption, supplied by "Blue Eagle" copper, while the company refused to negotiate with the striking miners.

38. Theodore Moran offers insightful analysis of corporate vertical integration and tensions of corporate and state policy (1974). See especially pages 50–55 for examination of copper pricing and relationships of risk avoidance. For analysis of Anaconda's rise to power in the 1930s, see "Anaconda Copper, Part 1" and "Anaconda Copper, Part 2."

39. For an excellent analysis of the Popular Front, see Klubock (1993, 421–515).

40. Klubock (1993,43–100, 421–515, 624–96) and Keen and Wasserman (1988, 338–54). State-sponsored industry benefited the working class, but the structure of the Chilean economy remained unchanged.

41. For examples of such reports and praise, see " Sangre y cobre," *La Pampa* (Chuquicamata), 10 July 1944, 2.

42. Personal interview, Butte, 1993.

43. Marcosson (1957, 220–50), *Annual Reports* 1941–1944, and "Anaconda Copper Mining Company in 1942 Will Produce over One-Third of U.S. Supply," *Fortune* (January 1942): 52–55+.

44. "Un aumento de sueldos es ahora completamente ilusorio," *La Pampa* (Chuquicamata), 14 February 1945, 1.

45. For comments on the decrease in Anaconda's net income as the result of the Office of Price Administration's (OPA) refusal to recognize and make necessary adjustments in price schedules, see also *Annual Report* 1945.

46. "Nuevas provocaciones en Chuqui y Sewell," *El Siglo* (Santiago), 5 March 1946, 1. See related reports in *El Siglo*, January to June 1946.

47. *Montana Standard* (Butte), 15 April 1946, 1.

48. *Montana Standard*, 19 April 1946, 1.

49. "Committee Says Communists Inspired Riots," *Montana Standard*, 24 April 1946, 1. As figure 8 shows, the piano was an upright, not a baby grand as many local storytellers claim.

50. See "Nuevas provocaciones en Chuqui y Sewell," *El Siglo*, 5 March 1946, 1; "Defensa de los culpables fue el informe del cobre," *El Siglo*, 7 April 1946, 1; "7,000 obreros de Chuquicamata son arrostrados a la huelga," *El Siglo*, 25 May 1946, 2; "Represalias inició la CHILEX," *El Siglo*, 28 May 1946, 1; and "El imperialismo intenta cercar por hambre a 25,000 Chilenos en Chuqui," *El Siglo*, 2 June 1946, 1.

51. On labor activism of white-collar workers, see, for example, "Solucionada: La huelga de la sección palas de la mina," *La Pampa* (Chuquicamata), 24 August 1946, 1, and "Pulsamos el ambiente para la huelga de los empleados particulares," *La Pampa*, 19 October 1946, 1.

52. For in-depth analysis on the political turns of the Gonzalez Videla government, see Klubock (1993, 624–96).

53. See "Cuatro compañías imperialistas obstaculizan el labor del gobierno," *El Siglo* 12 November 1946, 1; "Trust yanqui del cobre quiere dominar a

Chile," *El Siglo*, 22 November 1946, 1; "Otro espeluznante cuento se fabricó ayer en La Moneda: Huelga 'comunista' en Chuqui. Buscan pretexto para aplicar contra el pueblo las facultades extraordinarias?" *El Siglo*, 10 September 1947, 1; and "El gobierno decretó la censura al diario *El Siglo*," *El Siglo*, 6 October 1947, 1.

54. For summary text of the Law for the Permanent Defense of Democracy, popularly known as the *ley maldita*, see *La Pampa*, 30 April 1949, 1.

55. See for example "Represión contra comunismo ha continuado en la semana," *La Pampa*, 1 November 1947, 1; "Continua la represión contra el comunismo: En Calama fueron detenidos varios funcionarios públicos," *La Pampa* 14 February 1948, 1.

56. Notes from personal interview, Chuquicamata, 1993. I use the terms *Chuquicamatina* and *Chuquicamatino* (the women or men of Chuquicamata) as residents do, marking both gender and identification to place. It should be noted that there was growing women's activism throughout Chile from the mid 1930s through the late 1940s regarding women's suffrage. The creation of the *Movimiento pro Emancipación de Mujeres de Chile* (MEMCh) in 1935 and the *Partido Femenino de Chile* in 1947 highlighted this era of women's mobilization. Women won the right to vote in 1949. See Valdés and Weinstein (1993, 44–45) for a discussion. Women I interviewed did not speak to these particular movements. However, it is likely that these movements influenced other forms of women's social action as well.

57. Notes from personal interviews, Chuquicamata, 1993, 1994.

58. Notes from personal interview, Chuquicamata, 1994.

59. For critique of the Taft-Hartley Act, see "Move to Return Slavery in U.S.," *Oregon Labor Press*, 6 June 1947, 1. See also "Three Left-Wing Unions Expelled," *Montana Standard*, 16 February 1950, 1. For discussion of communist influence and interunion struggles, see "Why a Copper Strike?" *Fortune* (October 1951): 59; "Waging a Hot War on the Left Wing," *Business Week*, 11 June 1949, 100–102; and "Try, Try Again to Prove Communist Infiltration," *Business Week*, 24 November 1956, 74.

60. "Comenzó el éxodo de los obreros azuleados. Dramáticas despedidas hubieron esta mañana," *La Pampa*, 30 July 1949, 1.

61. *Annual Report* 1950; "Desaparecerá el mausoleo de los comunistas. Reconstruirán el edificio sindical el próximo mes," *La Pampa*, 29 October 1949, 1.

62. See also "Butte: New Mines, New Life," *Business Week*, 27 December 1947, 25; and Marcosson (1957, 272–29) on Greater Butte Project.

63. "Corporate Paytriotism," *Montana Labor News* (Helena, Mont.), 15 February 1951, 1.

64. Crisostomo Pizarro places the birth of the *Confederación Nacional de los Trabajadores del Cobre* (CTC) at the beginning of the 1950s (1986, 174). Klubock documents the conception of the CTC at a meeting of miners in Machali, near the El Teniente mines, in 1951(1993, 696). An oral history source in Chuquicamata set the date of the founding of the CTC as March 1953. Anaconda was also involved in its own negotiations at this time regarding diversification into the production of aluminum, a copper substitute. See Girvan (1974, 115–18).

65. For discussion of Anaconda's involvement in the Chilean government, see Laferrte and Ocampo (1951, 10). The report also addresses the corporate role in the fixing of copper prices and Chile's relative disadvantage as a producer of raw unmanufactured copper.

66. For analysis of Chilean political and economic concerns in the early 1950s, see Corporación Nacional del Cobre (1974, 36–39, 69–78), Moran (1974, 65–90), Girvan (1974, 107–30), and Tomic (1974, 131–58). On the strike in Butte and invocation of the Taft-Hartley Act, see *Montana Standard*, August to October 1951.

67. See "Anaconda y Braden estafan a Chile," *El Siglo*, 1 April 1953, 1; "La Anaconda alzó sus costos por sustraer 600 milliones a Chile," *El Siglo*, 4 April 1953, 1; "CEPAL revela acuerdo secreto entre Gonzalez Videla y compañías del cobre," *El Siglo*, 5 April 1953, 1; and "Boicot Yanqui contra el cobre chileno," *El Siglo*, 26 June 1953, 1.

68. Moran (1974, 75–90); "Se quiso impedir venta de cobre a la Argentina," *El Siglo*, 10 October 1953, 1; "La URSS mantiene oferta para comprar el cobre chileno," *El Siglo*, 25 October 1953, 1; Corporación Nacional del Cobre (1974, 72–75).

69. "Cias Yanqui paralizaron minas del cobre," *El Siglo*, 13 October 1953, 1; "Misión parlamentaria Yanqui asegura que solo se vendera nuestro cobre a los EE.UU.," *El Siglo*, 13 November 1953, 1.

70. "Ike's Brother Asks Aid for Latin America," *Montana Standard*, 20 November 1953, 1. For daily reports on Anaconda and the copper situation, see *El Siglo*, October and November 1953,

71. Personal interview, Chuquicamata, 1993.

72. Corporación Nacional del Cobre (1974, 75); "Vote Authorizes Strike Action," *Montana Standard*, 24 July 1954, 12.

73. It is important to note that, given the structure of the Chilean Labor code, sixty days was the legal limit of a strike.

74. As noted earlier, *obrero* and *empleado* roughly correspond to blue-collar and white-collar workers.

75. These themes were central to union men's accounts of labor history during my fieldwork in Chuquicamata. However, some Chuquicamatinos spoke more to the benefits of the ration card system than to its drawbacks.

76. On contract negotiations, see *Montana Standard*, July and August 1959, especially 13 August 1959, "Anaconda Officials Say Strike Will Be Long and Costly One." On interunion conflicts, see Anaconda Company Papers, MC 169, Box 73, File 1, MHSA and Butte Miner's Union File, LH 012, BSBPA.

77. The Andes Copper Mining Company, Anaconda's subsidiary in Potrerillos, Chile, had been in operation since the 1920s. By the late 1940s, the copper deposits were nearing depletion. Anaconda began developing its mining claims at nearby Indio Muerto mountain, site of the mine and community to be named El Salvador. See Marcosson (1957, 215–17).

78. On the earthquake, its effects in Butte, and the start of the strike, see Prodgers (1991, 59–60).

79. Personal interview, Butte, 1993.

80. Personal interview, Butte, 1993.

81. *People's Voice*, 18 September 1959, 1.

82. "Ratification Ends Copper Strike—Workers Are Returning to Jobs," *Montana Standard*, 16 February 1960, 1.

83. On Chuquicamata's favorite-child status, see *La Pampa*, "Partió con el pie derecho—Nuestra idea del monumento al trabajador del cobre," 4 July 1959, 1; "Chuquicamata, la ciudad capital mundial del cobre, no cuenta con un museo del cobre," 21 October 1959, 7; "Hoy se inaugurará el nuevo edificio sindical," 7 November 1959, 1; "Las viviendas y el progreso social en

Chuquicamata," 19 December 1959; and "Aporte al país de la gran minería del cobre en 1959," 15 April 1960, 3.

84. For concise synopsis of the Alliance for Progress, see Keen and Wasserman (1988, 532). See also Moran (1974, 110–30), Stallings (1978), and Gil (1966). Note also that there was a strike in Chuquicamata from October 1 to November 12, 1960. Pizarro recorded it as a strike over economic issues (1986, 177). In the *Annual Report* of 1960, company officials note that in the strikes in Butte and in Chuquicamata workers received virtually the same settlement that the company offered at the beginning of the negotiations. Several men in Chuquicamata recall a more interesting cause for the strike. They claim it was over the right to continue their practice of maintaining prostitutes in the single men's quarters. I return to this strike story in chapter 3.

85. Nathaniel Davis notes that approximately three million dollars was allotted by the United States via the CIA to the Christian Democrats in the 1964 election (1985, 20–21). Paul Sigmund notes that the CIA's contribution accounted for over half the campaign costs (1977, 34). Sigmund claims that Frei was unaware of the source of the funds.

86. Moran (1974:131) argued that the landed elites wanted to make the foreign companies rather than land ownership the target of blame for Chile's income inequalities.

87. For a discussion of Chileanization, see Corporación Nacional del Cobre (1974, 78–93), Alvear Urrutia (1975, 161–71), Tomic (1974, 215–34), *Annual Report* 1964, and *Oasis*, "Declaración conjunta sobre futuras," 26 December 1964, 2.

88. For an example of the conflicts that persisted after Chileanization, see Stefan de Vylder, who notes that in 1966 the United States forced Chilean President Frei to sell ninety thousand tons of copper as a contribution to the U.S. strategic reserve at a price of thirty-six cents per pound when the world price was seventy cents per pound (1976, 120–25).

89. See *Annual Report* 1964 for details on the partnership arrangements under the Chileanization plan. Corporate anxieties about the growing strength of the Communist Party in Chile and the risk of nationalization of the mines were revealed in the anticommunist attacks in the Butte press. For examples of such attacks, see *Montana Standard* 8 July 1964, 12. Norman Girvan notes that the annual average tonnage of copper produced in Anaconda's Chile operations was 344 thousand metric tons during 1960–1964 and 358 thousand metric tons during 1965–1969 (1974, 115, 122–23). He offers an insightful summary of Anaconda's window of opportunity during this critical period after Chileanization and before full nationalization of the copper industry.

90. See "La compañía informa al personal," *Oasis*, 28 June 1969, 2; "Anaconda Company Seals Deal with Chile," *Montana Standard*, 3 January 1970; Moran (1974, 146); and Sigmund (1977, 81–83).

91. There are numerous critiques made in *Oasis* during the Popular Unity government of the damages to equipment and operations in the last years of Anaconda. These critiques need to be viewed within the larger discourse of "old" and "new" order. See, for example, "Trabajadores chilenos reparan ruinas dejadas for los norteamericanos," *Oasis* 1973 (no date).

92. For data on the strike, see Pizarro (1986, 177). On the state of emergency, see *Oasis*, 20 November 20 1965, 2. Many people whom I interviewed in Chuquicamata made reference to this strike. As with other strikes both in Butte and Chuquicamata, accounts varied considerably concerning the actual period of the strike.

93. "Cada dia más feo lo de cobre," an article in *El Clarin*, a Santiago pro-labor newspaper, 5 May 1966, 2, reports on the arrest of union leaders in El Teniente, distrust of company officials, and calls by labor for nationalization of the mines.

94. See *El Siglo*, January — March 1966.

95. *El Mercurio*, 3 March 3 1966, 1.

96. *El Siglo*, 3 March 3 1966, 1, 5.

97. Personal interview, Chuquicamata, 1994. I did not find news accounts indicating that Allende was denied entry into Chuquicamata. However, an article in *El Loa de Calama*, 12 March 1966, 1, reported that Allende was denied entry into the Dupont Plant when he tried to visit the plant in his capacity as President of the Senate Commission on Hygiene and Health. He was turned away by company police and told that he must secure permission in Santiago.

98. *El Siglo*, 8 March 1966, 1l; *El Mercurio*, 8 March 1966, 1.

99. Personal interview, Chuquicamata, 1994.

100. *El Mercurio* and *El Siglo* offer dramatically contrasting accounts of the deaths. The incident triggered a special session of the Chilean Senate the following week. For detailed commentary on the event, its causes, and its aftermath, see República de Chile, *Diario de sesiones del senado, publicación oficial, legislatura extraordinaria, incidentes en el mineral El Salvador*, Sesión 78, Saturday, March 12, 1966.

101. For a thorough discussion of the Mine-Mill-Steelworkers merger, the politics of pattern bargaining, and the place of national security discourse and the Vietnam War in the 1967 strike, see Rosenblum (1995, 37–44).

102. Personal interview, Butte, 1991.

103. Quoted in pamphlet, "What the Copper Strike is All About," address by Joseph Maloney to the AFL-CIO 7th Constitutional Convention, December 12, 1967, BSBPA, LH005, Box 1.

104. War metaphors marked the media coverage of the strike as well. For example, the front page of the *Montana Standard*, 2 February 1968, features an article titled "Company Seeks Unconditional Surrender," which reports the acrimonious negotiations, alongside another article titled "Reds Killed 11.5 to 1," which reports the daily body count from Vietnam.

105. See "Nuevos perfiles para Chuquicamata," *Oasis*, 24 June 1967, 5–6; "Record en la mina," *Oasis*, 5 August 1967, 1; "Nueva cara para las pulperías de Chuquicamata," *Oasis*, 26 August 1967, 1; "La Exotica," *Oasis*, 14 October 1967, 4–5.

106. For coverage on the bargaining process among the Big Four copper companies, see the *Montana Standard*, 6–17 March 1968. For discussion of Phelps-Dodge's vulnerability because of a lack of foreign holdings, see the *Montana Standard*, 11 March 1968, 1. The other three had foreign copper holdings to sustain the domestic market. By March 16, 1968, Phelps-Dodge and Kennecott had reached a tentative agreement with the Steelworkers. It is important to note that under the Chileanization agreement with Kennecott, the Chilean government had acquired 51 percent ownership of the El Teniente operations in April of 1967. Thus Kennecott did not have the foreign "cushion" that Anaconda had. See Girvan (1974, 115).

107. For details on the 1967 strike, see the *Montana Standard*, June 1967 to April 1968; "Bitter Aftermath: End of a National Copper Strike," *Newsweek*, 15 April 1968, 80; "Toll of a Five-Month Strike: Who Is Hurt and How Much?" *U.S. News*, 11 December 1967, 94–96; Timmins (1970, 28–33); and

Guthals (1970). Of interest is "Chilean Unions, Company Eye U.S. Strike: Anaconda Dickers with Marxist-Controlled Blocs," front-page article in the *Montana Standard*, 23 March 1968, which reports on the interest of Chuquicamata's unions in the outcome of the Butte strike, their March 31 contract expiration date, and the points at issue in negotiations with Anaconda.

108. For data on voting patterns in the mining region, see Pizarro (1986, 201). His figures show that in the Antofagasta Region that encompasses the Chuquicamata mines, the voting averages by political party for the 1960s were Conservatives, 10.9 percent; Radical, 22.0 percent; Christian Democrats, 24.5 percent; and Socialists and Communists, 37.1 percent. Francisco Zapata (1975) argues that Chuquicamata's miners had instrumental ties to unions and leftist political parties. He sees their participation in the Socialist and Communist parties in terms of gaining and maintaining their own economic interests, rather than in terms of a critical class consciousness. Crisostomo Pizarro and Sergio Bitar (1986) critique the over-politicization of unions and the privileged status of the miners in explaining labor's discontent and eventual opposition to the Allende government.

109. Personal interview, Butte, 1991.

110. The Church Commission Report offers a detailed investigation of U.S. involvement in Chile from the time of Allende's candidacy to the military coup. Nathaniel Davis (1985), former U.S. ambassador to Chile during part of this time, has written a cautious account of his knowledge of and investigation into "official" U.S. involvement in Chile from 1970–1973. Davis acknowledges Nixon's visceral hostility toward Allende and recognizes CIA involvement (1985, 21). The CIA authorized nearly a half million dollars for antileftist campaigns during the 1970 elections. Nearly another one and a quarter million dollars was used to purchase radio stations and newspapers to support anti–Unity Party candidates in the important municipal elections of 1971. Another seven hundred thousand dollars went to *El Mercurio*. National Security Decision Memorandum 93, issued at Nixon's behest on November 9, 1970, established a policy of applying unacknowledged pressure on Allende's government to prevent its consolidation and to limit its ability to implement policies contrary to U.S. interests. Along with this informal blockade, a review of possible steps to drive down world copper prices was also ordered.

111. It is important to note that Allende's proposal won unanimous approval from a congress that was still dominated by a conservative majority.

112. For discussion of nationalization, see Moran (1974, 220–34); Corporación Nacional del Cobre (1974, 85–107); de Vylder (1976, 124–29); Vargas in Ffrench-Davis and Tironi (1974, 159–92); *Annual Report* 1971; "Chile: Copper Pays the Price of Nationalism," *Business Week*, 21 August 1971, 38–40; and *Oasis*, 11 July 1971, 1, and 17 July 1972, 7.

113. *Montana Standard*, 15 July 1971, 1; 12 July 1971, 1.

114. Personal interview, Butte, 1993.

115. For a discussion of the U.S. reaction to the nationalization of the mines, see de Vylder (1976, 128–30). De Vylder notes that the U.S. government and companies responded immediately with an informal blockade. He also notes that the companies exercised their right to appeal their case to the copper tribunal. Allende's charges of excess profits and denial of further compensation were upheld.

116. Sigmund and Davis play down the degree to which credit and assistance were denied to Chile, though both cite Nixon as having instructed the CIA direc-

tor to "make the economy scream," in a secret meeting shortly after Allende's election in September 1970 (Sigmund 1977, 103–4, 153; Davis 1985, 6–8, 31, 68, 308–10). Benjamin Keen and Mark Wasserman state that as a result of the nationalization of the mines, flow of private investment capital to Chile halted and credit from sources such as AID, the Export-Import bank, and the World Bank dried up (1988, 353–54). They cite testimony of William Colby, CIA director, before Senate subcommittee, confirming that the CIA spent eleven million dollars between 1962 and 1970 to prevent Allende's election. With Kissinger's authorization, the CIA spent eight million between 1970 and 1973 to "destabilize" the Chilean economy.

117. See Sigmund (1997), Davis (1985), and de Vylder (1976, 129–33).

118. According to de Vylder, not only was there a mass exodus of U.S. citizens working in Chuquicamata, but also Anaconda offered jobs to nearly one hundred Chilean professional and technical workers, who left as well (1976, 130–33). Davis describes the transition to Chilean management as chaotic at best (1985, 101–2). Though he acknowledges the effects of blockades on sale of parts, he claims the biggest problem was too much attention to political struggles and not enough to the business of mining.

119. De Vylder reports sixty-seven partial work stoppages in Chuquicamata in 1972 (1976, 130–35).

120. Sigmund (1977); Davis (1985); de Vylder (1976); and Pizarro and Bitar (1986). There also seems to be general agreement among residents of Chuquicamata with whom I spoke that the years of the Popular Unity government were chaotic at best, with many administrative problems exacerbated by shortages of basic goods.

121. See Verdugo (1989) for a well-documented account of the Caravan of Death.

122. Two powerful films, *Dance of Hope* (1989) and *Días de Octubre* (1991), document the everyday violence of the dictatorship and the demands for truth and justice. These themes are echoed in personal accounts given by residents of Calama and Chuquicamata.

123. For a detailed analysis of monetarism and the "Chilean economic experiment" under the guidance of Milton Friedman, see Gimpel Smith (1989). For an overview of the practices and effects of neoliberal economics and structural adjustment during the military dictatorship, see Quiroga Martínez (1994). As Sigmund euphemistically puts it, "The return to a free-market economy based on competition would have been impossible in a democratic system, but military rule seemed to provide the authoritarian control necessary to use classical methods to put an end to the chaos of the preceding regime, however painful it might be" (1977, 265).

124. See "Chile and Anaconda acuerdan arreglo por nacionalización de Chuqui y Salvador," *Oasis*, 27 July 1974, 1, and "Negociación favorable entre Chile y Anaconda," *Oasis*, 27 July 1974, 2, 10. Sigmund notes that in 1974, the Export-Import reopened its credit line with Chile, USAID asked for twenty-five million dollars in loans for Chile, and the IMF made a ninety-five million dollar standby loan (1977, 261). Sigmund argues this was not "political" discrimination but a response to a shift in Chile's "economic" policy.

125. See "A Private Recession That Plagues Anaconda," *Business Week*, 1 December 1975, 38–40. The article reports that Anaconda settled the loss of its mining operations with the Chilean government for 253 million dollars. It also got a good portion of the 159 million it claimed from OPIC.

126. For reports on Anaconda's downfall, see "Companies: An Ex-Banker Treats Copper's Sickest Giant," *Business Week*, 19 February 1972, 52–54; "The Private Recession Plagues Anaconda," *Business Week*, 1 December 1975, 38–40; "Banking on an Outsider: Business in the News," *Fortune* (June 1971): 33; and Malone (1985, 69–72).

127. See Madrick (1976, 58–60) and State of Montana, Department of Labor and Industry (1984).

128. See Baum and Knox (1992), Baum (1997), and Dobb (1996).

129. Personal interview, Butte, 1991. An article in the *Montana Standard*, 4 July 1991, says the purchase price was 5.2 million dollars. Dobb reports the "fire sale" price paid by Washington to ARCO as eighteen million dollars (1996, 45).

130. Personal interview, Chuquicamata, 1993.

131. Personal interview, Chuquicamata, 1994. Ongoing reports in *El Mercurio de Calama* during August and September 1978 give brief glimpses into the miners' acts of resistance and the numerous arrests. The tightly controlled press attributed the resistance to communist agitation.

132. Teresa Valdés and Marisa Weinstein describe the first national day of protest on May 11, 1983 (1993, 81). The act was organized by the Confederation of Copper Workers (CTC) and spurred the formation of the *Comando Nacional de Trabajadores*, a key act in shifting the political climate.

133. Personal interviews, Chuquicamata, 1994.

134. On the end of dictatorship and transition to democracy in Chile, see Politzer (1989), Angell and Pollack (1990), and Fernandez Jilberto (1991).

135. See *Oasis*, June to August 1993.

136. I draw this summary from Harvey (1989, 123–34).

3. MINING COMMUNITY

1. The chapter epigraphs are from Dempsey (1989, cover); Marcosson (1957, 194), permission to quote courtesy of Ayer Co. Publisher; and Harvey (1989, 123).

2. For insights on the meaning and power of community as practice, see Suttles (1972) and Cohen (1985). June Nash's ethnography *From Tank Town to High Tech* (1989) provides a helpful model for thinking about the collision and coalescence of corporate and on-the-ground visions of community. Roger Rouse's critical reading of an earlier version of this chapter has helped me develop the linkages between labor control and community building.

3. Rouse (1991; 1995) notes that community and space are always contingent. Equation of the two should not be uncritically assumed. For critical commentary on the concept of community in anthropology that challenges locality-bound models, see Roseberry (1991, 146–53).

4. Nicholas Dirks, Geoff Eley, and Sherry Ortner note that

> how we see ourselves as a basis for action and how we are addressed in the public arena are not fixed. Sometimes we recognize ourselves as citizens, sometimes as workers, sometimes as parents, sometimes as consumers, sometimes as enthusiasts for particular sports or hobbies, sometimes as believers in religious and other creeds, and so on; those recognitions are usually structured by power relations of different kinds; and they are usually gendered by assumptions placing us as women or men. (1994, 32).

Rouse (1995) addresses the making of workers, citizens, and consumers in the construction of flexible subjectivity. In this chapter and the following, I develop the interplay of community and subjectivity in the formation of social actors.

5. On Anaconda and the press, see Toole (1954, 28–29) and D. Anderson (1976, 20–22).

6. Anaconda operated the Chuquicamata weekly newspaper, *Oasis*, beginning in 1956. The company also strongly influenced the paper's predecessors, *La Pampa* and *El Pukará*. Benjamin Keen and Mark Wasserman note that the U.S. companies active in Chile maintained a close association with the Edwards family, the powerful clan that owned *El Mercurio*, along with a bank, investment corporations, insurance companies, industries, and two publishing houses (1988, 342). This close association was demonstrated in 1953 when, at the height of the conflicts over copper politics, the editor of *El Mercurio* arrived in Montana as a guest of the state department, for a tour of mining and ranching operations, with side trips to national parks. See "Chilean Editor Here as Guest of State Department," *Montana Standard*, 1 November 1953, 1.

7. For discussion of habitus, disposition, and the naturalization of the arbitrary through the dialectics of objectification and embodiment, see Bourdieu (1977, 78–90). I draw on Pierre Bourdieu's insights in considering residents' participation in this complex process of formation and distinction. Chuquicamatinos embodied resentments as well as an "acquired system of generative schemes" that fueled consciousness of the arbitrary as a key part of community disposition.

8. "Butte, America" is a popular community slogan displayed on bumper stickers, baseball caps, billboards, and tourist brochures.

9. On Butte's ethnic makeup in the early 1900s, see Calvert (1988, 60), M. Murphy (1997, 6–15), and Emmons (1989, 61–63). David Emmons's study of the Butte Irish offers an insightful analysis of class and ethnicity in the making of a mining community. Ray Calkins describes Butte's linguistic diversity (1982, introduction).

10. For excellent analyses of prostitution in Butte, its relationships to the broader service economy, and the shifting lines of respectability, see M. Murphy (1983; 1984; 1997, 71–90). Emmons notes that by 1905, Butte's red light district was second only the New Orleans's Corduroy Road (1989, 22).

11. Wide-open images of Butte were popularized in novels such as Dashiell Hammett's *Red Harvest* and Clyde Murphy's *The Glittering Hill*. The collected works presented in *Copper Camp*, a WPA popular history project, reinforced the images of Butte's hyperbolic history.

12. Mary Murphy's work "Surviving Butte" (1990) offers a richly detailed look at the place of gender in the making of mining life in Butte.

13. From Waldemar Kailaya, "Memoirs of Butte," unpublished manuscript, The Emily Kailaya Collection, BSBPA, LH021, Box 1.

14. Personal interview, Butte, 1991.

15. Personal interview, Butte, 1993.

16. Anonymous Irish toast, told by Kevin Shannon (1985, 41).

17. Personal interview, Butte, 1991.

18. Silver Bow County Board of Health, "Report on the Sanitary Conditions in the Mines and Community, Silver Bow County, December 1908 — April 1912," Typescript, MHSA; and "Report Showing Results of Inspection of

Dwellings, Hotels, Rooming Houses, and Boarding Houses and Their Surroundings," 1912, Typescript, MHSA.

19. "Young People Plan to Study Marxian Socialism," *Montana Socialist* (Butte), 22 May 1915, 5. Socialism was a strong political force in Butte at the time. Butte had a socialist mayor from 1911 to 1914.

20. T. I. Scee (1988) studied suicide rates in Butte between 1907 and 1914. She notes that nearly three times more men committed suicide than women. My own review of the coroner's records suggests that a similar pattern continued at least until 1920. A disproportionate number of Butte residents, the majority of them men, were committed to the state mental hospital in Warm Springs during this era. Certainly Butte's proximity to Warm Springs (a distance of thirty miles) would affect placement, but the numbers offer anecdotal evidence of deeper community issues as discussed by Scee.

21. *Anaconda Standard*, 22 April 1920, 1.

22. This pattern is described by Robert Lynd and Helen Lynd in *Middletown* (1929). *Middletown* is a community study worth revisiting for its prescient insights into the structured practices of labor control and community building.

23. See "Copper States Have Big Relief Rolls," *The Eye Opener*, 13 October 1935, 4. The article reports that Butte was second only to Phoenix, Arizona, in its percentage of residents receiving relief.

24. *The Eye Opener*, 17 March 1934, 1.

25. "Labor Observes May Day," *The Eye Opener*, 4 May 1935, 1.

26. "Anaconda Insures Peon but Not American Miner," *The Eye Opener*, 16 February 1935, 2.

27. The distinction of Big Shots and little guys is part of local parlance in Butte. I did not probe into how Butte people used the distinction during our conversations. It seemed obvious to me, because it is a distinction I use myself. It was both surprising and helpful to me when a reader reviewing this chapter commented that the distinction sounded "rude." The comment helped me to recognize something of my own "structure of feeling" and unarticulated sense of connection to community in Butte. To the Butte girl, the distinction may be fluid, but not rude. What happens, however, when the cultural scholar carries the Butte girl's knowledge out of bounds and commits it to print? Abstract discussions of discourse become concrete problems of representation.

28. *The Eye Opener*, 6 June 1934, 2.

29. For important discussion of socialization processes and development of regimes of capitalist accumulation from Fordism to flexible accumulation, see Harvey (1989, 123–97). David Harvey argues that a fully fledged and distinctive new regime matured during the post World War II boom, the pillars of which were a privileged workforce and state-sponsored reconstruction. He describes postwar Fordism as a way of life and an international affair.

30. See "Company Towns, 1956," *Time*, April 1 1956, 100–101. I return to the themes of discipline and play in discussion of Chuquicamata later in this chapter.

31. "Miners Certified for Surplus Food," *Montana Standard*, 2 October 1959, 1.

32. Clearly, it was a particular mix of white, European ethnic groups that constituted "American." Few of Montana's American Indian population found work in the mines. Older residents tell the story of a regiment of black soldiers sent to Butte near the end of World War II to work in the mines when copper was critical and labor was shorthanded. They say that the miners and the unions

blocked the soldiers' entry into the mines, refusing to work with them. A retired labor leader told me that Anaconda tried recruiting coal miners from West Virginia and Mexican miners with experience in the Arizona copper mines to work in Butte in the 1950s. He said that the company's recruitment efforts failed because these imported workers were a "different breed" and weren't accepted by the Butte miners.

33. Personal interview, Butte 1991.

34. Alvarez Vargas reports that in 1795 the border between Peru and Chile was established at the Rio Loa (parallel 21.27), which runs through the site of the city of Calama (1988, 25). During the 1860s and 1870s, various border treaties were negotiated and contested among Chile, Bolivia, and Peru, culminating in declaration of war in 1879.

35. For an overview of the early history of northern Chile and the mining region, see Alvear Urrutia (1975, 55–64).

36. This is a gross oversimplification of the political and economic conditions and practices leading up to the War of the Pacific. For a brief but more substantive overview, see Keen and Wasserman (1988, 223–227). See also Ramirez Necochea (1956).

37. See *Annual Reports* 1923–1928. The company did not provide similar data on Butte in its reports.

38. Personal interview, Chuquicamata, 1993.

39. For discussion of ethnic distinctions in Chuquicamata, see Latcham (1926, 146–48) and Gutiérrez and Figueroa (1920, 160–81). For unofficial census data on Chuquicamata and Calama in 1924, see Alvarez Vargas (1988, 61).

40. This is the stereotypic representation of Bolivians in the mining region expressed both in the cited historical accounts and in the stories of many Chileans in Chuquicamata.

41. Personal interview, Chuquicamata, 1993.

42. Personal interview, Chuquicamata, 1994.

43. Personal interview, Chuquicamata, 1994.

44. These competing claims reflect the disjunctures of community and difference as discussed by Young (1990, 307–17).

45. Letter from William Jurden, Chile Exploration Engineering Department, to William Wraith, Andes Copper Mining Co. (New York City Headquarters), August 21, 1925, Anaconda Company Papers, MC 169, Box 77, File 2, MHSA. Isaac Marcosson states that in 1948, 45 percent of the men in Chuquicamata were single and 55 percent were married, but that in 1957, 37 percent were single and 63 percent were married (1957, 204). He cites this as "evidence of community stability." It may also be evidence of Anaconda's ongoing preoccupation with gender balancing that required active corporate engineering.

46. Personal interview, Chuquicamata, 1993.

47. Based on accounts in personal interviews in Chuquicamata, 1993, 1994.

48. For a detailed discussion of the Butte Housewives League, see M. Murphy (1990, 33–45).

49. Data on the compensation is drawn largely from conversations with longtime residents of Chuquicamata. Alvear Urrutia notes that the *asignación familiar* was one of the benefits gained through union efforts in Chuquicamata (1975, 115–16). He writes that in 1953 the *asignación familiar* became a mandatory benefit for workers throughout the country. He describes the *compensación para cargas familiares* as an additional benefit based on the number of family members, which was provided by only a few mining operations. This fits with the personal accounts of the women's compensation in Chuquicamata.

50. For discussion of the benefit packages demanded by Chuquicamata unions, see "El pliego de peticiones," *Oasis*, 13 October 1956, 1. For discussion of the Kennecott operation and the distinction from Anaconda's practices of compensation, see Thomas Klubock's insightful analysis into gender and class among Chilean copper miners (1992, 65–77).

51. A discussion of the images constructed of miners is developed in chapter 4.

52. For a discussion of the politics of identification, see Visweswaran (1988).

53. A number of Chuquicamatinos offered their version of this story. At one gathering, when I asked if this were true, several men elaborated on details that lent a mythic quality as much as "truth."

54. "Company Towns, 1956," *Time*, 1 April 1956, 100.

55. Personal interview, Chuquicamata, 1993.

56. Personal interview, Chuquicamata, 1994.

57. Personal interview, Chuquicamata, 1994.

58. For a discussion of summarizing and elaborating symbols, see Ortner (1973).

59. Though Butte may not have had a "company store" per se, the labor press frequently pointed to the corporate monopoly created by Anaconda subsidiaries in Butte that impinged on local businesses.

60. Personal interview, Chuquicamata, 1993.

61. *Engineering and Mining Journal* 114 (5 August 1922): 221, cited in M. Murphy 1990, 203.

62. For a history of the Columbia Gardens, see J. Thompson (1987) and Boyer (1978).

63. On the shift to Miner's Field Day, see M. Murphy (1990, 204–6).

64. This suggestion was made in a full-page notice in the *Montana Standard*, 4 February 1968, 10, paid for by Anaconda. The notice, entitled "Proposals to Help Save Our Operations," presents a summary of the company offer. In bold-faced type, the ad notes that the Steel Workers were from Pittsburgh and that they put national bargaining goals ahead of Montana interests.

65. Personal interview, Chuquicamata, 1993.

66. Field notes from lecture by Bob McCarthy to the Butte Historical Society, March 18, 1993, with permission from the speaker.

67. *Montana Standard*, 4 July 1985, Special Supplement, 1.

68. When I asked people in Chuquicamata about the dance costumes, they told me that the ideas often came from movies that played in the Chile Theater. A former American Camp resident told me that *National Geographic* was popular with folks in Chuquicamata because of the wide variety of costume ideas it offered. Similar costumes are still used by dancers.

69. For explication of "the development of underdevelopment," see Gunder Frank (1967) and Cardoso and Faletto (1979).

4. MINING MEN AND DESIGNING WOMEN

1. For chapter epigraphs, see Campbell (1984, 97) and "My Madonna" excerpt from Robert Service (1907), quoted with permission of the estate of Robert Service, courtesy of Mr. M. William Krasilovsky. This excerpt appeared in promotional literature about Our Lady of the Rockies, a ninety-foot-tall religious monument that overlooks Butte.

2. On mining and masculinity, see Campbell (1984, 97–115), Klubock (1996), M. Murphy (1990, 52–190), and Yarrow (1991, 285–310).

3. For examples of miners and mining as subjects of songs and poetry, see Hand (1946, 1–25), Stegner (1967, 157–67), and Burke (1964).

4. *Daily Intermountain* (Butte), 13 June 1889, 1.

5. For a fictional account of Butte miners that plays on stereotypical images, see Richard O'Malley (1986).

6. *La Pampa*, 27 May 1944, 7. It is interesting to note that the copper miners also stand apart from Chile's coal miners, who labor in oppressive physical and economic conditions. There is little history of solidarity between the more economically "privileged" copper miners and the coal miners.

7. "Cartas a mi pueblo," the letters from "El Beño," was a weekly feature in *El Pukará* in the early 1960s. "Las inquietudes de Juan Minero," appeared weekly in *Oasis* during this era. Both presented miner's accounts of the fair and progressive operations of the company counterposed to the unreasonable demands of the unions.

8. The image and background of El Beño suggest his *"nortino"* heritage. He writes to his *morenita linda*, his pretty dark-skinned woman. His use of language is much less sophisticated than that of Juan Minero. Perhaps these two distinct masculine images reflect the corporate eye for detail and discrimination in marketing their antiunion message.

9. *El Pukará*, 11 January 1964, 6.

10. *Oasis*, 6 June 1964, 3.

11. *Los privilegiados* was a common description of miners of Chuquicamata. I heard the term throughout my fieldwork both in Santiago and in Calama.

12. Personal interviews, Chuquicamata, 1993, 1994. For numerous articles on the need to change the "work culture" in Chuquicamata, see *Oasis*, June to December 1993.

13. During a follow-up visit to Chuquicamata in 1995, I was struck by the many references to *vicios* in casual conversations about problems facing the mine and community. Some labor activists critically challenged this image of "vice." For many people, however, it seemed to fit well into the privilege and dependency script.

14. David Harvey describes late-twentieth-century capitalism in terms of flexible accumulation that demands flexibility in the labor force as well (1989, 121–97, 338–42).

15. I use *essential* loosely here, more in the sense of "boys will be boys" said with sarcasm and a roll of the eye than in any sense of masculine biology as unfaithful destiny.

16. Personal interview, Chuquicamata, 1993.

17. For discussion of a similar gender dynamic in the El Teniente mines, see Klubock (1992, 65–77).

18. Sonia Montecino argues the importance of *marianismo* in the constitution of gender identities and in the reproduction of values associated with the feminine (1993, 27).

19. Personal interview, Butte, 1991.

20. Excerpt from Teresa Jordan Oral History Collection, 1986, BSBPA.

21. June Nash (1979) describes a similar sense of identification rather than alienation among tin miners of Bolivia.

22. Personal interview, Chuquicamata, 1994.

23. Personal interview, Butte, 1993.

24. Personal interview, Butte, 1991.

25. Note the distinction here: People spoke of "you gringos" or "Anaconda" when recounting stories of racist practices vis-à-vis Bolivian laborers. When speaking on an individual level of bosses and workers, there is a discourse of meritocracy. People still recall by name those bosses who violated the code of respect in their labor practices.

26. Personal interview, Chuquicamata, 1993.

27. This line is from Pablo Neruda's "Los abogados de dólar" (1955), cited in Roseberry (1991, 105).

28. Personal interview, Butte, 1993.

29. Personal interview, Butte, 1991.

30. Personal interview, Butte, 1994.

31. Grant me rhetorical liberty here to juxtapose Bateson's psychological consequences of contradiction (schizophrenia) with Marx's necessary conditions of contradiction.

32. Basso's analysis focuses on labor-management negotiations at the Anaconda smelter, located in the town of Anaconda, Montana, twenty-five miles west of Butte. Basso argues that women were seen by management and labor men as the lesser of two evils. Management brought up importation of Mexican and black men only when the union membership balked at allowing women to work in the smelter. The union stalled on implementation, pushing the company to rely heavily on overtime work by the established white male workforce.

33. A feminist analysis of Catholicism in Butte and Chuquicamata is beyond the scope of this study. I refer the reader to Montecino's *Madres y hauchos* for a rich analysis of *marianismo* and the cultural import of the single mother, absent father, the body of the woman as locus of ethnic impurity, and the power of the *blanqueamiento cultural* (cultural whitening) in Latin America (1993, 27–67). See also Tarduccia (1993, 43–50) and Díaz (1993, 157–66).

34. On the strike of 1946 and women's participation, see chapter 2.

35. See for example "*La página feminina,*" *Oasis,* 7 March 1964, 5. Similar features appeared in *Oasis* and *La Pampa* throughout the 1950s and 1960s.

36. Cited with permission of Neil J. Lynch, author and publisher.

37. See *A Dream That Came True* (1986), Kearney (1990), and Lee (1992).

38. "The company" in 1979 to 1985, during Our Lady's construction phase, was Atlantic Richfield (ARCO), which purchased Anaconda in 1977. However, ARCO maintained some of Anaconda's practices, such as donating equipment and supplies to the grassroots efforts. Weeks after ARCO announced the layoff of five hundred employees, the company donated two hundred and fifty thousand dollars in supplies for Our Lady's construction.

39. Some tell a story of Butte's "miraculous" recovery, crediting Our Lady for the recuperation of mining and the expansion of small industry in Butte. Among some men, there is dark humor about Our Lady and the emasculation of labor with the collapse of union mining. Their bitterness may also relate to the growth in number of working women who became the sole supporters of their families once the mines closed.

40. The procession took place in Calama, with many people coming from Chuquicamata to participate. As Calama has grown, it has taken over as the center for social and cultural activities.

41. For examples of "Cartas a la mujer de Chuquicamata," see *Oasis,* June to October 1993.

42. Personal interview, Chuquicamata, 1993.

43. Pasties and empanadas are meat-filled pies. Pasties, a traditional miner's lunch, are still popular in Butte. Empanadas are a popular part of Chilean cuisine.

44. From personal interviews, Butte, 1991, 1993.

45. See *Chilex Weekly*, 16 November 1957, 4.

46. Personal interview, Chuquicamata, 1993.

47. Personal interview, Chuquicamata, 1993.

48. For examples of songs and lore, see Hand (1946, 1–25).

49. Personal interview, Butte, 1991.

50. Personal interview, Butte, 1993.

51. Personal interview, Chuquicamata, 1993.

52. Personal interview, Butte, 1993.

53. Personal interview, Butte, 1993.

54. Personal interview, Butte, 1993.

55. Personal interview, Butte, 1993.

56. Personal interview, Chuquicamata, 1994.

57. Longtime Chuquicamata residents, both men and women, told similar versions of this story with pride and humor. No one offered dates of the strikes, but all situated this activity in the 1940s and 1950s.

58. Personal interview, Chuquicamata, 1994. *Pacos* is the popular pejorative for police.

5. CRAFTING THE EVERYDAY

1. The chapter's initial epigraph is from the "Collected Poems of Sam and Lou," Typescript, courtesy of John McGinley. Permission to quote granted by the estate of Frances "Sam" McGinley. The second epigraph is from a personal interview with a member of the *agrupación* of Calama, 1994.

2. Alexander credits E. P. Thompson with this observation.

3. This view of actor and agency challenges Pierre Bourdieu's conception of agent as strategist. I draw from William Sewell (1992, 1–29) in developing a more complicated understanding of agency here.

4. I borrow the term *positionality* from Linda Alcoff, who argues that the position in which women find themselves can be actively utilized as a location for the construction of meaning. It is a place from which values are interpreted and constructed. See Alcoff (1994, 98–122).

5. I draw inspiration here from the work of Temma Kaplan and Caroline Moser on women's consciousness and action. Kaplan (1982) describes female consciousness as emerging from the sexual division of labor that assigns women the responsibility of preserving life. She argues that women with "female consciousness" accept the gender system of their society and engage in social practice to carry out their responsibilities and secure their rights within the system. Thus their social practice may have important consequences for social change as they politicize issues of the preservation of life. Making a similar argument, Moser (1987) portrays women's daily struggles to fulfill their obligations to preserve life in an urban squatter settlement in Guayaquil, Ecuador. She suggests that women build a common critical consciousness through these practices, such that the daily tasks of preserving family life become political tasks of building

infrastructure, both materially and politically. Female consciousness is not a fixed trait but a negotiated practice.

6. In his reformulation of Gidden's theory of structuration, Sewell was concerned with preserving the duality of structure and centrality of power while recognizing human agency, accounting for the possibility of change, and overcoming the divide between semiotic and materialist views of structure (Sewell 1992, 1–29).

7. Sewell argues that Bourdieu's own focus on *habitus* as the mutual reproduction of schemas and resources fails to fully consider how *habitus* itself might generate change (1992, 14–15).

8. Personal interview, Butte, 1993.

9. Personal interview, Butte, 1991.

10. Personal interview, Butte, 1991.

11. Personal interview, Butte, 1991.

12. I also conducted interviews with a number of women whose lives were not directly tied to mining. The theme of three-year cycles was never mentioned in their stories.

13. Personal interview, Butte, 1991.

14. Personal interview, Butte, 1991.

15. Personal interview, Butte, 1991.

16. Personal interview, Butte, 1991.

17. Personal interview, Butte, 1993.

18. Personal interview, Butte, 1991.

19. Personal interview, Butte, 1991.

20. Personal interview, Butte, 1993.

21. Personal interview, Butte, 1991.

22. In speaking of this creative remaking of the cultural materials at hand, I draw from anthropologist Claude Levi-Strauss's concept of *bricolage* (Levi-Strauss 1966).

23. Personal interview, Butte, 1991.

24. Personal interview, Butte, 1991.

25. Personal interview, Butte, 1991.

26. Personal interview, Butte, 1991.

27. Personal interview, Butte, 1991.

28. Personal interview, Butte, 1991.

29. This conundrum is reminiscent of the concept of "penetration" elaborated by Paul Willis: he argues that working class youth, in "figuring out" and opting out of the class structure of the school system, are, in fact, sealing their own fate of life on the factory floor (1981, 119–37). However, Willis's terminology is too masculine to serve in an analysis of women's social practice.

30. Personal interviews, Chuquicamata, 1994.

31. Personal interview, Chuquicamata, 1994.

32. Personal interview, Chuquicamata, 1993.

33. Personal interview, Chuquicamata, 1993.

34. Personal interview, Chuquicamata, 1993.

35. I employ the notion of domesticity as a public practice to challenge the gendered dichotomy of public and private, or as Sonia Montecino frames it, *"casas y calles"* (1993, 25). This publicness of domestic life is a key feature in distinguishing working-class women's experience from that of middle-class and upper-class women.

36. For a discussion of elaborating symbols, see Ortner (1973).

37. I borrow the phrase "weapon of the weak" from James Scott (1985).

38. The Chilean Labor Code set a sixty-day legal limit on strikes. Partial work stoppages were more frequent in Chuquicamata. General strikes were less frequent.

39. Personal interview, 1994.

40. Personal interview, Chuquicamata, 1994. She did not recall when this strike occurred but situated it during her growing up years in Chuquicamata in the 1950s and 60s.

41. Personal interview, Chuquicamata, 1993.

42. Personal interview, Chuquicamata, 1994.

43. Personal interview, Chuquicamata, 1993.

44. Personal interview, Chuquicamata, 1993.

45. Personal interview, Chuquicamata, 1994.

46. Personal interview, Chuquicamata, 1994.

47. Personal interview, Butte, 1993.

48. "Habla Berta Sierra, activo papel de la mujer en la nacionalización," *Oasis*, 10 July 1971, 1.

49. This discussion of women's social practice coincides with the argument developed by Kaplan (1982).

50. Personal interview, Chuquicamata, 1993. For a detailed account of the military operation responsible for the executions, known as the Caravan of Death, see Verdugo (1989).

51. Personal interview, Chuquicamata, 1994.

52. Personal interview, Chuquicamata, 1993.

6. MINER'S CONSUMPTION

1. The chapter epigraphs can be found in Hunter S. Thompson, *National Observer*, 1 June 1964; personal interview, Chuquicamata, 1994; and Karl Marx, "Alienated Labour" (1844) in McLellan (1977, 78).
For an overview of occupational hazards facing coal miners and similar concerns for hard rock miners, see "Black Lung: Mining as a Way of Death" (1969).

2. I draw insight from Susan Sontag (1978) here in thinking about the social implications of disorder and disease and the profound need to locate pathology in the individual. Perhaps the location of consumption in men's bodies created a model for locating other "problems of consumption" in a context of individual pathology.

3. *Montana State Department of Public Welfare Report* (1942, 9; 1960, 17).

4. *Mine-Mill Butte Miner*, 24 November 1956, 4.

5. See chapter 4, Marie's commentary that Anaconda collapsed because of weight at the top, where Big Shots with big pensions, men who never entered the mines, lived long.

6. *Butte Miner's Voice*, April 1959, 1, 2. *Blackspotting* refers to the appearance of black spots on the lungs during X-rays. The *Butte Miner's Voice* was a short-lived labor paper first published in April 1959 by "The Committee to Restore True Unionism in Butte."

7. Correspondence from vice-president of Chile Exploration Company, Santiago to general superintendent, Anaconda Reduction Works, 29 October 1949, Anaconda Company Papers, MC 169, Box 75, MHSA.

8. Ricardo Latcham (1926) also leveled severe criticism against Chile Exploration Company regarding health conditions in the mines. However, such

criticism is not heard from current residents, who have lived for more than thirty-five years with their state-of-the-art hospital as an icon of their community's status.

9. Statement by W. A. Clark, cited in Murphy (1990, 11).

10. Personal interview, Butte, 1993.

11. Personal interview, Chuquicamata, 1993.

12. I chose not to develop the role of middle-class and upper-class women's social practice in chapter 4, in order to focus on the common ground and important differences in the lives of working-class women. Working-class women's stories suggest a much stronger spatial and temporal contouring of life experience vis-à-vis corporate operations than did those of middle-class women. The intriguing history of *Chuqui Ayuda* deserves more analysis than it will be given here.

13. Personal interview, Chuquicamata, 1994.

14. Personal interview, Butte, 1993.

15. I am indebted to Mary Curran for alerting me to Johnnie Moore and Samuel Luoma's study. For a thorough discussion of public health issues in Butte, see Curran (1996).

16. Personal interview, Butte, 1993.

17. Personal interviews, Butte, 1993

18. Personal interviews, Chuquicamata, 1993.

19. The theme of distinctions in cultural and material capital is skillfully developed by Pierre Bourdieu (1984).

20. Personal interviews, Butte, 1993

21. Women's social mobilization around the politics of consumption is a key theme in previously mentioned works, including Blee (1985), Campbell (1984), Frank (1985; 1991a; 1991b), Kaplan (1982), Moser (1987), and Weinbaum and Bridges (1979). See also Safa (1990) for discussion of women's increasing political participation around human rights and collective consumption.

22. Personal interview, Butte, 1991.

23. Personal interview, Butte, 1993.

24. See "No Plans for Pit to Gobble Mining City," *Montana Standard*, 2 September 1970, 1; "Time to Level with Us," *Montana Standard*, 6 October 1970, 4; "Make Way for the Pit," *Montana Standard*, 5 November 1970, 1; "Swan Song," *Montana Standard*, 2 September 1973, 1; "Anaconda Company Not Selling Gardens," *Montana Standard*, 19 September 1973; "Continental Pit Expansion Remains Undecided," *Montana Standard*, 18 July 1974, 1.

25. Personal interview, Butte, 1993.

26. Personal interview, Butte, 1993.

27. Personal interview, Chuquicamata, 1993.

28. According to a Chuquicamata union activist, the CODELCO workforce increased by two thousand people between 1985 and 1990. He claims that the jobs went to friends and family members of military personnel. The present workforce is shouldering the blame for this crisis of overemployment that resulted from the military regime's hiring practices.

29. Personal interview, Chuquicamata, 1993.

30. Personal interview, Butte, 1993.

31. Personal interview, Chuquicamata, 1993.

32. Personal interview, Chuquicamata, 1993.

33. This message is strongly stated in numerous articles appearing in *Oasis* from July 1993 to July 1994. It was also stated directly by CODELCO management personnel during personal interviews in July 1994.

34. I return to analysis of this issue in chapter 7, where I address the practices of reclamation.

35. For further discussion of the Chilean experiment in monetarism and neoliberalism, see Gimpel Smith (1989), Green (1995), and Quiroga Martínez (1994).

36. Duncan Green cites *El Mercurio* (Santiago), 30 September 1993, as source of the World Health Organization report.

37. I borrow the phrase from the title of June Nash's book *We Eat the Mines and the Mines Eat Us* (1979).

38. For diverse perspectives on postmodernism and postmodernity, see, for example, Jameson (1984), Baudrillard (1988), Lyotard (1984), and Harvey (1989).

7. TRUST, BETRAYAL, AND TRANSFORMATION

1. The chapter epigraphs are from personal interview, Butte, 1991, and personal interview, Chuquicamata, 1994.

2. I refer intentionally to *men's* wisdom here. Though themes of trust and betrayal are part of women's stories as well, I am drawing from a dominant masculine discourse in this discussion. I do not see this theme as unique to the histories of Butte and Chuquicamata, but one common to many labor histories. What is interesting here is how this theme plays out.

3. For examples of corporate attacks on union leadership and credibility, see "Strike Protest March Urged for Today by Miners' Wives," *Montana Standard*, 18 August 1959, 1; "Miners' Wives March on Union Hall, Anaconda Company Offices," *Montana Standard*, 18 August 1959, 13.

4. Personal interview, Butte, 1991.

5. Personal interview, Butte, 1991.

6. Personal interview, Butte, 1991.

7. Personal interviews, Butte, 1991.

8. Personal interview, Butte, 1991.

9. For a sophisticated analysis of current environmental and social concerns in Butte, see Curran (1996).

10. See "La nacionalización garantiza y amplia derechos de los trabajadores del cobre," *Oasis*, 15 May 1971, 3.

11. See "Gobierno popular respeta y garantiza derechos de los trabajadores del cobre," *Oasis*, 25 May 1971, 4.

12. See "Otro trabajador ofrece un dia de sueldo para Chile," *Oasis*, 12 June 1971, 3.

13. See "Trabajador: No solo debes pensar en tu presente, sino en el futuro de Chile y de tus hijos. Produce más," *Oasis*, special supplement, 4 August 1971, 4.

14. See *Oasis*, July 1971 to April 1972, in particular "Participación de los trabajadores no existe. Sin solución seis huelgas: Burocracia," 29 April 1972, 14.

15. See "Assemblea de trabajadores se impusó del compromiso de acción," *Oasis*, 19 June 1972, 7–8.

16. See "Nacionalización en Chuquicamata," *Oasis*, 17 July 1972, 7. It is interesting to note that Silberman was thirty-three years old, an engineer from Santiago, and a Communist Party activist at the time of his appointment as general manager of Cobre-Chuqui.

17. See "El camino de la restauración nacional," *Oasis*, 3 November 1973, 4.

18. The "cultural transformation" is the brainchild of Fernando Flores, a former member of the Allende Popular Unity government who currently works as an international business consultant. He has helped developed reorganization plans for such organizations as IBM.

19. See *Oasis*, June 1993 to January 1994. For example, "Con todo y con todas, Chuqui cambia," *Oasis*, 23–29 October 1993, 12, 13; "Cambiando la vieja orden por el moderno acuerdo," *Oasis*, 17–23 July 1993, 6, 7.

20. During my return trip to Chuquicamata in July 1994, I spoke with several men in management posts in Chuquicamata. They were eager to tell me about the legacy of workforce problems they face as a result of Anaconda's corporate practices.

21. Workers' distrust was heightened when a scandal rocked the Chilean copper industry in January 1994. A corporate operative lost more than 260 million dollars on the copper futures market. The CEO of CODELCO and the minister of mining resigned under pressure as a result. See "La crisis en CODELCO," *La Epoca* (Santiago), 5 February 1994, 1–5 (B).

22. Personal interview, Butte, 1993.

23. I refer here to the historic devaluing of women's paid and unpaid labors. Clearly, I do not subscribe to essentialist views of masculine and feminine labor.

8. FOOD FOR THOUGHT AND ACTION

1. The chapter epigraph is from Derrida (1976, 158).

2. Peter McLaren offers this depiction of human subjectivity in a discussion of Freireian cultural politics. He cites Paulo Freire's emphasis on "the fact that human beings 'have the sense of project' in contrast to the instinctive routines of animals" (Freire 1985, 44).

3. Williams (1977, 130–133), Bourdieu (1977, 78), and Foucault (1980, 17–35, 92–102).

4. The centrality of issues of consumption in the politicization of women's social practice has been addressed by a number of scholars, including Abramovitz (1996), Blee (1985), Campbell (1984), Frank (1991a; 1991b), Kingsolver (1989), and Bookman and Morgen (1988).

5. Henry A. Giroux asserts that the cultural politics of Paulo Freire combine a language of critique and possibility (Giroux 1985, xiii, in McLaren 1994, 200). McLaren argues that this language of possibility and sense of a political project is lost in postmodernism's "retreat into the code" (1994, 193–201).

6. See, for example, Shirley (1990) and Stanford (1994).

7. For discussion of cross-border labor organizing in response to NAFTA, see Blum and Tanski (1994, 18–21) and Armbruster (1995).

8. For a discussion of convergence and counterpattern in empowering research methodologies, see Lather (1988).

Bibliography

ARCHIVAL SOURCES

ARCHIVO NACIONAL DEL SIGLO XX, SANTIAGO, CHILE

Ministry of the Interior, Monthly Correspondence, 1947–1949; 1953

BIBLIOTECA DEL CONGRESO NACIONAL, SANTIAGO, CHILE

Rare Books Collections

BIBLIOTECA NACIONAL, SANTIAGO, CHILE

Sección Chilena, includes unpublished working papers and theses relevant to copper history

República de Chile, Diario Sesiones del Senado, Publicación Oficial, Legislatura Extraordinaria, Incidentes en el Mineral El Salvador, Sesión 78, 12 de marzo de 1966

BUTTE-SILVER BOW PUBLIC ARCHIVES (BSBPA), BUTTE, MONTANA

Butte Historical Society, Photo Collection
Butte Labor History Project, Photo Collection
Butte Miner's Union File
Butte-Silver Bow County Coroner's Reports, 1921–1934
Emily Kailaya Collection
McGlynn Collection
Teresa Jordan Oral History Collection

MONTANA TECH OF THE UNIVERSITY OF MONTANA,
BUTTE, MONTANA

Annual Reports of the Anaconda Company, 1905–1983

MONTANA HISTORICAL SOCIETY ARCHIVES (MHSA),
HELENA, MONTANA

The Anaconda Company Papers
Jeannette Rankin Papers
Silver Bow County Board of Health, "Report on Sanitary Conditions in the
     Mines and Community, Silver Bow County, December 1908 – April 1912"
Silver Bow County Board of Health, "Report Showing Results of Inspections of
     Dwellings, Hotels, Rooming Houses, and Boarding Houses and Their
     Surroundings," 1912

MONTANA STATE LIBRARY, HELENA, MONTANA

Montana State Department of Public Welfare Report, 1942–1960

UNIVERSITY OF MONTANA MANSFIELD LIBRARY,
MISSOULA, MONTANA

Montana State Hospital for the Insane Report, 1921–1932, Special Collections

NEWSPAPERS

Anaconda Standard, Anaconda, Montana
The Butte Daily Post, Butte, Montana
Butte Miner's Voice, Butte, Montana
Chilex Weekly, Chuquicamata, Chile
El Clarin, Santiago, Chile
The Eye Opener, Butte, Montana
El Mercurio, Santiago, Chile
El Mercurio de Calama, Calama, Chile
Mine Mill Butte Miner, Butte, Montana
Montana Labor News, Helena, Montana
Montana Standard, Butte, Montana
Oasis, Chuquicamata, Chile
Oregon Labor Press, Portland, Oregon.
La Pampa, Chuquicamata, Chile
El Pukará, Chuquicamata, Chile
Reacción Social, Chuquicamata, Chile
El Siglo, Santiago, Chile
La Voz Sindical, Chuquicamata, Chile

LITERATURE

Abramovitz, Mimi.
     1996   *Under Attack, Fighting Back: Women and Welfare in the United
          States*. New York: Monthly Review Press, Cornerstone Books.

Alcoff, Linda.
    1994   Reprint. "Cultural Feminism versus Post-Structuralism: The Identity Crisis in Feminist Theory." In *Culture/Power/History: A Reader in Contemporary Social Theory*, edited by Nicholas B. Dirks, Geoff Eley, and Sherry B. Ortner. Princeton: Princeton University Press. First published in *Signs: Journal of Women in Culture and Society* 13 (1988): 405–36 (page references are to reprint edition).

Alexander, Sally.
    1994   Reprint. "Women, Class and Sexual Differences in the 1830s and 1840s: Some Reflections on the Writing of a Feminist History." In *Culture/Power/History: A Reader in Contemporary Social Theory*, edited by Nicholas B. Dirks, Geoff Eley, and Sherry B. Ortner. Princeton: Princeton University Press. First published in *History Workshop* 17 (1983): 125–49 (page references are to reprint edition).

Alvarez Vargas, Alejandro.
    1988   *Resumen de la historia de Calama*. Santiago: Editorial Universitaria.

Alvear Urrutia, Jorge.
    1975   *Chile, nuestro cobre*. Santiago: Editorial Lastra.

"Anaconda Copper Mining Company in 1932 Will Produce over One-Third of
    1942   U.S. Supply."
                 Fortune 25 (January): 52–55+.

"Anaconda Copper, Part 1."
    1936   *Fortune* 14 (December): 83–96+.

"Anaconda Copper, Part 2."
    1937   *Fortune* 15 (January): 71–77+.

Anderson, Benedict.
    1991   *Imagined Communities*. 2d ed. London: Verso Press.

Anderson, Don.
    1976   "Lee's Purchase of the Anaconda Dailies." *Montana Journalism Review* 19: 20–22.

Angell, Alan.
    1972   *Politics and the Labour Movement in Chile*. London: Oxford University Press.

Angell, Alan, and Benny Pollack.
    1990   "The Chilean Elections of 1989 and the Politics of Transition to Democracy." *Bulletin of Latin American Research* 9: 1–23.

Araya Carro, Elaba, Teresa Geraldo Orrego, Meigling Llajas, Maria Muñoz
    1973   Lagos, and Carmen Olmendo Assandron.
                 "Participación de los trabajadores en los comités de producción de Cobre-Chuqui." Memoria de prueba para optar al titulo de asistente social.Universidad de Chile de Antofagasta. Santiago: Biblioteca Nacional, Sección Chilena.

Armbruster, Ralph.
    1995   "Cross-National Labor Organizing Strategies." *Critical Sociology* 21: 75–90.

Arteaga, Ana Maria.
    1989   "Politicización de lo privado y subversión del cotidiano mundo de la mujer." In *Mundo de mujer: Continuidad y cambio*. Santiago: CEM.

Atherton, Gertrude.
    1914   *The Perch of the Devil*. New York: Frederick A. Stokes Co.
Ayquina: Historia y festividad del santuario de nuestra Señora Guadelupe de
    n.d.   *Ayquina*. Chuquicamata: Comité de Extensión Cultural.
"Banking on an Outsider: Business in the News."
    1971   *Fortune* (June): 33.
Baron, Eva.
    1991   "Gender and Labor History: Learning from the Past, Looking to
                the Future." In *Work Engendered: Toward a New History of
                American Labor*, edited by Eva Baron. Ithaca: Cornell Unversity
                Press.
Barros Garces, Raul.
    1986   *Amaras al cobre como a ti mismo*. Santiago: Editorial Andres
                Bello.
Basso, Matthew.
    1996   "'An Ounce of Prevention Is Worth a Pound of Cure': The
                Smeltermen of Anaconda in War and Peace, 1942–1945."
                Master's thesis, University of Montana.
Bateson, Gregory.
    1972   "Double Bind, 1969." In *Steps to an Ecology of Mind*. New
                York: Ballantine Books, 271–78.
Baudrillard, Jean.
    1988   *Selected Writings*. Edited by Mark Poster. Stanford: Stanford
                University Press.
Baum, Dan.
    1997   "Butte, America." *American Heritage* 48: 57–67.
Baum, Dan, and Margaret Knox.
    1992   "Butte, Montana, the Rebirth of a Blighted City." *Smithsonian*
                (November): 46–57.
Bell, Colin, and Howard Newby.
    1972   *Community Studies*. London: George Allen and Unwin, Ltd.
Bender, Thomas.
    1982   *Community and Social Change in America*. Baltimore: Johns
                Hopkins University Press.
Benería, Lourdes, and Martha Roldán, eds.
    1987   *The Crossroads of Class and Gender: Industrial Homework,
                Subcontracting, and Household Dynamics in Mexico City*.
                Chicago: University of Chicago Press.
Berger, Peter, and Thomas Luckman.
    1966   *The Social Construction of Reality: A Treatise in the Sociology
                of Knowledge*. New York: Anchor Books.
"Bitter Aftermath: End of a National Copper Strike."
    1968   *Newsweek*, 15 April, 80.
"Black Lung: Mining as a Way of Death."
    1969   *Nonferrous Report* (February): 4–5.
Blee, Kathleen.
    1985   "Family Patterns and the Politicization of Consumption Rela-
                tions." *Sociological Spectrum* 5: 295–316.
Blum, Albert, and Janet Tanski.
    1994   "Workers of the World Unite! Your Wages Depend on It!"
                Commonweal 121, no. 12: 18–21.

Bookman, Ann, and Sandra Morgen, eds.
  1988   *Women and the Politics of Empowerment*. Philadelphia: Temple
            University Press.
Bourdieu, Pierre.
  1977   *Outline of a Theory of Practice*. Translated by Richard Nice.
  [1972]   Cambridge: Cambridge University Press.
————.
  1984   *Distinction: A Social Critique of the Judgement of Taste*.
  [1979]   Translated by Richard Nice. Cambridge: Harvard University
            Press.
Boyer, Lynne.
  1978   "Butte's Columbia Gardens." *Montana Historian* 8: 2–7.
Briskin, Linda, and Lynda Yanz.
  1985   *Union Sisters: Women in the Labor Movement*. 2d ed. Toronto:
            Women's Educational Press.
Brown, Ronald.
  1979   *Hard Rock Miners: The Intermountain West, 1860–1920*.
            College Station: Texas A & M University Press.
Burke, Bill.
  1964   *Rhymes of the Mines*. 3d ed. Vancouver, Wash.: Bill Burke and
            Son.
"Butte: New Mines, New Life."
  1947   *Business Week*, 27 December, 25.
Calkins, Ray, ed.
  1982   *Looking Back from the Hill: Recollections of Butte People*.
            Butte: Butte Historical Society.
Calvert, Jerry.
  1988   *The Gibraltar: Socialism and Labor in Butte, Montana*. Helena,
            Mont.: Montana Historical Society.
Campbell, Beatrix.
  1984   *Wigan Pier Revisited: Poverty and Politics in the Eighties*.
            London: Virago Press.
Cardoso, Fernando Henrique, and Enzo Faletto.
  1979   *Dependency and Development in Latin America*. Berkeley:
            University of California Press.
Chaplin, Ralph.
  1920   "The Picket Line of Blood: Another Red Chapter of Labor
            History from Butte, Montana." *One Big Union Monthly* (June)
            9.
Chavez, Leo.
  1994   "The Power of the Imagined Community: The Settlement of
            Undocumented Mexicans and Central Americans in the United
            States." *American Anthropologist* 96: 52–73.
"Chile: Copper Pays the Price of Nationalism."
  1971   *Business Week*, 21 August, 38–40.
Cohen, Anthony.
  1985   *The Symbolic Construction of Community*. London: Tavistock.
"Companies: An Ex-Banker Treats Copper's Sickest Giant."
  1972   *Business Week*, 19 February, 52–54.
"Company Towns, 1956."
  1956   *Time*, 1 April, 100–101.

Connelly, Christopher.
   1938   *The Devil Learns to Vote*. New York: Civici-Friede.
Corporación Nacional del Cobre.
   1974   *El cobre chileno*. Santiago: CODELCO.
―――.

   1980   *Bodas de oro: órgano oficial del sindicato profesional único de
               empleados particulares, CODELCO-Chile*. Chuquicamata:
               CODELCO.
Cruzat, X., and Eduardo Deves, eds.
   1986   *Recabarren: Escritos de prensa, tomo 2, 1906–1913*. Santiago:
               Editorial Nuestra America y Terranova Editores.
Culver, William, and Cornel Reinhart.
   1989 ˙   "Capitalist Dreams: Chile's Response to Nineteenth-Century
               World Copper Competition." *Comparative Studies in Society
               and History* 31: 722–44.
Curran, Mary E.
   1996   "The Contested Terrain of Butte, Montana: Social Landscapes
               of Risk and Resiliency." Master's thesis, University of Montana.
Dance of Hope (Danza de Esperanza).
   1989   Documentary Film. Directed by Deborah Shaffer, produced by
               Lavonne Poteet. Santiago: Copihue Productions.
Davis, Nathaniel.
   1985   *The Last Two Years of Salvador Allende*. New York: Cornell
               University Press.
de Lauretis, Teresa.
   1984   *Alice Doesn't*. Bloomington: University of Indiana Press.
Dempsey, Al.
   1989   *Copper*. New York: Tom Doherty Associates.
Derrida, Jacques.
   1976   *Of Grammatology*. Translated by Gayatri Chakravorty Spivak.
   [1967]   Baltimore: Johns Hopkins University Press.
de Vylder, Stefan.
   1976   *Allende's Chile*. London: Cambridge University Press
Días de Octubre.
   1991   Documentary Film. Directed by Hernan Castro, produced by
               Wolfgang Pens. Santiago.
Días, Marcela.
   1983   "Sufrir y amar . . . la cruz. Dimensiones simbólicas en el discurso
               de Teresa de Los Andes." In *Huellas: Seminario mujer y antro-
               pología: Problematización y perspectivas*, edited by Sonia
               Montecino and María Elena Boisier. Santiago: CEDEM.
di Leonardo, Micaela, ed.
   1991   *Gender at the Crossroads of Knowledge: Feminist Anthro-
               pology in the Postmodern Era*. Berkeley: University of Cali-
               fornia Press.
Dirks, Nicholas B., Geoff Eley, and Sherry B. Ortner.
   1994   Introduction to *Culture/Power/History: A Reader in Contem-
               porary Social History*, edited by Nicholas B. Dirks, Geoff Eley,
               and Sherry B. Ortner. Princeton: Princeton University Press.
Dobb, Edwin.
   1996   "Pennies from Hell: In Montana, the Bill for America's Copper
               Comes Due." *Harper's Magazine* (October): 39–54.

Drake, Paul.
  1988   *Socialism and Populism in Chile, 1932–1952*. Urbana: Univer-
              sity of Illinois Press.
A Dream That Came True.
  1986   Directed by Dan Counter. Video. Butte, Mont.: Our Lady of the
              Rockies Foundation.
Emmons, David.
  1989   *The Butte Irish: Class and Ethnicity in an American Mining
              Town, 1875–1925*. Urbana: University of Illinois Press.
Falk, Richard.
  1993   "The Making of Global Citizenship." In *Global Visions: Beyond
              the New World Order*, edited by Jeremy Brecher et al. Boston:
              South End Press.
Faue, Elizabeth.
  1991   *Communities of Suffering and Struggle: Women, Men, and the
              Labor Movement in Minneapolis, 1915–1945*. Chapel Hill:
              University of North Carolina Press.
Fazio, Hugo.
  1995   "Frei: Chile país puente." *Encuentro XXI* 1: 57–65.
Fernandez Jilberto, Alex.
  1991   "Military Bureaucracy, Political Opposition, and Demo-
              cratic Transitions." *Latin American Perspectives* 18: 113–35.
Ffrench-Davis, Ricardo, and Ernest Tironi, eds. 1974.
  1991   *El cobre en el desarrollo nacional*. Santiago: Ediciones Nueva
              Universidad.
Finn, Janet.
  n.d.   "A Penny for Your Thoughts: Women, Copper, and Community
              in Butte, Montana." Unpublished ms., University of Michigan

———.
  1994   "The Promise of Participatory Research." *Journal of Progressive
              Human Services* 5, no. 2: 25–42.

———.
  1995   "Mining Community: The Cultural Politics of Copper, Class,
              and Gender in Butte, Montana, USA and Chuquicamata, Chile."
              Ph.D. diss., University of Michigan.
Fisher, Arthur.
  1923   "Montana: The Land of the Copper Collar." *The Nation* 117:
              20–22.
Forgacs, David.
  1988   *An Antonio Gramsci Reader: Selected Writings, 1916–1935*.
              New York: Schocken Books.
Foster, W. Z.
  1914   "The Miners' Revolt in Butte." *Mother Earth* 9 (September):
              216–20.
Foucault, Michel.
  1979   *Discipline and Punish: The Birth of the Prison*. Translated by
  [1975,   Alan Sheridan. New York: Random House, Vintage Books
  trans.   Edition.
  1977]

———.
  1977.   *Power/Knowledge: Selected Interviews and Other Writings,*

1972–1980. Edited and translated by Colin Gordon. New York: Pantheon.

————.
1990 *The History of Sexuality: An Introduction.* Vol. 1. Translated
[1976] by Robert Hurley. New York: Random House, Vintage Books
[trans. Edition.
1978]
Frank, Dana.
1985 "Housewives, Socialists, and the Politics of Food: The 1917 New York Cost of Living Protests." *Feminist Studies* 11: 256–86.

————.
1991a "Gender, Consumer Organizing, and the Seattle Labor Movement,1919–1929." In *Work Engendered: Toward a New History of American Labor*, edited by Eva Baron. Ithaca: Cornell University Press.

————.
1991b "'Food Wins All Struggles': Seattle Labor and the Politicization of Consumption." *Radical History Review* 51: 65–89.
Frias, Patricio.
1989 *El movimiento sindical chileno en la lucha por la democracia.* Santiago: Programa de Economia del Trabajo.
Freire, Paulo.
1985 *The Politics of Education: Culture, Power, and Liberation.* South Hadley, Mass.: Bergin and Garvey.
Frohman, Alicia, and Teresa Valdés.
1993 Democracy in the Country and in the Home: The Women's Movement in Chile." Santiago: FLACSO, Documento de Trabajo, Serie Estudios Sociales, no. 55.
Gallardo, Bernarda
1985 "Las ollas comunes de La Florida como experiencia de desarrollo de la organización popular." Santiago: FLACSO Documento de Trabajo, Serie Estudios Sociales, no. 248.
Galvez Naranjo, Joaquin.
1961 *Anaconda contraria a la creación de riquezas nacionales.* Santiago: no publisher listed.
Geertz, Clifford.
1973 "Deep Play: Notes on the Balinese Cockfight." In *Interpretation of Cultures.* New York: Basic Books.

————.
1983 *Local Knowledge: Further Essays in Interpretive Anthropology.* New York: Basic Books.
Giddens, Anthony.
1979 *Central Problems in Social Theory: Action, Structure, and Contradiction in Social Analysis.* Berkeley: University of California Press.
Giddens, Anthony, and David Held, eds.
1982 *Classes, Power, and Conflict: Classical and Contemporary Debates.* Berkeley: University of California Press.
Gil, Federico.
1966 *The Political System of Chile.* Boston: Houghton Mifflin.

Gilligan, Carol.
1982 *In a Different Voice: Psychological Theory and Women's Development*. Cambridge: Harvard University Press.

Gimpel Smith, Angélica.
1989 "Monetarism, Employment, and Unemployment: The Case of Chile, 1973–1983." Ph.D. diss., University of Sussex, England.

Ginsberg, Faye, and Anna Lowenhaupt Tsing, eds.
1990 *Uncertain Terms: Negotiating Gender in American Culture*. Boston: Beacon Press.

Giroux, Henry A.
1985 Introduction to *The Politics of Education: Culture, Power, and Liberation*, by Paulo Friere. South Hadley, Mass.: Bergin and Garvey.

Girvan, Norman.
1974 "Las corporaciones multinacionales del cobre en Chile." In *El cobre chileno en el desarrollo nacional*, edited by Ricardo Ffrench-Davis and Ernest Tironi. Santiago: CEPLAN.

Glasscock, C. B.
1935 *The War of the Copper Kings*. New York: Grosset and Dunlap.

Gordon, Deborah.
1995 "Border Work: Feminist Ethnography and the Dissemination of Literacy." In *Women Writing Culture*, edited by Ruth Behar and Deborah A. Gordon. Berkeley: University of California Press.

Gramsci, Antonio
1988 *An Antonio Gramsci Reader: Selected Writings, 1916–1935*. Edited by David Forgacs. New York: Schocken Books.

Green, Duncan.
1995 *Silent Revolution: The Rise of Market Economics in Latin America*. London: Cassell, Latin American Bureau.

Green, Linda.
1994 "Fear as a Way of Life." *Cultural Anthropology* 9: 227–56.

Guggenheim, Harry.
1920 "Building Mining Cities in South America: A Detailed Account of the Social and Industrial Benefits Flowing from the Human Engineering Work of the Chile Exploration Company and the Braden Copper Company — Organization, Administration, and Conception of Objects Sought." *Engineering and Mining Journal* 110: 204–10.

Gunder Frank, Andre.
1967 *Capitalism and Underdevelopment in Latin America*. New York: Monthly Review Press.

Gutfeld, Arnon.
1969 "The Speculator Disaster in 1917: Labor Resurgence at Butte, Montana." *Arizona and the West* 11: 27–38.

———.
1978 "The Murder of Frank Little: Labor Agitation in Butte, Montana, 1917." *Labor History* 19: 12–26.

———.
1979 *Montana's Agony: Years of War and Hysteria, 1917–1920*. Gainesville: University of Florida Social Science Monographs.

Guthals, Joel.
1970   "A Study of the 1967 Anaconda Copper Strike and Its Impact
           on Great Falls." Master's thesis, University of Montana.
Gutiérrez, Eulogio, and Marcial Figueroa.
1920   *Chuquicamata, su grandeza y sus dolores*. Santiago: Imprenta
           Cervantes.
Hammett, Dashiell.
1929   *Red Harvest*. New York: Grossett and Dunlap.
Hand, Wylan.
1946   "The Folklore, Customs, and Traditions of the Butte Miner."
           California Folklore Quarterly 5: 1–25.
Harvey, David.
1989   *The Condition of Postmodernity: An Enquiry into the Condi-
           tions of Cultural Change*. Oxford: Basil Blackwell.
Hawley, Amos.
1950   *Human Ecology: A Theory of Community Structure*. New
           York: Ronald Press.
Haywood, William.
1914   "The Battle at Butte." *International Socialist Review* 15:
           222–26.
Imagenes de El Loa.
n.d   Chuquicamata: Comité de Extensión Cultural.
Jameson, Frederic.
1984   "Postmodernism or the Cultural Logic of Late Capitalism."
           New Left Review 146: 53–92.
Kaplan, Temma.
1982   "Female Consciousness and Collective Action: The Case of
           Barcelona, 1910–1918." *Signs: Journal of Women in Culture
           and Society* 7: 545–66.
Kearney, Pat.
1990   *Miracle on the East Ridge*. Butte: Artcraft Printers.
Keen, Benjamin, and Mark Wasserman.
1988   *A History of Latin America*. Boston: Houghton Mifflin.
Kelly, Anthony, and Sandra Sewell.
1988   *With Head, Heart, and Hand: Dimensions of Community
           Building*. Brisbane, Australia: Boolarong Publishing.
Kingsolver, Barbara.
1989   *Holding the Line: Women in the Great Arizona Mine Strike of
           1983*. Ithaca: IRL Press.
Kinney, Ward.
1934   "Montana Challenges the Tyranny of Copper." *The Nation* 139:
           86, 99, 386–87.
Klubock, Thomas.
1992   "Sexualidad y proletarianización en la mina El Teniente."
           Proposiciones: Genero, mujer, y sociedad. Santiago: Ediciones
           SUR.

———.

1993   *Class, Community, and Gender in the Chilean Copper Mines:
           The El Teniente Miners and Working Class Politics, 1904–
           1951*. Ph.D. diss., Yale University.

———.

1996   "Working-Class Masculinity, Middle-Class Morality, and Labor

Politics in the Chilean Copper Mines." *Journal of Social History* 30, no. 2: 434–63.

Kornbluh, Joyce, ed.
1988   *Rebel Voices: An IWW Anthology*. Chicago: Charles Kerr Publishing.

Lafertte, Elias, and Salvador Ocampo.
1951   *El cobre de Chile: Nacionalización de Chuquicamata, Potrerillos y Sewell*. Santiago: no publisher listed.

Latcham, Ricardo.
1926   *Chuquicamata, estado yankee, visión de la montaña roja*. Santiago: Editorial Nascimento.

Lather, Patricia.
1988   "Feminist Perspectives on Empowering Research Methodologies." *Women's Studies International Forum* 11: 569–81

Lee, Leroy.
1992   *Our Lady Builds a Statue*. Butte, Mont.: Leroy Lee.

Levi-Strauss, Claude.
1966   *The Savage Mind*. Chicago: University of Chicago Press.

Limón, Jose.
1989   "*Carne, Carnales*, and the Carnivalesque: Bahktinian *Batos, Disorder*, and Narrative Discourses." *American Ethnologist* 16: 471–86.

Loveman, Brian.
1979   *The Legacy of Hispanic Capitalism*. New York: Oxford University Press.

Luxemburg, Rosa.
1972   *The Accumulation of Capital*. London: Monthly Review Press.
[1951]

Lynch, Neil J.
1979   *Butte Centennial Recollections*. Butte, Mont.: Neil J. Lynch.

Lynd, Robert, and Helen Merrell Lynd.
1929   *Middletown: A Study in Contemporary American Culture*. New York: Harcourt Brace.

Lynd, Robert, and Helen Merrell Lynd.
1937   *Middletown in Transition: A Study in Cultural Conflicts*. New York: Harcourt Brace.

Lyotard, Jean-Francois.
1984   *The Postmodern Condition*. Minneapolis: University of Minnesota Press.

Madrick, Jeffrey.
1976   "Inside Wall Street: The ARCO-Anaconda Merger Surprise." *Business Week*, 1 November, 58–60.

Malone, Michael.
1981   *The Battle for Butte: Mining and Politics on the Northern Frontier*. Seattle: University of Washington Press.

———.
1985   "The Close of the Copper Century." *Montana, The Magazine of Western History* 35: 69–72.

Marcosson, Isaac.
1957   *Anaconda*. New York: Dodd, Mead, and Company. Reprint, 1976, North Stratford, N.H.: Ayer Co. Publishers.

Marx, Karl.
1977   "Alienated Labour." Excerpt in *Karl Marx, Selected Writings*,
[1844]   edited by David McLellan. Oxford: Oxford University Press.
———.

1977   *The Eighteenth Brumaire of Louis Bonaparte*. Excerpt in
              Karl Marx, Selected Writings, edited by David McLellan.
              Oxford: Oxford University Press.
Marx, Karl, and Friedrich Engels.
1977   *The German Ideology*. Excerpt in *Karl Marx, Selected Writings*,
              edited by David McLellan. Oxford: Oxford University Press.
McCormick, Andrea.
1980   "Buckley Boardinghouse: Butte's Little Ireland." *Montana
              Standard* (Butte, Mont.), 16 March, 18.
McGinley, John.
1992   *The Prodigal's Journal*. Butte, Mont.: John McGinley.
McLaren, Peter.
1994   "Postmodernism and the Death of Politics: A Brazilian
              Reprieve." In *Politics of Liberation: Paths from Freire*, edited by
              Peter L. McLaren and Colin Lankshear. London: Routledge.
Milkman, Ruth.
1985   *Women, Work, and Protest: A Century of Women's Labor
              History*. Boston: Routledge and Kegan Paul.
Millis, Harry, and Emily Clark Brown.
1950   *From the Wagner Act to Taft-Hartley*. Chicago: University of
              Chicago Press.
Mintz, Sidney.
1985   *Sweetness and Power: The Place of Sugar in Modern History*.
              New York: Viking Press.
Montecino, Sonia.
1988   "Identidad femenina y modelo mariano en Chile." In *Mundo
              de mujer, continuidad y cambio*. Santiago: Ediciones CEM.
———.

1993   *Madres y huachos: Alegorias del mesitzaje chileno*. 2d ed.
              Santiago: Editorial Cuarto Propio, Ediciones CEDEM.
Moore, Johnnie, and Samuel M. Luoma.
1990   Hazardous Wastes from Large-scale Metal Extraction: The
              Clark Fork Waste Complex, MT." Paper presented at the 1990
              Clark Fork River Symposium, Montana Academy of Science,
              Missoula, Montana.
Moran, Theodore.
1974   *Multinational Corporations and the Politics of Dependence:
              Copper in Chile*. Princeton: Princeton University Press.
Moser, Caroline.
1987   Mobilization Is Women's Work: Struggles for Infrastructure
              in Guayaquil, Ecuador." In *Women, Human Settlements, and
              Housing*, edited by Caroline Moser and Linda Peake. London:
              Tavistock.
Mouffe, Chantal.
1988   "Hegemony and New Political Subjects: Toward a New
              Concept of Democracy." In *Marxism and the Interpretation of
              Culture*, edited by Cary Nelson and Lawrence Grossberg.
              Urbana: University of Illinois Press.

Murphy, Clyde.
    1944   *The Glittering Hill*. New York: E. P. Dutton and Co.
Murphy, Mary.
    1983   "Women on the Line: Prostitution in Butte, Montana, 1878–
                1917." Master's thesis, University of North Carolina, Chapel
                Hill.

———.
    1984   "Women's Work in a Man's World." *The Speculator* 1: 18–25.

———.
    1990   "Surviving Butte: Leisure and Community in a Western Mining
                Town, 1917–1941." Ph.D. diss., University of North Carolina,
                Chapel Hill.

———.
    1997   *Mining Cultures: Men, Women, and Leisure in Butte, 1914–
                1941*. Urbana: University of Illinois Press.
Nash, June.
    1979   *We Eat the Mines and the Mines Eat Us*. New York: Columbia
                University Press.

———.
    1989   *From Tank Town to High Tech: The Clash of Community and
                Industrial Cycles*. Albany: State University of New York.

———.
    1994   "Global Integration and Subsistence Insecurity." *American
                Anthropologist* 96, no. 1: 7–30.
Nash, June, and María Patricia Fernández-Kelly, eds.
    1983   *Men, Women, and the International Division of Labor*. Albany:
                State University of New York.
Neruda, Pablo.
    1955   "Los Abogados del Dólar." In *Canto general*. Vol. 1. Argentina:
                Losada.
Nicholson, Linda.
    1990   Introduction to *Feminism/Postmodernism*, edited by Linda J.
                Nicholson. London: Routledge.
O'Brien, Thomas.
    1989   Rich beyond the Dreams of Avarice: The Guggenheims in
                Chile." *Business History Review* 63: 122–59.
O'Malley, Richard.
    1986   *Mile High, Mile Deep*. Helena, Mont.: Century Lithographers.
Ore, Janet.
    1996   "The Quietest Strike in the United States: The 1934 Strike in
                Butte." Paper presented at the Montana History Conference,
                October 1996, Butte, Montana.
Ortner, Sherry.
    1973   "On Key Symbols." *American Anthropologist* 75: 1338–46.

———.
    1984   "Theory in Anthropology Since the Sixties." *Comparative
                Studies in Society and History* 26, no. 19: 126–66.

———.
    1989   *High Religion: A Cultural and Political History of Sherpa
                Buddhism*. Princeton: Princeton University Press.

———.
    1991   "Reading America: Preliminary Notes on Class and Culture." In

Recapturing Anthropology: Working in the Present, edited by Richard Fox. Santa Fe: School of American Research Press.

———.

1996   *Making Gender: The Politics and Erotics of Culture*. Boston: Beacon Press.

Ortner, Sherry, and Harriet Whitehead, eds.

1981   *Sexual Meanings: The Cultural Construction of Gender and Sexuality*. Cambridge: Cambridge University Press.

Pinto Vallejos, Julio, and Luis Ortega Martinez.

1990   *Expansión minera y desarrollo industrial: Un caso de crecimiento asociado (Chile 1850–1914)*. Santiago: Departamento de Historia, Universidad de Santiago de Chile.

Pizarro, Crisostomo.

1986   *La huelga obrera en Chile, 1890–1970*. Santiago: Ediciones SUR.

Pizarro, Crisostomo, and Sergio Bitar.

1986   *La Caída de Allende y la huelga de El Teniente*. Santiago: Ediciones del Ornitirrinco.

Politzer, Patricia.

1989   *Fear in Chile: Lives under Pinochet*. Translated by Diane Wachtell. New York: Pantheon Books.

Poulantzas, Nico.

1982   "On Social Classes." In *Classes, Power, and Conflict*, edited by Anthony Giddens and Peter Held. Berkeley: University of California Press.

"Private Recession That Plagues Anaconda."

1975   *Business Week*, 1 December, 38–40.

Probyn, Elspeth.

1990   "Travels in the Postmodern: Making Sense of the Local." In *Feminism/Postmodernism*, edited by Linda J. Nicholson. New York: Routledge.

Prodgers, Jeanette.

1991   *Butte-Anaconda Almanac: A Day-to-Day History of Montana's Two Greatest Mining and Smelting Towns*. Butte, Mont.: Jeanette Prodgers.

Quiroga, Patricio.

1995   "El nuevo tiempo historico: Cambio y confusiones." *Encuentro XXI* 1, no. 1: 30–38.

Quiroga Martínez, Rayén, ed.

1994   *El tigre sin selva: Consecuencias ambientales de la transformación económica de Chile, 1974–1993*. Santiago: Instituto de Ecología Política.

Ramirez Necochea, Hernan.

1956   *Historia del movimiento obrero en Chile, siglo XX*. Santiago: Austral Editorial.

Recabarren, Luis E.

1986   "En viaje al mineral de Chuquicamata." *Pampa de Antofagasta* (March 1913). Reprint in *Recabarren: Escritos de prensa, tomo 2, 1906–1913*, edited by Ximena Cruzat and Eduardo Deves. Santiago: Editorial Nuestra America y Terranova Editores.

Reiter, Rayna, ed.
1975   *Toward an Anthropology of Women.* New York: Monthly
            Review Press.
Rodo, Andrea, and Solange Hevia.
1991   "Consideraciones en torno a la participación de la mujer popu-
            lar en los espacios locales: Protagonismo o una nueva forma de
            subordinación?" Programa de la Mujer, SUR. Paper presented at
            international seminar, Mujer y Municipios, August 1991, in
            Quito, Ecuador.
Rosaldo, Michelle Zimbalist.
1974   "Woman, Culture, and Society: A Theoretical Overview." In
            Woman, Culture, and Society, edited by Michelle Zimbalist
            Rosaldo and Louise Lamphere. Stanford: Stanford University
            Press.
Rosaldo, Michelle Zimbalist, and Louise Lamphere, eds.
1974   *Woman, Culture, and Society.* Stanford: University Press.
Rosaldo, Renato.
1989   *Culture and Truth: The Remaking of Social Analysis.* Boston:
            Beacon Press.
———.
1990   "Celebrating Thompson's Heroes: Social Analysis in History
            and Anthropology." In *E. P. Thompson, Critical Perspectives*,
            edited by Harvey Kaye and Keith McClelland. Cambridge:
            Polity Press.
Roseberry, William.
1991   *Anthropologies and Histories: Essays in Culture, History,*
[1989]   *and Political Economy.* New Brunswick: Rutgers University
            Press.
Rosenblum, Jonathan D.
1995   *Copper Crucible: How the Arizona Miner's Strike of 1983
            Recast Labor-Management Relations in America.* Ithaca:
            IRL Press.
Rouse, Roger.
1991   "Mexican Migration and the Social Space of Postmodernism."
            Diaspora 1: 8–23.
———.
1995   "Thinking Through Transnationalism: Notes on the Cultural
            Politics of Class Relations in the Contemporary United States."
            Public Culture 7: 353–402.
Rubin, Lillian.
1978   *Worlds of Pain: Life in the Working-Class Family.* New York:
            Basic Books.
Sacks, Karen.
1975   "Engels Revisited: Women, the Organization of Production, and
            Private Property." In *Toward an Anthropology of Women*,
            edited by Rayna Reiter. New York: Monthly Review Press.
———. (Brodkin-Sacks).
1989   "Toward a Unified Theory of Class, Race, and Gender."
            American Ethnologist 16: 534–50.
Safa, Helen Icken.
1990   "Women's Social Movements in Latin America." *Gender and
            Society* 4, no. 3: 354–69.

Sahlins, Marshall.
  1981   *Historical Metaphors and Mythical Realities: Structure in the Early History of the Sandwich Islands Kingdom.* Ann Arbor: University of Michigan Press.
Salt of the Earth.
  1978   Screenplay by Michael Wilson, commentary by Deborah Silverton. New York: Feminist Press at City University.
Samagalski, Alan.
               Chile and Easter Island: A Travel Survival Kit. 2d ed.
  1990   Hawthorne, Victoria, Australia: Lonely Planet Publications.
Scee, T. I.
  1988   "The Story to Be Told of the End of the Line: Suicide in a Western American City, Butte, Montana, 1907–1914." Master's thesis, University of Montana.
Scott, James.
  1985   *Weapons of the Weak: Everyday Forms of Resistance.* New Haven: Yale University Press.
Scott, Joan.
  1988   "On Language, Gender, and Working-Class History." In *Gender and the Politics of History*, edited by Joan Scott. New York: Columbia University Press.
Service, Robert.
  1907   *The Spell of the Yukon.* New York: G. P. Putnam's Sons.
Sewell, William.
  1992   "A Theory of Structure: Duality, Agency, and Transformation." *American Journal of Sociology* 98, no. 1: 1–29.
Shannon, Kevin.
  1985   "The Mule in the Mine, a Miner's Tribute." *The Speculator* 2, no. 1: 41.
Shirley, Robert.
  1990   "Recreating Communities: The Formation of Community in a Brazilian Shantytown." *Urban Anthropology* 18: 255–76.
Sigmund, Paul.
  1977   *The Overthrow of Allende and the Politics of Chile, 1964– 1976.* Pittsburgh: University of Pittsburgh Press.
Sontag, Susan.
  1978   *Illness as Metaphor.* New York: Farrar, Straus, and Giroux.
Stallings, Barbara.
  1978   *Class Conflict and Economic Development in Chile, 1958– 1973.* Stanford: Stanford University Press.
Stanford, Lois.
  1994   "Transitions to Free Trade: Local Impacts of Changes in Mexican Agrarian Policy." *Human Organization* 53, no. 2: 99–109.
State of Montana.
  1984   *A Plant Closure Study: An Administrative Records Search of Five Plant Closures in Montana.* Helena: Department of Labor and Industry.
Steedman, Carolyn.
  1987   *Landscape for a Good Woman: A Story of Two Lives.* New Brunswick: Rutgers University Press.

Stegner, S. Page.
1967   "Protest Songs of the Butte Mines." *Western Folklore* 26 (July): 157–67.
Stewart, Kathleen.
1990   "Backtalking the Wilderness: Appalachian En-genderings." In *Uncertain Terms: Negotiating Gender in American Culture*, edited by Faye Ginsberg and Anna Lowenhaupt Tsing. Boston: Beacon Press.

———.
1996   *A Space on the Side of the Road: Cultural Poetics in an "Other" America*. Princeton: Princeton University Press.
Stolcke, Verena.
1988   *Coffee Planters, Workers, and Wives: Class Conflict and Gender Relations on São Paulo Plantations, 1850–1980*. New York: St. Martin's Press.
Stoler, Ann.
1985   *Capitalism and Confrontation in Sumatra's Plantation Belt, 1870–1979*. New Haven: Yale University Press.
Stoneall, Linda.
1983   *Country Life, City Life: Five Theories of Community*. New York: Praeger.
Strathern, Marilyn.
1988   *The Gender of the Gift: Problems with Women and Problems with Society in Melanesia*. Berkeley: University of California Press.

———.
1987   "An Awkward Relationship: The Case of Feminism and Anthropology." *Signs: Journal of Women in Culture and Society* 12: 276–92.
Susser, Ida.
1986   "Political Activity among Working-Class Women in a U.S. City." *American Ethnologist* 13: 107–17.

———.
1988   "Working-Class Women, Social Protest, and Changing Ideologies." In *Women and the Politics of Empowerment*, edited by Ann Bookman and Sandra Morgen. Philadelphia: Temple University Press.
Suttles, Gerald.
1972   *The Social Construction of Community*. Chicago: Chicago University Press.
Tarducci, Monica.
1993   "Sobre posmodernismo, feminismo y religión." In *Huellas: Seminario mujer y antropología: Problematización y perspectivas*, edited by Sonia Montecino and Maria Elena Boisier. Santiago: CEDEM.
Thompson, E. P.
1966   *The Making of the English Working Class*. New York: Vintage.
Thompson, Judith.
1987   "Goodbye to the Gardens." Senior seminar paper, University of Montana.

Timmins, William.
    1970   "The Copper Strike and Collective Bargaining." *Labor Law
                Journal* 21: 28–33.
"Toll of a Five-Month Strike: Who Is Hurt and How Much?"
    1967   *U.S. News and World Report*, 11 December, 94–96.
Tomic, Radomiro.
    1974   "Primeros pasos hacia la recuperación del cobre: El convenio
                de Washington de 1951." In *El cobre en el desarrollo nacional*,
                edited by Ricardo Ffrench-Davis and Ernest Tironi. Santiago:
                Ediciones Nueva Universidad.
Toole, K. Ross.
    1954   "A History of the Anaconda Copper Mining Company: A Study
                in the Relationships between a State and Its People and a
                Corporation, 1880–1950." Ph.D. diss., University of California,
                Los Angeles.
———.
    1972   *Twentieth-Century Montana: A State of Extremes*. Norman:
                University of Oklahoma Press.
Tristan, Flora.
    1983   *Worker's Union*. (Translation of *L'Union Ouvier*, published in
                Paris, 1837). Carbondale: University of Illinois Press.
"Try, Try Again to Prove Communist Infiltration."
    1956   *Business Week*, 24 November, 74.
United States Department of Interior.
    1934,   *Mineral Resources of the United States*. Washington, D.C.: U.S.
    1935   Government Printing Office.
Valdés, Teresa, and Marisa Weinstein.
    1993   *Mujeres que sueñan: Las organizaciones de pobladoras en Chile,
                1973–1989*. Santiago: Libros Flasco.
Valdez, Ximena, Sonia Montecino, Kirai de Leon, and Macarena Mack.
                Historias testimoniales de mujeres del campo. Santiago: Programa de
    1983   Estudios y Capacitación de la Mujer Campesina Indigena
                (PEMCI), Academia de Humanismo Cristiano.
Vargas, Edmundo.
    1974   "La nacionalización del cobre y el derecho internacional." In *El
                cobre en el desarrollo nacional*, edited by Ricardo Ffrench-Davis
                and Ernesto Tironi. Santiago: Ediciones Nueva Universidad.
Varney, Harold.
    1919   "Butte in the Hands of the IWW." *One Big Union Monthly*
                (March): 336–37.
Verdugo, Patricia.
    1989   *Los zarpasos del puma*. Santiago: Ediciones ChileAmerica.
Visweswaran, Kamala.
    1988   "Defining Feminist Ethnography." *Inscriptions: Special Issue on
                Feminism and the Critique of Colonial Discourse* 3/4: 2–43.
"Waging a Hot War on the Left Wing."
    1949   *Business Week*, 11 June, 100–102.
Warren, Roland.
    1978   *The Community in America*. Chicago: Rand McNally.
Weinbaum, Batya, and Amy Bridges.
    1979   "The Other Side of the Paycheck: Monopoly Capital and the

Structure of Consumption." In *Capitalist Patriarchy and the Case for Socialist Feminism*, edited by Zillah Eisenstein. New York: Monthly Review Press.

"Why a Copper Strike?"

1951   *Fortune* 44 (October): 59–60.

Williams, Raymond.

1977   *Marxism and Literature*. Oxford: Oxford University Press.

———.

1980   *Problems in Marxism and Culture*. London: New Left Books.

Willis, Paul.   Reprint. *Learning to Labor: How Working-Class Kids Get*

1981   *Working-Class Jobs*. New York: Columbia University Press. Original edition, Farnborough, England: Saxon House, 1977 (page references are to reprint edition).

Wright, Erik Olin.

1982   "Class Boundaries and Contradictory Class Locations." In *Classes, Power, and Conflict*, edited by Anthony Giddens and David Held. Berkeley: University of California Press.

———.

1989   "A General Framework for the Analysis of Class Structure." In *The Debate on Classes*, edited by Erik Olin Wright. London: Verso Press.

Writers Program, Work Projects Administration.

1943   *Copper Camp: Stories of the World's Greatest Mining Town, Butte, Montana*. New York: Hastings House.

Yarrow, Michael.

1991   "The Gender-Specific Class Consciousness of Appalachian Coal Miners: Structure and Change." In *Bringing Class Back In: Contemporary and Historical Perspectives*, edited by Scott G. McNall, Rhonda F. Levine, and Rick Fantasia. Boulder: Westview.

Young, Iris Marion.

1990   "The Ideal of Community and the Politics of Difference." In *Feminism/Postmodernism*, edited by Linda J. Nicholson. London: Routledge.

Zapata, Francisco.

1975   "Los mineros de Chuquicamata: Productores o proletarios?" Centro de Estudios Sociologicos, Colegio de Mexico.

———.

1979   "Trade Union Action and Political Behavior of the Chilean Miners of Chuquicamata." In *Peasants and Proletarians: The Struggles of Third-World Workers*, edited by Robin Cohen, Peter Gutkind, and Phyllis Braxier. New York: Monthly Review Press.

Zavella, Patricia.

1991   "*Mujeres* in Factories: Race and Class Perspectives on Women, Work, and Family." In *Gender at the Crossroads of Knowledge: Feminist Anthropology in the Postmodern Era*, edited by Micaela di Leonardo. Berkeley: University of California Press.

Zinn, Howard.

1980   *A People's History of the United States*. New York: Harper & Row.

Index

Compositor: BookMatters
Text: 10/13 Sabon
Display: Sabon
Printer and Binder: Data Reproductions Corp.